HOW
TO WATCH
TELEVISION

HOW TO WATCH TELEVISION

EDITED BY
ETHAN THOMPSON
AND **JASON MITTELL**

New York University Press

NEW YORK AND LONDON

NEW YORK UNIVERSITY PRESS
New York and London
www.nyupress.org

References to Internet websites (URLs) were accurate at the time of writing.
Neither the author nor New York University Press is responsible for URLs that
may have expired or changed since the manuscript was prepared.

LIBRARY OF CONGRESS CATALOGING-IN-PUBLICATION DATA
How to watch television / edited by Ethan Thompson and Jason Mittell.
pages cm
Includes bibliographical references and index.
ISBN 978-0-8147-4531-1 (cl : alk. paper) — ISBN 978-0-8147-6398-8 (pb : alk. paper)
1. Television programs—United States. 2. Television programs—Social aspects—United
States. 3. Television programs—Political aspects—United States. I. Thompson, Ethan,
editor of compilation. II. Mittell, Jason, editor of compilation.
PN1992.3.U5H79 2013
791.45'70973—dc23
2013010676

New York University Press books are printed on acid-free paper, and their binding
materials are chosen for strength and durability. We strive to use environmentally
responsible suppliers and materials to the greatest extent possible in publishing our
books.

Manufactured in the United States of America

Contents

III. TV Politics: Democracy, Nation, and the Public Interest

IV. TV Industry: Industrial Practices and Structures

V. TV Practices: Medium, Technology, and Everyday Life

Acknowledgments

Although only two names appear on this book's spine, it truly was a team effort. Coordinating forty people to do anything is challenging, but getting forty busy academics to commit to a shared approach to writing and a tight schedule of deadlines seemed particularly daunting. The eagerness with which the contributors jumped aboard is testimony to the commitment of each to improving media studies pedagogy. As editors, we were amazed at how smoothly the process went, and must extend our gratitude to our wonderful contributors for delivering such excellent work with minimal pestering or pushback. We would also like to thank those team members whose names only appear here—Eric Zinner, Alicia Nadkami, Alexia Traganas—and the rest of New York University Press's staff for their commitment to this project and hard work getting this book into your hands.

An earlier version of Noel Murray's essay on *M*A*S*H* appeared in *The A.V. Club*—we are grateful for their willingness to allow it to be revised and reprinted.

ETHAN:

I've wanted to make this book since my first stint as a teaching assistant in a TV class at USC, but it took many years and the right co-editor for it to happen. Many thanks to Jason for his help and hard work at every stage, from conceptualization, to expanding and securing the network of contributing scholars to the nuts and bolts of writing and editing. This book was also waiting for the right cohort of media scholars, and I am proud to count so many of the contributors as friends as well as colleagues. Thanks to my fellow faculty in the Department of Communication & Media and the administration of Texas A&M University – Corpus Christi, who have consistently supported my scholarship in television studies.

Finally, biggest thanks to my wife and primary TV-watching partner, Maria, and our three awesome kids, Jenna, Dax, and Mia. You all make me feel lucky and proud every day.

JASON:

I owe many thanks to Ethan for first devising the idea for this book and approaching me to contribute an essay—and then welcoming me as a co-editor in what has turned out to be a greatly rewarding collaborative process. It's rare to work so closely with someone where we agree on almost every decision throughout, and thus I have been spoiled for future collaborations.

My work editing and writing this book was undertaken while I was living in Germany, supported by the DFG in the framework of the Lichtenberg-Kolleg of the Georg-August-Universität Göttingen. I am grateful to my German friends and colleagues for their support and assistance throughout the process.

As always, I could not have accomplished my work without the love and support of my partner Ruth, who provided the time, energy, and German translation skills necessary for me to be able to focus on this book. And extra thanks to my children, Greta, Anya, and Walter, for everything they have taught me, including an appreciation of the complexities of *Phineas & Ferb*.

Introduction
An Owner's Manual for Television

ETHAN THOMPSON AND JASON MITTELL

Imagine that you just purchased a brand new television, and inside the box, along with the remote, the Styrofoam packaging, and various cables, was this book: *How to Watch Television*. Would you bother to open the cellophane wrapper and read it? Sure, you might scan through the "quick start" guide for help with the connections, and the new remote control may take some getting used to, but who needs instructions for how to *watch* what's on screen? Do-it-yourself manuals abound for virtually every topic, but TV content is overwhelmingly regarded as self-explanatory, as most people assume that we all just know how to watch television. We disagree. Thus, this is your owner's manual for how to watch TV.

First, a word of warning: this particular manual is not designed to tell you what to watch or not watch. Nor does it speak with a singular voice or seek to produce a consensus about what is "good" and what is "bad" on all those channels. In other words, the forty writers who contribute critical essays don't all agree on how to watch television. Despite the hundreds of years of cumulative TV-watching and dozens of advanced degrees among them, you can rest assured that, in many cases, they would disagree vehemently about the merits of one TV show versus another. This collection draws upon the insight of so many different people because there are so many different ways to watch TV and so much TV to watch. To be sure, the writers of many of these essays might "like" or "dislike" the programs they write about—sometimes passionately so. But we are all concerned more with thinking critically about television than with proclaiming its artistic or moral merits (or lack thereof). This book collects a variety of essays and presents them as different ways of watching, methods for *looking at* or *making sense of* television, not just issuing broad value judgments. This is what good criticism does—it applies a model of thinking to a text in order to expand our understanding and experience of it. In our book, those "texts," a term scholars use to refer to any cultural work, regardless of its medium, are specific television programs. Too often, people assume that the goal of criticism is to judge a creative work as

1

either "good" or "bad" and provide some rudimentary explanation why. Let us call this the "thumbs up/down" model of criticism. This model is useful if one is skimming television listings for something to pass the time, but not so useful if one wishes to think about and understand what's in those listings.

The "thumbs up/down" model reduces criticism to a simple physical gesture, possibly accented by a grunt. In contrast, we want to open up a text to different readings, broaden our experience of a text and the pleasures it may produce, and offer a new way to think about that text. Criticism should expand a text, rather than reduce it, and it is seldom concerned with simplistic good or bad judgments. In fact, most of the contributors to this volume would feel uncomfortable if they were forced to issue such a judgment on the programs they write about with a "thumbs up" or "thumbs down" icon next to the title of each essay. While most of the authors do provide some judgment of the relative worth of the program they analyze, those evaluations are always more complicated than a simple up or down verdict. One of the ironies of media criticism is that the individual who is probably more responsible than anyone else for the popularity of the "thumbs up/down" model is Roger Ebert, one of America's most thoughtful, articulate film critics from the 1960s until his death in 2013. Yet it was a succession of television shows starring Ebert and fellow critic Gene Siskel—first *Sneak Previews* (PBS, 1975–1982), then *At the Movies* (syndicated, 1982–1986) and *Siskel & Ebert* (syndicated, 1986–1999)—that popularized "thumbs up/down" criticism. How can we reconcile the fact that Ebert, an insightful critic and compelling writer, could also have helped reduce criticism to the simplest of physical gestures?

The answer, of course, is that Ebert didn't do it; a television program did, and television criticism can help us to understand why. If we examine the structure of these programs, we can see the usefulness of the "thumbs up/down" gimmick. Film, television, theater, and book reviews all have a long history in popular newspapers, magazines, and broadcasting, following the common model of making a value judgment and providing the reasons for that judgment. Sometimes the judgment is a vague endorsement of the work owing to particular qualities, while other times it is quantified—"3 out of 5 stars," for example. But in all those cases there are typically clear rationales, with the "stars" or "thumbs" providing a quick reference and reason to read further. There were movie critics on TV before *Sneak Previews*, but this program's innovative structure featured two critics discussing a number of films, with one critic introducing a clip and launching a conversation or debate about the film's merits. The "thumbs" metric provided a jumping off point for discussion, and guaranteed that the two had something concrete to agree or disagree about with a reliable and consistent structure for each review. At the end of each episode, the hosts recapped their judgments on each film, giving viewers a shorthand reminder to consider the next time they themselves were "at the movies." While "thumbs up/down" might be a reductive form of media criticism, it made for entertaining and sometimes useful TV, creating film criticism uniquely suited for the television medium. By looking at the various Siskel & Ebert TV shows and thinking about how "thumbs up/down" might have "fit" with the television medium, we can understand that program and appreciate it beyond whatever effect it might have had on narrowing the public's expectations about what media criticism does.

It is notable that while there have been television shows focused on film criticism and book criticism (like C-SPAN's *Book TV*), there has never been a TV program focused on television criticism. In fact, television criticism has an unusual history within popular media—traditionally, television reviews were published in newspapers upon the debut of a show if at all, rather than dealing with an ongoing series as episodes aired. Magazines like *The New Yorker* or *Newsweek* might run pieces analyzing an ongoing series, but not with any comprehensive structure or commitment to covering a series as it unfolds over time. The rise of online criticism in the twenty-first century has drastically changed the terrain of television criticism, as sites like *The A.V. Club* and *HitFix*, as well as the online versions of print magazines like *Time* and *Hollywood Reporter*, feature regular coverage of many series, reviewing weekly episodes of new shows and returning to classic television series with critical coverage to inspire re-watching them. Noel Murray's series "A Very Special Episode" at *The A.V. Club* is an example of such "classic television" criticism, featuring this tagline: "Sometimes a single TV episode can exemplify the spirit of its time and the properties that make television a unique medium." This book shares that critical outlook, and an expanded version of Murray's essay on "The Interview," a *M*A*S*H* episode, is included in this book.

Despite the rise in robust television criticism in popular online sites, academics have been less involved in such discussions of the medium. While the histories of academic fields like literary studies, film studies, art history, and music include many critical analyses of specific works, television studies as a field features far less criticism of specific programs. In part this is due to the series nature of most television, as the boundaries of a "text" are much more fluid when discussing a program that might extend across months, years, or even decades. Additionally, television studies emerged as an academic field in the 1980s and 1990s under the rubric of Anglo-American cultural studies, an approach that emphasizes contexts over texts, and thus much of television scholarship is focused on understanding the industrial, regulatory, and reception contexts of the medium more than critical analyses of specific programs. Books examining a particular program do exist, but critical works in television studies more typically focus on a format or genre (reality TV), a decade (the 1960s), or a methodology or area of study (industry studies). There are exceptions to this, of course; online academic journals like *FlowTV* often feature short critical essays on particular TV series. But we believe that there is a crucial role for television scholars to use our expertise about the medium's history, aesthetics, structures, and cultural importance to provide critical analyses of specific programs. Additionally, we want to see scholars writing for audiences broader than just other scholars, so we have commissioned shorter essays than typically found in an academic journal or book, and asked that they be written accessibly for students and a general readership.

While there is no single method employed by the dozens of authors found in this volume, most essays can be described as examples of *textual analysis*. The shared approach assumes that there is something to be discovered by carefully examining a cultural work, or "text"—in the case of this book's topic, that means watching a television program closely. In some cases, the text might be a single episode or two; in others, the essay looks more broadly at a particular series, or multiple programs connected by a key thread. But in each case, the author uses a "close watching" of a program to make a broader argument about television and its relation to other cultural forces, ranging from representations of particular identities to economic conditions of production and distribution. The goal of such textual analysis is to connect the program to its broader contexts, and make an argument about the text's cultural significance, thus providing a model for how you can watch television with a critical eye—and write your own works of television criticism.

A piece of television criticism, like the ones modeled in the rest of this book, can have a wide range of goals. Certainly all the book's authors believe that watching television is an important and pervasive facet of modern culture, and that taking time to analyze programming is a vital critical act. Some authors are more invested in understanding television as a specific medium, with industrial and regulatory systems that shape its programming, and its own unique formal system of visual and aural communication that forge TV's modes of storytelling and representation across a number of genres. Others regard television more as a window to broader social issues, whether by establishing norms of identity categories like gender or race or by framing political agendas and perspectives. These are not opposing perspectives, as television critics can think about the interplay between the medium itself and its broader context—indeed, every essay in this book hopes to shine a light on something about television itself as well as something broader within our culture, as we believe that knowing how to watch TV is a crucial skill for anyone living in our media-saturated world.

Of course, for many people reading this book, the idea of "watching television" might seem like an anachronism or a fossil from the previous century—what with so many electronic gadgets and "new media" surrounding us these days, why single out television? Television can seem to be an object from another era, quaint in its simplicity and functions. Such a response is the product of a very limited notion of what "television" is, and indeed, if you do think of TV as just a piece of furniture around which the family gathers each night, then there is something potentially outdated about television. However, television is (and always has been) more than just furniture, and now in our era of convergence among different technologies and cultural forms, there is more TV than ever. New or emergent forms of television work alongside the residual or "old," and it's important to remember that the majority of viewers still do most of their watching on traditional television sets. If we define the word "television" literally down to its Latin roots, it is often translated as "remote seeing." By thinking about television not as furniture but as "remote seeing" (and hearing) of sounds and moving images from a distant time or place, we can recognize that so many of our new media interactions are new kinds of television that we integrate into our lives alongside the familiar and pleasurable uses of TV we've known for so long.

Rather than radically reconfiguring our uses of media culture, new technologies and media forms emerge and find a place among and alongside those forms that already exist; a medium might ebb and flow in popularity, but seldom disappears altogether. And one of the most important aspects of all forms of media engagement, whether watching on a television set or mobile phone, is that these forms of engagement become part of our everyday lives, adapting to our geographical, technological, and personal contexts. Moreover, while new technologies might enable some to claim that they do not watch television, we believe that people who say they don't watch TV are either lying or deluding themselves. TV is everywhere in our culture and on many different screens, as we often watch television programs on our computers, or play videogames on our televisions. People who say they don't watch TV are usually suggesting they don't watch *those* kinds of TV shows that they assume less sophisticated viewers watch uncritically. But even as it gets reconfigured in the digital era, television is still America's dominant mass medium, impacting nearly everyone.

A brief anecdote about the dual editors' own media consumption practices while writing this introduction point to the role of television and other technologies in contemporary life. One of the editors of this book (Ethan) began writing the first draft of this introduction while watching a professional football game live via satellite television at a ranch in rural south Texas. The other editor (Jason) was at that very time travelling by train with his family across Europe, where they were watching Looney Tunes cartoons on an iPad. Ethan was watching a program via the latest digital high-definition TV technology, but in a highly traditional way—live broadcast to a mass audience sharing the same act of "remote seeing." Certainly one of the great pleasures of watching televised sports, which remains one of the most popular and prevalent forms of television today, is the sense of communal participation in an event as it occurs, shared by viewers both within the same room and across the globe; this experience depends on liveness, even at the cost of watching commercials and boring bits that modern technologies like DVRs can easily bypass. As a fan, Ethan watches for the sense of participation in what is happening at the time—a case of old-fashioned remote seeing enabled by new technologies.

Jason's experience is quite different, but still falls under the general category of "watching TV." As his kids watched Looney Tunes on a European train, they embraced one of television's longstanding primary functions: allowing children to see things beyond their personal experiences. This literally was "remote seeing," as his kids were watching something from a distant time and place: Looney Tunes were created as animated shorts screened in American movie theaters from the 1930s to 1950s, but they thrived throughout the second half of the twentieth century as a staple of kids' TV, and more recently through numerous DVD releases. Shifting these classic cartoons to an iPad enables a mobile viewing experience that trades the imagined community of the television schedule for the convenience of on-demand, self-programmed media consumption. While technically there is no "television" involved in watching cinematic cartoons on a mobile digital device, we believe that the cultural practices and formal elements established via decades of television viewing carry over to these new technologies, making watching TV a more prevalent and diverse practice in the contemporary era of media convergence.

These brief descriptions of watching television foreground our diverse viewing contexts, which help make watching TV such a multifaceted cultural practice—we multitask, watch on a range of screens in unusual places, and experience television programming across timeframes spanning from live to decades-old, and spatial locations from rural Texas to European trains and beyond. The rest of the book focuses less on specific viewing practices, and more on how we can use our expertise as media scholars to understand the programming that we might encounter in such diverse contexts. This is the goal of any form of criticism: to provide insight into a text, not to proclaim a singular "correct" interpretation. Indeed, there is no such "correct" interpretation, any more than there is a "correct" way to watch a football game or cartoon.

The essays in this book cover a representative sampling of major approaches to television criticism, and they are quite different from one another in terms of the TV they analyze and their methods of analysis. However, they do share some basic assumptions that are worth highlighting:

1. TV is complicated. This can mean many different things. Sometimes the text itself is formulaic, yet its pleasures are complicated. Other times, the

narrative of a TV program doesn't present a clear plot, yet attempting to puzzle out the story is a fundamental pleasure. Sometimes where a program comes from is complicated—the question of who created and is responsible for it can, for example, be less than straightforward. Or perhaps the meanings expressed by a show are complicated, presenting contradictions and diverse perspectives than can be interpreted. The bottom line is that television criticism seeks to understand and explain TV, no matter how simple or complex it might seem at first glance.

2. To understand TV, you need to watch TV. This might seem obvious, but there is a tradition of critics writing about television (usually to condemn it) without actually taking the time to watch much of it, or even to specify what TV texts they are criticizing. Judgments like these tend to be common amongst politicians, pundits, and anyone else looking to use television as a convenient "bad object" to make a point. Understanding TV requires more, though—and more than just watching TV, too. That is, some types of television require particular viewing practices to really understand them, such as the long-term viewing of serials and series, or the contextualized viewing of remakes or historically nostalgic programming.

3. Nobody watches the same TV. We watch a wide variety of programs, and even in those cases when we watch the same programs, we often watch them in vastly different contexts. Television is still a mass medium experienced by millions, but the specific experience of watching television is far from universal. While television in a previous generation was more shared, with events like the moon landing or the finale of *M*A*S*H* drawing the attention of a majority of Americans, even then our experiences of watching television were diverse, as viewers often think quite differently about the same texts.

4. Criticism is not the same as evaluation. You don't have to like (or dislike) a particular television program to think and write critically about it, and our goal is not to issue a thumb up or down. However, evaluative reactions to a text can be a useful way to get started thinking critically about television, as you attempt to figure out what you are reacting to (or against). Many of these essays foreground their authors' own evaluative reactions to programs that they love or hate (or even feel ambivalent about), but in every case, the critic finds his or her particular program interesting. Exploring what makes it so is a worthy goal for television criticism.

What follows in this book is a set of critical analyses that model how we might watch a particular television program that we find interesting. The programs represented are widely diverse and even eclectic, including undisputed classics, contemporary hits, and a few that you might not have heard of before. They cover a range of genres, from cooking shows to cartoons, sports to soap operas, and they span the medium's entire history. Even so, we do not claim to be comprehensive—there are countless other programs that might be the subject of such works of television criticism. We have focused primarily on American television, or in a few cases how non-American programming is seen in an American context, although given the pervasive reach of American television throughout the globe, we hope that international readers will find these critical works helpful as well. The authors are media scholars with a range of expertise, experiences, and backgrounds, offering a wide range of viewpoints that might highlight different ways of watching TV. Each essay starts with a brief overview of its content, and ends with some suggestions for further reading to delve deeper into the relevant topic and approach.

Each of these critical essays can be read on its own, in any order. We encourage readers to go straight to a particular program or approach that interests them. However, we have organized the book into five major areas to assist readers looking for essays that speak to particular issues or approaches, as well as instructors seeking to assign essays in relation to particular topics. Essays in the first section, "TV Form," consider aesthetics, analyzing visual and sound style, production techniques, and narrative structure, and showing how television style is crucial to understanding television content. The essays in "TV Representations" focus on television as a site of cultural representation of different groups and identities, including race, ethnicity, gender, and sexuality. Although many essays in the book are politically concerned, those in the "TV Politics" section look more explicitly at public affairs, government, and national and global boundaries in both fiction and factual programs. In "TV Industry," essays focus on economics, production, and regulation in historical and contemporary television culture. Those in "TV Practices" consider television in the context of everyday life, and the ways in which engagement with television texts carries across media and technologies. In the contemporary digital convergence era, it is increasingly important to think beyond a single television screen into a multiplication of media and devices.

Finally, while most owners' manuals get filed away and forgotten or thrown in the recycling bin unread, we hope this one will enjoy a more enduring presence. This book, the essays inside it, and the critical methods the authors employ, all seek to expand the ways you think about television. If the book itself doesn't earn a spot next to your remote control, we have no doubt that some essay inside it will form a lasting impression. Perhaps it will provoke you to think differently about a program you love (or hate), or it will make you a fan of a program you had never seen or even heard of before. Better yet, we hope *How to Watch Television* will prompt you to think critically and apply the methods you've read about in your own original way, while discussing or writing about a program of your own choosing. That is how this owners' manual can prove to be more permanent than others: as you flip through the channels, and especially when you stop to view a particular program, we hope that you cannot help but think critically about the television that you watch.

FURTHER READING

Butler, Jeremy G. *Television: Critical Methods and Applications*, 4th ed. New York: Routledge, 2011.

Gray, Jonathan, and Amanda D. Lotz. *Television Studies*. Boston: Polity, 2011.

Mittell, Jason. *Television and American Culture*. New York: Oxford University Press, 2010.

I

TV Form
Aesthetics and Style

1

Homicide
Realism

BAMBI L. HAGGINS

Abstract: One of the most critically acclaimed but low-rated dramas in network television history, *Homicide: Life on the Streets* approached the cop show genre by trying to remain true to actual police work and life in Baltimore. Bambi Haggins explores this commitment to realism by investigating the narrative and stylistic techniques employed by the show to create its feeling of authenticity.

Homicide: Life on the Streets (NBC, 1993–1999), one of the most compelling and innovative cop dramas ever aired on U.S. network television, occupies a significant, if often overlooked, position in the history of television drama. *Homicide* is the "missing link" between the quality dramas of the 1980s, such as *Hill Street Blues* (NBC, 1981–1987), and groundbreaking cable series unencumbered by network limitations, like *The Wire* (HBO, 2002–2008). While *Homicide* continues the "quality" tradition from its NBC dramatic forbearers—the multiple storylines, overlapping dialogue, and cast of flawed protagonists in *Hill Street Blues,* and the cinematic visual style and the city as character in *Miami Vice* (NBC, 1984–1989)—it manages to convey a sense of immediacy and intimacy that can be as disquieting as it is engaging. Based on David Simon's nonfiction book, *Homicide: A Year on the Killing Streets,* which chronicled his year "embedded" with Baltimore's "Murder Police," *Homicide* does little to assuage the audience's anxieties; rather, it brings a messy and unsettling slice of American urban life to network television. As a twentieth-century cop show, it offers an inspirational model for twenty-first-century television drama.

We might consider *Homicide's* commitment to realism in terms comparable to those of the "RealFeel" index, a meteorological measure that takes into account humidity, precipitation, elevation, and similar factors to describe what the temperature actually *feels* like. Thus, by examining the look, the sound, and, most significantly, the *sense* of *Homicide,* and by attending to facets of "emotional realism" and "plausibility, typicality, and factuality" of the series, we can describe its "RealFeel" effect. Though "RealFeel" synthesizes a variety of specific qualities, this essay focuses on signifiers of realism that build upon each other, resonate for the viewer, and make the televisual world of *Homicide*, its people, and its stories *feel* real: socio-culturally charged, unpredictable narratives with crisp and edgy dialogue; a *sense* of verisimilitude in terms of both the historical moment and the place; a cast of complex characters in a culturally diverse milieu; and the sampling of generic conventions combining dark comedy, gritty police drama, and contemporary urban morality tale within each episode.

These elements are not unique to this series—not when *Homicide* owes a debt to *Hill Street Blues*, and *The Wire* owes a debt to *Homicide*. While all three combine the highly evocative, and sometimes unsettling, visual style and the narrative complexity we have come to expect of quality television drama, each series builds upon the other, refining its sense of the real. The multiple storylines and flawed protagonists of *Hill Street Blues* give way to *Homicide*'s extended story arcs (across episodes and seasons), nuanced depictions of conflicted characters, and an incisive view of Baltimore in the 1990s. *The Wire* mobilizes—and expands upon—all of the aforementioned elements of "RealFeel" in its made-for-HBO drama.

Both the televisual milieu of *Hill Street Blues*, an inner city precinct in an unnamed urban space, and the multiple factions in *The Wire*, including Baltimore's police, government, unions, and schools, which are tainted to various degrees by corruption, resonate differently for audiences than the televisual milieu of *Homicide*. *The Wire* adheres closely to the multifaceted nature of the body of creator David Simon's journalistic work (which includes the corner, the precinct, and the press room), and, thanks to freedoms offered by the premium cable HBO network presents an unfiltered vision of Baltimore. *Homicide*, while undoubtedly ambitious, is more modest in its aspirations. Like the book upon which it is based, the focus is narrow: one work shift in one squad in one precinct, which makes the depiction of a small slice of Charm City more plausible and, arguably, more intimate.

Some might argue that the more controversial *NYPD Blue* (ABC, 1993–2005) covered similar narrative terrain and that its much-publicized instances of nudity and swearing pushed the boundaries of network television.[1] However, by utilizing the generic conflation of procedural and melodrama, *NYPD Blue* offers a more palatable—if provocative—televisual meal for primetime audiences. *Homicide*, a series in which issues of class and race are always part of the narrative roux, is often not easily digestible—nor is it intended to be. The lives and the work of homicide detectives are not easy: they deal daily with death. By spurning, for the most part, the violence of chases and shootouts typical of conventional cop shows, these Charm City stories achieve their "RealFeel" by offering a condensation of the *everyday* drama of being Murder Police—the cynicism, the frustration, the humor and the responsibility of "speaking for the dead. "

David Simon once said, "The greatest lie in dramatic TV is the cop who stands over a body and pulls up the sheet and mutters 'damn'. . . [T]o a real homicide detective, it's just a day's work."[2] From the very beginning of the series, *Homicide* endeavors not to lie. The signifiers of "RealFeel" can be seen in the opening scene of the first episode where we are thrown into a case in progress. In a dark, rain-drenched alley, Lewis and Crosetti are on the verge of calling off their half-hearted search for evidence—and the first lines of the series express their frustration:

> LEWIS: If I could just find this damn thing, I could go home.
>
> CROSETTI: Life is a mystery. Just accept it.

Beginning the series with a sense of frustration and disorientation captures the tone of daily life for Murder Police; neither the visual nor the narrative depiction is idealized. In physical terms, Crosetti and Lewis are clearly not the detective pinups of *Miami Vice*, nor do they have the unspoken closeness of the original troubled twosome of *NYPD Blue*. They are not the interracial partners favored by Hollywood films like *Lethal Weapon* (1987), in which the two who make up the odd couple come to know and care for each other. Lewis and Crosetti talk past each other, not really connecting with or acknowledging the other's views, with the result often playing as comedy. In the opening scene of the series, the quotidian woes of partnership are uppermost. Thereafter, Lewis and Crosetti continue to grouse, as the latter spouts his profundities and the former counters by casting aspersions on his partner's ethnic background (such as "salami-head"). The visual style matches the viewer's sense of the narrative flow—the camera pulls in as if trying to catch up to the two detectives, following their exchanges and their movement through the alley. The audience is drawn into a scene that, despite appearing mundane, is disorienting; while it is initially unclear what exactly the two are doing, their states of mind appear crystalline. Lewis is "done" in multiple ways: done searching, done listening, and, on some level, done caring. In contrast, Crosetti is waxing philosophical about the search.

As they move out of the alley and towards the light on the corner, a couple of uniformed cops and the victim, splayed on the ground with a bullet in his head, come into view. Lewis and Crosetti's tired banter, like the scene itself, creates the sense that solving murders is just another job—without the flourish of flashy crime-scene investigation or the romance of crusading cops. Overzealousness is seen as poor form. Lewis responds to the uniforms' attempts to engage him with thinly veiled hostility: "Ain't no mystery, the man who shot him wanted him dead." Crosetti's observation that the victim "tried to duck" meets with no sympathy from Lewis—"A lost art: ducking"—who mistakenly assumes that the shooting is drug-related. The scene is a commonplace for this pair and for the place, inner city Baltimore in the 1990s. The visual bleakness, the dark humor, and the casual lack of empathy shown by Lewis and Crosetti, for each other and for the victim, combine as signifiers for the "RealFeel" of *Homicide*.

The camera work in that premiere episode ("Gone for Goode," January 21, 1993) also contributes. With Academy Award–winning filmmaker, native Baltimorean, and series executive producer Barry Levinson as director, and with documentarian Jean de Segonzac as cinematographer, *Homicide's* signature visual style is established through the use of hand-held cameras. These swoop shakily in and out of the action at times, trying to capture all movement and thus constructing a frenetic scene; or at other times, they simply appear to record, without any stylistic flourish. Close-ups of the victims provide an intimate and unromantic view of the initial investigative process. Similar visual techniques capture the dance between the detectives and suspects during interrogation. Whether set in a back-alley crime scene, the drab squad room, or the claustrophobic minimalism of the "Box" (interrogation room), scenes are drained of color as if to signify the soul-sapping nature of the job. Jump cuts and play with perspective and point of view create a distinctive, raw, and artsy look for *Homicide* that functions in harmony with and in counterpoint to the narrative flow. The effect is part documentary, with the unflinching witnessing of *Harlan County USA* (1976), and part French New Wave, with the intimacy and evocative camera movement in *Breathless* (1960). Thus, the visual and narrative style act in concert to provide audiences with an understanding of the moment and of the place that has an aura of authenticity, and construction of character and situation feel emotionally realistic from the outset as well.

Indeed, *Homicide* marries the incisiveness of Simon's case studies and the collective vision of the creative team that was led by Levinson and included the award-winning television writer-producer and showrunner Tom Fontana, known for his groundbreaking television (*St. Elsewhere* and, later, *Oz*), as well as creator Paul Attanasio, who fictionalized Simon's book for the small screen and would later adapt *Donnie Brasco* (1997). Since early in his career, Levinson had been sending cinematic love letters to Baltimore through *his* visions of Charm City in *Diner* (1982), *Avalon* (1990), and, *Liberty Heights* (1999). By contrast, *Homicide's* vision of Baltimore is not colored by nostalgia; rather, the series, by design, depicts a city that is both a microcosm of 1990s urban America and a socio-culturally unique space.

Here, it is worth emphasizing that attempting to arrive at any singular definition of the "real" necessarily poses pragmatic, theoretical, and existential problems. Yet, it is possible to address the matter in another way by drawing on the work of media theorist Alice Hall, who describes a range of elements that establish how "real" a series *feels* to an audience: whether the events could have happened ("plausibility"); whether the characters are "identifiable" ("typicality"); and, the "gold standard" of television realism, whether the story is based on actual events ("factuality").[3] Indeed, Hall's "continuum of realism" offers a framework that encompasses signifiers of *Homicide*'s "RealFeel" such as the choice to shoot on location in Baltimore, the use of the term "Murder Police" (Baltimorean lingo), and the creation of an ethnically, economically, and racially diverse televisual milieu. Moreover, the construction of *Homicide*'s fictional detectives was informed by the actual ones described in Simon's book, which also adds to the series' verisimilitude.

However, the characters reflect the police force that one might *expect* to find in a city with a majority black population; thus, the majority white squad room from the book was diversified. Furthermore, the creative powers on *Homicide* did not succumb to the "majority hotness" requirement of most primetime dramas. In other words, the squad was cast to look the way that people actually do in real life, not on television. In the process of adaption of the book to the series, Lt. Gary "Dee" D'Addario became Lt. Al "Gee" Giardello, whose Sicilian lineage remained an essential part of the shift commander's persona; while the gender of Det. Rich Garvey was changed, Det. Kay Howard retained the reputation for putting down all of her cases, like her original; the white Det. Donald Waltemeyer, who played a minor role in the book, became Det. Meldrick Lewis, whose character provided a black Baltimorean view (from the projects to Murder Police) that differed significantly from that of Gee and of the highly educated New York transplant, Det. Frank Pembleton. *Homicide*'s varied (and progressive) depictions of black characters in an arguably idealistically integrated workplace were groundbreaking and remain uncommon. While endeavoring to capture the socio-political and socio-cultural complexity of the "Not quite North, Not quite South" urban space, the series plays with preconceived notions about urban American ills. The city of Baltimore depicted in the series still bears the scars of the 1968 riots, white flight, long-term unemployment, poverty, the scourge of crack cocaine in the 1990s, which has since waned, and the decades-long heroin epidemic, which has not. In Charm City, social problems are almost never as simple as they seem and, as seen in *Homicide*, the signifiers of "RealFeel," within the continuum of realism, reveal complexity, conflict, and contradiction.

The "RealFeel" of *Homicide* can also be understood in relation to Ien Ang's assertion that "what is recognized as real is not knowledge of the world, but a subjective experience of the world: a 'structure of feeling.'"[4] The inherent drama of *Homicide* and its "RealFeel" come into focus most clearly through nuanced—and seemingly incidental—exchanges: within backstories, idiosyncratic dialogue, and ticks of persona. Fleeting glimpses of detectives' internal angels and demons inflect the narrative: there is more to the characters' inner lives underneath the surface. Consequently, the audience's "subjective experience of the world" of *Homicide* is rooted in the worldview of Murder Police, for whom exposing the darker side of human nature is commonplace and for whom every victory is tinged with loss.

The characters in the series that best encapsulate the complexity, conflict, and contradiction of *Homicide* are Tim Bayliss and Frank Pembleton, arguably the program's central partners, due in no small part to the stellar performances of Kyle Secor and Andre Braugher, respectively. Bayliss and Pembleton can initially be viewed as binary opposites—idealist versus pragmatist, native versus transplant, white versus black, emotional versus intellectual. In the series premiere, Bayliss first enters the squad room as a transfer to the division, his box of possessions in hand, believing he will live his dream: "Homicide—thinking cops. Not a gun," he says as he points to his head. "This." His idealized vision of working homicide can be contrasted with Pembleton's monologue as he prepares to enter the Box, where he is king, with Bayliss:

> What you will be privileged to witness will not be an interrogation, but an act of salesmanship as silver-tongued and thieving as ever moved used cars, Florida swampland, or Bibles. But what I am selling is a long prison term, to a client who has no genuine use for the product.

While the actual interrogation is quick and manipulative, it provides the first demonstration of the differences in perspective between the new partners. Pembleton refuses to let Bayliss view this case in crisp, clean absolutes as he forecasts the young white male suspect's path through the system: his being re-cast by the defense attorney from murder suspect to an innocent seduced by an older male predator in a way that plays upon the predispositions of the jury pool and negates the voluntary nature of his actions. The case, with its cynical—and accurate—take on the course of justice, is the first of many that will make Bayliss question his beliefs in fundamental ways.

In Bayliss's first case as primary investigator, the victim, Adena Watson, is an eleven-year-old black girl with the "face of an angel." From the moment he flashes his ID and tentatively says, "Homicide," this case becomes his long-term obsession, extending throughout the life of the series. While trying to speak for Adena, Bayliss finds his adherence to a certain code of conduct challenged and eventually defeated.

In "Three Men and Adena" (March 3, 1993), an acclaimed, tension-filled episode penned by Tom Fontana and filmed almost entirely in the Box, Bayliss and

FIGURE 1.1.

Bayliss and Pembleton interrogate Risley Tucker in "Three Men and Adena."

Pembleton use every possible (legal) means to illicit a confession from Risley Tucker, an elderly black street vendor, who is known as the "Arraber" and is the only suspect in Adena's murder. In response to pressure to close the case and end his own obsession, Bayliss, in tandem with Pembleton, wages a twelve-hour interrogatory assault that makes the earlier interrogation seem like polite conversation. Both sides are firing in this verbal warfare. Tucker disparages Pembleton *as "one of them five-hundreds,"* after the detective tries to play on a sense of racial solidarity to coax an admission of pedophilia: "You don't like niggers like me 'cos of who we are, 'cos we ain't reached out, 'cos we ain't grabbed hold of that dream, not Doctor King's dream, the WHITE dream. You hate niggers like me because you hate being a nigger. You hate who you really are." As the deadline to release him grows nearer, Bayliss pulls the Arabber from his chair and almost uses a hot water pipe to coerce a confession. After this Tucker taunts Bayliss: "You from Baltimore, right? Do you say BAWL-mer or BALL-di-more? . . . Say Baltimore, and I'll tell you within ten blocks where you were born. . . . You got that home grown look. The not too southern, not too northern, not on the ocean but still on the water look with maybe a touch of inbreeding." After pushing Tucker to the brink of physical and emotional exhaustion, and getting him to confess his love for the young girl, the detectives lose their traction when the old man refuses to speak and their time runs out. In the end, Pembleton has been convinced that the Arabber is the killer, but Bayliss is no longer sure. (In season 4's "Requiem for Adena," it becomes clear that, in all likelihood, Tucker was not the killer.) Both Bayliss and Pembleton are changed by this interrogation—as partners and as individuals; the issues of race and class to which the Arabber refers in his barbs surface in their relationship to cases and to each other, reinforcing *Homicide*'s emotional realism. In "Three Men and Adena," Bayless, Pembleton, and Tucker speak to and from perspectives about race, class, and justice that are deeply rooted in their individual histories as well as the histories of Baltimore—and viewers have limited knowledge of each. Our experiences as longtime viewers of this genre are challenged: while we may always *feel* like we know more than we actually do—about the players, about the case, and about the city—the lack of certainty in these narratives (for the characters and for the viewers) imparts an uneasy ambiguity.

As Bayliss and Pembleton confront combustible issues, the viewer is forced to do the same—with no easy epiphany. In "Colors" (April 28, 1995), the partners clash when Bayliss's cousin shoots a drunk Turkish exchange student dressed as a member of the rock band KISS who tries to enter his house (mistakenly believing there is a party inside). Bayliss's unquestioning acceptance of his cousin's self-defense plea makes Pembleton question whether Bayliss can see racism in his family or on the job. This point is driven home for Bayliss when his cousin, cleared of the shooting, remarks, "Who'd have thought their blood was the same color as ours," as he washes it off his front porch. In "Blood Ties, Part 2" (October 24, 1997), Bayliss questions Pembleton's objectivity when a prominent black millionaire and humanitarian is embroiled in a case where the victim is a young woman who works and lives in his home and who is killed at an event honoring the patriarch. Due to the wealth of the family, their influence, and very good lawyers, no one is prosecuted, though Pembleton and Giardello know that the son is the killer and that they have been manipulated. Pembleton must admit that his judgment was colored on more than one level—by class and fame as well as race. However, the awareness of flawed perceptions, biproducts of greater social maladies, leaves issues unresolved—the characters, the narrative, and the viewer carry vestiges of these experiences. While the partnership between Pembleton and Bayliss, like those of the other detectives and the police and populace of Baltimore, dips into dysfunction as often as it reveals a kinship that is both tenuous and time-tested, we *feel* that their daily quest to get the "bad" guy in the Box is only part of the story.

While this essay can only begin to explore the concept of "RealFeel" as a way to talk about reading television drama, the uncomfortable pleasures of watching the televisual tales of the Murder Police, whose job is never really completed ("like mowing the lawn, you always have to do it again") and Baltimore, a not so safe space on the small screen and in "real life," does provide an analytical mother lode. Although the sense of the "real" in emotional, intellectual, visual, and narrative terms can be difficult to quantify, in *Homicide*, and in most quality drama from *Hill Street Blues* to *The Sopranos*, you can see how aspects of "Real-Feel" work in concert and at cross purposes. On the one hand, they conspire to synthesize backstories about culture, class, morality, and place in ways that feel comprehensible; on the other, the complexities of the narrative and the milieu depicted often cause those very assumptions to be called into question. In the end, *Homicide* elicits the aura of realism imbricated with a sense of knowing and not knowing simultaneously—a state of ambiguity not uncommon to everyday life—which makes these Charm City stories *feel* enticing, unsettling, and "real."

NOTES

1. See Jennifer Holt's essay on *NYPD Blue* in this volume.
2. Jim Shelley, "Is *Homicide: Life on the Street* better than *The Wire*?" *Guardian*, March 26, 2010, 10.
3. Alice Hall, "Reading Realism: Audiences' Evaluation of the Reality of Media Texts," *Journal of Communication* 53, 4 (December 2003): 634.
4. Ien Ang, *Watching Dallas: Soap Opera and the Melodramatic Imagination* (London: Methuen, 1985), 45.

FURTHER READING

Hall, Alice. "Reading Realism: Audiences' Evaluation of the Reality of Media Texts." *Journal of Communication* 53, 4 (December 2003): 624–41.

Lane, J. P. "The Existential Condition of Television Crime Drama." *The Journal of Popular Culture* (Spring 2001): 137–51.

Nichols-Pethick, Jonathan. *TV Cops: The Contemporary American Television Police Drama.* New York: Routledge, 2012.

Simon, David. *Homicide: A Year on the Killing Streets.* New York: Houghton Mifflin, 1991.

2

House
Narrative Complexity

AMANDA D. LOTZ

Abstract: In her analysis of the medical/procedural program *House*, Amanda Lotz shows how a procedural program can exhibit narrative complexity and innovative techniques of character development. Lotz examines how a single episode draws upon a variety of atypical storytelling strategies to convey meaning and dramatize a central theme of the series: "everybody lies."

In the 2000s, some U.S. dramatic television entertained its audiences with increasingly complicated characters. Series such as FX's *The Shield* (2002–2008), *Rescue Me* (2004–2011), and *Sons of Anarchy* (2008–present) and AMC's *Mad Men* (2007–present) and *Breaking Bad* (2008–2013) explored the complicated personal and professional lives of male characters and maximized the possibilities of television's storytelling attributes for character development. While several of these series can be properly described as character studies, other narrative forms also provided compelling examples for thinking about characterization, narrative strategies, and television storytelling. Series such as *CSI*, *Law & Order*, and the subject of this essay, *House, M.D.*, are organized episodically, so that they can be understood in individual installments, in stark contrast to the serialized character dramas on cable.[1] Yet even series that use limited serial components and instead structure their stories around solving some sort of legal or medical case within each episode can provide lead characters with the texture of depth and sophistication.

Episodically structured storytelling dominates the history of television, and this format has typically offered little narrative or character complexity; instead, characters are stuck in what Jeffrey Sconce describes as "a world of static exposition, repetitive second-act 'complications,' and artificial closure."[2] Such an assessment in some ways aptly characterizes the FOX medical drama *House, M.D.* (2004–2012, hereafter *House*). The basic features of an episode of *House* vary little: an opening scene involving characters and settings outside those common to the show begins each episode. These scenes introduce viewers to the case of the week and often feature some sort of misdirection—for instance, it is not the overweight, middle-aged man complaining of chest pains who will become this week's case, but his apparently healthy wife who will inexplicably collapse. The series' opening credit sequence rolls, and we return from commercials to find Dr. Gregory House's diagnostic team beginning their evaluation of the opening's patient. The remaining minutes of the episode focus on the team's efforts to identify the patient's ailment in time to save him or her, embarking upon a series of misdiagnoses along the way. Various interpersonal complications are introduced and addressed throughout the case; typically, they are related to evolving romantic entanglements among the primary cast, although few of these complications are likely to be resolved in one episode. At some point near the end of the episode, House has a conversation—typically with his friend Wilson—about some other matter and becomes suddenly quiet, having just stumbled upon the possible diagnosis evading the team. The condition is caught in time and alleviated (although in some rare cases the team fails to find the diagnosis in time), and the "artificial closure" Sconce notes is achieved.

As a series that chronicles the efforts of a master team of diagnostic doctors to identify and treat the rarest of illnesses, *House* emphasizes the plot goal of diagnosis in each weekly episode. Where many other series attempt to balance serial and episodic plotlines through a serialized, overarching mystery (*Murder One, Burn Notice, Monk*), *House* solves its mystery each week; the exploits of its misanthropic, drug-addicted lead character are what propel serial action instead. The implicit central enigma of its cumulative narrative—or the eight-season total story of *House*—is whether the series' eponymous lead can ever be properly civilized. Can House exist without painkillers? Can he cultivate meaningful relationships? Can he be brilliant and happy?

Most series that are dominated by this logic of episodic storytelling emphasize plot action and consequently leave characters fairly static over time. Yet in recent decades, even some episodically structured series have indicated the possibility for complex character development, and as Roberta Pearson outlines, mundane plot action can serve this end. In her case study of *CSI*'s Gil Grissom, Pearson presents a six-part taxonomy of elements that construct the character: psychological traits/habitual behaviors; physical traits/appearance; speech patterns; interactions with other characters; environment (the places the character inhabits); and biography (character's backstory).[3] She uses this taxonomy to create a language for exploring the particularities of television characters, which, along with techniques of characterization—beyond the case study—have been a significantly under-explored area in the field. She notes that the rudimentary taxonomy works for characters in all moving image forms, but that specific media or narrative strategies may vary techniques. For example, the ongoing storytelling process in television series allows for much more character growth and change than in the limited storytelling period available to realist cinema.[4] Pearson's case is valuable for illustrating that even though many episodic series place little emphasis on character depth, this is a creative choice rather than an inherent feature of episodically structured shows.

To better understand attributes of episodic television storytelling and techniques of characterization, this essay analyzes a single episode of *House*, focusing on how narrative strategies convey meaning on multiple levels. The episode "Three Stories" (May 17, 2005) conveys crucial character information in its basic plot, although the episode uses confounding techniques such as dream sequences, flashbacks, and imagined alternate realities—rarely clearly marked as such—to do so. The misdirection of these storytelling techniques reaffirms a central theme of the series: namely, that "everybody lies," which is House's personal outlook and dictates his particular approach to diagnostic medicine. Thus, this episode of *House* illustrates the complexity available to a series with a narrative structure that is generally rebuked for its reliance on formula and lack of nuance.

"Three Stories" is arguably the least routine episode of a series that normally maintains exceptional consistency. Although the selection of an aberrant case rarely offers sound footing for broader arguments, the unusualness of this episode underscores its significance and indicates the novelty of the series' approach to character development. Hence, it serves as the focus of this essay. The episode, the penultimate of the first season, finally explains the injury to House's leg, which has led to his chronic pain and perhaps his unhappiness—arguably his primary character traits. While this pain and unhappiness centrally define House, they are also what enable future serial storylines, such as his spirals through drug addiction, his efforts to get and remain clean, and his attempts to deal with human interaction and emotions without pharmaceutically induced numbness. House's struggles to alleviate his pain and his unhappiness—neither he nor the audience is ever fully aware whether these are separate conditions—are traced loosely in the cumulative narrative.

By the time "Three Stories" aired (twenty episodes into the first season) in May of 2005 and finally explained the origin of the lead character's primary character trait, *House* had established itself as a bona fide hit. The series benefited from airing during a post-*American Idol* timeslot, when the reality competition returned in January of 2005, but even this most enviable of lead-ins might not have been adequate to make such a contrary leading character so popular. Greg House remains the least conventionally heroic lead character to motivate a successful broadcast drama, although such flawed characters have been prevalent in recent years in the more niche-targeted storytelling space of original cable dramas.

House's personal misanthropy functions as a guiding ideology of the series, which stems from his requirement that his team of diagnosticians work from the assumption that "everybody lies." House encourages his team to dismiss medical histories reported by patients and instead sleuth through their homes to uncover the truth or think of things patients may be unwilling to tell doctors.

"Three Stories" begins exceptionally, but not in a way that informs viewers just how significant the exception will become. It opens in the middle of a conversation between House and chief of medicine, Dr. Lisa Cuddy, in a way that violates the well-established pattern of opening episodes with a non-regular character experiencing a medical emergency. The conversation in Cuddy's office establishes that a fellow doctor is ill and that Cuddy needs House to replace him and lecture on diagnostic medicine to a class of medical students. House characteristically tries to refuse, but accepts a release from doing clinic hours—an activity he finds distasteful due to the mundane ailments he encounters—in exchange for agreeing to lecture. House leaves Cuddy's office and finds a woman named Stacy, who we learn is his ex-girlfriend, in need of his diagnostic skills for her husband. Despite its atypical inclusion of regular characters, this pre-credit sequence offers two obvious potential patients—the ill doctor whom House must replace and Mark, husband to Stacy—although the deviation from the usual location external to the hospital suggests a greater break with conventional form could be occurring as well. A viewer could reasonably presume the still-young series was varying its conventional start, but the opening of "Three Stories" offers the ultimate misdirection, as the episode eventually reveals that the conversation between House and Cuddy involves the case of the week.[5]

After the opening credits, House begins his lecture to the medical students. He poses that there are three patients with leg pain and asks the students to diagnose the cause, as he gradually builds the stories of the patients. Although the series rarely uses techniques such as dream sequences, flashbacks, or imagined alternate realities, this episode eschews the realist techniques that normally characterize *House* by portraying characters whose conditions and embodiments shift each time House retells their scenarios. The cases begin as that of a farmer, golfer, and volleyball player, but House rewrites their histories and attributes each time he elaborates on the cases to the students, making "reality" difficult to discern. The actor playing the farmer (a middle-aged man) also appears as the volleyball player at first as well—although House describes the volleyball player as a teen girl. The golfer is actress Carmen Electra as herself, yet Doctors Foreman, Chase, and Cameron are interjected into the cases in a manner suggesting the scenario is real. Eventually three distinct actors embody the possible leg pain patients (none of whom are Electra) as House works through possible diagnoses, treatments, and consequences with the room of students.

FIGURE 2.1.

In an atypical episode, House eschews realist techniques by portraying characters whose conditions and embodiments shift as House retells their scenarios. Here, actress Carmen Elektra temporarily appears as an injured golfer.

Beyond the context of the lecture, this episode's inclusion of three different patients is uncommon, as the show usually features just one case. This unusual number of cases further confounds viewers' efforts to understand what is "really" going on, which isn't made clear until the episode is two-thirds complete. After multiple diagnoses and treatments of the farmer and volleyball player, House reveals the patient who began as a golfer, and is assumed to be a drug-seeker, has teak-colored urine. He offers a few additional indicators of the possible condition to the dumbfounded students when Dr. Cameron, a member of his diagnostic team, suggests "muscle death." House berates the students for not thinking of muscle death, while explaining that none of the man's doctors thought of it either, and that it took three days before the "patient" suggested it was muscle death. The episode then cycles back through vignettes in which the farmer and volleyball player are diagnosed and their doctors inform them that their legs may have to be amputated. When the episode turns back to the golfer/drug seeker/muscle death patient, Cuddy appears as the doctor. She delivers the news that amputation may be necessary. The scene transitions back to the lecture hall where House explains that an aneurism caused the muscle death, and a camera pan of the audience reveals all of House's team, Doctors Cameron, Foreman, and Chase, now seated in the back row, hanging on every detail. Foreman mutters, "God, you were right, it was House," and the scene cuts to House in bed as Cuddy's patient.

The remaining fourteen minutes of the episode shift to a more reliably realist style, although they do cut back and forth between flashbacks of House's treatment and his account of the tale to the class. In these scenes, the audience learns that Stacy was his girlfriend at the time of the aneurism, that House refused amputation—the better way to resolve the issue—and demanded a bypass to restore blood to the leg. But as Cuddy predicted, the pain was so great that he needed to be placed in a medical coma until the worst of it had passed. Stacy waited until

House was in the coma and, as his legal health-care proxy, allowed further surgery to remove the dead tissue. House's ongoing chronic pain results from the extent of the muscle removed in this subsequent surgery and the delayed diagnosis.

Beyond the idiosyncrasies of this particular episode, *House*'s treatment of character development is uncommon in a number of respects. First, it is most curious that the series waits until nearly the end of its first season to explain the origin of House's chronic pain. A conventional way to compensate for building the series around such a disagreeable protagonist would be to add layers to the character, to explain the origin of his pain, and/or to give it a cause that would warrant and justify the subsequent suffering and attitude that results.[6] Consider how CBS's *The Mentalist* (2008–present) explained the steady agitation of its less-than-personable protagonist as a result of the murder of his wife and daughter. This backstory is explained multiple times in the pilot and reemerges constantly throughout the series so that new or occasional viewers thoroughly understand the personality traits of the character and see how the exceptional tragedy he experienced justifies his focused search for the killer.

Instead of following such conventional explication and reiteration, the first season of *House* offers little explanation for House's physical or psychic ailments until this episode. The unconventionality of this strategy of under-explanation is furthered by the degree to which future episodes of the series do not recall House's origin story to audience members who missed this particular episode. Such recapping is easily and unobtrusively performed in other series by recalling crucial background details when new cast members are added. For example, in this case a new doctor could be informed of why House needs a cane by another character. Each episode of *House* introduces a new patient and in most cases provides a moment where House's poor bedside manner could be explained as a result of his chronic pain, including some details of its origin. However, the series does not recall this episode, or the information imparted in it again until late in season seven. In the interim, an entirely new group of doctors have become *House*'s primary team, and the series never depicts them inquiring about House's pain or another character explaining the limp.

It is also notable that this crucial origin story is told in such a convoluted manner. Viewers do not realize they are being told House's story until they are deep into it, and even once Foreman makes clear the significance of the story, the preceding deviation from realist narrative and inconsistent blending of three different stories make it difficult to identify what parts of the previous narrative of the golfer/drug seeker were real. Moreover, why confuse the story by suggesting the patient could be a drug seeker? Viewers know House as a drug addict, but he would not have been before the injury. The significance of the episode's more complicated techniques becomes clear if one considers the narratives and narrative techniques not chosen: House could have directly explained the incident in telling another character why he and Stacy broke up; the classroom technique could have been retained with just one case; all three cases could have been used without the constant variation in situations. These "easier" ways of incorporating the same information suggests the choice of complex techniques was deliberate.

The episode provides an explanation for House's devotion to his guiding mantra that "everybody lies," a crucial component of his character's psychology, in two different ways. First, the audience and lecture hall of medical students see that diagnosticians must face unreliable information from patients through House's repeated and varied presentations of the patient's situations and ailments. Patients, even when not trying to confuse a diagnostician, change their stories and omit vital details in ways that require physicians to reconsider everything they thought they knew. The deviation from realist storytelling illustrates to the viewer how diagnosticians might also feel that they don't "know" anything. With the things thought to be certain and true proven false, the episode appears to allegorize House's view of the world and justification for his conviction that everybody lies. The episode also depicts House's betrayal by Stacy, providing insight into his general distrust of people outside of diagnostics. Stacy acts in what she believes is House's best interest once he is comatose and defies his expressed treatment desire. His insistence upon the medical possibility of maintaining the leg and his life appears irrational—at one point she asks if he'd cut off his leg to save her, which he acknowledges he'd do—but his faith in medicine proves wise. The suspicion with which House regards self-disclosures begins to make more sense in the context of this tale in which his closest confidant betrays his clearly expressed desires.

The writers of House, including, notably, series creator David Shore, who penned this episode, use unconventional techniques to provide more than the morsels of character development commonly offered in each episode, thus helping to compel the audience to take an ongoing interest in the series beyond the short-term gratification of seeing the case of the week solved and whether the doctors are able to save the patient. But despite this structural variation, the episode perpetuates the general beliefs and outlook of the series.

The question for the critical analyst, then, is what is the consequence of this unconventional treatment of character? Throughout most episodes and seasons, the origins of House's bizarre actions are commonly attributed to "House being House." This phrase, used most often by those who have a long relationship with House, such as Doctors Wilson and Cuddy, refers to House's monomaniacal and socially unacceptable behavior, often to suggest that abnormal behavior is consistent with what characters can expect from him. Some characters know his story, which is presented as a defining cause of his behavior. Yet knowing the origin of House's injury does not change how his team approaches him. Moreover, other characters who join later and never learn the truth do learn how to "treat" House nonetheless. To handle the situation of House—to deal with a friend and coworker who suffers constant pain—it makes no difference whether that pain originated from a rare infection, a stabbing wound, or an aneurism. The series' handling of House's truth thus affirms the series' principle that understanding a history doesn't help understand an illness—knowing why House has pain doesn't help in dealing with or helping him. "Three Stories" illustrates the need to look beyond plot structure in assessing the simplicity or complexity of narrative and character. Although the staid features of episodic structure might allow for repetitive act structure and enforced conclusions, this episode illustrates the creative possibilities in character development and series outlook that can still be incorporated.

NOTES

1. Episodic shows have an industrial advantage because their ability to be viewed out of order and haphazardly yields larger audiences and thus license fees in syndication.
2. Jeffrey Sconce, "What If?: Charting Television's New Textual Boundaries," in *Television After TV: Essays on a Medium in Transition*, Lynn Spigel and Jan Olsson, eds. (Durham: Duke University Press, 2004), 97.
3. Roberta Pearson, "Anatomising Gilbert Grissom: The Structure and Function of the Televisual Character," in *Reading CSI: Crime TV Under the Microscope*, Michael Allen, ed. (London: I.B. Tauris, 2007).
4. Ibid., 49.
5. Just as this essay was completed, *House* aired episode 807, "Dead and Buried," in which it disregarded its usual opening structure for no apparent narrative reason.
6. For example, audience members could hardly shun House if his pain resulted from an injury suffered while saving a child or performing some other similarly heroic act.

FURTHER READING

DuBose, Mike S. "Morality, Complexity, Experts, and Systems of Authority in *House, M.D.*, or 'My Big Brain is My Superpower.'" *Television & New Media*, 11, 1 (2010): 20–36.

Mittell, Jason. "Previously On: Prime Time Serials and the Mechanics of Memory." In *Intermediality and Storytelling*, Marina Grishakova and Marie-Laure Ryan, eds. Berlin/New York: Walter de Gruyter, 2010.

O'Sullivan, Sean. "Broken on Purpose: Poetry, Serial Television, and the Season." *Storyworlds: A Journal of Narrative Studies* 2 (2010): 59–77.

Pearson, Roberta. "Anatomising Gilbert Grissom: The Structure and Function of the Televisual Character." In *Reading CSI: Crime TV Under the Microscope*, Michael Allen, ed. London: I.B. Tauris, 2007.

3

Life on Mars
Transnational Adaptation

CHRISTINE BECKER

Abstract: Remaking foreign programs is a common strategy for American television producers, but we must consider the contexts of each nation's industrial practices to fully understand such remakes. Christine Becker looks closely at both the British original and the American remake of *Life on Mars* to explore how contrasting norms of scheduling and serial formats help explain the differences in both storytelling and popular success between the two versions.

With the exception of the soap opera format, television dramas in Britain largely operate as short-run series, with as few as six episodes constituting a single "season," and only one or a handful of seasons making up the entirety of a program's run.[1] As a result, writers for such series can plot out prescribed endpoints to stories before launching production. In contrast to this "definite end" model, American network television generally operates through the "infinite middle" model, wherein writers for successful programs have to continually devise ways to delay the narrative endpoint in order to keep the show running for over twenty episodes a season, year after year, while also bearing in mind that a show could be cancelled at virtually any time. As Russell Davies, the creator of the British *Queer as Folk* (Channel 4, 1999–2000), said of the American remake (Showtime, 2000–2005) at the latter's onset: "The most important thing is to think of the U.S. version as a new show, a different show. Even before they'd written a word, a 22-episode series is a profoundly different thing, a different concept, to an eight-parter."[2]

American remakes of British dramas thus throw into relief the challenge of translating a show from one storytelling mode and industrial practice into another. In particular, the ABC remake (2008–2009) of the BBC's *Life on Mars* (2006–2007) offers a fruitful case study. Both versions have a nearly equal number of episodes: the British version ran for sixteen hour-long episodes split into two series units, and the U.S. season ran for seventeen 43-minute episodes before cancellation. The latter circumstance further offers an example of what can occur when an American series transitions from an infinite-middle to a definite-end model in response to advance notice of cancellation. Might a similar number of episodes and a similar chance to implement a definitive ending result in similar narratives?

To answer this question, I draw on formal analysis and consider industrial conditions in comparing the two *Life on Mars* productions in order to shed light on the impact that industry practices can have upon television narrative techniques. The essay will center in particular on narrative comparisons of three sets of paired episodes: the premiere episodes; two climatic middle episodes (in the British version, the series one finale and in the U.S. version, the last episode that aired before the two-month-long mid-season hiatus); and the series finales.

The initial premise of both series is the same: a police detective named Sam Tyler is hit by a car in the present day, and when he wakes up from the accident, he inexplicably finds himself in 1973. He is still in the same city and still Sam Tyler but assumed by those in his precinct, which is still the same as before the accident, to be a detective just arriving on transfer from a town called Hyde. Across the course of the series, Sam must figure out how he can get back to the present and keep his wits about him in the process. While this broad premise is the same in both versions, several differences in the opening episodes point to substantial influences from the infinite-middle versus the definite-end storytelling models.

Following the time travel opening, the primary narrative in each version of the first episode revolves around the 1973 search for a criminal suspect whom Sam believes to be responsible for kidnapping his fellow detective and girlfriend, Maya, in the present. Throughout both versions, Sam keeps seeing and hearing hospital sights and sounds, such as a heart monitor and doctors treating a patient, transmitted via radios and TV sets. Thus, it is implied that Sam is in a coma in the present and that the 1973 past is merely a creation of his unconscious imagination. Both Sams come to believe by episode's end that killing themselves in the past world will jolt them out of the coma. But in the U.K. version ("Episode One," January 9, 2006), a sympathetic police officer named Annie talks Sam out of jumping off the precinct building by convincing him that the 1973 world could be reality, and that perhaps he is part of it for a larger reason yet undiscovered. In the U.S. version ("Out Here in the Fields," October 9, 2008), it is Sam's swaggering boss, Gene Hunt, who intervenes by breaking up a situation in which Sam tries to get the criminal suspect to shoot him. One outcome of the British ending is that it places the series' central enigma squarely on the coma situation: is this reality or is Sam in a coma? In contrast, Hunt's intervention in the U.S. opener both plays down the coma possibility and emphasizes Sam's clash with Hunt, a conflict frequently exploited in the series.

In fact, the U.S. pilot advances more potential narrative threads right at the start of the series than the first U.K. episode. For instance, Sam's evident rapport with Annie, coupled with his conflicted relationship with Maya in the U.S. plot, clearly point toward an infinite-middle-model love triangle in past and present romantic relationships and a potentially endless "will they or won't they" scenario. Further tension is also prefigured by the characterization of a cop named Ray, who grumbles when Sam arrives because he fears the new arrival will block his promotion. The U.K. version does unspool these serial threads, but they're not all evident in the first episode. This difference calls attention to the industrial demands of the pilot system in the United States wherein a pilot has to lay its narrative cards on the table from the start or risk not being picked up to series. Conversely, the writers for the short-run British series knew they would have the full eight episodes to play out the stories and could thus utilize delayed exposition.

Following the opening, both series structure each episode's narrative largely as a police procedural, dominated by a crime of the week that often ties in with something Sam knows about from the present, while serial elements related to Sam's mysterious situation and interpersonal relationships constitute one-quarter or less of a typical episode. Many of the episodic elements in both versions are similar, as the American version drew liberally from the procedural stories of the original. However, the U.K. version keeps serially developing the coma as a logical explanation, while the U.S. version shifts away from that rationale without clearly defining what Sam might be experiencing. In the second U.S. episode ("The Real Adventures of the Unreal Sam Tyler," October 16, 2008), Sam lists off some possible options—mind experiment, time travel, extraterrestrials—and we get various hints pointing toward those options as the episodes continue.

What was clearly being laid in beginning of the American *Life on Mars* was the groundwork for a science-fiction series mythology for fans to try and piece together as the show continued, akin to *Lost* (ABC, 2004–2010). Indeed, it would appear that ABC hoped *Life on Mars* would offer life after *Lost*.[3] For a significant chunk of the U.S. version of *Life on Mars*, narrative elements point toward where future action could take Sam, while the episodic action continues largely parallel to that long-term storytelling. Conversely, the U.K. version uses its coma allusions, and the unification of past and present and the episodic and serial modes that they engender, to delve more vertically into Sam's character, deeper into his mental state. Here we can see a significant impact of series duration, wherein the infinite middle can allow for a wider range of serial options while the definite end encourages a narrower focus.

Such contrasts are further evident in the eighth and seventh episodes of the U.K. and U.S. versions respectively (the U.K. episode being a series one ender, the U.S. one a hiatus launcher). Both episodes present Sam re-experiencing a traumatic childhood incident that he now intends to prevent, as he tries to convince his violent father not to desert the family. While Sam does prevent one past certainty—namely, Vic viciously beating Annie—he fails to stop Vic from departing. In both episodes, four-year-old Sam gets the same speech from mom about dad leaving that he was always destined to get. But importantly, in the U.K. version ("Episode 8," February 26, 2006), Sam willingly lets Vic go in order to prevent his childhood self from seeing his dad sent to prison. In the U.S. version ("The Man Who Sold the World," November 20, 2008), Vic shoots Sam in order to escape. Given that U.K. Sam's anguish over whether to let Vic go or not is once again laden with more hospital sounds, it cements even more the likelihood that he is experiencing a coma vision. Subsequently, his decision to let his father go constitutes an acceptance of staying in that coma and in the past. This leaves the narrative open for a second series continuation of the show's central dilemma even as it provides a measure of emotional resolution if this was to have been the end of the series.

In the U.S. version's midpoint, there are no coma allusions, nor are we confronted with Sam's psychological torture over whether or not to let his dad go free. Instead, he tells Annie, "I thought this was the reason I was here, to stop my dad from leaving. But I think maybe it was to show me who he really was." Sam's connection to his father is thus stressed episodically, while the serial mythology resurfaces in the next scenes, when Sam follows a set of clues to an address and receives a phone call there from a mysterious, robotic-sounding male who tells him, "You're doing a good job, Sam. I need you to go to the basement. Go down to the basement, Sam." The episode ends, Christmas hiatus cliffhanger in place, with a tantalizing tease for where the show's mythology might take viewers next. The U.S. halfway point ends on a promise of more plot, while the U.K. midpoint dwells more on character emotion, with both options partly driven by scheduling requirements.

The next set of episodes in the U.S. version (episodes 8–11, January and February 2009) push even more heavily toward possible options for the show's mythology: information about Sam is being filed into something called the Aries Project; a Russian man whom Sam interrogates says that Sam previously worked on experiments that involved sending miniature robots into the human body to plant memories; a UFO expert says alien abductees commonly tell stories of being plucked from earth and dropped into the same place only years earlier; and Sam comes across a city councilman who claims he is from 2009. These elements don't all fully cohere together serially. Some could fit together, like the Aries Project and the councilman; some really couldn't, like the Russian experiment and the alien abduction. Even so, the serial mythology elements dominate viewer attention in this middle set of episodes, and it is evident that the writers were searching for expansive narrative options.

Strikingly, despite the U.K. first series' finale seemingly locking down the coma story, the initial second series' episodes complicate matters with the additions of the mysterious caller and a possible new explanation: Sam really is from Hyde and working undercover to root out corruption, but, suffering from amnesia due to a car accident, he has confused his cover story and his actual life. Head writer Matthew Graham said that he wanted to add more spice to the second season with this ambiguity, even as the coma story was still intended as the explanation all along.[4]

The good news for *Life on Mars* U.K. was that this serial nuance helped to keep viewer interest up. The bad news for *Life on Mars* U.S. was that its mythology teases were evidently not effective at drawing in *Lost* viewers or anyone else, as the ratings only kept dwindling. Accordingly, ABC publicly announced in early March that the show would be cancelled, infinite middle no longer required. However, the network did allow the producers to complete the seventeen-episode commitment, and the cancellation order reportedly came with a handful of episodes yet to be locked in, thus granting the writers the opportunity to provide a definite end to the story.[5]

The primary crime story of the U.K. series finale ("Episode 8," April 10, 2007) centers on Sam taking down Hunt for corruption and police brutality. At this point, Sam believes that his present coma self has a brain tumor, and the logic of the past-present analogy suggests that Gene Hunt is his tumor. Subsequently, an ill-fated crime sting that Hunt has devised goes awry, putting all of the cops' lives in jeopardy, and as Sam sees Hunt shot down, he is brought back to the present, awakening from his coma and recovering from what was indeed a tumor. Sam struggles to feel alive and involved in the present, however, and he's haunted by an unfilled promise to Annie that he would save her. Thus, in a stunning act, Sam jumps off the precinct roof, apparently putting himself in a coma again, and returns to 1973 to save Annie and the others. As with the series one finale, Sam once again reconciles himself to staying, only this time we recognize it's for good, as the car radio plays the sounds of Sam flat-lining in the present-day hospital and he drives off with his fellow detectives.[6]

The U.S. version ("Life is a Rock," April 1, 2009) is completely different. Sam is contacted by the mysterious caller again and told that if he completes a set of three tasks, he can go home. However, after completing the first two, Sam hangs up on the caller before receiving his third instruction, deciding that he prefers staying in 1973. He hugs Hunt in a gesture of reconciliation, the image suddenly pixilates, we hear audio flashbacks to key moments through the series, we see flashes of spaceship imagery, and Sam then awakens in an astronaut pod. The year is 2035, and Sam is in a space ship approaching Mars.

In the show's final scene, we learn that Sam has been traveling for two years on a mission to Mars—a development that nearly literalizes the show's title. To keep his brain engaged throughout the long trip, Sam was kept in a neuro-stimulation virtual reality dream state. "Sam 2035" chose to experience the virtual reality of being a cop in 2008 (the show offers no explanation why), but a meteor storm disrupted the program, which subsequently left Sam's 2008 virtual self surrounded by a 1973 virtual reality. As in *The Wizard of Oz*, most of the past 1973 characters have present 2035 counterparts. Most importantly, the man we knew as Gene Hunt is a fellow astronaut and—surprisingly—Sam's father. All of the astronauts converse as they awaken, with Sam being only slightly bothered, and more bemused, by what he has experienced.

In a moment of seriousness, Sam tells his father, "I really don't want to fight with you anymore, Dad." Thus, the U.S. version's serial elements add up not to a complex mythology or an existentialist tussling with reality, but instead are part of a dream simulation in the course of which Sam apparently came to terms with his relationship with his father. The show's creators have insisted that this was the ending they had in mind from the start, and certainly the space travel and rocket references are evident from the early episodes of the show.[7]

However, the middle episodes, produced before cancellation was a likelihood, unquestionably point toward a much more comprehensive explanation for Sam's predicament.[8] I believe that a more complex serial mythology would have been a necessity if the show had received a second season order. In comparison, episodes 12–15 only barely touch on the mythology aspect and are much more heavily episodic in nature. Whether this is because the writers suspected the show would be cancelled by the time of their production and didn't need to develop the wider mythology further or because the writers were just trying to stretch out the infinite middle in case of a renewal is unknown. But if the U.S. ending that was delivered had been the ending after multiple seasons, telling the audience that everything they had watched for season after season was fake, with relationships turning out to have minimal consequence and purpose, and with clues small and large being a huge collection of mere red herrings and brick wall diversions, fan outrage probably would have dwarfed the controversies surrounding other frustrating finales of shows like *Lost*, *Battlestar Galactica*, and *The Sopranos*.

In the end, even though both the U.S. and U.K. versions aired nearly the same number of episodes, Russell Davies's distinction about remakes being different shows still applies. Because the U.S. producers were initially planning for an infinite middle based on the industrial demands of American network television, the U.S. *Life on Mars* is a fundamentally different show than the U.K. one. The U.K. version's serial elements are primarily focused on character psychology, resulting in a thematically fused and rather dark story about existentialist alienation and liberation. British head writer Matthew Graham highlighted this emphasis in discussing his choice of ending with the predicted coma explanation: "For me, it

FIGURE 3.1.
The U.S. version's Sam writes out possible explanations for his situation, evoking the image of an American writer proposing plotlines on a writers' room whiteboard.

was much more important that there was a strong emotional closure to the story. That was more important than a massive twist."[9] Such intricate emotional cohesion is lacking in the lighter, truncated U.S. story. Instead, *Life on Mars*'s seventeen American episodes are fundamentally about plot, about what happened, not so much why it happened or how it affected its central character.

I suggest that this circumstance is at least partly borne of the industrial model of American long-form network television, in which seriality is about getting to next week and next renewal, not necessarily to the end of the story. Of course, the journey to that end still has the potential to be every bit as gratifying to viewers as a more focused short-run British drama, and *Life of Mars*'s U.S. writers certainly had ambitious creative visions for the series. But as the comparisons outlined in this essay indicate, writerly ambitions in both U.S. and U.K. television are usually subordinate to industrial demands, whether an untimely cancellation or a limited-episode order. And as this case thus further illustrates, only by marrying industrial analysis with narrative analysis can we properly understand seriality on American and British television.

NOTES

1. The term "season" is not used in Britain because their programming schedule is not dictated by the September-to-May cycle as it is in the United States. Instead, a grouping of successive episodes is called a "series."

2. Della Famina, "Enquiring Minds Want to Know," *Television Without Pity*, October 26, 2000, http://www.televisionwithoutpity.com/show/queer_as_folk_uk/enquiring_minds_want_to_know.php.

3. In fact, the show's producers reportedly called the serial elements "the *Lost* side" of the show when breaking story. Interview with Mark Ambrose, Vice President of Drama

Development, 20th Century Fox Television, February 21, 2011, Los Angeles, CA. Notably, ABC aired *Life on Mars* after *Lost* at midseason.

4. Ian Wylie, "*Life on Mars*: The Answers," *Life of Wylie*, April 17, 2007, http://lifeofwylie. com/2007/04/11/life-on-mars-the-answers/.

5. Josef Adalian, "ABC Gives Life on Mars a Finale," *TV Week*, March 2, 2009, http://www. tvweek.com/news/2009/03/abc_gives_life_on_mars_a_final.php.

6. Due to space limitations, I am not addressing the final reflexive shot that closes the episode.

7. Brian Ford Sullivan, "Interview: *Life on Mars* Executive Producer Josh Appelbaum, Part 2," *The Futon Critic*, October 6, 2008, http://www.thefutoncritic.com/interviews. aspx?id=20081006_lifeonmars.

8. As aired, the U.S. series' final revelation lacks coherence and was roundly mocked by the show's committed fans. After all, why would a virtual reality simulator create such a bizarre, spiraling set of paranoid circumstances for what is supposed to be a comforting state? Plus, in the final episode we see neither Maya's 2035 counterpart, nor that of Sam's 1973 father, nor does the virtual reality premise explain why we saw scenes that Sam wasn't a part of. I could go on.

9. Ian Wylie, "Life on Mars Was Wonderful," *Manchester Evening News*, April 11, 2007, http://menmedia.co.uk/manchestereveningnews/ tv_and_showbiz/s/1004158_life_on_mars_was_wonderland.

FURTHER READING

Dunleavy, Tricia. *Television Drama: Agency, Form, Innovation*. London: Palgrave MacMillan, 2009.

Nelson, Robin. *State of Play: Contemporary High-End TV Drama*. Manchester: Manchester University Press, 2008.

Newman, Michael. "From Beats to Arcs: Toward a Poetics of Television Narrative." *The Velvet Light Trap* (Fall 2006): 16–28.

Smith, Greg M. *Beautiful TV: The Art and Argument of Ally McBeal*. Austin, TX: University of Texas Press, 2007.

4

Mad Men
Visual Style

JEREMY G. BUTLER

Abstract: Through a detailed examination of how the visual look of *Mad Men* conveys the show's meanings and emotional affect, Jeremy G. Butler provides a model for how to perform a close analysis of television style for a landmark contemporary series. See our companion website, howtowatchtelevision.com for more images and a video clip to supplement this piece.

Much has been written about the look of *Mad Men* (AMC, 2007–present)—and not surprisingly, as the program has vividly evoked mid-century American life—the hairstyles and clothing, the offices and homes, and, of course, the chain-smoking and four-martini lunches of a particular, privileged segment of American society. However, *Mad Men* is more than a slavish reproduction of a bygone era. It sees that era through a contemporary filter that recognizes the despair and alienation that lay just beneath the surface. And it implicitly critiques the power structures of that time, which both casually and brutally subordinated working-class people, women, gays, and ethnic and racial minorities.

To understand how *Mad Men* accomplishes this critique, we need to look closely at its visual style. By "style," I don't mean just its fashion sense, although costume design is definitely a key stylistic component. Rather, I examine the program's style in terms of its mise-en-scene, or elements arranged in front of the camera, and its cinematography, or elements associated with the camera itself. Mise-en-scene covers set, lighting, and costume design, as well as the positioning of the actors on the set. Cinematography includes framing, camera angle, choice of film stock, and camera movement. In addition, it is also critical to attend to the program's editing design since editing determines what we see on the screen, for how long, and in what context. Together, then, mise-en-scene, cinematography, and editing are aspects of television style that showrunner Matthew Weiner, his crew, and his actors use to construct their twenty-first-century critique of 1960s American values.

To start an analysis of *Mad Men*'s mise-en-scene, we should look first at its set design, which serves the crucial function of establishing the program's time period. This is achieved both subtly—by the interior design of the rooms that characters inhabit—and not so subtly—by objects such as a March 1960 calendar that appears in close-up in the very first episode. Period authenticity is clearly important to showrunner Weiner, and the program contains remarkably few anachronistic objects, considering its relatively limited budget (when compared to feature films) and the grind of producing a weekly television program. However, period verisimilitude is not the only significant aspect of the set design. Equally important is the use of recurring sets to express the rigidity and repressiveness of early-1960s American society—as can be seen in the office of ad agency Sterling Cooper and the suburban home of Don and Betty Draper (both of which locales are replaced after season three).

The office set clearly reflects the power structure at the agency (figure 4.1). Secretaries are clustered together in a "pool," with their desks arrayed on an inflexible grid that mirrors the florescent lighting pattern above them. In this public space, they are at the mercy of the higher-ranking men of the office who make degrading, condescending comments about them, take their work for granted, and shamelessly ogle new hires, such as Peggy Olson in the first season. Except for the powerful and physically imposing office manager, Joan Harris, the women, including Peggy, have little control over their own space—unlike the men who move through it imperiously. The desk and lighting grids of the set design position them as if they were rats in an executive maze. Thus, the set design and the blocking of the actors' positions within it serve to dehumanize and contain the female characters.

The "mad men" are masters of their own spaces—afforded personal offices that physically separate them from the women. The higher up the corporate ladder, the more personalized these offices are, with agency head Bert Cooper's as the most distinctive. All who enter it are required, as per Asian custom, to remove their shoes, and then, once inside, they are confronted with Japanese erotic art and an abstract expressionist painting that is so mysterious and so massively expensive that employees sneak into Bert's office after-hours to stare at it in awe and incomprehension, while submissively holding their shoes in their hands.[1] Individual offices like Cooper's serve as spaces of authority, power, and privacy in contrast to the collective space of the secretarial pool.

Of course, Bert and the other men can move through the secretaries' space with impunity, as Pete Campbell does in figure 4.1. The social status and power attached to the private offices are made clear in Peggy's ascent from secretary to copywriter and full-fledged member of "Creative." Initially in the second season, she is forced to share space in what becomes the photocopy room, but eventually

FIGURE 4.1.
The rigid power struc-
ture of the ad agency
is visually manifested
in the office spaces of
Mad Men.

she gets her own office, and in the layout of the new Sterling Cooper Draper Pryce (SCDP) agency, she scores a prestigious one next to Don Draper's. However, the SCDP offices are not nearly as commodious as Sterling Cooper's. Contrasted with the wide-open space of Sterling Cooper's office, SCDP's diminished space visually echoes the diminished fortunes of the ad men as they struggle to start a new agency.

Mad Men's offices are not the only sets that repress and contain their characters. The homes and apartments of several characters serve important narrative functions as well. Central among these is the Draper home, the picture-perfect representation of affluent suburban existence, in which, however, the Draper family lives a less-than-perfect life. Indeed, with a disaffected daughter, a restless, adulterous mother, and a similarly adulterous father whose entire identity is also a fraudulent fabrication, the house is filled with melancholy and depression. In short, the idealized mise-en-scene of the Draper's home is frequently at odds with the despair of its inhabitants.

The pressures within their home finally result in divorce in the episode titled "The Grown-Ups" (November 1, 2009), which was the next-to-last episode of season 3 and included events that coincided with President John F. Kennedy's assassination on November 22, 1963. The episode contains a breakfast scene with a set design that exemplifies *Mad Men*'s style of decor in that it could have been lifted from a 1950s sitcom or a *Good Housekeeping* article. Pine-paneled walls, avocado-green appliances, and an oh-so-modern (electric!) stovetop with a skillet of scrambled eggs are part of the mise-en-scene, as are 1963-appropriate props such as a glass milk bottle, a loaf of Pleasantville(!) white bread, and various knickknacks. Into this mise-en-scene are inserted the conventional suburban "housewife" in her housecoat, the conventional urban "businessman" in his suit, and a pair of conventional children in their pajamas. But the previous scene has been anything but conventional, as Betty angrily tells Don, "I want to scream at you, for ruining all of this [the suburban life and home]" (figure 4.2), and, saying that she doesn't love him anymore, demands a divorce. The next morning, as Don exits the house through the kitchen for what will be the last time, he and the children speak, but the "grown-ups" of the episode's title exchange no dialogue. The bitter contrast between the scene's pessimistic emotional tone and its optimistic morning-time mise-en-scene characterizes *Mad Men*'s critique of mid-century America's superficial normalcy and repression of the messier aspects of human behavior in the name of conformity to the dominant social order. The mess still exists, but it's been pushed below the surface. As the 1960s progressed, however, that repression became less and less tenable. *Mad Men* feeds on our understanding of what is to come in the latter part of the rebellious 1960s, looking backwards and forwards simultaneously.

The dressing of *Mad Men*'s sets with time-appropriate objects creates the viewing pleasure of picking out period details, like the rotary-dial phones and IBM Selectric typewriters shown in figure 4.1. Details from the 1960s are necessary to construct the program's general time frame, but the program also uses objects in nuanced ways to anchor episodes to particular days in American history. "The Grown-Ups," for example, opens on an unspecified day in 1963. The year has been established earlier in the third season, and the characters complain about the lack of heat in the office, so we know it must be fall or winter. Then, in the background of a shot of Duck Phillips in a hotel room, we see the first of two televisions that are turned on and tuned to a live broadcast of *As the World Turns* (CBS, 1956–2010). The sound is off and the television has less visual impact than the ostentatious glass lamps in the foreground of the room—although the shot has been carefully framed to include the TV screen. The very next scene shows us Pete and Harry Crane, the head of Sterling Cooper's media-buying department, in Harry's cluttered office. A television is on in the background here, too, its presence emphasized when Pete asks Harry, "Can you turn that off?" Harry replies, "Not really," though he does turn the volume down. As Pete and Harry talk, a CBS News bulletin comes on in the background, but they are oblivious to it. In his hotel room, Duck turns off the same bulletin when Peggy arrives for a lunchtime assignation. It's not until the Sterling Cooper employees crowd into Harry's office—one of the few with a television—that Harry and Pete realize what has happened and that we viewers begin to see the impact of the event on *Mad Men*'s fictional world.

For the rest of the episode, televisions provide crucial narrative information and prompt characters to take, at times, extreme actions. Betty is particularly affected, with her confrontation of Don taking place beside a television tuned to funeral preparations (figure 4.2). Later, after seeing Lee Harvey Oswald killed on

FIGURE 4.2.
Mad Men's detailed mise-en-scene just barely contains the emotional upheaval below the surface of mid-century American "normalcy."

live television, she screams and exclaims, "What is going on?!" Motivated by the television violence she has witnessed and the collapse of her privileged world, she eventually leaves the house to meet Henry Francis, and he proposes to her. Thus, the television, an element of mise-en-scene, evolves in this episode from seemingly insignificant set dressing to major narrative catalyst, blending the personal crises of the characters with larger moments in American history.

The episode ends with one final comment on an object and its implicit reference to the assassination. After exiting the kitchen of his house in the scene discussed above, Don arrives at the empty and dark office, which is closed for a national day of mourning, and finds Peggy, who has come to escape her grieving roommate and relatives. The harsh, punishing florescent lights are off, and she is working by the natural light of a window, augmented by a desk lamp. Don examines the Aqua Net hairspray storyboards on her desk, one of which contains a high-angle view of four individuals in an open convertible (figure 4.3). Before he can offer an opinion, she anticipates his criticism: "It doesn't shoot until after Thanksgiving. We'll be okay." But Don authoritatively dismisses this delusion by shaking his head. The scene is rather elliptical unless the viewer is able to place this storyboard image within the iconography of 1963 and recognize how much it resembles widely circulated high-angle photos of the presidential convertible limousine in which Kennedy was shot (figure 4.4). Since none of those photos is shown in the episode, only viewers who associate the storyboard imagery with the visual vocabulary of 1963 will understand Don and Peggy's motivation for considering redoing the storyboard.

This short scene also illuminates *Mad Men*'s central preoccupation. It is a program about consumer products and the imagery attached to them through advertising. Moreover, *Mad Men* is obsessed with objects and their representation, and—by extension—with humans and their representations. Just as Don, who

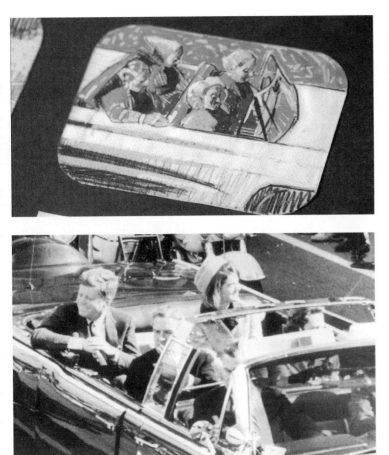

FIGURE 4.3.
Don nixes the plan
for a hairspray
commercial after
seeing a storyboard
that evokes widely
circulated photos
of the convertible
in which President
Kennedy was shot.

FIGURE 4.4.
Mad Men relies
on the viewer's
associations with
this photograph
of the Kennedy
motorcade.

was born Richard "Dick" Whitman, has *styled* himself as "Don Draper," so has Don mastered the ability to style products in a way that satisfies his clients and increases their revenue. One could even say that Don is a designer of his own mise-en-scene (his clothing, hair style, walk, the spaces in which he chooses to live and work, and so on), but, of course, Weiner and his crew and cast have actually constructed the mise-en-scene for both Draper and *Mad Men*.

The way that *Mad Men* is filmed and cut is distinctive, but unlike the show's mise-en-scene, its cinematography and editing do not mimic 1960s television. "The Grown-Ups" calls attention to this difference by giving glimpses of live, black-and-white television from 1963: *Mad Men* clearly does not look anything like *As the World Turns*. Rather, it uses a mode of production associated with contemporary high-budget, primetime dramas (e.g., *Lost*, *The Sopranos*, and the *CSI* programs) and with theatrical films. This single-camera mode of production allows for more precise visual control than is possible in the multiple-camera mode of production that was used by *As the World Turns* throughout its long run. That precision is evident in the final shot of "The Grown-Ups," where cinematography is used both to build a mood and develop characterization. After saying goodnight to Peggy in the main Sterling Cooper office, Don enters his own private office and hangs up his hat while the camera shoots him through the doorway. The camera then arcs slightly to the left to reveal a liquor cabinet as Don walks into the room. Not bothering to remove his coat, Don reaches for a bottle and begins mixing a drink (figure 4.5). The scene then cuts to black and the end credits roll while Skeeter Davis is heard singing "The End of the World": "Don't they know it's the end of the world 'cause you don't love me anymore?"

Episode director Barbet Schroeder and episode director of photography Christopher Manley use framing and camera angle to signify Don's isolation. Keeping the camera outside the room and surrounding Don with the frosted-window walls of the doorway frame have the effect of both emphasizing his remoteness and distancing us from him. As shown above in figures 4.1 and 4.2, *Mad Men* often shoots from a low camera angle that incorporates the ceiling in the frame. This shot is just below Don's eye-level, looking slightly up at him, which brings the ceiling into the top of the frame, blocking it off. The low-key lighting of the office—an aspect of mise-en-scene—works with the framing to blend Don into the darkness. In many TV programs and films, low angles emphasize the size and bulk and even heroic nature of a person or object, but in *Mad Men* the low angles more often make the ceiling close in on the characters, accentuating the repressiveness of their work and home spaces. In short, this scene's cinematography and mise-en-scene collaborate to generate an atmosphere of entrapment, despair, and alienation.

Mad Men's implementation of the single-camera mode of production allows for editing patterns that would be difficult or impossible in the multiple-camera mode used by soap operas. A breakdown of the kitchen scene previously described in which Don and Betty exchange no words (posted on this book's companion website) illustrates this point, and illuminates the narrative significance of characters looking at other characters.

As edited by Tom Wilson, the scene begins in the hallway as Don comes downstairs and walks through the dining room to the kitchen door. There, he pauses, unseen by his family. We see a point-of-view shot, over his shoulder into the kitchen. The next shot is a reverse angle from inside the kitchen, but not from anyone's point of view as he is still unobserved. We return to Don's point-of-view shot as he enters the kitchen and announces his presence: "Good morning." The children respond, but Betty pointedly does not. We cut to *her* point of view of Don even though she is looking down at the stove and not at him. The camera stays behind her, panning and tracking with Don as he crosses the room. During

this short walk, he looks directly at her, but she does not return his gaze. The camera movement comes to a rest from nobody's point of view, showing Betty, Don, and the kids; she looks straight ahead, and he and the children look at each other. The camera stays objective for four medium shots, with the fourth shot offering a subtle bit of camera work. Bobby looks at Sally, and when she turns around to look at Betty, the camera pulls focus from him to her—a distance of just a few feet. In terms of narrative motivation and the emotional rhythm of the scene, Sally needs to be sharply in focus as it is her look that motivates the next cut to Betty in a low-angle subjective shot where she looks back toward Sally and the camera. The scene concludes with a camera angle very close to the earlier one from Don's point of view, showing the entire kitchen as he sends one more unreturned look in Betty's direction before leaving.

This close examination of the ordering and framing of shots in the kitchen scene shows how important characters' looks—that is, whom they look at rather than how they look to others—are to this episode, the program, and television drama in general. And this dance of looks is achieved largely through editing, as in the eye-line match cut from Sally to Betty. Multiple-camera programs can also be fundamentally about looks, but this single-camera scene contains shots that would be too time-consuming or troublesome to capture during a multiple-camera shoot. Specifically, the camera has been moved to several positions well inside a four-walled set, showing us the Draper kitchen from virtually every angle. Multiple-camera shows, with their three-walled sets, cannot bring the camera as close to the characters' perspectives as *Mad Men* does. A seemingly simple shot such as the low-angle, medium close-up of Betty with a camera positioned deep inside the set would be nearly impossible to achieve in a multiple-camera production, whether that production be *As the World Turns* in 1963 or a twenty-first-century multiple-camera program such as *Two and a Half Men* (CBS, 2003–present).

Much like Douglas Sirk's melodramas in the 1950s, *Mad Men* makes sophisticated use of visual style—mise-en-scene, cinematography, and editing—to mount a critique of American consumer culture. The mise-en-scene of "The Grown-Ups," in particular, is about the significance of objects and about characters gazing at them and at each other. Built around looks at television sets, the episode provides an implicit commentary upon the medium's increasing social significance in the 1960s and the terrors that it would bring into our living rooms. Betty's horrified gaze as she watches the killing of Oswald from her suburban couch can be extrapolated to the viewing of televised violence of the Vietnam War and the assassinations to come in the later 1960s. On a personal level, the emotional and narrative power of looks—both returned and unreturned—is featured repeatedly in *Mad Men*. And its mode of production allows the program's crew to maximize that power through creative cinematography and editing. The sleek look of *Mad Men* and its reproduction of 1960s modernity might initially draw us to the program, but it is the characters' looks at one another that weave the emotional fabric of its stories. By dissecting the program's style, we can better understand *Mad Men*'s affective impact and its astute visual critique of mid-century America.

NOTES

1. The Japanese woodcut is Hokusai's *The Dream of the Fisherman's Wife,* and the abstract painting is an untitled one by Mark Rothko.

FURTHER READING

Bordwell, David, and Kristin Thompson. *Film Art: An Introduction*, 10th ed. New York: McGraw-Hill, 2013.

Butler, Jeremy G. *Television Style.* New York: Routledge, 2010.

Edgerton, Gary R. *Mad Men: Dream Come True TV.* London: I.B. Tauris, 2010.

5

Nip/Tuck
Popular Music

BEN ASLINGER

Abstract: Most analyses of television programs focus on a program's visual and narrative construction, but neglect the vital element of sound that is crucial to any show's style and meaning. Ben Aslinger listens closely to *Nip/Tuck*'s use of music, exploring how it helps shape the program's aesthetics and cultural representations.

Nip/Tuck's (FX, 2003–2010) pilot episode featured an extended sequence in which The Rolling Stones' "Paint It Black" plays as Sean McNamara and Christian Troy perform a facial reconstruction on a man who they find out later is a child molester trying to mask his identity. Most reviewers of the pilot (July 22, 2003) drew attention to the importance of popular music to the program's style, noting "the eerie use of The Rolling Stones' 'Paint it Black' to dramatize a facial reconstruction even before mentioning the plot or the performances."[1] *Nip/Tuck*'s emphasis on surgery, style, and music was even reinforced in promotional materials, most notably the flash-based "Can you cut like a rock star?" game on the FX website. The uses of popular music in *Nip/Tuck* distinguish the series from older medical dramas such as *Dr. Kildare* and more contemporary series such as *ER*, as well as point to the ways that industrial imperatives surrounding popular music licensing impact the formal properties of contemporary television texts.

Some critics have argued that the tracks used in *Nip/Tuck* are perfect sonic illustrations of the skin-deep, youth-obsessed, superficial Miami culture chronicled by the program. However, television scholars should be skeptical of critical commentaries that sum up popular music licensing and scoring practices in broad strokes but fail to pay sufficient attention to specific production practices. While such trade and popular press pieces might work to get at a superficial sense of a show's use of music, they fail to address the complex ways that popular music interacts with visual elements to convey meanings, and the multiple ways that

FIGURE 5.1. The fundamental link between music and *Nip/Tuck*'s "edgy" style was reinforced in promotional materials such as this game on the show's website.

producers and music supervisors use licenses to strategically add weight to key plot points, visual sequences, and dialogue exchanges.

Feminist media scholars have analyzed the ways that *Nip/Tuck* works to define beauty in dominant terms that privilege whiteness and an unattainable size and shape.[2] These scholars have analyzed gender performances in *Nip/Tuck* and makeover shows that enlist the medical gaze in order to create aspirational narratives and police beauty standards; however, analyses of television textuality must take into account not just visual elements and scriptwriting practices, but also the ways that television sound is constructed for meaning-making effects. By addressing the popular music soundtrack in *Nip/Tuck*, I add to previous analyses centering on the visual culture of the program and further explore how program producers imagined surgical and embodied aesthetics in the series. Popular music tracks work in *Nip/Tuck* to initiate surgical sequences, to "soften" surgical sequences by aestheticizing the penetration of the body, and to bridge *Nip/Tuck*'s focus on appearance with psychological interiority and character identifications. In order to connect industrial imperatives to textual outcomes, I begin by discussing how executive producer Ryan Murphy's collaboration with music supervisor P. J. Bloom created strategies for deploying popular music tracks. I then draw on existing scholarly work on the soundtrack in order to analyze how specific examples of licensing work to complicate viewer perceptions of *Nip/Tuck*'s narrative and diegesis (the storyworld it creates and inhabits).

Critical to establishing *Nip/Tuck*'s "edge" was the way the series used popular music and editing strategies to turn surgeries into televisual spectacles.[3] Murphy had previously produced *Popular* (1999–2001) for the WB, a network that was very influential in establishing the importance of popular music to 1990s definitions of "quality" production practices and strategies for targeting niche demographics. By drafting P. J. Bloom as the series music supervisor, Murphy worked to make the series edgy and to emphasize the meaning-making capacity of the popular music soundtrack.[4]

According to Bloom, music supervision typically abides by certain norms and conventions that are defined by the producer and are specific to a particular series. Given the timeline needed to secure music licenses, prepare temp tracks, and create a final, polished soundtrack, a clear sonic palette expedites decision-making and the production process.

Bloom argued that setting up the "sonic fingerprint" and "musical tone" for the series was one of the strategies that guided his work as a music supervisor.[5] "Most of the time, we try to use songs that speak lyrically to the procedures being conducted in the operating room," he said. "On occasion, we'll use music that speaks to the characters' individual tastes; but most often the songs are a satirical look at whatever cosmetic procedure the patient is undergoing."[6]

According to Bloom, two major strategies for *Nip/Tuck* were to use "classic" rock tunes for ironic and/or satirical effect and to use "cool" newer tunes (mainly electronic music) to depict the superficial, slick world of South Beach and certain surgeries. Murphy and Bloom also repurposed songs that older audiences would remember from their original contexts and that could be viewed during the burgeoning 1970s and 1980s nostalgia trend by audiences too young to remember their original radio and MTV airplay. The series' Miami location and the use of classic rock and pop songs may have reminded older viewers of the strategic deployment in *Miami Vice* (NBC, 1984–1989) of popular songs such as Phil Collins's "In the Air Tonight," but *Nip/Tuck* depicted a much grittier Miami than the earlier "big three" network series, which was produced during the decline of the classic network system, whereas *Nip/Tuck* was produced during what Amanda Lotz calls the transition to a "post-network era."[7]

Bloom and Murphy decided to use the Bang Olufsen stereo in the operating room as a character of sorts in the series, and the music that the stereo plays is an important part of most surgical sequences.[8] These sequences often begin with either anesthesiologist Liz Cruz or one of the nurses waving a gloved hand in front of the device in order to activate it and then zoom in on a spinning CD that is also the sync point for the start of the master recording. In effect, the program's surgical sequences are set in motion by powering up audio technologies.

In addressing the textual and stylistic importance of highlighting the selection of music and the handling of listening technologies on the screen, Ken Garner argues that Quentin Tarantino's films, especially *Reservoir Dogs, Pulp Fiction,*

FIGURE 5.2. Activation of the Bang Olufsen stereo in the operating room draws attention to the series' use of popular music to help turn surgical sequences into televisual spectacles.

and *Jackie Brown*, devote screen-time to the act of musical selection in ways that heighten the meaning of the music played, linking the process of playing music more directly to onscreen actions, character identifications, and narrative incidents.[9] Extending Garner's point to television style in *Nip/Tuck*, we can see Murphy and Bloom employing the Bang Olufsen stereo to call attention to the visual and sound styles of each particular surgery. For viewers who might otherwise ignore the popular music soundtrack or miss its textual significations in other parts of the episode, the visual representation of the process of musical selection here emphasizes the role of popular music in establishing surgical aesthetics by incorporating audio technology in the diegesis. We pay more attention to the music because we see the moment that Garner describes, the particular circumstances in which music is played, and the way that music is activated; thus, we are visually primed to think about what we will hear during the surgical sequence. Activating the stereo sets the plastic surgery in motion and prepares viewers for shots of scalpels and medical technologies penetrating the surface of the body.

The sounds that emanate from the Bang Olufsen stereo directly affect our understanding of narrative and embodiment. The deployment of songs creates a critical commentary on what racialized, classed, and gendered bodies matter most in the cityscape of Miami, twists the meanings of pop and rock tunes, and calls attention to the construction of both the onscreen bodies and the televisual spectacle. In "Montana/Sassy/Justice" (October 7, 2003), Rod Stewart's "Hot Legs" plays during a surgery on a woman's "cankles." In the second season premiere ("Erica Naughton," June 22, 2004), the Bang Olufsen stereo plays Billy Idol's "Eyes Without a Face" during a facial reconstruction on Libby Zucker to repair some of the physical damage from a gunshot wound. These songs fit part of the "sonic fingerprint" of the series in that they use older songs for ironic/satirical effect; however, these songs may also work to treat surgical procedures as grotesque.

The often upbeat songs, guitar riffs, and rock production aesthetic may render these sequences more disturbing and alienating for the viewer, as upbeat popular music achieves a contrapuntal quality when juxtaposed with the images.

Popular music gains some of its representational power from the lyrical allusion to embodiment, but this is not the only way that popular music affects meaning in the series. Popular songs that have been previously featured in high-profile soundtracks carry their previous significations into *Nip/Tuck*. For instance, during the third season premiere ("Momma Boone," September 20, 2005), "Stuck in the Middle with You" plays in the McNamara/Troy operating room as Sean performs a silicone implant replacement surgery. Sean takes over five hours to remove all the leaking silicone from just one breast and then has to put in a new implant before he can even move on to the other breast. Silicone sticks to his surgical gloves, forcing him to stop, put on new gloves, and continue to work. This sequence, with its disturbing visuals, encourages the viewer to link plastic surgery with mutilation. The song's prior usage in Quentin Tarantino's *Reservoir Dogs* further encourages this reading as Tarantino famously used the song to highlight a scene where one protagonist tortures a captured cop and cuts off the cop's ear. Thus, Murphy and Bloom draw not only on the 1970s classic rock hit, but also on intertextual allusions linking the song to forms of mutilation in the minds of many of *Nip/Tuck*'s audience members. Yet, even without knowledge of the intertextuality at work here, audience members are likely to be disturbed by the juxtaposition of the singer's throaty voice, danceable guitar rhythms, and early 1970s folk/rock sound with the visual track of the episode and be prompted to consider whether plastic surgeons are healers or carvers. This sequence can also be seen as setting up one of the central themes of the season, which features a serial killer called the Carver and openly questions what value should be attached to plastic surgeons and their craft.

The song lyrics themselves often remind us that we are watching bodies being opened and reconstructed onscreen. The use of "Poison Arrow" by the British New Wave 1980s band ABC in the episode "Antonia Ramos" (October 14, 2003) further illustrates the role that lyrics in classic songs play in emphasizing the embodied aesthetics of surgery. Featured prominently in the first four minutes of the episode, the nondiegetic song plays as Sean and Christian are called to a hotel room on the seedy side of Miami to take care of a woman (Antonia Ramos) whose breast implants are leaking heroin. Ramos had agreed to smuggle heroin for Escobar Gallardo (a druglord) in exchange for a contract with what turns out to be a non-existent Miami modeling agency. The lyrics of ABC's New Wave pop song are about romantic love and the potential for partners to hurt each other with the "poison arrow" of words. On one level, the placement of this song works to connect emotional and physical pain. For Antonia Ramos, the "poison arrow" is both a physical and a psychological one—surgery to have heroin-filled implants placed in her breast, unexpected complications that lead to her near death and a long recovery, surgery to have the implants removed, and imminent deportation once it is discovered that she has no work visa and the modeling agency doesn't exist. To sum up the textual role of "Poison Arrow" as ironic/satirical is to ignore the song's larger role in the narrative, where it further highlights the female, poor, and Latina bodies that "count" less in the Miami cityscape. While such bodies are marginalized within the real Miami, in *Nip/Tuck* they are also used as "exotic" plot points and "disposable" one-off characters in a series largely about the anxieties of middle-aged white heterosexual professionals.

Murphy and Bloom also make musical choices that take advantage of lyrical allusions and reward insider musical knowledge. Using music that is well known to target demographics deepens narrative comprehension for specific audiences and works to treat embodiment and plastic surgery as politically and socially contested terms within the series. In "Sophia Lopez, Part II" (September 23, 2003), for example, the title of Tori Amos's "A Sorta Fairytale" is itself resonant, but Murphy and Bloom's choice of this song also draws on Amos's star positioning and her politicized fanbase. The music of Tori Amos, a recording artist with a huge gay, lesbian, and feminist audience who has done active political work for gender and sexual rights, is used to highlight Lopez's struggle for belonging and comfort in her own body. In the episode, Sophia Lopez, a recurring character, is undergoing gender reassignment surgery. Earlier in the season, Sophia had helped to expose Sean's mentor, who operated an unsafe and unsanitary practice and who had butchered members of the Miami transgender community. When Sophia expressed her misgivings about helping Sean try to shut down his mentor—namely, that for her and other working-class men and women this surgeon was their only option—Sean agreed to perform the rest of Lopez's surgeries pro bono.

Before the song begins, an operating room controversy erupts when a nurse tells Sean that Sophia has smuggled in something underneath her gown. Sophia confesses, revealing a picture of her son Raymond, and Sean tells the nurse to wrap the framed picture in a sterile bag and let Sophia hold it in the surgery. As Lopez counts back from ten while Liz administers the anesthesia, "A Sorta Fairytale" begins playing.

This sequence exhibits one common pattern of music licensing in contemporary television drama, where an extended song clip accompanies a montage to close the episode. Thus, while Amos's "A Sorta Fairytale" may be perceived as diegetic music, occurring within the fictional world of the program (although we don't always see the stereo being turned on in every surgery scene), the song becomes part of the nondiegetic soundtrack once we leave the operating room and we see Sean and Christian in their homes. In the operating room, Amos's song calls attention to the politically contested nature of embodiment. The content of the song, about an emotional breakup, is far from the romantic fairytale implied by the song title and refrain. Amos's performance on the Bosendorfer piano and backup musicians' performances on acoustic and electric guitar, bass, and drums work to create a kind of dreamy soundscape. While the refrain invokes Lopez's fantasy of social acceptance, the repetition of the lyrical refrain, "a sorta fairytale," along with the plaintive to wistful to morose quality of Amos's vocals call attention to the fact that even after this surgery, Sophia Lopez will have to fight for social acceptance and for bodies like hers to be valued in the public sphere.

The song, together with the visuals—the framed picture of the patient's son, our previous knowledge of Lopez as a recurring character in the series—highlight the economic, psychological, and physical struggles faced by transgender men and women, and calls attention to the precarious and ambivalent relationship transgender patients have historically had with the medical system.[10] Amos's star text and the lyrics of the song encourage audiences to consider Lopez's pursuit of gender reassignment surgery as a brave act and to consider whether Lopez will ever achieve social acceptance, what value will be placed on bodies like hers, or if, for contemporary America, Lopez's dream of equality is still "a sorta fairytale." My argument here is not that most audience members will extract this meaning from the sequence; rather, it is that music supervisors and executive producers can draw on lyrical allusions and discourses of musical meaning that are tied up in genre or artist/performer identity to create evocative effects for particular groups of the audience.

Occasionally, Murphy and Bloom decide to use classical music or no music to call attention to difficult and experimental surgeries in the series—surgeries that often fail. These exceptions bear out the rule that most of the music in the program is popular recorded music from the latter half of the twentieth century and highlight the ways that non-musical forms of sound can be used for narrative and stylistic effect. Two examples of classical music include the surgery to separate Siamese twins attached at the head that ends in both girls dying on the table ("Rose and Raven Rosenberg," August 17, 2004) and the face transplant surgery on Hannah Tedesco ("Hannah Tedesco," November 15, 2005). After Hannah's body rejects the transplant later in the episode and the transplant must be removed from the teen girl's face, Liz says, "I can't find any music that feels appropriate right now." This marks one of the few times the producers chose not to use music of any kind and instead incorporated the diegetic sounds of the operating room, particularly the respirator and the heart monitor, over flashes of the surgical sequence. This notable exception to the program's sonic style illustrates that while popular music licensing is the general trend in the program, producers do on occasion deviate in order to try something different. These deviations also illustrate that the sounds and images in all surgical sequences are carefully planned and that the musical choices in these sequences have much to tell us about the ways that *Nip/Tuck* constructs the embodied aesthetics of surgery.

The use of diegetic nonmusical sound in the surgery to remove the face transplant stands in stark contrast to most surgical sequences, where the volume of direct diegetic sounds is either lowered or muted. Popular music tracks played through the Bang Olufsen stereo are diegetically motivated, but as film music scholars Claudia Gorbman and Robynn J. Stilwell argue, music often crosses back and forth between the diegetic and the nondiegetic.[11] While music in the McNamara/Troy operating room is diegetically motivated, the music video–style editing and shot scale choices call attention to the camera shutter and the construction of particular shots as well as the disjunction between the passage of musical time and narrative time. Diegetic music is often viewed as more organic, as it belongs to the story world and the characters; in contrast, the nondiegetic score is sometimes interpreted as manipulative, as the nondiegetic score is used to establish preferred readings of onscreen action for the audience. In *Nip/Tuck*, thinking of the music as traversing the diegetic/nondiegetic boundary raises questions about how the sounds and images onscreen are being manipulated and brings into focus the tensions between organic bodies and bodies disciplined by plastic surgery. To see music cross the diegetic/nondiegetic boundary during surgery raises the question of what constitutes the organic, "real" body. That music in the series seems to cross this boundary as surgery ensues draws greater attention to the physical boundary crossing of the scalpel penetrating flesh.

By placing music strategically in surgical scenes, Murphy and Bloom use sound to think through the representation and politics of plastic surgery. *Nip/Tuck* provides an excellent example of how contemporary television producers and music supervisors craft musical sounds to fit a series and deploy popular music tracks for specific narrative effects. Series such as *Mad Men* (AMC, 2007–present) or *The O.C.* (Fox, 2003–2007) may use popular music tracks to create a sense of a historical era or to appeal to a demographic market, but the shape and sound that music licensing takes depend on production norms and narratives. Television criticism must wrestle with the industrial norms and cultural connotations of licensed music to more fully understand how licensed tracks mobilize meaning.

NOTES

1. Tom Lowry, "Finding Nirvana in a Music Catalog," *BusinessWeek*, October 2, 2006.
2. Kim Akass and Janet McCabe, "A Perfect Lie: Visual (Dis)Pleasures and Policing Femininity in *Nip/Tuck*," in *Makeover Television: Realities Remodeled*, Dana Heller, ed. (London: I.B. Tauris, 2007).

3. Matthew Gilbert, "*Nip/Tuck* Is Not Afraid to Look the Ugly in the Eye; *Nip/Tuck* Diagnoses the Human Condition," *Boston Globe*, September 5, 2004.

4. P. J. Bloom, http://www.myspace.com/pjbloom.

5. "Exclusive Q&A with P. J. Bloom," http://www.niptuckforum.com/sitemaps/message53125.html.

6. "Exclusive: *Nip/Tuck* Music Supervisor P. J. Bloom Interview," http://rcrdlbl.com/2008/01/11/exclusive_nip_tuck_music_supervisor_pj_bloom_interview.

7. Amanda Lotz, *The Television Will Be Revolutionized* (New York: New York University Press, 2007).

8. "Exclusive: Nip/Tuck Music Supervisor P. J. Bloom Interview."

9. Ken Garner, "Would You Like to Hear Some Music?' Music in-and-out-of-Control in the Films of Quentin Tarantino," *Film Music: Critical Approaches*, K. J. Donnelly ed. (New York: Continuum, 2001), 189.

10. Joanne Jay Meyerowitz, *How Sex Changed: A History of Transsexuality in the United States* (Cambridge, MA: Harvard University Press, 2002).

11. Claudia Gorbman, *Unheard Melodies: Narrative Film Music* (Bloomington: Indiana University Press, 1987); Robynn J. Stilwell, "The Fantastical Gap Between Diegetic and Nondiegetic," in *Beyond the Soundtrack*, Daniel Goldmark, Lawrence Kramer, and Richard Leppert, eds. (Berkeley: University of California Press, 2007).

FURTHER READING

Altman, Rick. "Television/Sound." In *Studies in Entertainment: Critical Approaches to Mass Culture*, Tania Modleski, ed. Bloomington: Indiana University Press, 1986.

Chion, Michel. *Audio-Vision*. Claudia Gorbman, trans. New York: Columbia University Press, 1994.

Cook, Nicholas. *Analysing Musical Multimedia*. Oxford: Clarendon Press, 1998.

Donnelly, K. J. *The Spectre of Sound: Music in Film and Television*. London: BFI Publishing, 2005.

Frith, Simon. "Look! Hear! The Uneasy Relationship of Music and Television." *Popular Music* 21 (2002): 277–90.

6

Phineas & Ferb
Children's Television

JASON MITTELL

Abstract: While critics often condemn children's television as a hyper-commercial and lowbrow electronic babysitter, they often neglect to analyze how such programs actually engage young viewers. By looking at the narrative structure of *Phineas & Ferb*, Jason Mittell suggests that children's television can engage its audience with more sophistication and intelligence than might appear at first glance.

One of the primary ways that people think about television is in comparison to other media, with television typically serving as a cultural "bad object" when viewed next to literature, film, or other media regarded with more respect and legitimacy. When held up to such cross-media scrutiny, television is frequently dismissed as crass, hyper-commercial, formulaic, and catering to the lowest common denominator. Of course, those who make such dismissive generalizations rarely take the time to look closely at television programming, differentiating among distinct shows and genres that might challenge such conventional wisdom. Instead, television is regarded from afar and painted with a broad stroke using the framework that was most famously articulated by FCC Commissioner Newton Minow in 1961: television is a "vast wasteland."[1]

Within the television medium itself, some genres themselves function as bad objects, derided in comparison with more respected genres like serious dramas, sophisticated comedies, informative public affairs programming, or legitimate sports broadcasting. Daytime soap operas, trashy talk shows, and exploitative reality TV are all placed on the low end of cultural hierarchies that help legitimate television's more respectable programming. But probably no genre has been the object of more moral hand-wringing and cultural scorn throughout the medium's history than children's television. Countless books and editorial columns have decried the perceived damage that television has allegedly inflicted on generations of children, and such lamentations have fueled policymaking aimed at protecting kids from the worst of what television might do to them. Such condemnations treat children's television as an undifferentiated mass of lowbrow shows aimed at turning already slack-jawed, zombified kids into brainwashed consumers, junk food eaters, and cultural illiterates.

Are there programs that warrant such condemnation? Certainly there are many horrible children's programs—just as there are horrible primetime dramas, news programs, and documentaries, not to mention films, novels, and works in every other creative medium. It would be easy to redeem the genre of children's television by highlighting the exceptional examples of shows that succeed in educating their young viewers and appealing to parents as well, as with groundbreaking educational programs like *Sesame Street* (PBS, 1969–present) and *Blue's Clues* (Nickelodeon, 1996–2006). But the bulk of children's programs, especially those aimed at school-age viewers, aim to entertain far more than to educate, so to complicate these blanket condemnations of the genre, we need to look closely at a show whose goals are more commercial and entertaining than educational. To understand how children's television operates on its own terms, we need to ask what appeals to kids and to take into consideration how they engage with popular programs. Thus, let's take a close at one of the most popular children's shows of today: Disney Channel's *Phineas & Ferb* (2007–present).[2]

At first glance, *Phineas & Ferb* seems to live up to the most dismissive caricatures of children's television. The show is incredibly repetitive and formulaic, with nearly every episode offering only a slight variation on the main plot structure. The characters are broad caricatures, with unsophisticated animation highlighting hyperactive dialog and action rather than nuanced visuals. The content is fairly crass, focused on children breaking rules, contentious sibling rivalry, and clichéd espionage action. And Disney has capitalized on its success by extending the brand through licensed merchandise, including numerous CDs, videogames, DVDs, clothing, websites, and enough action figures to fill a toy-store aisle. In short, when critics dismiss children's television as mindless, formulaic, hyper-commercialized pap, *Phineas & Ferb* seems to fit the bill as a prime example.

However, we must go beyond the first glance—*Phineas & Ferb*'s young fans certainly do. Just as soap operas make little sense to novice viewers glancing at a random episode without the benefit of serialized backstories and relationships, a show like *Phineas & Ferb* becomes much more complex and nuanced once you can appreciate it in the context of an ongoing series. Children typically watch their favorite shows regularly and repeatedly, viewing the same episode frequently within the multiple times that a show may air on a given day or week, or replaying the same DVDs endlessly. *Blue's Clues* leveraged this preference for repetition for educational aims, creating an episode structure which young children could learn and follow easily, and then predict behaviors based on repeated viewing.[3] *Phineas & Ferb*'s structure is not designed with cognitive or developmental benefits in mind. At the same time, while the creators seem to know that kids enjoy a certain degree of repetition and predictability in their storytelling—a lesson learned from generations of bedtime stories and fairytales—*Phineas & Ferb* does not merely offer simple formulas for the sake of pleasing undiscerning young viewers; instead, the show's pleasures stem from a complex interplay of repetition and variation.

To understand the nuances of the show's narrative form, we need to look closer at the show's core formula. The title characters are stepbrothers of an unspecified age (probably around ten), and every episode is set during their seemingly eternal summer vacation. After an initial bout of boredom, the brothers come up with a "Big Idea," announced by Phineas, whose catchphrase is "Hey Ferb, I know what we're gonna do today!" Notably, Phineas is the talkative brother, with Ferb saying at most one or two lines per episode. They then build an elaborate invention, such as a shrinking submarine or an escalator to the moon, or undertake a fanciful mission, like becoming a boy band sensation or searching for the lost city of Atlantis, while their fifteen-year-old sister Candace tries in vain to "bust" her brothers to their mother, Linda. Candace also has her own goals, which typically involve getting Jeremy, her crush, to pay attention to her, and Phineas and Ferb's big ideas often inadvertently interfere with her plans. Meanwhile, the family's pet, Perry the Platypus, is secretly Agent P, a spy who slips away every episode to get a mission from Major Monogram to defeat arch villain Dr. Doofenschmirtz. Perry gets temporarily captured by Doofenschmirtz, who offers a monologue about his plans to take control of "the tri-state area" through evil plots, like stealing all of the region's zinc or making everybody else's voice higher, and using inventions like the Monkey Enslave-inator, Make Up Your Mind-inator, or Turn Everything Evil-inator, as well as typically providing a flashback to his troubled childhood in the German village of Gimmelshtump to provide a rationale for his evil ways. Invariably, Perry escapes and foils Doofenschmirtz's evil plans (prompting another repeated catchphrase, "Curse you, Perry the Platypus!"), with a side effect of the evil plot impacting Phineas and Ferb's big idea in a way that undermines Candace's attempts to bust the boys at the last possible moment. For instance, in "The Flying Fishmonger," the boys dig a giant gorge in their backyard, but due to the malfunctioning of Doofenschmirtz's machine that kicks sand in people's faces (the Who's-Crying-Now-inator), it gets filled up just as Candace brings her mother to bust them. Episodes typically end with Perry rejoining the family and Phineas saying, "Oh, there you are, Perry," resetting the narrative for the next installment.

This elaborate summary of the basic *Phineas & Ferb* formula applies to the majority of the show's storylines, with most episodes comprised of two independent eleven-minute segments that follow this plot structure, as well as containing numerous repeated catchphrases, running gags, brief song segments, and familiar callbacks to other episodes. Not only is the show quite silly in its plots and characters (and dialogue, songs, and gags), but it is highly repetitive and formulaic—viewers know what to expect in any given story within fairly rigid parameters. And yet it's incredibly pleasurable, fun, and clever in its own way. It's easy to imagine that critics who regard children's television with typical skepticism would see such use of formula and repetition as markers of the show's poor quality, but I would argue that repetition serves different functions within the series. The success of *Phineas & Ferb* shows how formula and form can function within a creative work not as markers of mass production or laziness, but as parameters that enable creativity. This is a common notion in other media, wherein the rigid structures of poetic forms like sonnets or haiku, for example, or the strict formal requirements of various song types in both classical and popular music create frameworks for creative innovations. Nobody condemns a Shakespearean sonnet because the rhyme scheme or meter is predictable; instead, we admire how poets can work within formal constraints to create moments of inspiration and surprise.

I am not suggesting that *Phineas & Ferb* is the cultural equivalent of a Shakespearean sonnet, but rather that there are more ways to define creativity than sheer originality or lack of formula. For the show's fans (young and old), one of its chief pleasures is seeing how each episode mines its predictable structure and expected repetitions in new ways. It is the pleasure of "theme and variation," involving a response to how norms are subtly adjusted in each episode, rather than an experience shaped by a fully unpredictable narrative. This type of storytelling is particularly appealing to children, whose repetitive viewing and learning styles privilege the discovery of patterns and rules—by repeatedly watching or hearing stories, kids learn what to expect from a narrative and how subtle variations can make a difference. Through this repetition, little variations in *Phineas & Ferb* pay off with pleasurable humor and reward long-time viewers for paying close attention. For instance, Phineas and Ferb's friend Isabella usually enters an episode with her tagline, "Hi guys, whatcha doin'?" spoken in a distinctive (and highly imitable by her young fans) sing-song voice. But in a number of episodes, other characters say the line or a variant of it, which often triggers a moment of reflexive self-awareness, such as one in which Isabella scolds someone for stealing her line. Such subtle variations not only create moments of pleasure among fans who recognize the show's patterns but also reward long-time careful viewers by acknowledging the show's embedded formulas.

Rather than addressing a dumbed-down viewer inattentive to the show's formulaic repetitions, *Phineas & Ferb* treats its young fans as savvy and sophisticated, attuned to the details and patterns inherent in the show's form. The plots are frequently ludicrous, but often the point of an episode is to anticipate the ridiculous ways that the competing outlandish inventions of Doofenschmirtz and the young brothers eventually intersect and cancel each other out, even though only the silent Perry is aware of the two different events and sets of characters. Young viewers watch episodes knowing full well that eventually the two plots will come together at the story's climax, but not knowing precisely how. In "The Fast and the Phineas" for instance, Doofenschmirtz's Deflate-inator seems to have little to do with Phineas's participating in a high-profile auto race in his mother's tricked-out remote-controlled car—until Doofenschmirtz's gun causes a blimp to crash into a broadcasting tower, cutting out the signal to the race's TV coverage just as Candace is showing Phineas racing to Linda. While the dual plotlines in *Phineas & Ferb* are designed to be watched by viewers who know full well that they will formulaically converge in the end, the show's formula invites kids to speculate and imagine how the plotlines will come together in unpredictable ways, what previous episodes will be referenced, and which of the show's conventions will be varied.

Such an approach to storytelling that focuses less on "what will happen?" than "how will the story be told?" is part of a larger trend of narrative complexity in television, where savvy viewers marvel at the storytelling machinery as well as getting immersed in the story. This approach has been termed "the operational aesthetic," and it is typically found in adult primetime programs like *Lost*, *The Sopranos*, and *Breaking Bad*.[4] For its part, *Phineas & Ferb* offers a junior version of the operational aesthetic, catering to kids who watch television programs intently and repeatedly. The plot mechanics of multiple threads coming together at the episode's climax is reminiscent of complex adult sitcoms like *Seinfeld*, *Arrested Development*, and *Curb Your Enthusiasm*, in which a central pleasure comes from anticipating the payoff of an elaborate, multi-threaded narrative machine. While certainly more casual viewers might enjoy the goofy humor and catchy songs of *Phineas & Ferb*, the show's narrative design offers savvier fans of all ages the more elaborate and expansive pleasures that come from embracing the complexity and variety beneath the repetitions and formula. This differs from other kids' media that embeds adult references to amuse parents while kids enjoy slapstick humor or goofy characters—a strategy common to *Looney Tunes* and *Sesame Street* alike. By contrast, *Phineas & Ferb* gives both kids and adults the same pleasures of complex construction and payoff from narrative anticipation.

Not all episodes of *Phineas & Ferb* follow its formula precisely, however. While most episodes present variation and innovation within the smaller moments of new inventions, unlikely plot collisions, shifts in the character catchphrases, and expectation of Ferb's saying his single line, a few episodes violate the show's core formulaic plot structure and key story events. For instance, in the episode "Phineas and Ferb Get Busted!" (March 13, 2009), Candace finally succeeds in busting her brothers, resulting in an entirely distinct plot structure: the boys are sent to reform school, and Candace guiltily decides to bust them out, and despite there being no explicit B-plot with Perry, Candace sees Perry and Doofenschmirtz battling during their escape in a scene that finally reveals Perry's secret identity to the family. Of course it all turns out to be a dream (first Candace's and then Perry's), but the episode offers a significant variation to the show's formula and thus shatters expectations for fans used to its standard plot structure and character roles. Such non-formulaic episodes are distinctly pleasurable in the context of the show's normal strict adherence to patterns—which is to say that if every episode were less formulaic, such violations would not be such significant and fun exceptions.

One common element in such non-formulaic episodes is reflexivity, where the show "winks" at the audience about its plot formulas or expectations. In "Phineas and Ferb Get Busted," such reflexivity emerges early, as Candace and her mother talk about how boring it is that the same thing happens every single day, with Candace trying to bust her brothers and Linda finding no evidence of wrongdoing. After Linda does see the boys' mischief, however, she mentions how frequently Candace claims they are up to something, and a quick montage of flashbacks to nearly every episode in the first season appears, in effect acknowledging that viewers are fully aware of the show's formulas. Reflexivity has been a key part of animation for decades, from Bugs Bunny directly addressing the audience to *The Simpsons* referencing past episodes and poking fun at its corporate parent, Fox. *Phineas & Ferb*'s particular brand of reflexivity focuses mostly on the show's use of repetition, calling attention to what some critics might see as a weakness as being a source of creative variation and viewing pleasure instead.

Two non-formulaic episodes that highlight the show's use of repetition and pleasures of variation are "Phineas and Ferb's Quantum Boogaloo" (September 25, 2009) and "Rollercoaster: The Musical!" (January 29, 2011). Both of these episodes engage directly with the events of the show's very first episode, "Rollercoaster" (August 17, 2007), revisiting the original's plot and key events through complex storytelling. The story of "Rollercoaster" established the show's basic formula: the boys create a gigantic (and physically impossible) rollercoaster, Candace tries to get Linda to see the coaster, and Perry foils Doofenschmirtz's plan involving a massive magnet and the world's largest ball of aluminum foil in a way that makes the coaster disappear before Candace's eyes. "Quantum Boogaloo" is a time-travel story, with the boys going twenty years into their future, only to enable adult Candace to travel back in time to bust her brothers in their very first summer adventure: the events of the "Rollercoaster" episode. Adult Candace's successful busting also inadvertently saves Doofenschmirtz, which creates a dystopian future where he is in control of the tri-state area. Complications pile up, leading to three versions of Candace all fighting over whether to bust or save Phineas and Ferb, but everything is eventually put back into temporal order for the next episode. While "Quantum Boogaloo" is one of the program's most complex and convoluted episodes, as befits a time-travel tale, it would be even more confusing to a novice viewer who doesn't know the show's formula and the initial story of "Rollercoaster." Thus, in such instances, episodes work to appeal to fans who accumulate knowledge about the show's storytelling strategies.

"Rollercoaster: The Musical!" is even more reflexive and intertwined with the show's initial episode. The latter episode starts with Phineas nostalgically remembering the fun they had building the rollercoaster and saying, "We should do it again, but this time as a musical!" The rest of the episode replays the events of "Rollercoaster" with minor variations, but with nine musical numbers added. The songs are particularly reflexive, being primarily centered on often repeated catchphrases like "Whatcha Doin'?" or "Hey Ferb, I know what we're going to do today," or focused on the show's formulaic plotlines, as in "Mom Look," in which Candace sings about all of the mischief that her brothers have done throughout the summer (and that previous episodes featured). There is no doubt how the plot will turn out, as it's a virtual replay of the initial episode, but the episode's joy is watching the familiar story replayed with character's meta-commentary on the action through song. Like so many *Phineas & Ferb* episodes, "Rollercoaster: The Musical!" asks its viewers to focus less on what might happen but more on *how* the story will be told, especially in relation to past episodes and well-established formulas.

Thus *Phineas & Ferb* presents an interesting conundrum: every episode is almost identical on the level of plot and character, and thus you can understand the show easily after watching only a single episode, but you need to watch many episodes to understand the show's deeper and more complex appeals. Arguably, this pattern is an extreme version of a broader tendency within American television, wherein complex serialization and cumulative backstories are common in many of today's most acclaimed primetime shows. *Phineas & Ferb* is far from being a serial, as most episodes can be watched out of order, but the cumulative effect of watching the show is attuning yourself to the serial build-up of its formal dimensions rather than remembering ongoing plot events and character developments.

Steven Johnson has argued that much of contemporary popular media make a positive cognitive impact on viewers, specifically suggesting that videogames and narratively complex television "make us smarter."[5] It's impossible to know whether these claims are accurate without undertaking direct experimental research on viewers, and even such research methods would fall short of proving direct cognitive effects. But when watching a show like *Phineas & Ferb*, and talking with its

FIGURE 6.1.
Phineas & Ferb's first episode
"Rollercoaster" starts a running
gag with an adult authority asking Phineas, "Aren't you a little
young to be a rollercoaster engineer?" to which he replies, "Yes,
yes I am." The revisionist "Rollercoaster: The Musical!" restages
the familiar scene as a musical
number, complete with dancing
engineers.

young fans, it seems hard to imagine that the program is causing the cognitive
damage that anti-television detractors might claim. It certainly makes you pay
attention, think about the connection between episodes, and be mindful of television's formal dimensions in ways that contradict the negative effects of children's
television that many critics take for granted. Researchers have suggested that a
key impact of children's media is to teach children how to learn, even if the contents of what is learned are relatively inconsequential, like cataloguing the range
of creatures found in *Pokémon*.[6] A show like *Phineas & Ferb* doesn't teach kids
direct real-life lessons like reading or geography, but it does train kids to be careful and savvy consumers of narrative, preparing them for more adult stories that
range from complex primetime serials to literary fiction, and even developing an
awareness of how storytelling strategies factor into non-fiction forms like news
and sports.

So is *Phineas & Ferb* just another example of formulaic lowbrow children's television striving to sell merchandise to unwitting kids? Certainly the show is a product of a hyper-commercial television system that strives to generate ratings and promote merchandise. But creatively, it builds on storytelling strategies that have emerged in recent years to make television more demanding and sophisticated. *Phineas & Ferb*'s adaptation of narrative complexity for elementary schoolers highlights general strategies that television uses to engage children while keeping them entertained, and in ways that counter the stereotypical vision of passive couch potatoes watching an electronic babysitter. The series demands that viewers pay attention to follow a complex narrative structure, contradicting the assumed role of commercial children's television as bad object.

NOTES

1. Newton Minow, "Television and the Public Interest," speech presented at the National Association of Broadcasters, Washington, DC, May 9, 1961, http://www.americanrhetoric.com/speeches/newtonminow.htm.
2. The show regularly ranks among the highest-rated kids' programs on cable, and the 2011 original made-for-TV movie *Phineas & Ferb Across the 2nd Dimension* ranked as one of the most-watched cable movies ever aired.
3. Daniel Anderson, "Watching Children Watch Television and the Creation of *Blue's Clues*," in *Nickelodeon Nation: The History, Politics, and Economics of America's Only TV Channel for Kids*, Heather Hendershot, ed. (New York: New York University Press, 2004).
4. See Jason Mittell, *Complex TV: The Poetics of Contemporary Television Storytelling* (New York: New York University Press, forthcoming), for more on this style of primetime programming.
5. Steven Johnson, *Everything Bad is Good for You: How Today's Popular Culture is Actually Making Us Smarter* (New York: Riverhead Books, 2005).
6. Joseph Jay Tobin, ed., *Pikachu's Global Adventure: The Rise and Fall of* Pokémon (Durham: Duke University Press, 2004).

FURTHER READING

Buckingham, David. *After the Death of Childhood: Growing Up in the Age of Electronic Media*. Cambridge: Polity Press, 2000.

Hendershot, Heather, ed. *Nickelodeon Nation: The History, Politics, and Economics of America's Only TV Channel for Kids*. New York: New York University Press, 2004.

Johnson, Steven. *Everything Bad is Good for You: How Today's Popular Culture is Actually Making Us Smarter*. New York: Riverhead Books, 2005.

Seiter, Ellen. *Sold Separately: Children and Parents in Consumer Culture*. New Brunswick, NJ: Rutgers University Press, 1993.

7

The Sopranos
Episodic Storytelling

SEAN O'SULLIVAN

Abstract: *The Sopranos* is one of television's most acclaimed series, ushering in the rise of the twenty-first-century primetime serial and helping to elevate the medium's cultural status. But Sean O'Sullivan problematizes our understanding of the show's seriality, highlighting episodes that function more as short stories than as chapters in a novel, and thus illuminating how the program's story structures and themes explore and challenge the norms of television narrative.

When Jennifer Egan discusses her inspirations for *A Visit from the Goon Squad*, the winner of the 2011 Pulitzer Prize for Fiction, she often cites *The Sopranos* (HBO, 1999–2007). Egan's book has nothing to do with mobsters or federal agents. Rather, it is a loosely connected series of thirteen chapters, tracing over several decades a group of people affiliated with the music business. When it came out, there was considerable debate about whether the book should be called a novel or a collection of short stories. The style and point of view can vary drastically from chapter to chapter; characters that may have seemed "major" sometimes drop out and sometimes reappear, with "minor" characters at times taking over the reins. It was this structural restlessness, this ambivalence about linear connection, that Egan found appealing in the HBO show: "The lateral feeling of it, [and] not to have to always be focused on the forward thrust. There were whole episodes where you had no idea why this was going to be important in the bigger scheme of things, and yet it was fascinating; I loved the idea . . . of letting it feel meandering."[1] Egan points here to the powerful anti-serial riptide at the center of the most widely celebrated serial drama of the last decade, its resistance to the accumulative forces of consequence, continuity, and progression that nineteenth-century installment fiction and twentieth-century soap opera marketed as their defining features. This essay will spotlight two episodes from the show's initial season, each of which operates "laterally" in relation to the rest of that season.

The first of these is the most highly praised of all episodes of *The Sopranos*; the second is one of the least beloved. That gulf in reception illustrates the attractions, perils, and effects of rupturing serial conventions.

Egan's diagnosis would undoubtedly please David Chase, creator and show-runner of *The Sopranos*, since his aversion to the traditional television business drove the design and ethos of the show. Chase described his early creative differences with the channel:

> There was a little bit of friction the first season between myself and HBO, because they were more interested in the serialized elements and I was not. "What's going to happen from one episode to the next?" "Are they going to kill Tony or not?" "Who planned it?" Or: "What's the result of what happened in episode 2?" I was more interested in discrete little movies.[2]

If Egan uses a metaphor of movement—the "lateral" rather than propulsive tendency of a narrative—Chase offers an arboreal image:

> If you look at a Christmas tree, people don't care about the trunk of a Christmas tree; they only care about the lights and the balls and the tinsel. But the trunk has to be there. So we always referred back to that; we had this continuing story, which people seemed to get involved in. I didn't intend to do a soap opera.[3]

Chase's notion of "people" here is helpfully contradictory. On the one hand, "people" got involved in the continuing story—namely the trunk of the tree; on the other hand, "people" care only about the surrounding baubles, those visual delights that make the trunk pleasingly invisible. This conflict between what "people" want—perhaps different kinds of people, or more likely the same people in different moods of narrative consumption—speaks directly to *The Sopranos*' self-conscious shifts between satisfaction and dissatisfaction.

The most famous hour of the series, and Exhibit A of Chase's stand-alone storytelling preferences, is "College" (February 7, 1999), the show's fifth episode. Composed of just two storylines, rather than the typical model of three or four, "College" follows Tony and his daughter, Meadow, during her college tour in Maine and Tony's wife, Carmela, during her dangerous flirtation with Father Phil Intintola back in New Jersey. The dramatic core of the episode is Tony's discovery of a former mob informer, ensconced in rural New England thanks to the witness protection program; Tony tracks the "rat" down and garrotes him while Meadow is being interviewed at Colby College. *Time*'s James Poniewozik reflected a critical consensus in 2007 when he ranked "College" as the best episode in the series' history, citing its riveting opposition "between the family and Family parts of Tony's life."[4] "College" precisely fits Egan's sense of *The Sopranos*' commitment to "lateral" movement, since the psychiatric environment and particular Mafia conflicts of the show's first four episodes are absent. Chase deemed it the show's "most successful episode . . . a film noir in and of itself"; critically, "it has nothing to do with anything that happened beforehand, and it has nothing to do with anything that happened later . . . To me, that was the ultimate *Sopranos* episode."[5]

In terms of the show's central figure, "College" produces ripples neither in the area of plot—there is no event-consequence to Tony's actions here—nor in the area of character—Tony does not "discover" something about himself at this point, and there appear to be no psychological aftershocks. But if we think of "character" not just as a fictional person's mental or emotional conditions, but as a relationship between that fictional person and a viewing audience, in fact "College" had significant ramifications for what "happened later." As Chase tells it, this storyline represented another major conflict with HBO in the inaugural season; channel executive Chris Albrecht worried that the gruesome, hands-on execution of the informant would harm Tony's "relatability," destroying the audience's ability to connect with the series' main character. Chase stuck to his guns, on the grounds of verisimilitude, saying that "if we're really gonna believe this guy is a credible mobster, he's gotta kill people. In real life, that's what these people do."[6] That conflict between creator and channel illustrated how "character" can mean something very different in two different contexts, whether in the show's internal world or diegesis, as championed by Chase, or in the world inhabited by the shows' viewers, foregrounded by HBO.

Five weeks after "College," another episode of *The Sopranos* would also enact the lateral move, Chase's preference for the "discrete little movie": "A Hit Is a Hit" (March 14, 1999), the show's tenth hour. The chief preoccupation of "A Hit Is a Hit" is music, and specifically the music industry—as advertised by the title, which reflects the impossibility of understanding why some music succeeds commercially, and why some does not. The two chief storylines are bridged by the gangsta rapper Massive Genius—someone who truly has nothing to do with what happened beforehand, or with what happened later, since he appears nowhere else in *The Sopranos*. One of the two plots involves his attempts to get "reparations" from Tony's friend Hesh Rabkin, a Jewish mob associate who exploitatively managed R&B bands in the 1950s; the other involves Christopher Moltisanti's attempts to get his girlfriend, Adriana La Cerva, started as a music producer, with Massive operating as an advisor who is frankly more interested in Adriana herself. Massive essentially takes control of *The Sopranos* at this juncture, operating as the central agent of plot and serving as the focus of tension and desire. Structurally, the show borrows here from the anthology format, a televisual genre wherein each episode produces a self-contained story, with no relation to predecessor or successor episodes. Contemporary viewers of *The Sopranos* would have been uncertain about how much to invest in Massive's character and story-lines. Does he matter, in the grand scheme of things? The answer to that question depends on what we imagine *The Sopranos* to be.

Given the central role of music in the episode, it is worth noting that music in *The Sopranos* was a defining authorial concern for David Chase. He made clear that getting a significant music budget was critical to his original deal with HBO, and that "music and this particular cast of actors" were his favorite parts of the series.[7] The show's use of diverse, pre-existing musical sources—from Bruce Springsteen to Radiohead to opera—meant that each song or selection required no direct reference to the preceding or succeeding one; each musical cue was "discrete," just as Chase wanted for the episodes themselves. A familiar score in a series, with familiar melodies and practices, helps create continuity; we might think of the recurring musical intensification that typically led to commercial breaks on *Lost* (ABC, 2004–2010), giving that show—which roamed across many genres and styles—an auditory serial thread for the audience, a welcome contact with the familiar. Chase's aversion to this kind of continuity even applied to his original plan for the title sequence, where he wanted to feature a different song every week. He characterized the televisual convention of using a single initial theme every week as "bourgeois"; but HBO insisted on "something identifiable" at the start of each episode, and he relented.[8] Music's ability to signal familiarity or change, in other words, represents another version of the continuous and the discontinuous. The cluster of material that we call an album offers a musical par-allel to the structural tension between the novel and a series of short stories. A "concept album," like a novel, promotes connectivity, the promise that the order of the songs is crucial, that everything is linked—a start-to-end logic that mimics one version of serial drama. A collection of singles or separate pieces, like a series of short stories, fractures connectivity, minimizing the importance of sequence and allowing individual songs to be freely excerpted from the group. The first season of *The Sopranos* tested the boundaries between novel and short stories, between concept album and singles collection, and "A Hit Is a Hit" proved to be a particularly problematic case.

"A Hit Is a Hit" appears nowhere in any roll call of the show's most cherished moments. The *TV Guide Sopranos Companion* summarized and lamented it thusly: "Gangsta rapper meets boy gangster in this rather contrived episode of culture clash that pulls us away from the compelling intrigues of recent episodes."[9] This judgment expresses a typical way in which serial viewers compartmentalize and justify opinion and evaluation. "College" also depends on contrivance, and on pulling away—from the serendipitous re-encounter with the mob rat to the circumstances under which Carmela and Father Phil spend a night under the same roof. But "contrivance" in that earlier context is forgiven because the pay-off or pleasure trumps, for many viewers, the artifice of accident on which the plots of "College" rest. The schism of reaction between "College" and "A Hit Is a Hit" illustrates the risk/reward of abandoning televisual convention; Chase's inclination toward a "discrete" rather an integrated hour of events, topics, or people defines what we might call the conflicted or restless television serial, a twenty-first-century phenomenon of which *The Sopranos* has been the most vivid exponent. The most prominent successor, in the conflicted/restless vein, may be *Mad Men* (AMC, 2007–present). That show's creator, Matthew Weiner, was a staff writer for the final seasons of *The Sopranos*, and his series frequently disrupts expectations of serial momentum and narrative convention. "I don't want there to be a formula," Weiner has said. "I don't want people to know what to expect ever when they turn the show on."[10]

"A Hit Is a Hit" parallels "College" in terms of subject matter, and in terms of season placement. Both episodes obsessively examine art and culture, from an apt quotation from *The Scarlet Letter* that Tony sees on a wall at Bowdoin College during Meadow's interview to debates over authorship and musical inspiration that occupy the later episode. "A Hit Is a Hit" intensifies the attention to art that we see in "College," moving from a flurry of allusions to a focus on how art is made, and how art works. And structurally each episode functions as a break, interrupting a defined four-episode serial sequence. "College" follows the first quartet of shows, which depict the illness and death of acting boss, Jackie Aprile, and Tony's clever orchestration of Uncle Junior's rise to boss; "A Hit Is a Hit," meanwhile, appears just when the conflict between Tony and Uncle Junior is on the verge of exploding. Those two placements within the season, however, are not exactly analogous. One crucial difference is that of accumulation. Four hours into cooking a serial season, when the flavors have yet to take hold, we may be tolerant of something new. But after nine hours we are much more likely to grow impatient; Chase's commitment to the "discrete" film produces distinct problems at distinct points of a thirteen-episode story. A second difference is one of consequence, or aftermath. While "College" may have "nothing to do with" plot and character in terms of the major serial developments of the season, it has a great deal to do with character in terms of our relation to Tony; by contrast, "A Hit Is a Hit" will leave no wake of any kind. In many ways, it is the more radical of the two episodes, and the one that comes closer to performing the subversive job of rejecting serial conventions, within the guts of a singularly successful serial edifice, than anything else Chase and his team attempted. That struggle between freedom and form is explicitly addressed in "A Hit Is a Hit" when a record producer advocates for the clear, connective structure of a song like The Beatles' "She Loves You" while the lead singer of Adriana's band, Visiting Day, argues for something "introspective" and unschematic—another version of serial conformity contrasted with a rejection of recognizable pattern.

Even more than music, one might say that the main topic of "A Hit Is a Hit" is performance—the performance not just of songs, but of identity categories like race, class, and ethnicity. Massive Genius performs a designated street persona but has a degree in Urban Planning; Hesh declares that, as a Jew, he was "the white man's nigger" long before hip-hop. In a third story, Tony feels that he is asked to put on a lower-class, goomba minstrel show in front of his rich neighbors, especially the Cusamanos, in order to gain access to their country club. The emphasis on performance, and on the instability of identity, connects to the episode's focus on the destabilized meanings of capitalism, status, and art in the postmodern world—the arbitrary value of money after the disappearance of the gold standard, of status after the 1960s social revolutions, and of art after the collapse of aesthetic hierarchies. "A Hit Is a Hit" is the first *Sopranos* episode to begin in New York City, the American epicenter of capitalism, status, and art, and the precipitating incident of the plot is the unexpected seizure of a huge pile of cash. Even the "D" story, the smallest element of the episodic interweave, touches on money and value as Carmela gets involved in the gossipy suburban world of hot stock tips. Each of these plots points to the fluctuating, possibly arbitrary nature of worth, meaning, and desire. Christopher offers another version of the problem of distinguishing how we know what matters, what fixed values things have or lack, when he laments the imponderables of Adriana's potential new business: "Music—it's not something you can hold in your hands, you know. Like football betting cards, or coke." Gambling chits and illegal drugs are the new gold standard; art, money, and status are an indecipherable mess.

"A Hit Is a Hit" essentially serves as a televisual essay on late twentieth-century culture more broadly, including treasured objects such as Murano glass, bidets, Versace clothing, and the *Godfather* films. *The Sopranos*, of course, would soon become such an object itself, a register of cultural acuity for those sharp enough to subscribe to HBO or purchase the DVDs; the episode, produced in the vacuum before the first season was aired, divined that a work of television might also turn into a valuable and tradable commodity, a nugget of knowledge that is worth something if we think it is worth something. "A Hit Is a Hit" ends with a clear gesture of viewer-teasing, as Tony—who is eventually frozen out of the Cusamanos' social circle—asks his neighbors to do him "a solid" by hiding a wrapped box, without revealing its contents. We know that the box is filled with sand, but they regard it with terror: "What is it? Heroin?" "A weapon? Could be anything." That box represents the uncertain condition of the entire episode, its immersion in the traumatic but inescapable state of American current affairs, where things mean what they mean only by context, or by shared guesswork.

FIGURE 7.1.

Just as Tony Soprano toyed with his neighbors by asking them to hide a mysterious box (harmlessly filled with sand), episodes of *The Sopranos* occasionally presented viewers with characters and plot-lines whose relationship to the serial narrative was opaque.

This is a world—both on- and off-screen—where the intrinsic seems opaque or antique, and we can know only by relation. Likewise, a serial episode of a television drama "means" what it means in relation to its seriality, to its relational context with preceding and succeeding episodes. An episode like "A Hit Is a Hit," which rejects its serial place, may seem to its detractors to create a void of meaning; "A Hit Is a Hit" is unbeloved precisely because it troubles our understanding of what *The Sopranos* is, as a serial narrative enterprise.

The episode shows us that *The Sopranos* is not a collection of characters, in the way that, say, *Six Feet Under* (HBO, 2001–2005) is a collection of characters; rather, *The Sopranos* is a way of thinking about serial narrative. That distillation of the show may be discomfiting. In a sense, "A Hit Is a Hit" is not so much the companion episode to "College" as its inversion. If that earlier episode appeared to institutionalize our relationship to Tony as the cornerstone of the show, the later one disrupts our sense that any single element, or even any stable cluster of elements, can define the show's essence. One legacy of "College" and "A Hit Is a Hit" is "Pine Barrens" (May 6, 2001), a late third-season episode involving Christopher and Paulie's pursuit of a Russian through snowy woods—a Russian who disappears and is never found. "Pine Barrens" was number two on James Poniewozik's list of *The Sopranos*' greatest hits—a fact for which he apologized, calling it the "most un-*Sopranos*-like of *Sopranos* episodes," a "distinctly contained short story. . . in a series that unfolds like a novel."[11] As I have been claiming, *The Sopranos* does not unfold like a novel; it unfolds like *A Visit from the Goon Squad*, a text that hovers deliberately on the boundary between short story and novel. It is precisely the "un-*Sopranos*-like" episodes that most fully define the series' narrative interests.

Within the genre of the lateral move, "Pine Barrens" may be closer to "College"; both episodes feature familiar characters in a rural setting trying to kill, in alternately comic and grim fashion, a problematic foe whom the audience has never encountered before and will never see again. And both seem to be "about" a core territory of the show—underworld assassination—as opposed to being "about" something irrelevant—the world of music—even though David Chase manifestly cares a lot more about music than he does about underworld assassination. Perhaps the most radical consequence of withholding context and consequence can be found in a very different kind of *Sopranos* episode, one featuring a hugely important serial event. In the sixth-season "Kennedy and Heidi" (May 13, 2007), a major character dies, and Tony ends up on a guilt-ridden, drug-driven escapade in Las Vegas; the episode concludes with him in a peyote haze, staring at a Western sunrise and proclaiming, "I get it!" This grand scene of epiphany suggests a moment of reckoning; surely we'll find out, a week later, what Tony "got." Instead, in the next episode, it's as if that epiphany never happened.

"Kennedy and Heidi" gives the lie to narrative nostrums of "arc" and "development," screenwriting-manual simplifications of how people operate and how lives happen; surely, it is more "real"—to use the key term that David Chase used to justify the central plot of "College"—to suggest that we as people often end up exactly where we started, that we change very little, that epiphanies are fleeting and delusive and ignored. And which is more "artificial": the episode that wanders off course, or the episode that obeys the authorial click-clack of plot sequencing? "A Hit Is a Hit" valorizes the disruption and the pause, over the flow. Its model—the collection of singles—taps into our current moment of iTunes, and the crumbling of the album as a serial object. "A Hit Is a Hit," as an anti-serial serial episode, in 1999 anticipated the digital atomization of culture consumption. Is a season a concept album? Or is a season a collection of singles? Can it be both at the same time?

NOTES

1. Boris Kachka, "*A Visit from the Goon Squad* Author Jennifer Egan on Reaping Awards and Dodging Literary Feuds," *New York,* http://www.vulture.com/2011/05/jennifer_egan_goon_squad_inter.html.
2. *The Sopranos*, "David Chase Interview" (Season 1 DVD, HBO Video, 2001).
3. Ibid.
4. James Poniewozik, "Top 10 *Sopranos* Episodes," *Time.* http://www.time.com/time/specials/2007/sopranos/article/0,28804,1602923_1602896_1602904,00.html.
5. *The Sopranos*, "David Chase Interview."
6. Peter Biskind, "An American Family," *Vanity Fair* 560 (2007): 282–83.
7. David Chase, *The Sopranos: Selected Scripts from Three Seasons* (New York: Warner Books, 2002), x.
8. *The Sopranos*, "David Chase Interview."

9. *TV Guide Sopranos Companion* (New York: TV Guide, 2002), 47.

10. Alan Sepinwall, "*Mad Men*: Talking 'Out of Town' with Matthew Weiner," *What's Alan Watching?* August 16, 2009, http://sepinwall.blogspot.com/2009/08/mad-men-talking-out-of-town-with.html.

11. Poniewozik, "Top 10 *Sopranos* Episodes."

FURTHER READING

Chase, David. *The Sopranos: Selected Scripts from Three Seasons.* New York: Warner Books, 2002.

Lavery, David, ed. *Reading The Sopranos: Hit TV from HBO.* London: I. B. Tauris, 2006.

O'Sullivan, Sean. "Broken on Purpose: Poetry, Serial Television, and the Season." *Storyworlds* 2 (2010): 59–77.

Polan, Dana. *The Sopranos.* Chapel Hill, NC: Duke University Press, 2009.

Yacowar, Maurice. *The Sopranos on the Couch: The Ultimate Guide.* New York: Continuum, 2006.

8

Tim and Eric's Awesome Show, Great Job!
Metacomedy

JEFFREY SCONCE

Abstract: Sketch comedy is a staple of American television, with styles ranging from mainstream to alternative and even experimental forms that target a young, predominantly male audience. Jeffrey Sconce explores the highly experimental approach of *Tim and Eric's Awesome Show, Great Job!*, connecting it to the history of metacomedy as playing with comedic form with reflexivity and ambiguity.

In the fall of 1975, the premiere episode of *Saturday Night Live* (NBC, 1975–present) featured a somewhat puzzling performance in the show's final half-hour, an "act" befitting the program's ambition to showcase comedy generally considered "not ready for prime time."[1] As immortalized in the unlikely biopic *Man on the Moon* (1999), comedian Andy Kaufman stood alongside a portable record player on an otherwise empty stage, remaining more or less inert for some fifteen seconds after his off-camera introduction by house announcer Don Pardo. Kaufman then dropped the needle on a record—a scratchy 45rpm of the theme song from *Mighty Mouse*. The first laugh is one of recognition—the audience pleasantly surprised by this unexpected sonic memory of what had been a staple of U.S. television since the mid-1950s. Twenty-seven seconds into the bit, the song arrives at its chorus and most memorable hook, a moment when Mighty Mouse himself joins the singers to announce: "Here I come to save the day!" Here Kaufman suddenly erupted into a grandiloquent performance of lip-syncing, miming the rodent superhero word for word while extending his arm heroically aloft. Kaufman then resumed his awkward silence. Twenty seconds later, the song appears to return to Mighty Mouse's musical cue. A nervous Kaufman prepares to repeat his miming act. But it's a false alarm—the song goes into another verse without the singing mouse—and Kaufman looks slightly embarrassed at having missed his mark. A full thirty seconds pass until once again Kaufman and Mighty Mouse exclaim, "Here I come to save the day!" Realizing now this is the entire "act," the audience response is even more enthusiastic at this second repetition. Having mimed the line twice (and with one flub), Kaufman takes advantage of an instrumental break to drink a well-earned glass of water. The chorus returns once again, and in the "rule of threes," Kaufman silently belts out the signature line a final time. With that, in just under two minutes, the "routine," the "bit," the "act," is over. Having been won over by this audacious performance of essentially nothing, the audience erupts in thunderous applause.

A resolutely underwhelming performance delivered "poorly" (again, Kaufman screws it up at one point), Kaufman's low-key pantomime evoked a series of enigmatic questions, both for its audience in 1975 and for subsequent commentators on comedy and culture. Was this performance "for real" or was it a hoax of some kind? Was this meant to be "funny" or "not funny," or was it funny precisely because it wasn't actually all that funny? Discussions of Kaufman are as liable to reference conceptual art as television comedy, elevating Kaufman as the most esoteric performer among a group of comedians emerging in the early 1970s who increasingly subjected comedy to the logic of avant-garde performance. Filmmaker/actor Albert Brooks, for example, began his career appearing on talk shows as a terrible ventriloquist (and then later as a "talking" mime). Steve Martin's early stand-up integrated shtick learned while working at Disneyland (prop comedy, animal balloons, juggling) with a persona alternating between low idiocy and high Dada. Michael O'Donoghue, the original head writer for *Saturday Night Live,* occasionally closed the show by doing impressions of various celebrities subjected to six-inch steel spikes driven into their eyeballs. Writing in *Time* in 1981, critic Richard Corliss dubbed this sensibility the "Post-Funny" School of Comedy.[2] Philip Auslander has described such routines as "anti-comedy," a practice focused on the vulnerabilities and potential "failures" of public performance.[3] Given that audiences often found (and still find) these performances to be extremely funny, perhaps the most useful term would be "metacomedy": stand-up, sketch, and even narrative comedy that is explicitly about the art of comedy itself, a foregrounding of its expectations, conventions, and execution.

Elements of metacomedy have continued to thrive among various "alternative," "underground," and "edge" comedians over the past thirty years. Though very different in terms of their material, Gilbert Gottfried's archly stylized Catskill classicism and Sarah Silverman's blankly feigned naïveté both draw attention to the conventions of stand-up and the mechanics of the joke. Sasha Baron Cohen's turns as Ali G, Borat, and Bruno, meanwhile, continue the Kaufmanesque interest in blurring the line between performance and reality (even if, as is the case with Cohen, the audience is always "in" on the joke). Perhaps the most sustained recent exploration of the anti/metacomedy sensibility has been the television work of Tim Heidecker and Eric Wareheim, a team from Philadelphia who have produced two series for the Cartoon Network's *Adult Swim* block: *Tom Goes to the Mayor* (2004–2006) and *Tim and Eric's Awesome Show, Great Job!* (2007–2010). "Tim and Eric" (as they are typically billed) are also regular contributors to the online/HBO collaboration *Funny or Die,* and in 2011, they completed work on their first motion picture, *Tim and Eric's Billion Dollar Movie.* For the moment, the fifty episodes of *Tim and Eric's Awesome Show, Great Job!* (henceforth *TAEASGJ!)* remain their best known work. Ostensibly in the genre of sketch comedy, each episode features an often dizzying eleven minutes of sketches, sight gags, parodies, animation, guest "stars," and free-form improvisation. Some episodes purport to have a "theme" or return briefly to a central story spine; others do not. Even with this anarchic play of elements, however, certain recurring themes and devices appear from episode to episode, joined together by a comic style that both builds on and extends their metacomedic sensibility.

While much of *TAEASGJ!* conforms to the quality standards of professional television, the series also frequently cultivates the look and feel of "public access" TV by foregrounding the odd personalities, awkward performances, technical mistakes, and obsolescent technologies that typify such low-budget productions. *Uncle Muscle's Hour,* a recurring bit across the series' five seasons, is perhaps the most emblematic of this approach, each installment featuring a poorly performed video of a song by Casey, an apparently mentally challenged and/or emotionally disturbed teenager, and his "brother," whose contribution to each performance is to dress in a costume appropriate to that week's song. Filled with frame rolls, glitches, and tracking errors, the performances appear to have been shot and edited on poor quality VHS tape, augmented with cheap graphics and Chiron effects that date the videos to the 1980s. Further complicating matters, *TAEASGJ!* also features a handful of recurring and one-off performers who either do have a background in public access (singing ventriloquist David Hart) or who occupy the lower echelons of "showbiz" that one typically associates with the access ethos (comedian James Quall). These segments also frequently make use of the high-key lighting and dated graphics typical of low-budget studio production, reaffirming the "non-professional" status of these performers who, in the end, are rather difficult to decipher in terms of intent and execution.

One might argue that this emphasis on the impoverished style and talent associated with public access is simply a form of parody—an exaggeration of access conventions for comic effect. And yet the conflation of Tim and Eric's invented personas with the seemingly "real" guest appearances—all embedded in the program's rapid cycling of other sketches, bits, and cutaways—works to obscure the status of any single performance. Much as Kaufman's performances compelled viewers in the broadcast era to question what was real and what was not, *Tim and Eric's* vacillation between performing "fake" ineptitude and showcasing apparently authentic amateurism elicits a similar confusion in the era of multichannel cable. One of Kaufman's more notorious bits, for example, involved "sabotaging" a live late-night variety show (ABC's *Fridays*—a short-lived competitor to NBC's *Saturday Night Live*) by refusing to play "stoned" in a sketch and then getting into a fight with cast member Michael Richards and stage manager Jack Burns. Such a stunt would be difficult if not impossible to stage today—Internet spoilers would doubtlessly give away the joke either before or immediately after the incident, while the fragmentation of the broadcast audience into ever smaller niches would make the hoax, even if "successful," an isolated incident on an isolated channel far away from the attention of any cultural mainstream. One could argue *TAEASGJ!*'s highly fragmented structure has adapted this metacomedic strategy of confusing "reality" and "performance" to the environment of a 100+ channel cable system, replicating a logic of channel-surfing that also so often suspends viewers between the real and the parodic. Though Tim and Eric themselves are clearly "performing" their various roles (especially for regular viewers of the show), figures like Hart and Quall maintain the ambiguities of intent and execution once associated with Kaufman—are they "for real" or not? Are they in on the joke? These ambiguities are further cultivated by shuffling these moments of apparent amateurism within other familiar and equally degraded media forms, such as the infomercial, the public service announcement, and the corporate training video. Whether Tim and Eric *intend* to fool viewers by walking the thin line between real and parodic uses of public access or authentic and fake infomercials is not really important; the very look and structure of each *TAEASGJ!* episode effectively camouflages these sketches within the larger anonymous flows of the cable universe, thus making them available for various misapprehensions and confusions.

Each time Casey and his brother take to the stage to sing a recent composition ("Cops and Robbers," "Hamburgers and Hot Dogs," "Big Spider"), the performance invariably ends with a sweaty (and perhaps snotty) Casey spontaneously vomiting, seemingly overwhelmed by a sudden burst of anxiety or emotional trauma. Ostensibly a more disgusting version of comedy's patented "spit take," Casey's vomit variations (ranging from discrete burps to full-out projectile launches) speak to *TAEASGJ!*'s interest (one might say "fixation") with what is generally regarded to be the lowest form of comedy: "bathroom humor"—fart, shit, piss, cum, menstruation, snot, and vomit jokes, frequently made in conjunction with the various "naughty" body parts that produce these substances. Freud famously argued that all jokes are ultimately about displaced aggression and/or sexuality. In this respect, Tim and Eric's comedy is decidedly "pre-genital," distilling "toilet humor" into a particularly stylized and self-conscious form of regressed sexuality. Emulating the style of an educational public service spot for children, for example, Tim and Eric dress as small boys and rap about the benefits of sitting down while "peeing." A fake infomercial extols the virtues of the diarrheaphram—a device for preventing diarrhea flow—that, in the cloacal logic of young childhood, conflates a butt-plug with a woman's diaphragm. Leaving no orifice unprobed, a group of seniors on a double-date learn the benefits of the Cinch "food tube," a device that allows diners to avoid the stabbing dangers of the fork by having their food mixed in an industrial blender (with "softening cream") and pumped directly into the stomach (but only after first having all their teeth removed to better accommodate the tube's insertion down the esophagus). Such sketches and other cutaways frequently enhance this fascination/revulsion with the body's functions and fluids by amplifying various bodily sounds (kissing, lip-smacking, sniffing, stomach growls, churning intestines) extremely high in the mix, making them all the more alien and even unsettling.

Many have argued that "low" body humor typically works to deflate—if only symbolically and temporarily—those people and institutions that profess to have power over others (kings, popes, and presidents, after all, still have to go to the toilet). *TAEASGJ!* seems to take populist innovations in toilet humor as a challenge. Consider the "poop tube." Reversing the logic of the earlier "I sit down when I pee" rap spot, this bit presents a fake commercial for a device that allows the user to defecate while standing and even remaining fully clothed. While the existence of such a ridiculous device may or may not be humorous in and of itself, the ad continues with a laborious description of how the contraption's constituent parts ("fecal pump," "liquefier," and "flow spout") actually operate, accompanied by images of men sloppily spraying their liquefied waste into urinals and trash cans. Somewhat inexplicably, the "poop tube" has been designed so that its "flow spout" vents to the front of the user, thereby making the device even more disgusting (and thus more comedic) in its operation. As a decidedly "anal" form of humor grounded in the forbidden (and thus repressed) sexual fascination with the pleasures and processes of defecation, "shit" jokes are typically the product of a more or less clever process of "displacement" (the "joke work," as Freud called it) that makes these underlying associations return in ways that are surprising and thus amusing. Here, however, the shit joke undergoes little to no such revision. What is usually approached obliquely in such humor is made crudely explicit—the sights and sounds of shitting; the juvenile punning typical of excretion humor (the commercial's pitchman is B. M. Farts, son of Whetty Farts); the revulsion of contamination (a boy is seen with liquefied feces dripping down his face); and even the infantile rebellion of missing the toilet (a man attempts to aim his flow spout at a public urinal, but unfortunately the device does not allow for great accuracy). The "poop tube's" ostensible target may be the never-ending parade of useless "As Seen on TV" products advertised day and night on cable—but as a metacomedic gag, the bit works more to call out the existence and conventions of shit humor generally, taking a usually simple joke and making it both overly graphic and overly complex. It is, in this respect, an extremely intricate and even sophisticated treatment of the lowest of the "low" gags in comedy's repertoire.

A similarly reflexive logic informs some of the "character work" on *TAEASGJ!*, in particular a recurring bit featuring Tim and Eric as the "Beaver Boys," two young men who share a love of shrimp and white wine. Dressed in white from head to toe and donning caps bearing the image of their favorite crustacean, Dilly and Krunk spend much of their time in clubs performing their signature dance move—the "beaver bounce"—in an attempt to attract women. "Beaver Boys" can trace its origins, at least in part, to an influential sketch appearing in the early years of *Saturday Night Live*. While comedy teams dating back to the days of vaudeville and silent cinema have exploited male anxiety over approaching women, Steve Martin and Dan Aykroyd's "Wild and Crazy Guy" routines of the late 1970s cohered a set of conventions that have remained staples of this sketch genre ever since. Martin and Aykroyd played Nortek and Georg Festrunk, Czech brothers who had recently escaped from behind the Iron Curtain and relocated to the United States. Dressed in distinctly outmoded foreign outfits and speaking with exaggerated eastern European accents, the brothers seemingly dedicated all their time and energy on a quest to score "fox-es" and their "big American breasts." Though they typically failed to "score," each installment nevertheless ended optimistically with Nortek and Georg sharing their celebratory catchphrase, "We are two wild and crazy guys!" Given that sketch comedy on U.S. television continues to court and thus cater to a male adolescent audience, this stock premise—two men/boys united by a shared subcultural wardrobe and limited worldview futilely attempting to impress and seduce women—has remained an extremely durable formula in American comedy. Beavis and Butt-head, Wayne and Garth, and the Roxbury Guys all provide unique inflections on this basic formula; Sasha Cohen's "Borat" continues the Festrunks' difficulties with language and women while shedding the amplifying device of the brother/friend.

Given this extensive lineage of brothers and buddies comically attempting to attract unattainable women by performing their various versions of "cool," Tim and Eric's "Beaver Boys" routine becomes, in its simplicity, surprisingly more complex. On one level, the Beaver Boys are yet another entry in this long tradition of sketch humor, two more guys hopelessly unable to perform whatever it is that they think women will find attractive. In their first appearance, for example, the Boys approach two women sunbathing on the beach and simply begin demonstrating (without invitation) various postures they know how to do. Their posing, however, has less to do with the sexual "peacocking" associated with beach culture than with a child's attempt to impress his mother (Dilly shows the girls

FIGURE 8.1.

As enamored with shrimp and white wine as they are with women, Tim and Eric's "Beaver Boys" parodically replicate earlier acts like Steve Martin and Dan Aykroyd's "Wild and Crazy Guys."

that he can walk sideways like a crab). The Beaver Boys can certainly be enjoyed as yet another exercise in moronic masculinity, and yet their drastically reduced stylization suggests—in true metacomedic style—that the bit is as much a parody and/or commentary on this particular form of sketch comedy. For example, while most of their predecessors created and occupied fairly elaborate subcultural worlds (eastern-block emigrants, stoner kids, Long Island club rats, Kazakhstan) complete with accompanying lingo and wardrobe, Dilly and Krunk appear united by nothing more than an odd affinity for shrimp and white wine—their commitment to this imaginary "lifestyle" reaffirmed in their pledge to wear white clothes and a shrimp cap wherever they go. Essentially prelingual, they have no catchphrases (although while they are dancing in the club, an off-screen computer types and reads out the various moves the two are performing, including, of course, the "beaver bounce"). The duo demonstrated little to no "development" over their appearances, although in their final bit, Dilly and Krunk did somehow manage to attract a "hot" pair of identical twins. This seeming success, however, is only fleeting as the premise once again reasserts its inviolable logic. Out to dinner with these no doubt hard-earned dates, Dilly and Krunk notice a waiter serving shrimp entrees at a nearby table. In a comic series of repeated double takes, they look (in unison) back and forth from their dates to the nearby entrees, vacillating between excited exclamations of "twins!" and "shrimp!" The arrival of a chardonnay at the next table seals their fate, compelling the two to abandon their dates in order to binge on the shrimp and white wine. In disgust, the hot twins get up and leave. While other recurring bits in this genre have worked to find novel variations for what is an essentially "one-joke" structure, Tim and Eric's "Beaver Boys" instead foreground the rather relentlessly repetitive logic of such shtick—even reducing it to a pure form of mathematics: "hot girls = shrimp" but "shrimp + white wine > hot girls."

Nigel Tufnel and David St. Hubbins, guitarists for the renowned (mock) metal band Spinal Tap, once famously observed, "It's such a thin line between stupid and clever." In *TAEASGJ!* and their other projects, Heidecker and Wareheim's focus returns again and again to this thinnest of lines. When the routines work, they produce some of the cleverest stupidity on television; when they fail, the bits can be insufferably stupid, even painful. Of course, judgments of "success" and "failure" are subjective, perhaps nowhere more so than in comedy—a genre particularly sensitive to the likes and dislikes of personal taste. But this, too, is emblematic of the contemporary turn to metacomedy. *TAEASGJ!* can certainly be enjoyed strictly as "low" comedy—a carnival of pratfalls, funny voices, and gross-out gags. But the series also positions itself as a form of "avant-garde" humor, a comedy less interested in transgressing social propriety than the formal rules and conventions of comedy itself. In this respect, it epitomizes sociologist Pierre Bourdieu's distinction between "avant-garde" and "popular" taste.[4] Bourdieu argues the "avant-garde" (as both a style and a community) values form over function, and thus approaches an art object (be it painting, theater, film, or even television) with a more detached consideration of technique and convention (what Bourdieu calls "the aesthetic disposition"). "Popular" taste, on the other hand, values function over form, expecting form to remain essentially invisible as the work enacts the desired function of entertainment (through laughter, drama, beauty, sentiment, etc.). Crucially, Bourdieu argues these tastes are not innate, but are instead linked to issues of class and education. The "aesthetic disposition," in other words, must be learned, and the opportunity to master it is afforded only to those with the time and resources necessary to study the history and forms of art.

TAEASGJ! suggests that even television—long-considered the lowest and most debased of the visual and performing arts—has both "artists" and an audience who have now cultivated such a disposition. For some, no amount of discussion or defense will make the "poop tube" anything other than an infantile gross-out gag. For connoisseurs of comedy and television, however, such gags speak to an ongoing appreciation for valuing form over function, making *TAEASGJ!*—like so much other "avant-garde" production—an uncertain study in the cleverly stupid and stupidly clever.

NOTES

1. In the early day of *Saturday Night Live* the show's cast was billed as "the not ready for prime time players," a comic riff on the competition on ABC (Howard Cosell's "Prime-Time Players"), but more importantly a comment on both the talent of the players and the expectations of primetime formats.

2. Richard Corliss, "Comedy's Post-Funny School," *Time* (May 25, 1981): 86–87.

3. Philip Auslander, *Presence and Resistance: Postmodernism and Cultural Politics in Contemporary American Performance* (Ann Arbor: University of Michigan Press, 1992).

4. Pierre Bourdieu, *Distinction: A Social Critique of the Judgment of Taste* (Cambridge: Harvard University Press, 1987).

FURTHER READING

Auslander, Philip. *Presence and Resistance: Postmodernism and Cultural Politics in Contemporary American Performance.* Ann Arbor: University of Michigan Press, 1992.

Freud, Sigmund. *The Joke and Its Relation to the Unconscious.* London: Penguin Classics, 2003.

Hendra, Tony. *Going Too Far.* New York: Doubleday, 1987.

Keller, Florian. *Andy Kaufman: Wrestling with the American Dream.* Minneapolis: University of Minnesota Press, 2005.

Marc, David. *Comic Visions: Television Comedy and American Culture.* Malden, MA: Wiley-Blackwell, 1997.

II

TV Representations
Social Identity and Cultural Politics

9

24

Challenging Stereotypes

EVELYN ALSULTANY

Abstract: Critical discussions about television's patterns of representation some-times devolve into reductive assessments of "positive" or "negative," "good" or "bad" images. In this essay, Evelyn Alsultany describes how the action-drama *24* employed innovative strategies to avoid stereotypes of Arab/Muslim terrorists, but argues that sympathetic portrayals of individuals won't alleviate television's consistent representation of Arabs and Muslims primarily within the context of terrorism.

Since September 11, 2001, a number of TV dramas have been created with the War on Terror as their central theme, depicting U.S. government agencies and officials heroically working to make the nation safe by battling terrorism.[1] Although initially created prior to the 9/11 attacks, *24* (FOX, 2001–2010) became the most popular of the fast-emerging cycle of terrorism dramas. The program centered on Jack Bauer, a brooding and embattled agent of the government's Counter-Terrorism Unit, who raced a ticking clock to subvert impending terrorist attacks on the United States.

In 2004, the Council on American-Islamic Relations (CAIR) accused *24* of perpetuating stereotypes of Arabs and Muslims.[2] CAIR objected to the persistent portrayal of Arabs and Muslims within the context of terrorism, stating that "repeated association of acts of terrorism with Islam will only serve to increase anti-Muslim prejudice."[3] Critics of CAIR retorted that programs like *24* reflected one of the most pressing social and political issues of the moment, the War on Terror, with some further contending that CAIR was trying to deflect the reality of Muslim terrorism by confining television writers to politically correct themes.[4]

The writers and producers of *24* responded to CAIR's concerns in a number of ways. For one, the show included sympathetic portrayals of Arabs and Muslims, in which they were the "good guys," or in some way on the side of the United States. Representatives of *24* said that the program "made a concerted effort to show ethnic, religious and political groups as multi-dimensional," and noted that "political issues" were "debated from multiple viewpoints."[5] The villains on the eight seasons of 24 came from around the globe and included Russians, Germans, Latinos, Arabs/Muslims, Euro-Americans, Africans, and even the fictional president of the United States. Rotating the identity of the "bad guy" was one of the many strategies used by 24 to avoid reproducing the Arab/Muslim terrorist stereotype (or any other stereotypes, for that matter).[6] 24's responsiveness to such criticism even extended to creating a public service announcement that was broadcast in February of 2005, during one of the program's commercial breaks, and featured lead actor Kiefer Sutherland staring into the camera, reminding viewers that "the American Muslim community stands firmly beside their fellow Americans in denouncing and resisting all forms of terrorism," as well as urging all viewers to "please, bear that in mind" while watching the program.

24 proved innovative in portraying the Arab/Muslim terrorist threat that has defined the War on Terror, while seeking not to reproduce the stereotype of the Arab/Muslim terrorist. This essay outlines some of the representational strategies 24 used to accomplish this, including portraying Arab and Muslim Americans as patriotic Americans or as innocent victims of post-9/11 hate crimes, humanizing Arab/Muslim terrorists, and presenting an array of terrorist identities. On the surface, such innovative strategies seem to effectively subvert stereotypes. However, a diversity of representations, even an abundance of sympathetic characters, does not in itself "solve" the problem of racial stereotyping. As Ella Shohat, Robert Stam, Herman Gray, and other scholars have shown, focusing on whether or not a particular image is either "good" or "bad" does not address the complexity of representation.[7] Rather, it is important to examine the ideological work performed by images and storylines beyond such binaries. If we interpret an image as simply positive or negative, we can then conclude that the problem of racial stereotyping is over because of the appearance of sympathetic images of Arabs and Muslims during the War on Terror. The reality is much more complex, though, and an examination of such images in relation to their narrative context reveals how sympathetic portrayals themselves participate in a larger field of meaning about Arabs and Muslims. That is, combating stereotypes is more complex than including positive and nuanced Arab/Muslim characters and storylines. Such efforts can have only a minimal impact so long as the underlying premise of the story hinges on an Arab/Muslim terrorist threat.

The most common way that writers of 24 showed that they were sensitive to negative stereotyping was by creating "positive" Arab and Muslim characters. These characters generally take two forms: a patriotic Arab or Muslim American who assists the U.S. government in its fight against Arab/Muslim terrorism, either as a government agent or civilian; or an Arab or Muslim American who is the innocent victim of a post-9/11 hate crime or harassment. For example, on season six of *24*, Nadia Yassir, a Muslim woman from Pakistan who has lived in the United States since she was two years old, is a dedicated member of the Counter-Terrorism Unit, where she works to prevent a terrorist attack orchestrated by the Arab/Muslim Abu Fayad. In addition to her portrayal as a patriotic Muslim American, she is also framed as an innocent victim of the post-9/11 backlash against Arabs and Muslims when she is falsely suspected of leaking information to the terrorists, tortured by her colleagues during interrogation, and restricted access to the computer systems when she returns to work. Nadia is a "good" Muslim American: she is patriotic, likable, and we sympathize with her plight.

This strategy of representing Arabs and Muslims as patriotic Americans and as victims of violence and harassment is also evident in a fourth-season episode of *24*. Jack Bauer and Paul Raines, in the midst of a blackout and looting in Los Angeles, seek shelter in a gun shop while corporate commandos try to kill them. Two Arab American brothers own the gun shop. Tired of being unjustly blamed for the terrorist attacks, the brothers insist on helping to fight terrorism alongside Jack Bauer. "If you find the people who caused today's bloodshed, then we'll help you," they say. They are also given lines such as "You don't understand. For years we've been blamed for the attacks by these terrorists. We grew up in this neighborhood. This country is our home."[8] This emphasis on victimization and sympathy challenges both long-standing representations of Arabs/Muslims as terrorists and a sense of celebration that otherwise surfaces when Arab/Muslim characters are killed.

Writers and producers of *24* also sought to diminish the Arab/Muslim terrorist stereotype by humanizing Arab/Muslim terrorist characters. Most Arab and Muslim terrorists in films or on television shows before 9/11 were stock villains, one-dimensional bad guys who were presumably bad because of their ethnic background or religious beliefs.[9] In contrast, post-9/11 terrorist characters are shown in a familial context as loving fathers and husbands; they are given back-stories; we are offered a glimpse into the moments that have brought them to the precipice of terror. In 2005, *24* introduced viewers to a Middle Eastern family in a recurring role for the first time on U.S. network television; the family appeared for most of the season as opposed to a single episode. In their first scene they seem like an "ordinary" family eating breakfast together. The mother, Dina, and father, Navi, discuss how their son, Behrooz, is forbidden from dating an American girl. At first it appears that this is for religious or cultural reasons, but it is soon revealed that they are a sleeper cell and that the son is forbidden from dating the American girl because they do not want anything to get in the way of their mission.

Behrooz's task is to deliver a briefcase containing a device that will activate a nuclear power plant meltdown. If all 104 U.S. power plants melt down, they

FIGURE 9.1.
In *24*, terrorist characters
are humanized by por-
traying them in a familial
context.

will release radiation that will kill millions and make regions of the United States uninhabitable for years. Portraying terrorists doing ordinary things like having a family discussion over breakfast helps make terrorist characters multidimensional. In the episodes to come, each family member's relationship to terrorism is explored. The father is willing to kill his wife and son in order to complete his mission; the mother will reconsider her involvement with terrorism only to protect her son; and the teenage son, raised in the United States, is portrayed as having an evolving sense of humanity that ultimately prevents him from being a terrorist. Such nuances show one means whereby writers and producers of *24* have tried to avoid reinscribing stereotypes.

They have also challenged the Arab/Muslim terrorist stereotype by "flipping the enemy," a strategy that leads the viewer to believe that Muslim terrorists are plotting to destroy the United States, and then reveals that those Muslims are not Arab, or that they are merely a front for Euro-American or European terrorists or part of a larger network of international terrorists. During season two of *24*, Bauer spends the first half of the season tracking down a Middle Eastern terrorist cell, ultimately subverting a nuclear attack. One of the key terrorist suspects is Reza Naiyeer, who is Middle Eastern (though his country of origin is not named) and about to marry a blond white American woman, Marie Warner. Suspicious of Naiyeer, Warner's sister hires a private investigator to run a background check on him. The private investigator finds that he appears to know a man named Syed Ali, who has links to terrorist activities. Naiyeer is not a particularly likable character, which adds to his portrayal as a terrorist suspect. However, as Naiyeer seeks to prove his innocence, he discovers that his fiancée, Warner, the last person who would be suspected of terrorism, is the one collaborating with Syed Ali on a terrorist attack. In the second half of the season, we discover that European and Euro-American businessmen are behind the attack, attempting to goad the United States to declare a war on the Middle East and thereby themselves benefit from the increase in oil prices. Flipping the enemy operates first by confirming cultural assumptions that Arabs/Muslims are terrorists and then challenging that assumption by revealing an unsuspected terrorist identity. This strategy conveys that terrorism is not an Arab or Muslim monopoly.

Other common strategies 24 used to circumvent stereotyping include representing U.S. society as multicultural and leaving the country of the terrorist characters unnamed. For several seasons, the U.S. president was African American and his press secretary Asian American. The Counter-Terrorist Unit was equally diverse, peppered with Latinos and African Americans throughout the show's eight seasons. The sum total of these casting decisions created the impression of a United States in which multiculturalism abounds, people of different racial backgrounds work together, and racism is socially unacceptable. Fictionalizing or simply not naming the terrorists' country is another strategy that can give a show more latitude in creating salacious storylines that might be criticized if identified with an actual country. In season four of 24, the terrorist family is from an unnamed Middle Eastern country; in season eight, the fictional country "Kamistan" is a source of terrorist plots. This strategy rests on the assumption that leaving the nationality of the villain blank eliminates potential offensiveness; if no specific country or ethnicity is named, then there is less reason for any particular group to be offended by the portrayal.

These representational strategies are not exhaustive, nor are they all new to our post-9/11 world. Rather, they collectively outline some of the ways in which writers and producers of 24 have sought to improve representations of Arabs (and other racial and ethnic groups). These strategies present an important departure from deploying stereotypes to creating more challenging stories and characters, and, in the process, reflecting a growing sensitivity to the potential negative impact of stereotyping. These strategies seek to make the point—indeed, often with strenuous effort—that not all Arabs are terrorists, and not all terrorists are Arabs. However, for all the show's innovations, 24 remains wedded to a script that represents Arabs and Muslims only within the context of terrorism and therefore does not effectively challenge the stereotypical representations of Arabs and Muslims.

Stuart Hall has claimed that even with the best of intentions, writers and producers who seek to subvert racial hierarchies can inadvertently participate in inferential racism, which Hall defines as "apparently naturalized representations of events and situations relating to race, whether 'factual' or 'fictional,' which have racist premises and propositions inscribed in them as a set of unquestioned assumptions."[10] The persistent unquestioned assumption in these TV dramas is that Arabs and Muslims are terrorists or linked to terrorism, despite writers' efforts to create a wider range of Arab and Muslim characters. The primary objective of television writers and producers is not education, social justice, or social change. Rather, the goal is to keep as many viewers watching for as long as possible, thereby producing successful commercial entertainment. Television must therefore strike a balance between keeping its products as engaging as possible while not offending potential viewers. Writers thus seem to be constrained and influenced by two factors: audiences have been primed for many years to assume that Arabs/Muslims are terrorists, and therefore writers create what viewers expect and what will sell. At the same time, some viewers are particularly sensitive to and critical of stereotypes, and therefore writers are faced with the challenge of creating a more diverse world of characters. The results are some modifications to avoid being offensive, while still perpetuating core stereotypes that continue to have cultural resonance. Post-9/11 television is testimony to the fact that stereotypes that held sway for much of the twentieth century are no longer socially acceptable—at least in their most blatant forms. But this does not mean that such stereotypes (and viewers' taste for them) have actually gone away; they have only become covert.

Inserting a patriotic Arab or Muslim American or fictionalizing Middle Eastern countries are ineffectual devices if Arabs, Muslims, Arab Americans, and Muslim Americans continue to be portrayed solely through the narrow lens of good or bad in the fight against terrorism. The result of the good/bad coupling is startling: at its most effective, the strategy creates an illusion of post-racism that absolves viewers from confronting the persistence of institutionalized racism in a way that echoes Herman Gray's argument about how representations of the black middle class family in television sitcoms of the 1980s and 1990s contributed to an illusion of racial equality.[11] Gray acknowledges *The Cosby Show* for successfully recoding blackness away from images of the "welfare queen" and the drug dealer, while simultaneously noting that it participated in rearticulating a new and more enlightened form of racism, and contributed to an illusion of "feel-good multiculturalism and racial cooperation."[12] Similarly, while I acknowledge that *24* took important steps in diversifying its portrayal of Arabs and Muslims, we cannot go as far as assuming that such efforts actually solve stereotyping. Sympathetic images of Arabs and Muslims after 9/11 give the impression that racism is not tolerated in the United States, despite the slew of policies that have targeted and disproportionately impacted Arabs and Muslims.

Many other post-9/11 TV shows use these strategies, from terrorist-themed shows like *Sleeper Cell* (Showtime, 2005–7) and *Homeland* (Showtime, 2011–present) to broader-themed shows with occasional terrorist motifs like *Law and Order* (NBC, 1990–2010) and *The Practice* (ABC, 1997–2004). In effect, then, such strategies have become standardized. Nonetheless, while representational strategies that challenge the stereotyping of Arabs and Muslims were being broadcast, circulated, and consumed, real Arabs and Muslims were being detained, deported, held without due process, and tortured. According to the FBI, hate crimes against Arabs and Muslims multiplied by 1600 percent from 2000 to 2001.[13] Across the decade following 9/11, hate crimes, workplace discrimination, bias incidents, and airline discrimination targeting Arab and Muslim Americans have persisted. In addition to individual citizens' taking the law into their own hands, the U.S. government passed legislation that targeted Arabs and Muslims (both inside and outside the United States) and legalized suspending their constitutional rights.[14] The USA PATRIOT Act, passed by Congress in October 2001 and renewed multiple times since, legalized the following (previously illegal) acts and thus enabled anti-Arab and Muslim racism: monitoring Arab and Muslim groups; granting the U.S. Attorney General the right to indefinitely detain non-citizens suspected of having ties to terrorism; searching and wiretapping secretly, without probable cause; arresting and holding a person whose testimony might assist in a case as a "material witness"; using secret evidence without granting the accused access to that evidence; trying those designated as "enemy combatants" in military tribunals (as opposed to civilian courts); and deportation based on guilt by association rather than actions.[15] To put it mildly, the explicit targeting of Arabs and Muslims by government policies, based on their identity as opposed to their criminality, contradicts claims to racial progress.

Certainly not all Arabs and Muslims were subject to post-9/11 harassment. Nonetheless, these multiple representational strategies do not in themselves solve stereotyping and racism, and can actually perform the ideological work of producing the illusion of a post-race moment that obscures the severity and injustice of institutionalized racism as outlined above. Such TV dramas produce reassurance that racial sensitivity is the norm in U.S. society, while simultaneously perpetuating the dominant perception of Arabs and Muslims as threats to U.S. national security. So long as Arabs and Muslims are represented primarily in the context of terrorism, our current crop of representational strategies—for all of their apparent innovations—will have a minimal impact on viewers' perceptions of Arabs and Muslims, and far worse, will perpetuate a simplistic vision of good and evil under the guise of complexity and sensitivity.

Surely, one show alone cannot undo a history of stereotyping, even as the representational strategies employed by the creators of *24* did constitute steps toward subverting them. Nonetheless, although some television writers certainly have humane motives, and although some producers honestly desire to create innovative shows, devoid of stereotypes, such efforts are overwhelmed by the sheer momentum of our current representational scheme. Thus, representations of Arab and Muslim identities in contexts that have nothing to do with terrorism remain strikingly unusual in the U.S. commercial media. There have been a few sitcoms and one notable reality television show that have aimed to break out of prevailing molds: *Whoopi* (NBC, 2003–2004), *Aliens in America* (CW, 2007–2008), *Community* (NBC, 2009–present), and *All-American Muslim* (TLC, 2011–2012) all offer broader portrayals of Arabs and Muslims. Three out of these four programs were short lived; still, they are examples of representations of Arabs and Muslims outside of the context of terrorism and homeland security. If there were a more diverse field of representations of Arab and Muslim identities in the U.S. media, then those representations in the context of terrorism as seen on *24* would not provoke as much concern over perpetuating stereotypes because they would no longer dominate the representational field. But despite a few exceptions, *24's* model of framing Arabs and Muslims within the field of terrorism still is the dominant mode of media representation.

NOTES

1. *24*, FOX, November 2001–2009; *Threat Matrix*, ABC, September 2003–January 2004; *The Grid*, TNT, July–August 2004; *Sleeper Cell*, Showtime, December 2005–December 2006; *The Wanted*, NBC, July 2009.
2. "Fox TV Accused of Stereotyping American Muslims," *Free Republic*, January 13, 2005, http://www.freerepublic.com/focus/f-news/1320357/posts.
3. "24 Under Fire From Muslim Groups," *BBC News*, January 19, 2007, http://news.bbc.co.uk/2/hi/entertainment/6280315.stm.
4. Critics of CAIR include www.jihadwatch.org and www.frontpagemag.com.
5. "24 comes under Muslim fire," *Northern Territory News* (Australia), January 29, 2007, 23.
6. I use "Arab/Muslim" not to suggest that these identities are one and the same, but rather to point to how Arab and Muslim identities are portrayed as conflated.
7. See Ella Shohat and Robert Stam, *Unthinking Eurocentrism: Multiculturalism and the Media* (New York: Routledge, 1994), and Herman Gray, *Watching Race: Television and the Struggle for Blackness* (Minneapolis: University of Minnesota Press, 1995).
8. "Day 4: 7pm–8pm," *24*, FOX, March 14, 2005.
9. See Jack G. Shaheen, *Reel Bad Arabs: How Hollywood Vilifies a People* (Northampton, MA: Interlink Publishing Group, 2001).
10. Stuart Hall, "Racist Ideologies and the Media," *Media Studies: A Reader*, 2nd ed., Paul Marris and Sue Thornham, eds. (New York: New York University Press, 2000), 273.
11. Herman Gray, *Watching Race*.
12. Herman Gray, "The Politics of Representation on Network Television," in *Media and Cultural Studies: Keyworks*, Meenakshi Gigi Durham and Douglas Kellner, eds. (Oxford: Blackwell Publishers, 2001), 449.
13. Marcy Kaptur, "Kaptur Bill Safeguards Civil Liberties for All: H. Res. 234 Seeks to Protect Against Religious, Ethnic Persecution," press release by Congresswoman Marcy Kaptur (D-Ohio), May 15, 2003, http://www.adc.org/index.php?id=1803.

14. For reports on the government's practice of detaining and deporting Arabs and Mus-lims after 9/11, see, for example, American-Arab Anti-Discrimination, "ADC Fact Sheet: The Condition of Arab Americans Post-9/11," March 27, 2002, http://www.adc.org/index.php?id=282.

15. Council on American-Islamic Relations, "The Status of Muslim Civil Rights in the United States 2002: Stereotypes and Civil Liberties," Civil Rights Report, 2002, http://www.cair.com/CivilRights/CivilRightsReports/2002Report.aspx. For a summary of such government initiatives, see Anny Bakalian and Mehdi Bozorgmehr, *Backlash 9/11: Middle Eastern and Muslim Americans Respond* (Berkeley: University of California Press, 2009).

FURTHER READING

Alsultany, Evelyn. *Arabs and Muslims in the Media: Race and Representation after 9/11.* New York: New York University Press, 2012.

McAlister, Melani. *Epic Encounters: Culture, Media, and U.S. Interests in the Middle East since 1945*, 2nd ed. Berkeley: University of California Press, 2005.

Shaheen, Jack G. *Reel Bad Arabs: How Hollywood Vilifies a People.* Northampton, MA: Inter-link Publishing Group, 2001.

Shohat, Ella, and Robert Stam. *Unthinking Eurocentrism: Multiculturalism and the Media.* New York: Routledge, 1994.

10

The Amazing Race
Global Othering

JONATHAN GRAY

Abstract: *The Amazing Race* is one of the most successful reality shows in American television history, and arguably no other program has spent so much time outside of the United States or introduced U.S. audiences to so many non-Americans. Jonathan Gray applies a postcolonialist critique to the show's images and characters, finding plenty to criticize, while also pointing to moments that suggest the potential to challenge age-old images of crazy and exotic foreigners.

American television was never just American, but in recent years, its production, distribution, and reception have all globalized in a more concerted way. In terms of American television's onscreen representations, though, its interest in and use of the rest of the world are still starkly limited. Vancouver and Toronto stand in for American cities when Canadian tax breaks help Hollywood out. *Law and Order: SVU*'s Elliot Stabler takes a trip to Prague to bust a child pornography ring and spy or military shows jaunt around the globe to capture nefarious evil-doers, portraying the globe as a problem to be fixed by American law enforcement. Reality television and the news, meanwhile, also seem most interested in the world at large when it is corrupt and violent, corrupt and dying, corrupt and depraved, and/or willing to supply a judge for a competition reality show. Or occasionally the rest of the world justifies coverage when it is stunningly beautiful, exotic, and free of people, as in *Survivor* and many nature shows or documentaries.

I generalize, of course, but so does American television. Exceptions can be found, but they are few and far between, largely because depictions of the rest of the world are themselves few and far between. In the 2011–2012 television season, for instance, every scripted program on American primetime network television was set in America, with only the retro airline drama *Pan Am* and the spy shows *Chuck* and *Nikita* leaving American shores even occasionally. Network reality programming offered us a quick trip overseas on *America's Next Top Model*; it gave us a lush yet unpopulated South Pacific in *Survivor*, and *The Amazing Race* (CBS, 2001–present). As is often the case, and as had become de rigeur by the show's nineteenth season (in its eleventh year on television), the heavy lifting of representing the world and its people on network television was left to *The Amazing Race*.

Over those nineteen seasons, *The Amazing Race* regularly brought in 10–12 million viewers a week, according to Nielsen ratings, and won the Primetime Emmy for Outstanding Reality-Competition Program nine out of ten times after the award was introduced in 2003. The show's format is relatively simple, filming several teams on a race around the world. The race is broken into legs in different countries with tasks to be completed before advancing, movement by all manner of modes of transport, and ultimately a footrace at the end of each leg to the *Amazing Race* mat where host Phil Keoghan and a festively costumed local await, ready to eliminate the last-placed team in most instances. The teams set out from the United States, and the first team back to the final mat in the United States wins a million dollars. The race requires the competitors to interact with locals to get ahead, and the series regularly portrays the competitors' thoughts and opinions on the places they visit. As a result, it is a remarkably rare entity on American network television in this supposedly globalized era: a program that spends time in other countries, depicting the locals of those countries while doing so, and showing an interest, however fleeting and caricatured at times, in the rest of the world. As one of the few shows on American television to do so, it carries significant representational "weight" in speaking of, for, and about the world at large. Like it or not, outside of the news, the *Amazing Race* crew are one of the key sources on American primetime television for messages about the world and its various citizens.[1]

What, then, does it say about the world? Jordan Harvey argues that its depiction is mostly without merit, stereotypical, and Orientalized.[2] I agree to a point and will illustrate how deeply nationally chauvinist the program can be, through analyzing season seven, broadcast from March to May 2005. However, I will not "only" critique *The Amazing Race*; I will also focus on moments in season seven when it realizes progressive potential for depiction and challenges rather than re-iterates tired clichés about the rest of the world in ways that highlight the multiplicity inherent in most television representations.

In his groundbreaking analysis of the discursive conquest of the Middle East by centuries of Western writing about the area and its peoples, Edward Said notes how this conquest happened in part by denying non-Westerners the right to speak for themselves, as knowledge was constructed for and about them in the West instead.[3] While everyday discussion about depictions and representation can often turn to noting the presence of "stereotypes" and to the rating of depictions as either "good" or "bad," one of Said's most helpful offerings was to remind us that much of the symbolic violence done to those being depicted begins when they are denied the right to speak for and of themselves and is exacerbated by the need to reduce complex, varied cultures to singular signs that take on the status of representativeness. Significant cultural diversity is thus reduced, for instance, to the singular depiction of the angry, irrational, despotic, and barbaric "Arab" seen in fictional texts written by non-Arabs. However, cultural identity is always in such flux, characterized by variation and difference, that any attempt to depict a group of people will at the least prove inadequate, and at the worst do great damage to an understanding of the diversity of identity. Said observes how large swathes of Western literature, "science," and travel accounts engaged in a process by which cultural differences within the Middle East were flattened out and reduced to a monolithic group ("the Oriental") that was then regarded as a knowable, singular entity and to a rhetoric that justified colonization and subjugation. And though Said's initial work was primarily historical and concerned with the Middle East, subsequent work by Said and others shows the continuation of this into the present day (witness how rarely, for instance, Iraqis are invited to discuss Iraqi culture or society on American cable news), and the extension of Orientalism to multiple foreign groups. If the nation is, as Benedict Anderson famously notes, "an imagined community,"[4] much of the work that goes into nation-building takes the form of imagining those who are not like us and projecting onto them all manner of unsavory attributes, so that we can then flatter ourselves with the contrast we see between the savage them and the noble us.

In many ways, *The Amazing Race* takes an active part in this process of nationally chauvinistic projection, all the more so because it wears the badge of being "reality." Yet many of the show's more egregious moments of representation let us see how such depiction has often become a self-confirming process. The premise of *The Amazing Race* suggests that we will see competitors in "real" situations with "real" people around the world, but instead they are often interacting in highly contrived situations. In an early leg of season seven, for instance, teams face a challenge in which they must lead llamas a short distance in Peru. Rather than read this instruction in the Lima airport and be forced to find llamas, llama herders, and so forth, the teams are guided to a specific location in the countryside where the llamas await them, and where only those Peruvians hired or otherwise allowed "on set" by the producers may interact with them. The producers often hire the locals beforehand; for example, the bushmen from whom the teams can select for lessons on spearing a swinging sack in South Africa were preselected by the producers. While we can understand this choice for logistical reasons, the result is that the producers have *chosen* many of the locals to whom both the teams and we as viewers are introduced to represent their culture, and we would be naïve to assume they were chosen at random. *The Amazing Race* requires an amazing feat of international organization and stage design (hence its many Emmy awards); before the cameras even arrive, therefore, the producers have already played a key role in deciding exactly what we will or even *can* see. They decide what is worth depicting from a country, and hence they decide what should be represented, leaving the country and its people little and sometimes no room to speak for themselves.

This stage design is especially notable in the challenges, as complex cultures are reduced to a small set of tasks that are habitually described as "common" and "traditional" by Keoghan. South Africa, for instance, gives us a "Tunnels or Tribes" Detour challenge, introducing South Africans to us literally as cavemen, or as primitive tribal elders who demand those most stereotypical of tribal belongings: necklaces, drums, pipes, and bowls (rather than iPods, say). In Botswana, the "Food or Water" Detour challenge reductively implies that the people are so poor that their life and cultural being has been reduced largely to the search for food and water. And India gives us "Trunk or Drunk," exoticizing the country as a land of elephants, vibrant color, and mysticism. Of course, producers also decide *where* in different countries the teams will visit, and these decisions have considerable impact on the resulting image of the country and its people as well. Whether the nation is presented as traditional, simple, and rural, or as commercially vibrant, modernized, and urban comes down entirely to the producers' choice. And then there is the mat, where Keoghan waits sternly for the teams, flanked by a local who is usually in traditional dress and limited in task to waiting several hours with the host before turning on a smile and welcoming the teams to his or her country. "Mat talk" will often ensue between Phil and the racers, and this usually entails retrospective commentary on the day's tasks, yet the "native" welcomers are never invited to contribute to these discussions, nor to provide further context or additional information. Moreover, because of the speed of the race, many interactions with locals along the way reduce them to passive pointers; we rarely see or hear a local rise even to the level of supporting character in an episode. Surely more interactions occur along the way during the race, but the editing leaves audiences with heavily restricted *and directed* vision.

The locals quite often function as backdrops alone. One reply to the criticism that we learn so little about the locals is that the show ultimately isn't about them—it's about the American racers. Interpersonal dynamics between the racers, both within groups (witness Ray and Deanna's spats in season seven) and between them (witness Alex and Lynn's hatred of Rob and Amber), frequently take center stage, and the locals are merely obstacles around which the racers and their attitudes must maneuver. This reduction of "the Other" to backdrop, though, has been a key component of the simplistic rendering of foreign cultures for centuries. Thus, for example, Chinua Achebe notes critically of Joseph Conrad's *Heart of Darkness* that the Africans are poorly rendered in order to make them more ideal as backdrop for the central concern with the hero Marlow's psyche.[5] Conrad's novel may be critical of colonial governance, as such, but it never shows a true interest in colonial *subjects* of that governance; instead, the novel renders them in broad, crude strokes. Similarly, in *The Amazing Race*, non-Americans are rarely if ever allowed to become true characters. Rather, the world becomes a sounding board for the American subject, and the world's people appear as objects to be looked at, smiled at, or occasionally frowned at, yet never fully fleshed-out individuals.

Season 7's episode entitled "We Have a Bad Elephant!" offers one case in point, with editing and stage design forcing the various Indians on the show into a series of unsavory positions. Rob claims ownership over a local serving as guide, worrying that another team might "steal" him. A challenge requires teams to push ornately decorated wooden elephants through the streets, co-opting locals to push for them. Gretchen ends up atop the elephant, yelling at Indian children to push harder, presenting us with a shocking colonial era tableau. Later, a Fast Forward challenge requires Joyce to submit to having her head shaved, which leads to shots of an Indian man standing above the prone, crying Joyce, cutting off her hair, in a disturbing image that evokes countless tales of foreign male sexual aggression against "our" women. Finally, after a camel race with dancing, colorfully dressed Indians looking on, the teams arrive at the mat, where they are greeted by an old Indian man whose moustache connects to his sideburns, and whose welcome suggests little command of English. Few of these subalterns are allowed to speak, save to confirm their ownership by Rob in the former case, or to welcome racers in the latter, and none serves as anything more than local color.

As this criticism suggests, a key disappointment with *The Amazing Race* is its failure to live up to its potential to offer better chances to hear from and of non-Americans. Small modifications could make for such interesting moves forward in the presentation of foreign nationals to the viewing audience. What if, for example, Phil's companions on the mat debriefed the racers instead of Phil? What if locals joined the team members for an entire leg? What if not all teams were American? What if they were rewarded more systematically and significantly for learning about the cultures and people around them? And what if less of the action was staged?

Certainly, when the race finds itself in spaces that the producers cannot control, we often see the show working at its best. Throughout the show's many seasons, passersby in markets have fueled some of the more captivating interactions,

FIGURE 10.1.
A competitor yells
from atop her
elephant at locals
to push harder.

as they speak for themselves and not according to script. In season seventeen, one task involving a set of Russian babushka potato farmers was brought to life by subtitled translations of the babushkas' plucky commentary and mockery of the racers. Camera work and editing in the cracks between challenges often give us better, if fleeting, access to the locals' perspectives as well. As with all reality shows, one risks falling into a trap by focusing on the set-up of *The Amazing Race* alone, as much of the art of reality television lies in its editing. Reality as genre specializes in judgment by editing, wherein insensitive and stupid comments are rendered as such by a quick cut to someone else's judgmental glare. Here, the show's editing regularly rewards the culturally sensitive and interested racers, and chastises the insensitive and ignorant. In many of these brief moments, viewers are invited to identify with the locals, not the racers, and to see the Americans and their behavior as the spectacle. Thus, for example, when "the hillbillies" boisterously start singing on a pickup truck serving as a bus in Peru, the camera captures numerous scornful and bemused looks from their fellow Peruvian passengers. And throughout season seven, Lynn's derogatory comments about, for instance, Peru being "donkeys and blankets" or Johannesburg being "a real city" and not just "like chickens and camels and whatever" are habitually met either by admonishment from his partner Alex or with a quick cut to a disapproving local taxi driver. In such moments, the show can break from offering a racer's eye-view of the race, and it often becomes most amusing when doing so.

The show works against stereotype at other points, too. Season seven, after all, is not all llamas and bushmen. Rather, Keoghan and the camera introduce several cities by focusing on their outstanding architecture, commercial centers, technology, and modernization, hence refusing to label those attributes as American only. Occasionally, the show also gives cultural and political history in ways that could expand its audience's understanding of a country. One of the tasks in Chile, for example, begins with Keoghan noting the country's many award-winning novelists, while a visit to Soweto leads to a history lesson (albeit extremely brief) on the city's political past. Lynn's comment that Johannesburg isn't just "chickens and camels and whatever" may be especially cringe-worthy, but it stands alongside many moments in the run of *The Amazing Race* when racers have commented with awe at how a place or people have defied their expectations and stereotypes. Such moments may be offset and outnumbered by tasks that play into stereotype, but here we see how easy it is and would be for the show to more systematically *challenge* received knowledge about the rest of the world and give us an expanded sense of what to expect outside the United States.

Meanwhile, the show's initial and final legs always take the teams through the United States, where we see American passersby treated entirely akin to foreign passersby. American cabbies' incompetence can often decide the race as much as (or, due to placement at the end of the race, seemingly more than) foreign cabbies; Americans become backdrop and passive pointers; American cities and regions are reduced to simplistic tasks; and each season therefore ends with Americans filling in the same roles as their foreign counterparts. The representational weight of such in-country depictions are lighter than those of foreign locations, of course, as most viewers have likely seen countless other depictions of Miami (in the case of season seven), but astute viewers may at least be taught in these final legs that the show's depictional mode is just that—a mode and a visual grammar—rather than accurate representation.

Everything happens so quickly on *The Amazing Race* that racers often voice a desire to return to the country and "really" see it later. Such moments actively frame the show's depictional mode as superficial, and thereby gesture to depths of cultures and countries that *The Amazing Race* is not showing. While this framing does not excuse the show's choice to paint in broad strokes, and while we still might be left wondering why, for instance, the show doesn't offer us an entire race in only one country in order to allow for more depth, the acknowledgment of the show's inability to represent the world is still important. Just as we are all surely aware by this point in reality television's history that the camera doesn't show us everything about each person, *The Amazing Race* invites us to realize that we haven't seen everything about the countries it visits. Moreover, as evidenced by Travelocity's multi-season sponsorship of *The Amazing Race*, the show encourages viewers to fill in the gaps themselves by traveling more and seeing more. A glance at most *Amazing Race* fan discussion boards also indicates that the show offers viewers the chance to sit back in judgment both of its representations, as fans often compare what they saw in their own travels in a featured country to what the show depicts, and its racers' social strategies in interacting with locals, as such behavior is commonly central to fan reactions to cast members. And as with its CBS reality partner, *Survivor*, the show invites us to imagine how much better we'd be as contestants in terms of both speed and ethics.

Where are we left, then? With a show that can easily fall into an age-old rut of belittling other people and cultures in an attempt to lift up America and Americans, and yet one that is also capable of subverting elements of that process. As one of the few American primetime shows that regularly takes Americans outside of their own country, it is therefore simultaneously disappointing and promising. While it would be "neater" to conclude with either condemnation of the show or praise, it deserves both, albeit at different moments. More broadly, though, its failures point to a larger shared failure of American network television to cope representationally with globalization. After all, while *The Amazing Race* deserves criticism for its worse moments and for frustratingly falling short of its potential, its colleagues on primetime television deserve criticism for not even bothering. Hollywood is happy to take the world's money, it seems, and to export its American-centric brand of television far and wide, but it is still largely disinterested in creating a truly global television. When representations of the world at large and of the billions of people outside of America are restricted to *The Amazing Race*, the news, rewards on *Survivor*, nature shows, images of Anthony Bourdain eating in other countries, the imported *Locked Up Abroad*, and little more, U.S. television is failing both the world and the United States.

NOTES

1. See Jonathan Gray, *Television Entertainment* (New York: Routledge, 2008), 109.

2. Jordan Harvey, "*The Amazing 'Race'*: Discovering a True American," in *How Real is Reality TV? Essays on Representation and Truth*, David S. Escoffery, ed. (Jefferson, NC: McFarland, 2006) 212–29.

3. Edward Said, *Orientalism* (New York: Vintage, 1979).

4. Benedict Anderson, *Imagined Communities: Reflections on the Origin and Spread of Nationalism* (New York: Verso, 1993).

5. Chinua Achebe, "An Image of Africa: Racism in Conrad's *Heart of Darkness*," in *Hopes and Impediments: Selected Essays, 1965–1987* (Portsmouth, NH: Heinemann, 1988).

FURTHER READING

Hall, Stuart, ed. *Representation: Cultural Representations and Signifying Practices.* Thousand Oaks, CA: Sage, 1997.

Harvey, Jordan. "*The Amazing 'Race'*: Discovering a True American." In *How Real is Reality TV? Essays on Representation and Truth.* David S. Escoffery, ed. Jefferson, NC: McFarland, 2006.

Havens, Timothy. *Global Television Marketplace.* London: British Film Institute, 2008.

Murray, Susan, and Laurie Ouellette, eds. *Reality TV: Remaking American Culture*, 2nd ed. New York: New York University Press, 2008.

Roy, Ishita Sinha. "*Worlds Apart*: Nation-Branding on the National Geographic Channel." *Media, Culture and Society* 29, 4: 569–92.

11

The Cosby Show
Representing Race

CHRISTINE ACHAM

Abstract: Few sitcom families in television history have been as widely loved as the wholesome, wealthy, black family of *The Cosby Show*. Christine Acham re-examines the politics of *The Cosby Show* in the historical context of the Reagan-Bush era, in conjunction with the comedic persona and politics of star/creator Bill Cosby.

On April 30, 1992, I tuned in to watch the last episode of *The Cosby Show* (NBC, 1984–1992). The LA riots had begun the day before, and news coverage of the on-going chaos was broadcast during the commercial breaks. With the Rodney King verdict and the reaction of African Americans to continuing racism in American society televised twenty four hours a day, why would anyone choose to watch what seemed in 1992 to be an antiquated sitcom about a wealthy black family? I grew up with *The Cosby Show* and could recall vividly the earliest of episodes, such as when Rudy's fish dies or when Denise makes a horrible replica of a designer shirt for Theo. While I had not watched the show regularly in years, it seemed appropriate to bid farewell to what was one of the most significant representations of a black family seen on U.S. television thus far. *The Cosby Show* was the top-rated program on television from 1985 to 1989, beloved by a cross section of the American audience, yet a battle over the meaning of blackness expressed in the program had raged since its debut on September 20, 1984.

Television's images of African Americans reveal a convergence of factors, including the legacy of black representation in American media, the ideology of the producers, and American social realities. *The Cosby Show* is a product of this amalgamation. In order to have a more nuanced understanding of *The Cosby Show*, it is essential to survey the social, economic, and political history from which this show emerged, while remaining cognizant of the comedic history of Bill Cosby and the influence he would have over the creation of the program.

The late 1970s found the United States in the midst of an economic crisis, the cause and solution of which became major points of contention between Jimmy Carter and Ronald Reagan in the 1980 presidential election. Reagan's slogan "Let's Make America Great Again" symbolized the rhetoric and reasoning of the campaign. The voter was meant to ask, what caused the downfall of this great nation? Reagan placed the blame squarely on the shoulders of the Carter administration and its investment in progressive social welfare programs. His flawed premise was that the liberalism of the post–civil rights era resulted in inflated government-supported entitlements, given to so-called undeserving minorities who were allegedly draining the economy.[1]

Since his 1976 bid for the Republican nomination, Reagan began to coalesce this cultural image of the undeserving minority with that of black people. One of Reagan's favorite stories was that of a Chicago "welfare queen" who abused the system and lived a wealthy lifestyle. During the election period, Reagan used such hyperbolic anecdotes to appeal to whites struggling in a failing economy, suggesting that whites were the victims of reverse discrimination and being negatively impacted by such policies as affirmative action.[2]

The rhetoric of Reagan successfully cemented the strong racial division within American society, and his policies as president reversed many of the gains the black population had made in the post–civil rights era. With the support of television news, which emphasized stories of the failing black family, welfare cheats, and inner city-crime, blackness was increasingly demonized and criminalized in the Reagan eighties.

The Cosby Show seemingly offered the perfect antidote for a black image in crisis through its presentation of a wholesome and wealthy black family led by the well-known assimilationist comic Bill Cosby. While his early routines used some racially based humor, he evolved in the 1960s into a monologist who told stories of, amongst other topics, his childhood and family life without overt markers of race. Television was seen as the way to truly cross over to mainstream audiences, and in 1963 Cosby had that opportunity with a successful appearance on NBC's *The Tonight Show* (1954–present) that led to other television appearances and an article in *Newsweek*.

Cosby's early success came at the specific time in African American history when black frustration with the lack of social progress triggered the rise of the Black Power Movement. Many African American artists and public figures spoke out about the injustices in American society, but the social and political milieu had little overt impact on Cosby's comedy. Indeed, in a 1963 interview on the Canadian Broadcasting Company (CBC), Cosby related a story that illustrates his political outlook: he was an athlete travelling with his team through the South when he and another black player were refused service on the patio of a restaurant and were told to eat in the kitchen. While they first refused, they eventually ate in the kitchen, and it turned out to be the best meal they ever had. On the way back they stopped at the same restaurant, and this time the coach demanded that they be allowed to eat on the patio with the rest of the team:

> COSBY: Well of course we didn't want to eat on the patio knowing what the
> kind of meal we were going to get in the kitchen. The punch line of the
> whole story is that we boycotted the place.
> INTERVIEWER: (laughing) Because they wouldn't let you eat in the kitchen.

This joke is problematic on many levels, yet instructive to the type of comedy Cosby was known for in the 1960s. While countless African Americans struggled for their basic civil rights, that Cosby could so easily make a joke that depoliticized the meanings of the lunch counter boycotts is disturbing.

As African American historian Mel Watkins argues, "Cosby's outward congeniality was crucial to his quick ascendency. At a time when racial confrontations were escalating in the streets, his relaxed, chatty style and surface image of a clean-cut, sanguine black man was the antithesis of the menacing figures on the street."[3] In 1965, this image was parlayed into his first acting role, one part of an undercover duo with white actor Robert Culp on *I Spy* (NBC, 1965–1968). Cosby's character was a Rhodes scholar who was not only proficient in martial arts, but also spoke seven languages. Cosby's portrayal was uplifting, especially considering that the African American roles on television had thus far generally been stereotypical, laughable buffoons and put-upon servants.

As Cosby's career continued in television, he took control over his own image. When he signed on to do *The Bill Cosby Show* (NBC, 1969–1971) and the cartoon *Fat Albert and the Cosby Kids* (syndicated, 1972–1985), he made sure that he was the executive producer, a role that no other African American had attained thus far. He was consequently able to hire actors and shape the storylines. Cosby would take this hands-on approach to *The Cosby Show*, the most significant program of his career. How would Cosby's personal politics impact *The Cosby Show*? Would the show, which began in the midst of the Reagan era of the 1980s, address blackness, especially considering Cosby's direct decision to avoid the issue throughout his career?

The Cosby Show tells the story of husband and doctor, Heathcliff ("Cliff") Huxtable, wife and lawyer, Clair, and their five children. This upper-middle-class black family was unique to American television. Previously, mostly working-class, single-parent, and often poor black families were portrayed in programs that were abundant in the 1970s, such as *Good Times* (CBS, 1974–1979) and *What's Happening!* (ABC, 1976–1979). From the initial planning stages for *The Cosby*

Show, Bill Cosby's control and influence were evident in his roles as star, executive consultant, co-creator, and co-producer with direct control over every script. The scripts were based on a Cosby-developed scenario, which he would share with the writers who would then create a script around his ideas. Cosby hired Alvin Poussaint, an African American psychiatrist from Harvard University, as a consultant on the show, "to review the show's scripts for psychological consistency, racial authenticity, and freedom from unintended insult."[4]

Considering that in the Reagan era, black images on television and within the American imagination were commonly demonized, *The Cosby Show* presented an oppositional narrative. Here was an upstanding, independent, and hard-working family contrasting the numerous perceptions of welfare families who were said to be draining the American economy. Unlike black-cast sitcoms of the 1970s, such as *Sanford and Son* (NBC, 1972–1977) or *The Jeffersons* (CBS, 1975–1985) that relied on race-based humor, *The Cosby Show* chose to ignore the impact of race on the family. When Cosby was forced to address the question of race in interviews, he suggested that the very question was flawed: "Some people have said our show is about a white family in blackface. What does that mean? Does it mean only white people have a lock on living together in a home where the father is a doctor and the mother is a lawyer and the children are constantly being told to study by their parents?"[5]

The comedy presented on *The Cosby Show* corresponded with Cosby's stage persona, and the show portrayed characters and storylines that white Americans could accept and more importantly empathize with. Co-star Phylicia Rashad (then Ayers-Allen) reflected Cosby's sentiment:

> Our show is not about black people, it is about human beings . . . I've been at press conferences with him [Cosby] and I noticed that people kept trying to narrow what he had to offer to an ethnic group. Well, he's bigger than that . . . He doesn't concoct humor that only one group of people can identify with. He deals with human circumstances. I don't blame him for getting annoyed when people try to make his humor less universal.[6]

These narrative qualities and ideas of universality were evident from the beginning of *The Cosby Show* and can be seen in the pilot episode (September 20, 1984). Most of the episode revolves around the challenges of parenting a lively bunch of children—for example, how to get the kids to stop teasing each other, and how Cliff will react to daughter Denise's date. However, the primary crux of the episode is son Theo's poor report card and Cliff's handling of the problem. Theo states that he might not go to college and instead be a "regular person." Cliff then tries to teach Theo the reality of living on a limited salary by giving him Monopoly money, then taking it away as Theo acknowledges expenses that he would have, until Theo ends up with nothing. Theo realizes he will not have enough money but says to Cliff in a touching speech that while his father is a doctor and his mother is a lawyer, they should love him even if he is just a "regular person." Cliff responds, "That's the dumbest thing I ever heard in my life. It is no wonder you get D's in everything . . . I am telling you, you are going to try as hard as you can and you're going to do it because I said so. I am your father. I brought you into this world. I'll take you out." In this episode there is an understated but clear commentary on class. One of the great American myths is that anyone who just tries hard enough will succeed, that if one just pulls oneself up by the bootstraps, one can achieve the American dream. Cliff wants his son to do better than "regular people," who hold jobs like bus driver or gas station attendant. While Theo suggests he can get such a job if he does not go to college, Cliff needs Theo to understand that there is a better life for those who try harder.

Other episodes emphasized the similarity between the Cosby clan and mainstream American society, regardless of race. In "Is that my Boy?" Cliff is excited when his son tries out for the football team, although it turns out that Theo is far from the star quarterback. In "Goodbye Mr. Fish," Rudy's fish dies, and the family has a funeral in the bathroom, and in "How Ugly is He?" Denise dreads bringing her boyfriend home to meet her father who she is convinced will ruin her relationship.

While clearly appealing to a universal audience, *The Cosby Show* was still a black show. Beyond the cast's race, this was evident primarily in setting, but also in terms of some storylines and the casting of guest roles. Paintings by African American artist Varnette Honeywood—copies of paintings from Cosby's own residence—hung in the Huxtable home. There were also framed pictures of African American historical figures such as Martin Luther King and Frederick Douglass. In the children's rooms were posters of 1980s-era African American youth icons such as Michael Jackson, Prince, Mr. T., and Whitney Houston. The Huxtable home was often filled with jazz music, and even the children would refer to African American authors and poets such as Richard Wright, Toni Morrison, Jamaica Kincaid, and James Baldwin. African American artists such as Lena Horne, Stevie Wonder, and Sammy Davis, Jr., were a few of the show's significant guest stars.

The success of *The Cosby Show* during the first season indicated a working formula that Bill Cosby intended to follow in the upcoming seasons, building on the upper-middle-class black family's appeal to audiences. At the start of the second season, series director Jay Sandrich indicated in an interview that he would, "like to deal a little more with what is really happening in some schools today. I would like to deal a little more with prejudice. They don't acknowledge that they're a black family."[7] Questioned by the reporter for the same article, Cosby wondered why the Huxtables should have to deal with issues that other sitcom families did not have to and responded, "Everybody knows that they're black; why does this family have to deal with that?" A spokesman for Cosby later described the incident as "a case of preference not a source of tension."[8] Nonetheless, this difference in viewpoint does illuminate one of the key points of contention over *The Cosby Show*'s representation of blackness. Should this show, with its worldwide appeal, challenge the mainstream audience to deal with the question of race, even if only occasionally? After all, black people were struggling, with the unemployment rate for blacks more than twice that of whites in 1985.[9] Bill Cosby's answer was a clear "no."

While Bill Cosby was not willing to use *The Cosby Show* as a platform for a dialogue on race, conservatives eagerly manipulated the meanings of *The Cosby Show* in their own agenda on race. For example, in May of 1986, when Gary Bauer, Education Undersecretary and Chair of the Working Group on Family in Ronald Reagan's administration, addressed a group of Wisconsin educators, he noted that

> The Bill Cosby show and the values it promotes may ultimately be more important to black children's success than a bevy of new federal programs. . . . The set of character traits, which we refer to as the Protestant work ethic has been ridiculed and debunked by self-proclaimed intellectuals. But the facts clearly show that it works for minorities and poor children as well as the children of the suburbs.[10]

Bauer's words are frightening on a few levels. First, for everyone who would argue that it was just a TV show, here was a man in the administration of the government who not only referred to a TV show in a speech on policy, but also suggested how it could in essence replace federal programs for the poor—programs that were already in political jeopardy. By drawing parallels between *The Cosby Show* and the positive outcome for minorities and the poor who exhibited a strong work ethic, Bauer used *The Cosby Show* and its black family as evidence to make a comment on race and poverty in American society. As the fictional minorities on *The Cosby Show* seemed to indicate, if you just worked hard enough you could achieve the American Dream. While Bill Cosby wanted his series to ignore race, it was inevitably a part of the American dialogue on race and class throughout its tenure on the network.

By 1990, however, the television landscape had changed, and the presence of two popular sitcoms, *Roseanne* (ABC, 1988–1997) and *The Simpsons* (FOX, 1989–present), drew the audience's attention to issues of class. In the seventh season, *The Cosby Show* opened its doors to a cousin of Clair's from the inner-city neighborhood of Bedford-Stuyvesant and finally took a chance at addressing

FIGURE 11.1.
Cousin Pam moves out
of the inner-city and into
the luxury of the Huxtable
home.

class differences in black society. In the episode "Period of Adjustment" (October 11, 1990), Pam moves in to the Huxtable home for the foreseeable future as her mother must go to California to stay with Pam's grandmother, who is ill. Pam is clearly taken aback by the size of the Huxtable house and tells Clair that they could fit her entire apartment into one half of the Huxtable living room. Pam also marks her name on her food to make sure that no one eats it. She hangs out with friends from her old neighborhood—these teenagers speak with some black vernacular and an urban cadence—and thus the audience gets a glimpse of what black life looks like outside of the idealistic Huxtable doors. In "Attack of the Killer B's," Pam deals with the high cost of college, and in "Pam Applies for College," she has to face the fact that her poor grades before entering the Huxtable home may prevent her from going to the same college as her best friend. It is significant to note that Pam's guidance counselor makes it abundantly clear to Pam that she cannot use the fact that she is from a disadvantaged neighborhood and the product of a single-parent household as excuses for not making good grades. Many students from her neighborhood, like her best friend Charmaine, she is told, are going to good schools—they just worked harder. Although *The Cosby Show* seemingly broaches questions of race and class, the conclusions drawn in the episode indicate an unwillingness to challenge the conservative dialogue on race, suggesting that one's class status is solely a matter of individual choice rather than the result of a systemic problem.

Outside of the incorporation of Pam's character, *The Cosby Show* did not change very much in terms of the ideological stance established in its first season. Critics of the show highlight the potential impact *The Cosby Show* could have had, if it had chosen to say something concrete about race and class in U.S. society, especially at a time of such political backlash against black progress. This point was illuminated in a 1992 study that was ironically funded by a Bill Cosby grant to his Alma Mater, The University of Massachusetts, Amherst. The authors of the study concluded that while *The Cosby Show* superficially promoted an attitude of racial tolerance amongst white viewers and brought pride to many African Americans, "Among white people, the admission of black characters to television's upwardly mobile world gives credence to the idea that racial divisions, whether perpetuated by class barriers or by racism, do not exist. . . . The Cosby-Huxtable persona . . . tells viewers that, as one respondent put it 'there really is room in the United States for minorities to get ahead, without affirmative action.'"[11] Bill Cosby held on to the belief that his show should not engage with the political and social realities of race. What he did not take into account was *The Cosby Show's* very existence in the highly racialized climate of post–civil rights America, in which these representations could never be separated from race.

That much of mainstream America responded with surprise at the rage of the LA riots at least partially indicates the power of the illusion of race created by *The Cosby Show*. The images of the LA riots brought the unvarnished reality of race and class back to American television, disrupting Cosby's fantasy of post-racial harmony that had dominated the Nielsen ratings for years. The presence of these stark oppositional images on television the same night—one fictional, the other documentary—is a reminder of the powerful role that television plays in mediating Americans' perceptions of such key issues as race and class on a daily basis.

NOTES

1. For more on the politics and policies of Ronald Reagan, see Thomas B. Edsall and Mary D. Edsall, *Chain Reaction: The Impact of Race, Rights, and Taxes on American Politics* (New York: W.W. Norton 1991).

2. Herman Gray, *Watching Race: Television and the Struggle for Blackness* (Minneapolis: University of Minnesota Press, 1995), 17.

3. Mel Wakins, *On the Real Side: A History of African American Comedy from Slavery to Chris Rock* (Chicago: Lawrence Hill Books, 1994), 505

4. William Rasberry, "Cosby Show: Black or White?" *Washington Post*, November 5, 1984, A27.

5. Sally Bedell Smith, "Cosby Puts His Stamp on a TV Hit," *New York Times*, November 18, 1984, section 2, p. 1.

6. Arthur Unger, "Phylicia Ayers-Allen: Getting Beyond the Race Question," *Christian Science Monitor*, November 23, 1984, On TV, 39.

7. Morgan Gendel, "Cosby and Co.: What Makes a Show a Hit?" *Los Angeles Times*, September 26, 1985, F1.

8. Ibid.

9. John Hope Franklin and Evelyn Brooks Higginbotham, *From Slavery to Freedom: A History of African Americans* (New York: McGraw Hill, 2011), 584.

10. Keith B. Richburg, "Cosby Show Values Lauded; Reagan Aide Extols Effect on Black Children," *Washington Post*, May 31, 1986, A6.

11. Sut Jhalley and Justin Lewis, *Enlightened Racism: The Cosby Show, Audiences, and the Myth of the American Dream* (San Francisco: Westview Press, 1992), 135.

FURTHER READING

Acham, Christine. *Revolution Televised: Prime Time and the Struggle for Black Power.*Minneapolis: University of Minnesota Press, 2005.

Bogle, Donald., *Prime Time Blues: African Americans on Network Television.* New York: Farrar, Straus and Giroux, 2001.

Dyson, Michael Eric. *Is Bill Cosby Right? Or Has the Black Middle Class Lost its Mind?* New York: Basic Civitas Group, 2008.

Gray, Herman. *Watching Race: Television and the Struggle for Blackness.* Minneapolis: University of Minnesota Press, 1995.

Jhalley, Sut, and Justin Lewis. *Enlightened Racism: The Cosby Show, Audiences, and the Myth of the American Dream.* San Francisco: Westview Press, 1992.

12

The Dick Van Dyke Show
Queer Meanings

QUINN MILLER

Abstract: The television sitcom is typically considered a conservative form that reaffirms the status quo. In particular, network era sitcoms' normative constructions of gender and sexuality are assumed to be antithetical to queer representation. In this examination of an episode of *The Dick Van Dyke Show* informed by historiography, gender studies, and transgender criticism, Quinn Miller shows how textual and intertextual details in the fabric of postwar sitcoms create a type of queer representation that differs from the LGBT (lesbian, gay, bisexual, and transgender) characters TV producers commonly develop today.

Like many narrative forms, television deploys a hierarchy of characters. In addition to crafting main roles and a supporting cast, actors in minor appearances portray stock types. Comedy conventions allow secondary characters to deviate from norms in ways that main characters seldom do. With more minor parts, writers and actors have more freedom. As media scholar Patricia White has shown, such narrative conventions can produce queer meaning in popular texts.[1] The term "queer" describes energies that protest norms and trouble conventional ways of thinking. A queer approach to television texts exposes the simplified understandings of gender and sexuality that make complex TV representations seem to fit conventional notions of what "straight," "gay," "lesbian," "bi," or "trans" identity and behavior entail. As a strategy for sparking radical change to social norms, which construct difference through dichotomies, queer criticism seeks to challenge conventional identity categories. Working with the minutia of television, this critical strategy reveals anti-normative perceptions, presentations, and desires within programming that is commonly understood as both "normal" and neutral.

This essay presents a queer critique of *The Dick Van Dyke Show* episode "I'm No Henry Walden" (March 13, 1963). The classic sitcom *Dick Van Dyke* (CBS,

1961–1966) depicted the life of Rob Petrie, who lives with his wife, Laura, and son, Ritchie, in suburban New York and pens scripts for *The Alan Brady Show*, a popular comedy variety series, at an office in the city. "Walden" debunked assumptions that cultural norms applied to everyone by representing variations across different characters' perceptions of gender and sexuality. An analysis of "Walden" informed by transgender studies and queer historiography demonstrates how moments of self-reflexive television comedy complicate binary understandings of identity and culture. My discussion shows that queer meanings can interfere with deeply ingrained social constraints within the space of TV programs. Queer meanings in individual television episodes are an important part of both queer history and TV history. Comedic moments and brief references to contextual material can bring queer culture to life in a manner often absent from more straightforward LGBT representations.

Dick Van Dyke regularly compared TV to other media in ways that reworked ideological views on gender and sexuality. "Walden" addresses cultural divisions between television and literature. When Rob is mysteriously invited to a glitzy fundraising event for a literary foundation hosted at a fancy Park Avenue apartment, he frets about "real" writers judging his profession. In showcasing Rob and Laura's anxiety in the company of pontificating scholars, offbeat poets, and cosmopolitan novelists, the episode explores differences in class, status, and sense of humor. The episode opens in the Petries' bedroom, as Rob and Laura prepare for the party. Rob grows nervous and worries that he was invited by accident, while Laura tries to calm and compliment him. The next sequence takes place at the event, where host Mrs. Huntington, a socialite with a big personality, repeatedly calls Rob "Bill Petroff," introducing him as the author of *The Town Crier Weeps No More* (a presumably serious book with an unintentionally funny title). Huntington, who presumptuously acts as if she knows better than Rob how to pronounce his name, remains oblivious to his attempts to correct her mistake. Being addressed as a novelist when he is really a television writer confirms Rob's expectation of feeling out of place, and the people they meet further alienate him and Laura with their disdain for TV. One particularly haughty guest calls Rob's boss "Mr. Brody" (instead of Brady) and implies that a "television machine" is a worthless object alien to her refined sensibility. At the end of the episode's first act, Huntington calls for donations to the Henry Walden Literary Fund, and Rob accidentally pledges a blank check to the charity effort.

After a post-party scene back in the Petries' bedroom, the setting shifts to the *Alan Brady Show* office, where Rob receives a surprise visit from Walden, a character whose name references Henry David Thoreau, the nineteenth-century activist and author of *Walden* whose work, as Michael Warner argues, "repeatedly expressed a longing for self-transcendence through the love of another man."[2] In a comic and poetic reversal of expectations, Walden condemns the pretentious beliefs of his cohort and asks Rob to collaborate with him on a broadcast special that will treat television comedy as an important national art form, an invitation that heals Rob's bruised ego. The invitation also represents an enlightened view of TV that combats elitist beliefs that the medium is rubbish and its popularity a sign of social ruin. The episode's coda brings Walden's appreciation of television to the fore at a second party in the same Park Avenue apartment by uniting the *Alan Brady* writers with the literati for a celebratory screening of "The History of American Humor." In the end, the series suggests that Rob *is* a "Henry Walden," despite the episode's title, because he is a respected artist in his medium. In making this argument, "I'm No Henry Walden" represents a culture of queerness within and beyond its fictional literary party.

Throughout, "Walden" represents social distinctions in ways that destabilize social conventions around gender expression and cultural value. Issues of class, prestige, and sexuality arise frequently, prefaced by Rob's flirtatious comment to Laura that even if they are out of place at the party, their presence will happily "prove . . . television writers marry the prettiest girls." Voicing Rob's wariness of "serious" writers, this line implies that the Petries' marriage will remain strong during their encounter with the literary world. This is a conventional sentiment, yet it is expressed through associations that resist social norms. While suggesting that Rob enjoys one marker of success (i.e., Laura) that places him above people with bigger incomes and reputations, the line also implies—despite popular notions of middle-class prudishness and affluent decadence—that their physical pleasure exceeds that of bohemians and aristocrats.

In an example of queer meaning that arises from sitcom self-reflexivity and TV's hierarchy of characters, Carl Reiner and Frank Adamo, two people with ongoing roles behind the scenes on *Dick Van Dyke*, play minor characters who, along with a host of other supporting players, challenge the suburban family mindset Rob and Laura Petrie represent. Reiner, who scripted "Walden" and created *Dick Van Dyke* based on his own experience (and would have starred in the show had the network not deemed him "too Jewish"), plays Yale Sampson, a cultural critic who believes realism—the television industry's bread and butter—is dangerous. For the role of fey poet H. Fieldstone Thorley, the show's producers cast Adamo, who was Dick Van Dyke's personal assistant and often stepped in for bit roles on the series—thus becoming a point of backstage trivia for fans (particularly following Nick at Nite's kitschy publicity of his appearances). The plotting of "Walden" generates narrative space for its writers, directors, editors, costumers, and actors to cultivate eccentric characters that comment on its own backstory.

As "Walden" depicts characters' perceptions of social markers through relatively intangible cultural cues, it fashions roles reminiscent of extratextual queer figures. The episode's cast of characters reflects a vision of avant-garde diversity that contrasts with the image of white middle-class nuclear families associated with television programming. Two black guests, for example, who are prominent considering the white-centrism and overall lack of racial integration in fictional series during this period, recall Harlem Renaissance authors like Nella Larsen, Zora Neale Hurtson, Langston Hughes, and Bruce Nugent, as well as James Baldwin, whose novel *Another Country*, which features multiple queer characters, came out the same year "Walden" aired. As the Petries venture into a social space outside their normal routine, the series explores conceptual terrain generally deemed beyond the realm of the era's family comedies. While such intertextual references may be obscure to most viewers, the queer history implicit within them remains a part of programming in spite of this obscurity.

This episode's intertexts and wordplay denaturalize commonplace assumptions about social differences by stressing connections between gender and sexuality norms on the one hand, and cultural hierarchies around occupation and status on the other. "Walden" draws particular attention to Adamo's portrayal of the poet "H." *Dick Van Dyke*'s producers convey queer authorship through this character's comportment and manner of speaking, as well as through his undone, slightly askew bowtie and the titles of his two books of poetry, *Lavender Lollipops* and *Point Me to the Moon*. These titles constitute queer content in their camp treatment of gay coding (lavender), sexual metaphor (lollipops), and social abjection in the era of the space race (*Point Me to the Moon*). The writer's abbreviated name reinforces these associations with gender and sexual nonconformity, given its sense of anonymity and the resonance of "H." with both canonical gay author W. H. Auden and the queer avant-garde writer and filmmaker H.D. With his stock "beatnik" characteristics, H. also serves as a doppelganger for Allen Ginsberg, the queer writer and activist whose publisher was charged with obscenity in 1957 for the "cock and endless balls" in *Howl and Other Poems*. *Dick Van Dyke* includes H. as the final author spotlighted in "Walden's" party sequence and accents his presence by including multiple reaction shots from the protagonists.

Directly before Rob is caught up in the blank check debacle, he and Laura sit slightly apart from the rest of the group, looking relatively comfortable. The visual economy of the couple's view of H. is integral to the only moment of the party when the couple would not rather be "canning plums" or "taking in a movie." With its characterization, "Walden" suggests that H. is not any more bizarre than his peers, even if he appears further afield of gender norms. As an eyebrow raise from Laura indicates, H. is indeed unusual compared to the other people at the party. In being eccentric, however, he blends in with his unorthodox compatriots. In particular, apart from Rob and Laura, none of the attendees appears to be married. Despite broader cultural emphasis on presumed differences between wedded couples and unattached or ambiguously attached artists, the editing, acting,

FIGURE 12.1.
The party guests applaud H. (standing in the second row) after he announces his contribution to the literary cause. Directly in front of him are Yale (Reiner) and Walden (Sloane), while behind him a man in a headdress signifies "Eastern" metaphysics, one of Hollywood's go-to emblems of worldliness and general "otherness" in the 1960s.

and direction of the episode constructs H., along with Walden, as a marker of the comfort that Rob and Laura, who feel like outsiders at the party, might find in the context of an exceedingly urbane milieu. While *Dick Van Dyke* is generally assumed to represent a conventional world to which queer figures were antithetical, "Walden" demonstrates the way in which queer characters, while marginal, were nonetheless central to episodes dealing with the arts.

As part of the "high" culture scene, Rob and Laura participate in conversations that queer gender and cultivate unconventional erotics. As they talk to Thomas Evelyn, for example, a French modernist in a black dress and pearls, their bourgeois perspective shows. They register surprise at a woman named Tom, whereas the other characters fail to register anything unusual and remain oblivious to the couple's uneasy reaction. In other words, the incongruity that Rob and Laura perceive goes unnoticed by the literati, thereby indicating the couple's suburban sense of gender norms, which obviously differs from that of the more sophisticated crowd. This disparity is heightened by the "Petrie/Petroff" mix-up, which results in Laura being referred to, like Tom, with a name traditionally given to men. Rob repeatedly attempts to state his name after he is mistaken for Bill, but people think he is introducing his wife. Thus Laura is called Rob—or "Rob, darling," in the parlance of the upper crust. This nonchalance around gender situations that might be perceived as confusing, contradictory, or transgressive creates a space within which queer forms of transgender and transsexual meaning are possible. As the *Dick Van Dyke Show* writers and performers normalize Tom through the reactions of the party attendees, their characters make room for gender transitions and genderqueer identities and embodiments.

In addition, as the error of the party attendees renders the Petries a couple with two "male" names, "Walden" maintains unconventional currents of homoeroticism, creating what Gayle Salamon has called "homoerratic" interactions.[3] In first responding to Tom and then attempting to convey Rob and Laura's actual names, Van Dyke and Moore play gender anxieties for laughs, thereby drawing out butch-femme exchanges during which an erotics of difference situated beyond essentialized sex categories becomes evident between women as well as between the Petries. After the couple becomes known as "Bill and Rob," for example, Rob, occupying the position of "Bill," calls his wife by his own name in jest. This diegetic joke compounds the couple's denaturalized "difference" erotics with a momentary erotics of sameness. In other words, the dialogue detaches the characters' masculine-feminine rapport from their status as "male" and "female," and this sexual dynamic queers the masculine-masculine and feminine-feminine vibes cultivated by Laura's comic masculinization as "Tom" and Rob's comic emasculation in connection to the "feminine" medium of television.

While these fleeting moments may seem inconsequential, their significance becomes clearer in the context of additional queer referents for "Walden's" ensemble. For example, in the context of Tom's last name, which is Evelyn, her "male" first name points to the feminized connotations, at least in the U.S. context, of British author Evelyn Waugh's typically "female" moniker. Beyond this literary connection, the fictional title of Tom's book, *I Love to Love to Love to Love*, calls up the modernist prose of Gertrude Stein, who was legendary in the 1960s for writing "Rose is a rose is a rose is a rose" and notable for her queer gender presentation and negotiation of heterosexism. While *Dick Van Dyke* does not present a fictionalized version of either Stein or Waugh—or of Ginsberg, Auden, or H.D.—the Tom and H. characters do clearly reflect the producers' (and perhaps some viewers') understandings of a literary world that included queer figures.

"Walden's" queer meanings are additionally produced through traits in its supporting characters that are not directly related to gender or sexual non-conformity. This is most evident with Reiner's Yale Sampson. Extratextual reference points for Sampson riff on the era's cultural stereotype of the incoherent "egghead," a derogatory caricature of academics. Reiner's comic delivery of Yale's intellectual monologue, which is intermittently unintelligible, conjures public intellectuals as diverse as Clement Greenberg and Marshall McLuhan. Yale's rant includes words like "penetrability" and "ostentation," as well as several neologisms. Later, Rob imitates Sampson's arrogance and manner of speaking, listing traits he associates with the literati they encountered including "vulnerability" and "flamboyance." As with H.'s *Lavender Lollipops*, these adjectives encode the queer element of the episode's minor characters' collective cultural difference. Rob's irritability at their "flamboyance"—after being dismissed as an artist and taken for a donation he and Laura cannot afford—and Sampson's emphasis on the word "penetrability" signal queerness through their intertextual citation of popular discourses constructing homosexuality. At the same time, when Rob rants in parody and frustration, he represents the partygoers as unapologetic about their behavior, a stance that undercuts these same homophobic discourses.

In the context of the episode's ensemble, issues of artistic reputation and income surface in connection with queerness, such as when the Petries discuss their finances following Rob's accidental donation. Building on the themes of cultural identity and socio-economic differences running through "Walden," Rob confesses that he bought the tuxedo he is wearing, telling Laura, "They won't let you on Park Avenue in a rented tux!" Worrying that if his check bounces he will "lose his reputation," Rob recalls the charity's goal of raising $250,000 (well over a million dollars today) and tells his wife that Huntington could fill his check out "for two thousand bucks," using slang terms that exaggerate his class identity. Laura reminds him that most of the donors pledged royalties rather than concrete amounts, quipping that H.'s royalties for *Lavender Lollipops* "couldn't amount to more than a dollar and twenty cents." While acknowledging bias against queer-coded cultural production in the marketplace, Laura's comment troubles received notions of economic value in "high" art along with popular discourses constructing queers as a threat.

Unsettled themes of class, talent, and reputation again collide during Walden's visit to Rob's office and in the episode's brief coda. These scenes further destabilize divisions between apparently normal and abnormal people, high and low class demeanor, and respectable and repellant media. With his first lines of the episode, Walden reveals himself to be an oddly plain-talking poet laureate with an appreciation for popular culture and a sense of humor that the other "serious" writers lack. Showcasing characteristics that blur seemingly intractable social distinctions, he uses colorful language ("hoodwinked, bamboozled, hornswoggled") to describe Huntington's method of procuring Rob's pledge and shows surprising respect for the illustrious vaudeville and early TV careers of Rob's writing partners, Buddy and Sally, by reciting a string of accolades that praise the showbiz credentials of Morey Amsterdam and Rose Marie, the actors who play these characters. Walden cracks no less than ten jokes in five minutes, including a risqué one about Huntington that, in reversing stereotypes based on classed expectations for sexual expression, serves as a bookend to the Petries' own display of affection at the episode's outset. Just as Walden's vernacular aligns with Rob's Midwest-inflected speech (evident in Rob's reference to a novel he "ain't never gonna finish no how"), this element of sexuality establishes connections across perceived cultural divides.

While its content questions cultural hierarchies, "Walden's" overall reflexivity emphasizes the "high" elements of "low" media and the "low" elements of "high" culture. Walden's quips are penned—and Sampson is performed—by Reiner, who, as a TV writer, is the type of writer that his fictional intellectuals are expected to be above. H. is acted by Adamo, who, as the assistant to the show's star, occupies a position relative to his marginalized character, but would appear to have less artistic clout. When Walden lands a punch line, and when Yale and the others congratulate Rob after viewing the co-authored television special, it is not only television (and the people who write it and support its production) that appear newly praiseworthy, but also those viewers who will risk social stigma by exhibiting a sophisticated appreciation for the medium. In scripting characters like Tom, H., and Yale and then highlighting their differences from Rob and Laura, "Walden" spotlights both the respect Rob and Laura feel toward celebrated writers and the outrage they experience when snobs lacking in quick wit dismiss TV writing. In effect, the queer meanings attached to its minor characters allow *Dick Van Dyke* to cultivate tensions between popular culture and respected mediums of self-expression while also pointing out the absurdity of the distinctions on which these tensions are based.

The series' comparison of Rob and Yale (whom Rob accidentally calls "Harvard," in a passing swipe at Ivy League pedigree), for example, operates through dichotomies that it ultimately redefines. Rob's belief that Sampson has nothing of real value to say yet receives kudos for being obscure distinguishes Rob's work from Yale's. In the context of Sampson's dismissal of mass culture and realist conventions, and his fan Venetia Fellows' way of turning her nose up at TV, "Walden" intensifies Rob and Yale's character differences, implying that educated people with discerning tastes often miss the artistry of television writing when it takes the form of light entertainment. Walden, however, rejects this norm, arguing that Rob, as a "first-class television writer," has more talent than the "third-rate novelist" Petroff. This belief is confirmed in the final scene by applause from Yale, H., and the others at a screening of "The History of American Humor" that features Sally and Buddy as representatives of comedy's "low" art.

Through indirect renderings of queer artists, *Dick Van Dyke* contributed to a television discourse that goes beyond "high" and "low." With the awkwardness (from a conventional perspective) and unremarkableness (from the sophisticates' perspective) of H.'s *Lavender Lollipops* and women with "men's" names, "Walden" ventured into a self-reflexive space around authorship, cultural norms, and non-conformity. The associations "Walden" invokes between art and queerness support *Dick Van Dyke*'s self-presentation as a high form of low culture, but its abstract and satirical representations undermine the high/low distinction itself. Looking at popular art that complicates markers of social distinction shows non-normative worldviews embedded in TV from the network era. It also shows that divisions between "high" and "low" class, taste, and talent make the overall matrix of gender and sexual differentiation seem far more straightforward than

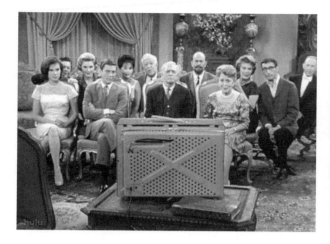

FIGURE 12.2.
In "Walden's" final scene, key players watch a TV set suggestively placed in front of a book. From right to left, they include: Laura, Buddy, Sally, Rob, Tom, Dr. Torrance Hayward, Walden, Yale, Mrs. Huntington, Venetia, H., and an unnamed butler.

it actually is. When artists break down assumed distinctions between high and low culture, they often throw the norms that stabilize gender and sexuality into question as well. The same is true of queer television criticism that addresses the instability of common beliefs and binary logics of identity and difference. Illuminating unexpected challenges to straight conventions and spaces of non-conformity within norms, queer analysis of TV changes the way we see conventional representations in past eras and cultural history as a whole.

NOTES

1. Patricia White, *UnInvited: Classical Hollywood Cinema and Lesbian Representability* (Bloomington: Indiana University Press, 1999).
2. Michael Warner, "Thoreau's Bottom," *Raritan* 11, 3 (1992): 53.
3. Gayle Salamon, *Assuming a Body: Transgender and Rhetorics of Materiality* (New York: Columbia University Press, 2010), 71.

FURTHER READING

Doty, Alexander. *Making Things Perfectly Queer: Interpreting Mass Culture.* Minneapolis: University of Minnesota Press, 1993.

Salamon, Gayle. *Assuming a Body: Transgender and Rhetorics of Materiality.* New York: Columbia University Press, 2010.

Sedgwick, Eve Kosofsky. *Tendencies* (Durham, NC: Duke University Press, 1993.

Warner, Michael. "Thoreau's Bottom." *Raritan* 11, 3 (1992): 53–79.

White, Patricia. *UnInvited: Classical Hollywood Cinema and Lesbian Representability.* Bloomington: Indiana University Press, 1999.

13

Eva Luna
Latino/a Audiences

HECTOR AMAYA

Abstract: In this examination of the highly successful Spanish-language program *Eva Luna*, Hector Amaya argues for the politically progressive potential of the *telenovela* as a serial melodrama. Ultimately, however, he critiques *Eva Luna*'s failure to meaningfully engage with contemporary topics of relevance to Latino audiences.

The telenovela *Eva Luna* (2010–2011) marks a new direction for Univision's primetime programming and a relative departure from its narrative traditions. Since its inception in 1961, Univision, originally named Spanish International Network (SIN), has relied on telenovelas from Latin America to fill its primetime schedule. The majority of these telenovelas, often from Mexico's Televisa, are conventionally conservative, rags-to-riches stories that scholars in Latin America have criticized for reconstituting traditional gender, racial, and class prejudices. Because Univision relies on these problematic shows, Latino media activist organizations argue that Univision cannot possibly meet the cultural and ethnic demands of Latinas/os living in the United States, who require programming that reflects their reality and that can help them navigate U.S. society and culture. But due to factors that include the growing political, cultural, and economic clout of Latinas/os in the United States, and changes in the Spanish-language media landscape, Univision is now interested in expanding their U.S. production capabilities.[1] *Eva Luna* is partly the result of Univision's effort to produce more of its own primetime programming while continuing its ratings successes.[2]

Eva Luna clearly met the ratings challenge, drawing an average of 5 million viewers per episode and 9.7 million in its finale.[3] These numbers indicate that Univision's primetime programming, and *Eva Luna* in particular, has reached the level of mainstream programming, competing with the rest of the networks and often winning the ratings race. This essay analyzes *Eva Luna* as part of Univision's new programming strategy and evaluates its politically progressive potential by examining several of *Eva Luna*'s key textual characteristics. It asks the question: Does *Eva Luna* address the media needs of Latinas/os? At first glance, the answer seems to be "yes." It is set in contemporary California, where Eva González, an immigrant from Mexico, struggles to fulfill her dreams of happiness and success. Although Univision's effort to engage with issues important to Latinos seems commendable, this essay shows how *Eva Luna*'s use of genre conventions undermines the show's progressive potential—that is, its potential to propose or explore political ideas that can enhance social, class, sexual, gender, or racial equality. This essay proposes that to read a text like *Eva Luna*, one needs first to understand the telenovela as a genre with a history, within which the genre's progressive potential can be found.

Like many other telenovelas, *Eva Luna* is a serial melodrama that tells the story of a young dispossessed woman who has to fight to acquire both the man of her dreams and a higher status in life. Eva is the daughter of an undocumented immigrant and, like her father, picks apples for a living. Set first in the orchards of southern California and later in Los Angeles, the telenovela brings together the world of the undocumented with the glamorous life of California's wealthy Latino classes. The telenovela quickly uproots Eva from the orchards to the mansions where the young beauty meets Daniel Villanueva, the wealthy, talented, handsome, morally outstanding, and white widower who will become Eva's love and, 111 episodes later, husband.

Eva faces a rollercoaster of events that constantly threaten her and her family's well-being, as is common to the genre. In the first episode, her father is killed by a car. Soon, her younger sister, Alicia, becomes involved with a young man of dubious character. Because of her pride, Eva cannot hold a job; when she does get one, she falls into the web of trickery of her nemesis, Marcela Arismendi, who controls the ad agency where Eva will eventually work, and who is the manipulating mother of Victoria, Daniel's fiancée. But overcoming these threats is simply a baseline that the narrative uses to show Eva's resourcefulness and mettle. The heart of the narrative is Eva's quest to move from poverty to riches, and from single to married. The means that she uses to achieve this include an intelligence that allows her to grow up as a fruit picker and also have the cultural capital to create a very successful slogan to advertise apples, recognize Picassos, and possess the know-how to do exquisite stitching that Victoria, a model, puts to good use.

The narrative is committed to Eva to a degree that even her weaknesses are used to further her case for deserving success. In the first few episodes, for instance, Eva must get a job to support her young sister, but is fired several times because of her pride and her unwillingness to tolerate what she considers mistreatment by wealthy clients. Pride, this moral weakness, functions in Eva's case

FIGURE 13.1.
Eva looks adoringly into Daniel's eyes.

to show that she values herself to the point that she would rather risk her economic well-being and her sister's than tolerate the assumption that the rich have the right to treat working class people poorly. In Eva's balance, morality and basic manners outweigh crass materialism. In *Eva Luna*'s imaginary, by contrast, success is bound to material wealth.

The riches in this story are generated in the advertising world by the famed publicity agency owned by Don Julio Arismendi. Daniel, Eva's romantic interest, is the agency's most successful publicist and the fiancée of Victoria Arismendi, daughter of the agency's owner and a successful model. *Eva Luna,* then, is a story of substitution in which Eva, a poor immigrant, will come to occupy Victoria's social location. Over the course of the narrative, Eva wins the heart of Victoria's father, Don Julio, who eventually treats Eva as a daughter, giving her control and ownership of the agency. Besides substituting for Victoria in the daughter role, Eva also becomes a successful model and Daniel's wife. By the end of the narrative, Victoria has been fully displaced by Eva, who is consistently empowered by Don Julio, the patriarch. Don Julio is represented, like Eva and Daniel, as a moral individual who, given the proper information, will make the right choices and will invest affection and money on the proper individuals—Eva in particular. Importantly, the telenovela shows that Don Julio, like Eva, began poor and only through hard work and talent came to occupy the role of wealthy patriarch.

Understanding the politics of these plotlines requires some background in the genre of the Latin American telenovela, the direct descendent of the Cuban radionovela (radio-novels), which in turn descended from the European serial melodrama of the nineteenth century.[4] All of these serial melodrama forms emerged at the intersection of economic, political, and social transformations that created the space for the appearance of this influential cultural form. The form brings together the melodrama, a narrative style centered on morality plays and heightened emotion, and the serial, a mode of writing and publishing rooted in media industry necessities.

The European melodrama originated as a response to the new social arrangements wrought by the industrial revolution and the moral void created by rural to urban migrations.[5] However, melodrama was not only a response to morality issues within the home. Jesús Martin-Barbero notes that in the first half of the nineteenth century, melodramas often addressed the social challenges of the city, which people increasingly interpreted through a political prism.[6] Barbero is particularly interested in the European serial melodrama, which was delivered in episodes and distributed by an increasingly robust popular press and was thus a novelistic form proper for, and responsive to, the popular classes. Most serial melodramas featured stories about the struggles of the poor to survive and succeed in the exploitative new urban environment of the industrial age. In Charles Dickens's stories, for instance, the hero is typically a dispossessed man, woman, or child who must struggle to survive the extremely harsh labor environment of London (*Oliver Twist*) or the political complexity of the city and its maddening legal system (*Little Dorrit*). But the popular classes were not only the inspiration for writers; they also affected and shaped writing. Readers used letters to the editor to suggest narrative developments and new characters, making the serial melodrama the first mass participatory media.

The serial melodrama, like its genre successors, the radionovela and the telenovela, is neither intrinsically conservative nor progressive. Its conservative potential, according to critics like Umberto Eco, lies in the fact that this popular cultural form can quickly become "a series of montages designed for the continual and renewable gratification of its readers."[7] This aspect of the popular novel disconnects readers from the actual social reality that the serial melodrama is meant to explore. In Eco's view, this popular literary form makes palatable the underprivileged existence of the popular classes without actually fostering political changes.

The progressive potential of the serial melodrama, according to Barbero, is rooted in the fact that throughout history this popular form also became an important depository of popular memory and modern ways of reflecting on the politics of the moment. For these reasons, serial melodramas, like those written by Dickens or Dumas, should be treated not simply as massified, debased culture (as Eco implies), but as popular culture that does the difficult job of helping the popular classes make sense of their situation. "Popular memory" here refers to the way a community uses culture to memorialize a vision of its history to help understand its location in time and in society. The serial melodrama's progressive potential depends, then, on the ability of specific texts to act as repositories of popular memory—a job that in pre-industrial times was carried on by folklore—and on the ability of serials to narrativize political problems and political options. These two standards are still relevant and can be used to evaluate the serial melodrama's successor, the telenovela.

Like nineteenth century European melodramas, telenovelas are morality plays that invite moral and political reflection. And, like the older serials, telenovelas are shaped by the necessity of the media industry to have a faithful consumer base—in this case, television viewership. Such popular success is possible only when the text delivers meaningful narratives, but meaningful is not the same as politically progressive. Mindful of Barbero's ideas, I ask: Is *Eva Luna* responsive to the popular memory of Latinas/os? And is *Eva Luna* sensitive to the political needs of Latinas/os?

Here I concentrate on popular memory that intersects with politics and use the term "politicized popular memory" (PPM) to designate this confluence. PPM is a way of codifying a community's political past and present in a cultural text. Popular memory is not simply about going back in time; instead, it is about linking past and present to reflect a community's circumstances. When popular memory directly engages with the way power is distributed and the manner this distribution shapes the life of a community, popular memory becomes a depository of the political. Sometimes PPM engages with standardized aspects of political life such as labor policy or elections. But PPM also has the potential of constituting new political objects by emphatically discussing how elements of daily life can result in unjust power distribution. This is the case with, for instance, the complex comments about standards of beauty that became central to the popular dramedy *Ugly Betty* (ABC, 2006–2010). It follows that for any televisual text to be a depository of PPM, it must help viewers meaningfully reflect on a relevant aspect of the powers they confront, whether these powers are traditionally thought of as political or not. Measured by the standard of PPM, *Eva Luna* is a cultural patchwork that ultimately does more to disconnect Latinas/os from their reality than help them reflect on it.

Eva Luna potentially offers PPM based on language, locality, and setting. Language is an important bridge between a community and its past, and, for linguistic minorities such as Latinas/os, language becomes a particularly meaningful connector among communities in the present. Telenovelas like *Eva Luna* function as community rituals that bring together Spanish-speakers in Miami, Los Angeles, Tulsa, or Lincoln. They connect people across regions, but also across national origins. Spanish language media allows for Latinas/os of Dominican, Puerto Rican, Cuban, Argentinean, or Mexican descent to remember that their cultural roots have always been partly shaped by their colonial origins. I am not suggesting that Latinas/os of different national origin ought to disregard their cultural differences, but I suggest that language and Spanish cultural ancestry are meaningful common denominators for Latinas/os in the United States.[8] Because of its ethnically diverse casting, *Eva Luna* itself tries to bring this Latino national diversity into one linguistic platform. Members of the main cast have roots in Mexico, Brazil, Argentina, Puerto Rico, Venezuela, and Cuba, and though their accents are tempered, Spanish-speaking Latinas/os can often hear the difference.

The significance of having television in Spanish is amplified when we consider the way Spanish, and English with accented Spanish, are treated in mainstream English-language media. Spanish is often used to codify racialized negative characteristics.[9] TV shows use Spanish to tell viewers a character's class, moral character, sexual proclivities, and general otherness. In English-language television, Spanish is spoken by gardeners, maids (like Rosario in *Will and Grace*), criminals (any episode of *Law and Order*), and sexualized bombshells (Gloria in *Modern Family*). Only rarely do you hear professors, honest politicians, detectives, teachers, or physicians speak Spanish or English with a Spanish accent.

Spanish alone does not make a televisual text work as popular memory. All programming shown in Univision during primetime is in Spanish, and the majority is imported from Latin America. Spanish has added relevance because *Eva Luna* was made in the United States and set in California. Perhaps obviously, watching a show made locally is more likely to help viewers reflect on and understand their present contexts. The cultural needs of a national community cannot be fully served by culture produced by and for other nations, regardless of whether these nations are the viewers' ancestral homes. Local programming is more likely to reflect on reality in a manner that makes sense to a local community and that takes into account a community's values and history.

In locally producing *Eva Luna*, Univision is amplifying the chance of having television that can act as popular memory, but this opportunity is squandered. At first glance, *Eva Luna* seems to engage with issues that would help Latinas/os connect immigration, a common narrative of origin in Latino communities, to understanding their present, which is partly filtered through the political challenges of immigration law. The story is set in Southern California, a place defined by immigration, and some of the first characters we see are undocumented immigrants working in an apple orchard. But nothing in the way these settings are photographed reflects the actual economic conditions of farm labor or the social stigmas inherent in being undocumented. The characters are clean, handsome, and happy. The orchard seems to be run by the workers and, without supervisors in sight, it appears mostly as an idealized site of labor, far from the way that Dickens, for one, depicted workplaces in nineteenth-century London. The working conditions that undocumented workers have to face today, as scholars and activists have noted, actually resemble those of nineteenth-century London more closely than those seen in *Eva Luna*. They tend to be exploitative, dirty, unsafe, and back-breaking.[10] And, as I have written elsewhere, the legal framework that sustains this exploitation is as irrational as the framework explored in *Little Dorrit*.[11] By contrast, apple-picking is depicted in *Eva Luna* with the textual characteristics of the pastoral: a pleasant, romanticized narrative frame that pleasantly connects people to the landscape, or, in this case, that romanticizes the connection between labor and the orchard.

To make matters worse, *Eva Luna* further disregards the importance of reflecting on undocumented labor by quickly moving away from the orchard. Of the 111 episodes produced between November 1, 2010, and April 11, 2011, all but one are set in the wealthy suburbs of Los Angeles. And, in 111 hours of narrative, there are no mentions of the political fights about undocumented immigrants happening in the United States, or a sense that these political issues might be relevant to Eva. Instead of engaging in a Dickensian narrative, *Eva Luna* concentrates on melodramatic representations of what have to be called fantasies of economic and social success. This is not the L.A. of the middle classes. The Arismendi mansion, which is the setting of around one-third of the scenes in *Eva Luna*, is a palace more often found in regressive TV shows such as *The Real Housewives of Beverly Hills* (Bravo, 2010–present). In this, *Eva Luna* follows the narrative traditions of Venezuelan or Mexican telenovelas, replicating the fantasies of economic and social success common in Venevision and Televisa. Instead of using this cultural platform to engage, even minimally, in exploring popular memory, *Eva Luna* seems committed to rehearsing the fantasies of others.

Further diminishing this text's progressive potential is the way *Eva Luna* replicates racial imaginaries found in other Univision programming that consistently marginalizes non-whites. Mexican and Venezuelan telenovelas famously cast their characters based on race, systematically normalizing the location of whites above the location of mestizos, Indians, and blacks. *Eva Luna* does the same by connecting notions of success and failure to racial characteristics. Like most serial melodramas, *Eva Luna* depicts a world of moral confrontations where the protagonist must face undue challenges and prove, repeatedly, that she deserves the rewards of her proper moral choices. In this telenovela, the system of punishment and rewards is partly represented by the physical characteristics and surroundings of Eva and Daniel. Eva is played by Blanca Soto, a real-life Mexican beauty queen and model, who is coded as underprivileged partly because of her brown skin. Eva, however, lacks any other socially-recognized stigmas of poverty such as bad diction, poor manners, violent proclivities, or lack of ambition. She is an intelligent, well-spoken, and driven young woman who is interested in advertising and who, we eventually learn, has a knack for it. Eva, put simply, embodies the potential for success. Yet, true to gender and racial conservatism, success will not be signified by showing how Eva acquires a privileged position in the advertising world. Her success needs a man, Daniel, whose whiteness can truly symbolize a woman's success. Daniel stands here not simply as Eva's romantic interest, but also as an emblem of Eva's success. Daniel embodies this success and defines it in terms of class, beauty, race, and education—a model that further separates Eva's original world of fruit pickers from her dream world of advertising.

Eva Luna is a complex televisual text that has some progressive elements, including language and localism, which connect people to popular memory. Yet, *Eva Luna* ultimately squanders the potential to be treated as politicized popular memory because of the way it treats its geographic, political, and labor settings. To make matters worse, this show further betrays its potential by codifying success in terms of race and class in ways that reconstitute the economic and social marginalization of most Latinas/os, who embody racial and class markers quite different from those of *Eva Luna's* cast.

I want to conclude by briefly noting the paradoxes inherent in analyzing popular culture, which is culture that becomes meaningful partly because of the number of people who are exposed to it. By this measurement, *Eva Luna* was a resounding success at the national and global levels. It averaged 5 million viewers during 111 episodes and has been exported to eight nations, including Mexico, where it showed in Televisa's primetime lineup. But the reason media scholars are interested in popular culture also relates, like Eco and Barbero note, to what popular culture may do for the people that consume it. By linking the telenovela to the serial melodrama, this article shows that there is nothing inherently conservative or reactionary about telenovelas. It argues that the telenovela, like other examples of popular culture, can bring about or facilitate positive political effects for those who consume it. But the lesson is that in order for telenovelas to have this positive, progressive effect, they must have specific textual characteristics. They must be responsive to a community's popular memory, and must be willing to problematize and present relevant political issues. *Eva Luna* fails on these two important measurements and can thus be defended only as a smart articulation of Univision's economic needs.

NOTES

1. Luis V. Nuñez, *Spanish Language Media after the Univision-Hispanic Broadcasting* (New York: Novinka Books, 2006).

2. *Eva Luna* is a co-production between Univision and Venevision, Venezuela's most influential TV network and the second largest supplier of telenovelas to the U.S. market after Televisa.

3. Rafael Romo, "The Beginning of an Era? Hispanic Soaps Gain Popularity," *CNN Enter-*

tainment, April 19, 2011, http://articles.cnn.com/2011-04-19/entertainment/hispanic.soap. operas_1_soap-operas-hispanic-population-hispanic-marketing-expert?_s=PM:SHOWBIZ.

4. Rosa Marta Alfaro, "The Radio in Peru: A Participatory Medium without Conversation or Debate," *Television & New Media* 6, 3 (2005): 276–97.

5. Ben Singer, *Melodrama and Modernity: Early Sensational Cinema and Its Contexts* (New York: Columbia University Press, 2001), 30.

6. Jesús Martín-Barbero, "Memory and Form in the Latin American Soap Opera," in *To Be Continued . . . Soap Operas around the World*, Robert Allen, ed. (London: Routledge, 1995), 276–84.

7. Umberto Eco, *The Role of the Reader: Explorations in the Semiotics of Texts* (Bloomington: Indiana University Press, 1984), 134.

8. Vicki Mayer, "Please Pass the Pan: Retheorizing the Map of Panlatinidad in Communication Research," *The Communication Review* 7 (2004): 113–24.

9. Hector Amaya, "Television/Televisión," in *Flow TV: Television in the Age of Media Convergence*, Michael Kackman et al., eds. (New York: Routledge, 2011), 183–98.

10. Abel Valenzuela, "La Esquina (The Corder): Day Laborers on the Margins of New York's Formal Economy," *The Journal of Labor and Society* 9, 4 (2006): 407–423.

11. Charles Dickens, *Little Dorrit* (New York: Oxford University Press, 1953).

FURTHER READING

La Pastina, Antonio, and Joseph D. Straubhaar. *Gazette: The International Journal for Communication Studies* 67, 3 (2005): 271–88.

López, Ana. "Our Welcomed Guests: Telenovelas in Latin America." In *To Be Continued . . . Soap Operas around the World*, Robert Allen, ed. London: Routledge, 1995.

Martín-Barbero, Jesús. *Communication, Culture and Hegemony: From the Media to Mediations.* Newbury Park: SAGE Publications, 1993.

14

Glee/House Hunters International
Gay Narratives

RON BECKER

Abstract: One key cultural function of television is to represent different identities, especially marginalized groups; here Ron Becker considers one interesting type of contemporary gay representation. By connecting seemingly disparate texts of *Glee*, *House Hunters International*, and the online It Gets Better movement, we can see how media construct messages of optimism and hope that can have powerful impacts on viewers.

In 2010, syndicated advice columnist Dan Savage and his partner, Terry Miller, posted a video to YouTube in an effort to reach out to teenagers dealing with anti-gay bullying and thoughts of suicide. The fortysomething couple shared their own painful experiences being consistently harassed and feeling ostracized at school. Their main goal, however, was to provide hope for gay teenagers by assuring them that things will improve. "It gets better," Savage avowed, "and it can get great and it can get awesome. Your life can be amazing, but you have to tough this period of it out and you have to live your life so you're around for it to get amazing. And it can and it will." The video went viral and kick-started a social movement that has brought unprecedented national attention to the problems of gay teen suicide and anti-gay bullying. Thousands of people posted videos to the It Gets Better Project website, and millions viewed the videos and donated money.

This essay is not about the It Gets Better campaign per se, but rather the fundamentally optimistic social message at its core. Most of this essay will, in fact, focus on two television series: *Glee* (2009–present), Fox's campy musical "melodramedy" about the joys and pains of a high school glee club in Lima, Ohio, and *House Hunters International* (2006–present), HGTV's formulaic, real-estate reality show in which people looking to relocate to distant places like Dubai or buy second homes in tropical spots like St. Lucia tour three homes before deciding

which one to buy. I connect these two disparate programs—one, a primetime network mega-hit that had as much buzz as any show during the 2010–2011 season;
the other, just one of a dozen inexpensive, home-centered, lifestyle shows steadily
repeated on cable networks like HGTV, TLC, and Bravo—because I believe that
they work together to support the same optimistic vision of contemporary gay
life as the It Get Better Project does. While *Glee* portrays the pathos of gay teens
seeking a better life, *House Hunters International* gives viewers an aspirational
glimpse of what that life could be.

Chris Colfer, the openly gay actor who plays Kurt Hummel, the openly gay
high school student on *Glee*, was one of the first celebrities to post a video to
ItGetsBetter.org. His prominent participation seemed appropriate. By the fall of
2010, the hit FOX series had become well known for its depiction of high school
bullying and as a champion of kids who don't fit in—themes that are firmly established in the pilot episode. In fact, Kurt is introduced to viewers as a bullying
victim in one of the series' first scenes. As the pilot's narrative opens, we see Kurt,
a look of panic on his face, standing next to a dumpster and surrounded by nine
tall jocks in letterman's jackets ("Pilot," May 19, 2009). Kurt seems to know the
drill, but insists that they wait for him to take off his Marc Jacobs jacket before
throwing him in the garbage. The scene also introduces viewers to the unique
mix of melodrama and satiric comedy that *Glee* would become known for. While
Kurt's ashen face at the start of the scene suggests real fear, the upbeat score, the
sunny lighting, and the bullies' seeming respect for designer couture give the
scene a comedic incongruity.

Our introduction to Rachel Berry (Kurt's soon-to-be glee club teammate) captures the pathos of being an outsider at McKinley even more powerfully. We get
to know Rachel through a flashback montage that juxtaposes her self-confident
optimism and ambition to be a star against the cruel abuse she experiences at
school. The sequence is framed by Rachel's audition for glee club in which she
sings the pathos-filled ballad "On My Own" (from the "seminal Broadway classic
Les Mis"). In voiceover narration, Rachel enthusiastically explains her rich life
(e.g., she was "born out of love" by two gay dads who "spoiled her in the arts";
she doesn't have time for boys because she posts videos of her performances to
her MySpace page every night to hone her skills). Alongside Rachel's description,
however, viewers see that there is more to the story. Rachel's earnest MySpace
video, for example, becomes fodder for cyber-bullying by cheerleaders who post
comments like "Please get sterilized." As the sequence ends, we return to Rachel's
audition at its emotional climax, the lyrics now connected to Rachel's own story.
While Rachel belts out the line "A world that's full of happiness that I have never
known," we see a flashback of her reading the mean girls' comments. The hurt
expression on her face and the pathos of her performance of the lyric belie her

bravado. The moment, however, is disrupted by a somewhat violent exclamation point. Just as Rachel ends the lyric's final note, the scene abruptly cuts to a shot of Rachel having a slushie thrown in her face as she turns around. The scene is traumatic—certainly to Rachel, but it might also be for the viewer who is meant to be startled by the unexpected edit and the sudden silence of the scene.

While bullying becomes endemic at McKinley High (e.g., all of the glee club members eventually get slushied), Kurt is singled out for special abuse because of his sexuality and his refusal to conform to traditional gender norms. In a later first season episode, when word gets out that Kurt is competing for the chance to sing "Defining Gravity" (a song traditionally sung by a woman), his father receives an anonymous phone call from a guy who states, "Your son's a fag." Although his dad is worried, Kurt is not so shaken; he tells his dad, "I get that all the time" ("Wheels," November 11, 2009). The anti-gay bulling increases in season 2, however, when Kurt is repeatedly harassed by Dave Karofsky, a football player who we eventually learn is gay himself, although highly closeted. The harassment intensifies over the course of several episodes, with Karofsky even threatening to kill Kurt. When official policy limits what school officials can do, Kurt's father decides to pull him from McKinley and the glee club. As the series developed, Kurt's storyline became perhaps the most powerful way for the series to explore the central themes of high school bullying and the pain of being an outsider. "When we did the 'Preggers' episode, when Kurt tries out for the football team," remembers Brad Falchuk, *Glee* co-creator and executive producer, "that's where I think we really understood who Kurt was and how much of an emotional anchor he was going to be for the show."[1] As stories about gay-teen bullying and suicides grew in the 2010, Kurt's story and *Glee* gained even wider resonance.

Glee doesn't simply focus on the problem of high school bullying, however. In describing the series' narrative philosophy, executive producer Ryan Murphy explained: "It's four acts of darkness that take a turn and have two acts of sweetness. It's about there being great joy to being different, and great pain."[2] The series' sweetness, of course, is written into the optimism of its underlying premise: that the glee club is a safe space where you can embrace who you really are despite the bullies. It is also woven into the series' longer-term story arc—the idea that this ragtag group of misfits can win nationals and in the process create a future for themselves where things are better. As Kurt explains to his father, "Being different made me stronger. At the end of the day, it's what's going to get me out of this cow town" ("Wheels").

Glee includes more specific scenes of sweetness—elements one might describe as moments of magical-musical realism. "Preggers" (September 23, 2009), for example, provides a joyously queer version of a high school narrative cliché. In an effort to impress his father, Kurt joins the football team and discovers an innate talent for kicking the ball. Meanwhile, the football coach believes that learning choreography from Mr. Schuster might make the football team (the glee club's re-peated tormentors) "perform" better on the field and help them end their embarrassing losing streak. The players resist, fearing they will look "gay." But down six points in the final second of the big game, they decide to go with it. As Beyoncé's "Single Ladies" blares over the speaker system, the team breaks into a choreographed dance routine, confusing their opponents enough to help them score a dramatic touchdown. It is then up to Kurt, who dances up to the ball Beyoncé-style and kicks the winning field goal. The crowd erupts, and for a moment, the effeminate gay kid is the high school football hero.

Many of the musical numbers have such magically joyous qualities and seem to function as wish fulfillments. In "Born This Way" (April 26, 2011), for example, Kurt returns to McKinley High from Dalton Academy, the idyllic, gay-embracing, all-boys private school Kurt had transferred to when he needed to escape Karofsky's harassment. As Kurt is welcomed back by his glee club friends on the steps outside McKinley, his boyfriend, Blaine, and the other members of Dalton's all-boy show choir make a surprise appearance and serenade him with an emotional rendition of "Somewhere Only We Know." For the length of the performance, the narrative and "normal" life at McKinley High are suspended, and the scene offers a vision of the world where things are better.

In *Glee*, such scenes are momentary; the music ends, and life returns to "normal." Kurt and the power of dance may have helped win the game on Friday, but the football players will slushie the glee kids on Monday. Blaine may get to declare his love for Kurt through a choreographed Keane song in the schoolyard, but homophobia doesn't disappear. At prom, for example, Kurt is elected prom queen as a practical joke. "Don't you get how stupid we were?" Kurt asks Blaine, in tears. "We thought that because no one was teasing us or beating us up that no one cared. Like some kind of progress had been made. But it's still the same . . . all that hate. They were just afraid to say it out loud, so they did it by secret ballot" ("Prom Queen," May 10, 2011). Such reversals are narrative necessities. As a continuing series, *Glee* needs to keep its antagonists as important sources of narrative tension. If a series predicated upon the struggle for a better future is to come back for another season, that better life must continually be deferred.

Observers have criticized the series for what they see as poor writing, pointing to episodes with incoherent plot developments, jarring shifts in tone, or inconsistent character motivations.[3] While I sympathize with some of this criticism, for me the pleasures offered by the pathos of such narrative reversals and the anticipation of more magical realism compensate for any sense of contrivance or narrative inconsistency. I would also argue that such inconsistency might actually speak to the disorienting experience of homophobia and the indirect and ultimately uncertain path of progress. In fact, part of *Glee*'s appeal, I think, is that

FIGURE 14.1.
Openly gay actor
Chris Colfer, seen
here in the *Glee*
pilot, was one of the
first celebrities to
post an It Gets Bet-
ter video.

chris colfer

alongside its peppy musical score, campy comedy, and upbeat musical numbers, there is an underlying "darkness" that suggests that things don't always get better.[4]

While *Glee* invokes hope in a future where things get better for gay kids like Kurt, home-centered reality shows like *House Hunters International* present an already existing world where things aren't only better for gay men and women, they are actually terrific. Gay people are commonly included as designers and clients on makeover design shows like *Curb Appeal: The Block*, *Design Star*, *Flipping Out*, and *Color Splash*, and as homeowners and house seekers on real-estate shows like *Million Dollar Listing*, *Selling L.A.*, *Bang for Your Buck*, and *Income Property*. Although gay people are often central characters in these programs, the narrative tension never relies on the struggles they face because they are gay. Instead, viewer interest is maintained through anticipation: Will Jane and Mary love their newly landscaped backyard? How excited will the family be by the remodeled kitchen the show's gay host David designed? Which house will Patrick and Brian purchase? Given the format of these shows, we always get our answer by the end of the episodes, and the answers to such questions are typically "yes," "yes," and "the house of their dreams."

The fact that such shows are edited to guarantee happy endings is not surprising. After all, they rely heavily on sponsorship from the home improvement industry, a sector deeply interested in making home renovation and ownership look appealingly effortless. Such shows also tend to represent a decidedly upscale sector of home ownership; for instance, *Bang for Your Buck* might compare three $75,000 master suite renovations, *Flipping Out*'s Jeff Lewis renovates only million-dollar LA homes, and *Curb Appeal: The Block* spends $20,000 on each front yard make-over. It is likely much easier for the producers and network executives to attract both advertisers and viewers (especially those viewers advertisers most want to reach) with aspirational images of home ownership. Thus, the gays and lesbians featured in these programs are almost always successful professionals and relatively affluent homeowners living the dream.

A 2011 episode of *House Hunters International*, entitled "Family-Friendly Living in Hellerup, Denmark," (June 19, 2011) illustrates these points well. The family in question includes "lifetime partners" Paul and Meinhard St. John. According to the host's voiceover commentary, Paul, a software engineer from Colorado, and Meinhard, a part-time actor and model from Denmark, "started off worlds apart, but destiny brought them together." As we watch the two tall, thin, attractive middle-aged men stroll down the cobblestoned streets of Stockholm, Sweden, purchase cheese from a deli, and drink beer with a circle of friends, the host explains that the couple is adopting a baby boy, Liam, and has decided to move to Denmark to start their new family. The couple looks blissfully happy, but the host informs us that trouble may be brewing. It seems that the couple has different priorities when it comes to picking their dream house. "Will disputes over location versus renovation create a divide? Or will they find happiness in the perfect home?" the host asks, establishing the episode's narrative tension. "Find out when *House Hunters International* heads to Hellerup, Denmark."

Consistent with the series' rosy representation of home ownership, Paul and Meinhard's story ends happily. Although their real estate agent warns us that the couple's seemingly ample $2 million budget might make it tough to find the perfect home in Denmark's hot housing market, the couple tours three massive homes in the affluent Copenhagen suburb. As the host anticipated, the couple does disagree. Paul doesn't like the closed-off kitchen in the first house. Meinhard doesn't like the casement windows in the second house. Both love the third house, but Paul hates the fact that it sits next to a busy freeway. In the end, however, Paul and Meinhard agree completely and purchase the third house for "only" $1.8 million. In the episode's coda, we get to check in on the couple eight months later. Liam has arrived, and the family has settled into their dream house. As we watch idyllic images of the couple feeding their chubby-cheeked son and entertaining friends, Meinhard describes their new life as a family: "You think that you're prepared, but it's never what you imagined. It's been a gift. It's been a blessing."

Glee and *House Hunters International* intersect with the It Gets Better campaign in various ways. When put together, these gay characters (Kurt's fictional story and Paul and Meinhard's reality-edited story) create a larger narrative that echoes Dan Savage and Terry Miller's personal story and those of many of the people who contributed to the website. Many It Gets Better video testimonials follow the same narrative structure. In act one, they recount painful memories of being bullied as a teenager; in act two, they describe when things started to get better; and in act three, they explain how good their current life is. In this context, one can read Paul's successful family and house hunt as the culmination of

FIGURE 14.2.
"Lifetime part-
ners" Paul and
Meinhard reflect
on how good their
life is in Denmark
on *House Hunters
International.*

the journey Kurt is starting. The last shot of the couple—they are framed in a two
shot sitting beside each other in their living room, reflecting on the joys of family
life in their new home—strongly recalls the visual look and themes of the video
testimonials. Kurt Hummel's dream of escaping the oppressive homophobia of
Lima, Ohio, is realized in the globe-hopping life of Colorado-native Paul St. John.

Kurt's dream is also realized in the real-life experience of Chris Colfer. As
Colfer's video testimonial makes clear, he had a very painful experience as a gay
kid growing up in Clovis, California. His high voice made him a target of bullies; his only friends were the high school lunch ladies. Since getting cast on *Glee*,
however, his life has improved dramatically. "It's very therapeutic," Colfer explains. "Outside of work I'm getting the praise and acceptance I've always wanted.
And at work, I've got my first set of friends ever. What I am is a true Cinderella
story."[5] Thus Colfer's real-life path working on *Glee* supports the show's underlying optimism that being true to yourself will eventually pay off, and the message
that things get better.[6]

My training in media criticism encourages me to be skeptical of television's
images of gay life. Media scholars, myself included, have been understandably
hesitant to equate the increased number of gay men and lesbians on television
with political progress, arguing that increased cultural visibility doesn't mean
that discriminatory public policies have been overturned or that anti-gay attitudes have disappeared. Critics have also been right to point out how television's
images of gay life are problematically shaped by commercial imperatives; *House
Hunters International*'s representation of an affluent global gay elite serves as one
clear example of this dynamic.[7]

While it is always important to be skeptical, the It Gets Better campaign encourages me to value the importance of strategic optimism as well. Things don't always get better for gay people, of course. Gay adults sometimes face intense discrimination at work, rejection by friends and family, and an underlying social system that disadvantages non-heterosexual people (especially those who aren't white, upscale, or gender normative). Yet the It Gets Better campaign is predicated on the idea that struggling gay kids can find real emotional support by hearing from people who survived such challenges. Television images of gay life can play a similar role. Colfer, for example, recounts the many moving letters he receives from gay viewers explaining how Kurt helps them feel that it is okay to be who they are. "With all due respects to my castmates," Colfer states, "they don't get the letters like I get—the letters that not only say 'I'm your biggest fan' but also 'Kurt saved my life' and 'Kurt doesn't make me feel alone' from 7-year-olds in Nebraska."[8] The emotional impact of the It Gets Better videos and *Glee* encourages me to consider programs like *House Hunters International* in another light. Yes, few gay people have access to the web of socio-economic privileges that helped Paul and Meinhard build their happy family in their $1.8 million Danish house. And I have no idea whether the perfect family life promised by the end of the episode is actually real or just the product of effective editing. At the same time, programs that normalize idealized images of gay life can offer real hope and emotional support for gay viewers who live in a culture where inspiring role models and positive reinforcements may be lacking.

The line between being delusional and being optimistic can be a very fine one. American commercial television can be decidedly delusional. It is subsidized, after all, by a commercial logic that claims that there is a product out there to solve any problem you might have. It is important to be highly skeptical of that logic—to interrogate its claims and to call out the delusions it supports. At the same time, our critical approach to the media's distorted representation of the world shouldn't lead us to discount the strategic value of television's optimism and to believe that things can, and are, getting better.

NOTES

1. Tim Stack, "Chris Colfer Makes Some Noise," *Entertainment Weekly*, November 12, 2010, 46–48.

2. Erik Hedegaard, "*Glee* Gone Wild," *Rolling Stone*, April 15, 2010, 42–49.

3. See, for example, Robert Bianco, "*Glee* Loses Its Voice in the Chaos," *USA Today*, March 3, 2011, D1.

4. At the pilot's main narrative turning point, quarterback Finn Hudson stands up to his football teammates when they try to force him to quit glee club. "Don't you get it, man?

We're all losers," he tells them. "Everyone in this school. Hell, everyone in this town. Out of all the kids who graduate, maybe half will go to college and two will leave the state to do it. I'm not afraid of being called a loser, because that's what I am. But I am afraid of turning my back on something that actually made me happy for the first time in my sorry life." Although the speech helps deconstruct the kind of hierarchy that enables bullying, it also has a certain fatalism, a recognition that not everyone will get to leave Lima. In this regard, Finn serves as a counter-balance to Rachel and her insistent optimism that she will become a star. So too do many of the show's adult characters—none of whom seem to be living out their dreams. Whether or not the show sustains this balance through later season is debatable.

5. Hedegaard, "*Glee* Gone Wild."

6. That Chris Colfer's and Kurt Hummel's lives would merge in this way is not surprising since *Glee* producers created the role for Colfer and used specific experiences Colfer had in crafting storylines for Hummel.

7. See Ron Becker, *Gay TV and Straight America* (New Brunswick: Rutgers University Press, 2006); Suzanna Duanta Walters, *All the Rage: The Story of Gay Visibility in America* (Chicago; University of Chicago Press, 2001).

8. Stack, "Chris Colfer Makes Some Noise."

FURTHER READING

Becker, Ron. *Gay TV and Straight America*. New Brunswick: Rutgers University Press, 2006.

Gorman-Murray, Andrew. "Queering Home or Domesticating Deviance? Interrogating Gay Domesticity through Lifestyle Television." *International Journal of Cultural Studies* 9, 2 (2006): 227–47.

Walters, Suzanna Duanta. *All the Rage: The Story of Gay Visibility in America* Chicago; University of Chicago Press, 2001.

15

Grey's Anatomy
Feminism

ELANA LEVINE

Abstract: Looking at how *Grey's Anatomy*'s representations of gender and race go beyond simple notions of positive or negative images, Elana Levine argues that the hit medical drama serves as a fantasy space for imagining a world free of discrimination and power imbalances, and thus offers a more nuanced set of representations than might first appear.

Contemporary entertainment television often tells stories of professionally accomplished women who, despite their successes, lament the missing men, children, or home life that would make them feel complete. Whether in Ally McBeal's dancing baby dreams of the 1990s or Carrie Bradshaw's boyfriend troubles in the early 2000s, female characters have frequently expressed frustration with the lack of "balance" between their personal and professional lives. At the same time as they have faced such struggles, many of these same characters have found empowerment, whether by embracing a (hetero)sexually attractive appearance and the command it allows them over men, or by enjoying confidence boosts and pleasure through shopping and other forms of decadent consumerism made possible by their privileged economic status.

While viewers have found such depictions entertaining, some audiences, including some media scholars, have criticized these representations for the ways that they implicitly—and sometimes explicitly—suggest that our society no longer needs the critical take on gender roles provided by the feminist movement. In this sort of "postfeminist" mindset, either feminism is identified as the cause of women's problems, in that the movement's embrace of women taking on greater professional roles purportedly failed to account for how to fit a personal life within such accomplishments, or feminism has succeeded so well that it no longer applies. For example, according to this line of thinking, women who present themselves as sexual objects do so by their own choosing and not due to societal pressures to appear attractive to men, as feminism has supposedly erased those kinds of gender inequalities. Media scholars and other critics have charged that such assumptions that feminism is "done" actually work in the interests of the male-dominated social structure known as patriarchy.[1] Such postfeminist thinking makes even the suggestion of gender inequalities seem outdated or even discriminatory in its own right, and fails to account for the experiences of under-privileged women, especially in terms of class status. As a result, many persistent inequalities are allowed to continue all the more powerfully, with little hope of challenge to their power.

The hit medical drama *Grey's Anatomy* (ABC, 2005–present) is a product of this postfeminist cultural environment. The world it presents is in many ways one that has been changed by feminism. But instead of suffering from these changes, or using such changes as a means of revalidating conventional expectations of gender, sexuality, and also race, *Grey's* provides a feminist-friendly fiction or *fantasy*, allowing us to imagine a world in which identity-based discrimination has been defeated to women's benefit, rather than at their expense. In its early seasons, *Grey's* overtly tapped into the postfeminist cultural context that had helped make programs like *Sex and the City* (HBO, 1998–2004) into hits. This is most clear in the early seasons' opening credit sequence, which paired markers of medical expertise with those of sexualized femininity: a pair of red stiletto heels disrupts a row of surgical booties, an eyelash curler is laid alongside surgical instruments, an IV drip dissolves into a martini being poured into a glass, intertwined male and female feet caress at the edge of a gurney. The sequence characterized the fictional world as more concerned with sexual hijinks than medical drama, one in which the sexualized femininity of the female leads would supersede, or at least always accompany, their professional endeavors.

But the fictional world that actually follows the opening credits does not adhere to such a model; instead, this world leans more toward a feminist fantasy than a typical postfeminist compromise. While the characters' sexual relationships are central from the beginning, none of the female leads are conventionally sexualized. All of the characters wear scrubs in most of their scenes, and the flowing tresses of characters like Cristina and Izzie are typically tightly secured in knots and ponytails. The sexual attractiveness of former lingerie model Izzie is deliberately downplayed—she wears little visible make-up and her body is most overtly displayed when she blows up in anger at her colleagues for ogling a modeling spread she posed for as a medical student. Angrily stripping down to her underwear to show the mundaneness of exposed flesh, she pointedly notes that working as a model has left her debt-free while her fellow interns deal with hundreds of thousands of dollars in loans ("No Man's Land," April 17, 2005). While many representations of women in postfeminist culture depict femininity and

FIGURE 15.1.
The first-season credit sequence of *Grey's Anatomy* included images of sexualized femininity (like these red heels alongside surgical booties) that were contrary to the show's depiction of women doctors as medical professionals ahead of sexualized beings.

sexual attractiveness as women's foremost sources of liberation, in *Grey's Anatomy*, empowerment comes when the women doctors are seen as medical professionals ahead of sexualized beings. Izzie's victory is in getting her colleagues to take seriously her skills as a doctor, despite her modeling; she does not need her work as a model to prove her sexual appeal despite her professional success.

As much as the series traffics in the personal travails and romantic dramas of its characters, the female protagonists nearly always privilege their careers over their personal lives. This is in opposition to many of the male characters, who openly yearn for love and family in a characterization directly descended from daytime soap opera, where male characters tend to have similar desires. In many instances of postfeminist culture, women who are excessively invested in their careers must "pay" for this investment with some kind of debilitated or dysfunctional personal life, as on the aforementioned *Ally McBeal* (FOX, 1997–2002). Yet the women of *Grey's* are rarely punished for their professional focus. As the most aggressively careerist of her peers, Cristina repeatedly rejects her male partners' efforts to get her to devote more time and attention to her personal life, whether this be in her initial reluctance to marry Burke or in her unambiguous decision to have an abortion following each of two unplanned pregnancies. Meredith, the title character of this ensemble show, is equally career-focused. She insists that Derek treat her as a resident, not as his wife, when she expresses discomfort at dealing with a patient; she puts off attending to her (even more careerist) mother who is suffering from Alzheimer's; and she long resists Derek's efforts to get her to marry him. The active and satisfying sexual and romantic lives of these characters challenge the postfeminist assumption that career and interpersonal happiness are either incompatible or that they require super-woman perfection. The female characters of *Grey's* are flawed, beset with troubles, and frequently unhappy, but their work as surgeons is never represented as a mistake or even as a particularly costly choice. It defines them and makes them proud, another nod to daytime soap opera, with its accomplished career women who suffer unrelated personal travails.

Part of the way that *Grey's* makes such a nonjudgmental representation of career-focused women possible is that it presents a fantasy world nearly free of discrimination of all kinds. In the first season, Cristina wryly notes the gender imbalance amongst surgeons ("A Hard Day's Night," March 27, 2005), Meredith attacks the sexist Alex for his assumptions ("Winning a Battle, Losing the War," April 10, 2005), and Izzie has to prove herself as more than a pretty face and voluptuous body. But such overt attention to inequalities quickly fades, and the series spends very little time concerned with such obstacles. The program even more overtly resists any acknowledgement of racial inequalities or differences. The series has been well publicized for having an unusually high number of racial minorities amongst its cast and for "blindcasting" many roles, such that actors of different races might have been cast as particular characters. Onscreen, inter-racial romantic relationships are common, and the characters' racial differences are never an issue between them. When the Asian-American Cristina and the African-American Burke are forced to confront their differences, the show focuses on his neatness and her slovenliness, amongst other non-racially marked qualities.[2] Their racial difference is unnamed, as is that between Cristina and her white husband, Owen, in the program's later seasons.

Critics of postfeminist and "post-racial" thinking would argue that the denial of gender- and race-based discrimination in the world of *Grey's* ultimately works to excuse or diminish the significance of the real-world discriminations that continue to exist, particularly those faced by people less privileged than the typical characters of primetime TV, such as racial profiling by law enforcement or unequal treatment by employers. While largely blind to the problems (and the pleasures) of difference, the program does not condemn or dismiss the efforts of past (or present) feminist or civil rights movements. Instead, it presents a world in which such efforts would be unnecessary, in which the politicizing of identity is not needed. In this respect the program offers a fantasy space—what we might think of as a feminist fantasy of a world beyond inequalities of gender, sexuality, and race. In this respect, the program matches a conception of popular entertainment as offering utopian fantasies responding to "real needs *created by society*." When film scholar Richard Dyer used this concept to explain the appeal of Hollywood musicals, he also argued that the utopia offered by such entertainments leaves out real world dissatisfactions of class, race, and patriarchy.[3] In the case of *Grey's*, however, the utopic view on offer in fact engages with some of those very dissatisfactions, albeit in compromised ways.

An imagined world beyond such dissatisfactions is taken for granted in most *Grey's* episodes. However, select episodes and moments highlight these inequalities, placing them safely in the past or in a world apart from that of the surgeon protagonists, preserving the hospital itself and the work of medicine as a utopic sphere. For instance, the series seems to blame Meredith's mother, Ellis, for being selfish and career-obsessed, as Meredith's own fears of commitment and motherhood seem to stem from her mother's hurtful influence. Yet as the series proceeds, we learn that Meredith's father was also to blame for her dysfunctional home life, and that Ellis did the best she could to mother Meredith while also succeeding in the cutthroat and male-dominated world of surgery.

The sexism—and racism—of the past, as well as Ellis's struggle to deal with her competing roles, are made most clear when former chief of surgery Richard Weber recounts to the staff his and Ellis's experience with an AIDS patient in 1982, before the disease was named or understood ("The Time Warp," February 18, 2010). In the ensuing flashbacks, we learn more about Richard's affair with Ellis, about the racism and sexism each faced in their training (Richard is the sole person of color amongst his cohort; Ellis the only woman), and about the presence of discrimination more broadly, as most of the staff refuses to treat the AIDS patient. While we see Ellis walk away from a needy, young Meredith, we also see that this is not easy for her, and that Meredith's father is in part to blame. Ellis's position is made especially sympathetic when she and Richard argue after he tells her she cannot leave her husband because of Meredith, and that he will handle their surgery so that she can attend to her distraught daughter. At this, Ellis declares, "I gave birth to a child, Richard. That makes me a mother. It doesn't make me inept; it doesn't make me less of a woman. It doesn't make me less of a surgeon. No matter how much everyone wants it to." Ellis's fury and her refusal to see her roles as incompatible are feminist responses to a discriminatory situation. That she nonetheless thrives and that Meredith comes to follow in her path suggest that—for all their tensions—the feminist struggles of the earlier generation have made for a better world.

The feminist fantasy of the hospital-centered world of *Grey's* manifests itself in multiple ways. The final three episodes of season 7 amply demonstrate these tendencies ("White Wedding," May 5, 2011; "I Will Survive," May 12, 2011; "Unaccompanied Minor," May 19, 2011). In this set of episodes, Derek and Meredith decide to adopt an orphaned African baby who has been brought to the hospital for treatment; lesbian partners Callie and Arizona get married; and Cristina discovers she is pregnant and plans to have an abortion. These events, and the developments surrounding them, are representative of the program's handling of three matters that contribute to its functioning as a feminist fantasy space and that resonate with the historically feminized genre of soap opera: straight men's commitments to women and family, non-traditional conceptions of marriage, and women's connections to one another as mothers, daughters, and friends.

FIGURE 15.2.
One way in which *Grey's Anatomy* functions as a "feminist fantasy space" is through its dramatization of nontraditional conceptions of marriage, such as that between characters Callie and Arizona.

Throughout the series, many of the lead male characters assert their commitments to the women they love and their willingness to devote time and attention to rearing a family. Derek, nicknamed "McDreamy" by the women interns in the early seasons, is not only a star surgeon and a handsome charmer; he is also a devoted partner and, we determine in these episodes, a dedicated father. Unlike other male characters, Derek is never unfaithful to his romantic partners and easily commits to Meredith; in their relationship, she is the one with commitment issues. When he treats baby Zola, he feels an instant bond and persuades Meredith that they should adopt her ("White Wedding"). That it is Derek's connection to the baby, not Meredith's, motivating the adoption makes the character even more appealing as a romantic, yet feminist-friendly, fantasy figure.

When Cristina's husband, Owen, tells her how committed he would be to the child they have unintentionally conceived and offers to interrupt his career as a surgeon both to care for the child and to preserve Cristina's commitment to her own (less advanced) career, he, too, demonstrates such fantasy qualities. While he tries to persuade Cristina to have the baby, he does not try to persuade her to change her ambitions as a result. When she schedules the abortion without discussing it with him, his anger is not directed at her unwillingness to fulfill a traditional role ("Unaccompanied Minor"). Rather it comes from her unwillingness to engage in a full, equal partnership that would consider his concerns and commitments as equal to hers. Not only does this story represent another straight man wholly invested in an equal partnership and primary child-raising duties, but it also depicts a woman who does not want to be a mother, a stance for which she is not villainized.

The conceptions of marital partnership and parenting at the center of Owen and Cristina's dispute are also central to these episodes' feminist tendencies. This three-episode sequence begins with the lavish wedding of Callie and Arizona, a couple whose tribulations had been central to major storylines of season 7. When the two were broken up, the bisexual Callie slept with her best friend, Mark, with whom she had been involved previously. While their sexual involvement did not indicate a romantic relationship to either of them, they accidentally conceived a child and decide to raise that child together. Once Arizona and Callie reunited, Arizona also agreed to parent the child. The program offers this unconventional arrangement as an ideal situation all around, allowing Arizona and Callie to build a home together with their daughter while allowing Mark to be a devoted father, a newfound passion for the former playboy—in this storyline, Mark becomes yet another of the series' handsome men devoted to child-rearing. Callie's mother's disapproval of her out-of-wedlock child and her same-sex relationship provides the central conflict in the wedding episode, demonstrating that the show does occasionally represent identity-based prejudices, though typically roots them in an older generation.

Still, the episode centers on the joyful connection between Callie and Arizona, with Mark and their daughter key members of their newly configured family. That the brides' white gowns and traditional ceremony are juxtaposed with the wedding of Derek and Meredith, who realize that being legally married will assist their adoption of Zola, further accentuates the program's progressive conception of marriage and commitment. Derek and Meredith's wedding, held at City Hall, in their street clothes, in front of a judge, at the end of a busy work day, provides a compelling contrast with Callie and Arizona's ("White Wedding"). When the straight, white couple treats legal marriage as little more than a procedural matter while the interracial lesbian couple treats their not-legally-sanctioned wedding as a celebratory ritual, the program presents a fantasy world in which convention, tradition, and even law become insignificant in light of the bonds of love and commitment.

These episodes also highlight another ongoing theme of the series—women's relationships to other women, especially as mothers, daughters, and friends. While the storylines that occupy these episodes are centered on romantic relationships (as well as workplace drama), kinship and friendship connections between women also play significant roles. When Callie is devastated by her mother's rejection of her life, her friend and colleague Miranda helps her to move forward with her plans. Meredith's series-long struggle to come to terms with her own now-deceased mother comes to a head as she begins to identify as Zola's potential mother. We see Meredith's anxiety about her own maternal worth and see her carry on Ellis's legacy when she tells Zola's social worker, "I'm a surgeon. And I'm a good surgeon. And I want to be a good mother. Honestly, I don't know much about it. But I am ready to learn, and I'm a fast learner. And I will do whatever it takes to be a good mom" ("I Will Survive").

Meredith's tentative effort to be a mother and a surgeon comes to a head in "Unaccompanied Minor," when the ties between Meredith and Cristina and that between Meredith and Zola intertwine. In the second season, when Meredith agrees to be Cristina's "person"—the support person required by the clinic where Cristina is to receive her abortion—the two form a lasting bond, even as they compete with each other for access to surgeries and other workplace honors ("Raindrops Keep Falling on My Head," September 25, 2005). While the two eschew hugging and other conventional markers of female friendship, they support one another unconditionally, and often rely on one another before and apart from their romantic relationships with men. As season 7 concludes, not only have Owen and Cristina broken up, but so too have Meredith and Derek, after Derek discovers a work-related choice Meredith made that potentially jeopardizes both of their careers and the hospital. Just after Meredith and Derek's split, Meredith is permitted to take Zola home on her own. Cristina also comes "home" to Meredith's house, seeking comfort and security. The season ends with the two women together again, bonded more to each other than to their male partners, each in her own way facing the daunting task of choosing to be a mother, or not. The season ends with its two female leads simultaneously quite lost and calling upon their inner strengths, leaning upon each other and the traditions of the many women before them.

If we can agree that Grey's offers this vision of a space beyond the inequalities of gender, sexuality, and race, how might we account for this fantasy? American television is hardly known for its progressiveness of outlook, and most often contemporary popular culture pairs some sort of backlash with its representation of a world changed by feminism and other progressive social movements. We might account for Grey's Anatomy's vision by considering the perspective of the program's creator and showrunner, Shonda Rhimes, one of the few women, and few African Americans, to head a primetime network drama series in television history. While the identity of a program's leader is only one of many factors that shape it, we have so few examples in television of an African American woman's leadership that it is difficult to know what impact Rhimes's particular perspective may have. The program's outlook may also be the product of a new phase in postfeminist culture, one that is finally able to let go of the many recriminations and costs that more typically have accompanied media tales of women's empowerment and independence. Grey's does not present a perfect feminist picture, but it does provide a fantasy of a world truly changed by feminism—a welcome relief in a reality that too often fails to live up to such promise.

NOTES

1. For example, see Angela McRobbie, "Postfeminism and Popular Culture: *Bridget Jones* and the New Gender Regime," in *Interrogating Postfeminism: Gender and the Politics of Popular Culture*, Yvonne Tasker and Diane Negra, eds. (Durham: Duke University Press, 2007), 27–39, and Rosalind Gill, *Gender and the Media* (Cambridge, UK: Polity, 2007).

2. For more on the series' use of blindcasting, see Kristin Warner, "Colorblind TV: Prime-time Politics of Race in Television Casting," (Ph.D. diss., The University of Texas at Austin, 2010).

3. Richard Dyer, "Entertainment and Utopia," in *Genre: The Musical*, Rick Altman, ed. (London: Routlege, 1981), 184.

FURTHER READING

Gill, Rosalind. *Gender and the Media*. Cambridge, UK: Polity, 2007.

Levine, Elana. "*Buffy* and the 'New Girl Order': Defining Feminism and Femininity." In *Undead TV: Essays on Buffy the Vampire Slayer*, Elana Levine and Lisa Parks, eds. Durham, NC: Duke University Press, 2007.

Moseley, Rachel, and Jacinda Read. "'Having it *Ally*': Popular Television (Post-) Feminism." *Feminist Media Studies* 2, 2 (July 2002): 231–49.

Tasker, Yvonne, and Diane Negra, eds. *Interrogating Postfeminism: Gender and the Politics of Popular Culture*. Durham, NC: Duke University Press, 2007.

16

Jersey Shore
Ironic Viewing

SUSAN J. DOUGLAS

Abstract: One of the most popular shows among young audiences in its day, *Jersey Shore* raises numerous questions about boundaries of taste and quality in both "real" behaviors and television. Susan Douglas argues that by looking closely at how the show addresses its audience with an assumed ironic distance, we can see how the series both transgresses and reinforces traditional social norms.

On December 8, 2009, MTV unveiled another "reality" TV show with a highly conventionalized format: select a group of male and female twentysomethings, put them in a house together, make sure the bar is fully stocked, mount cameras everywhere, see what happens, and edit for maximum drama. This was a formula that, since the premiere of *The Real World* in 1992, had served the network quite well. But while the formula remained roughly the same, the cast didn't. Unlike *The Real World*, which over the years had come to traffic in juxtaposing different "types"—the naive country bumpkin, the urban African American woman, the homophobe, the player, the blond party girl—or *Laguna Beach* and *The Hills*, which featured primarily blond So-Cal rich kids, *Jersey Shore* (MTV, 2009–2012) took quite a different tack. This time, MTV selected self-identified "Guidos" and "Guidettes," lower-middle-class or working-class Italian Americans, the kind of young people rarely seen on TV, and threw them all together in a beach house in Seaside Heights, New Jersey.[1]

Amidst controversy about ethnic stereotyping (not to mention poor taste), the show quickly became a sensation and MTV's top-rated series of all time. By the time of the show's fourth season in the summer of 2011, which transported the cast to Florence, Italy, the trade press was labeling Thursday night television "Jerzday"; not only did the show beat its broadcast competition on Thursday night, but for weeks it was the most watched program on cable. Just as important, it was the top overall television show among that most coveted demographic, teens and young people between the ages of twelve and thirty-four.[2]

How are we to account for the success of this show? After all, by nearly any conventional standard, *Jersey Shore* is dreadful: it is structurally formulaic, the characters cartoonish, their behaviors crude, often anti-social, and repetitive. Each episode consists of recurring déclassé elements like excessive drinking often resulting in vomiting, grind dancing in bars, fist fights (among the women as well), multiple sexual encounters, and melodramatic conflicts over the most trivial issues, like who said what to whom in what tone of voice. Nonetheless, when a show, however banal, becomes a big hit, we need to think about what kinds of anxieties and aspirations it may be revealing and managing.[3] This is particularly true when a popular cultural form is denounced by traditional arbiters of taste as trashy, inauthentic, and cynically manufactured. Now, there is every reason to believe that *Jersey Shore* was indeed all of these things, but it still must have been doing some kind of cultural and ideological work to be so successful.

One must always place media texts within their historical context to fully appreciate what contemporary issues they might be working through, standing back from the shows to examine how they address their audiences. Why are the cast members compelling? What behaviors, and disputes about behaviors, are the main focus of the show? How does it balance predictability and surprise? What norms does it reinforce and what taboos does it violate? And do the conflicts and behaviors tell us anything about the situation young people (and not just "Guidos" and "Guidettes") find themselves in at this particular moment in history?

Before attempting to answer these questions, we need to review the appeal of "reality TV" programs. From an industry perspective, they are cheaper to produce than scripted programs as they don't require elaborate sets and locations, or high-priced talent. And from *Super Nanny* to *The Real Housewives* (of wherever) to *The Real World*, reality TV shows use idiotic, arrogant, or self-destructive behaviors which we are urged to judge and which are designed to make us feel much better about ourselves: however dumb or selfish we were today, at least we weren't like *that*. Indeed, unlike complicated economic or political debates, the dramas and conflicts on these shows hail us as absolute, knowledgeable authorities about right and wrong, what should and should not be tolerated. In particular, the "confessional" mode of address, when the various cast members talk to us directly, evokes what John Fiske has called "enunciative productivity": completing the meaning of the show by exclaiming, along with other viewers, our scandalized sense of outrage, of who was right and who was wrong.[4] Another pleasure is guessing what's "real," what's been staged, how much of the drama has been exaggerated, and the like: these shows wink at us, invite us to be puzzle-solvers, much the way celebrity gossip magazines do, as we try to assess what might be true and what is just made up.[5]

This is a key component to the pleasure of many reality TV shows: the cultivation of the ironic, knowing viewer. This deliberate, self-conscious industry strategy became much more pervasive in the early twenty-first century, as a way to legitimate cheaply produced shows that showcased stupid or inappropriate behaviors. Irony offers us the following fantasy: the people on the screen may be rich, or spoiled, or beautiful, or allowed to party nonstop, but you, oh superior viewer, get to judge and mock them, and thus are above them. Many MTV shows elbow the viewer in the ribs, saying, "We know that you know that we know that you know that this is excessive and kitschy, that you're too smart to read this straight and not laugh at it."[6]

Because *Jersey Shore* is so self-consciously over the top, with its endless scenes of hot tub hooking-up, bar brawls, public drunkenness, relentless interpersonal conflict, and displays of total ignorance, the show demands that you simultaneously mock and distance yourself from the cast members, yet hunger to know what on earth they might do next. By the time they get to Florence, one of the world's epicenters of high art and culture, they marvel that "God, everything is in another language!" and wonder if a building they are looking at is the Vatican, which knowledgeable viewers know is in Rome. MTV deliberately draws attention to such cluelessness; it offers this irony as a shield, as irony means that you can look like you are absolutely not seduced by the mass media, while then being seduced by the media, while wearing a knowing smirk. In addition, the show certainly cultivates the "third person effect," or the conceit among viewers that they watch the show ironically and aren't taken in by it while other, presumably more naïve viewers must take it utterly at face value. Thus viewers can feel superior not only to the cast members, but also to other viewers imagined to be less sophisticated than they.

So on to the show itself. The first season began with eight very carefully selected cast members, and the story lines and roles for the different characters settled in quickly. Sammi Giancola, a.k.a. "The Sweetheart," and Ronnie Ortiz-Magro, an Italian American and Puerto Rican man from the Bronx, entered a turbulent on-again, off-again relationship spanning several seasons; Mike Sorrentino, better known as "The Situation," was the player, constantly trying to score with women; he was joined in these efforts by Paul DelVecchio—Pauly D—from Johnston, Rhode Island, and Vinny Guadagnino, from Staten Island. Angelina Pivarick was the self-important Diva whom the others came to hate; Jennifer Farley, better known as JWoww, who reportedly—and obviously—got herself breast augmentation surgery for her twenty-first birthday, struggled to remain faithful to her boyfriend. Nicole Polizzi, or Snooki, a Chilean girl adopted by an Italian family in New York, became the group's mascot, vulnerable and easily hurt, prone to excessive drinking, and getting in trouble in ways that compelled the others to rally around her in solidarity. Thus the show offered repeated narrative cycles of conflict, retribution, and reconciliation that comingled predictability and surprise. While the male cast members were obviously chosen for their bulging biceps and ripped six packs, and the women for their enormous boobs and long hair, none of them is conventionally beautiful. Snooki, in particular, is the polar opposite of the tall, svelte blondes who dominate the fashion magazines and Victoria's Secret ads. Clearly this is one of the secrets of her appeal to so many young women: her absolute defiance of the prevailing corporate definitions of beauty and femininity that police us all.

Various signifiers mark these young people as quite apart from the wholesome, scrubbed kids of the Disney Channel or the upper-crust characters in *Gossip Girl*. These are not people we're supposed to emulate or envy. Their speech is working class, regional, and ethnic: they drop their final Gs, as in their references to "fist pumpin'," "hatin'," the ever-present "fuckin'," and in phrases like "she's disrespectin' you." Door is pronounced "doah," and downstairs "downstayes." Various people say "ain't," and other incorrect locutions include "my girl is more cuter" than his, "if I was you," and, as Snooki says of JWoww and her boyfriend, "I don't get them two."

More importantly, they are emphatically and proudly defiant about their deviance from mainstream, conformist, middle-class mores about appearance, decorum, and ethnicity. The men wear "wife beaters," or T-shirts, and wouldn't be caught dead in a three-button, collared polo shirt with any kind of logo on it. They are anything but modest, especially about their self-proclaimed attractiveness to women, and the women are anything but demure. All characters are sexually aggressive to such a degree that it makes viewers wonder how much they were coached to inhabit these bragging and strutting personas.

Interestingly, we get an odd working-class version of the metrosexual, in which these insistently macho guys nonetheless indulge quite readily in various feminine practices like hair care and wearing jewelry to enhance their appearance and sexual capital, muting any threat to their manhood by taking command of such behaviors and folding them into a new, dominant masculinity.[7] The cast members emphasize the centrality of what they call "the Guido lifestyle." For Pauly D, whose hair stands straight up on his head like a rock-solid mesa (a.k.a., a "blow out"), this means "family, friends, tannin' and gel." He has "a [fuckin'] tannin' bed" in his place because "that's how serious I am about being a Guido and living up to that lifestyle." He's a DJ who wants the Guidettes to "cream their pants" when they hear his music. He doesn't try to steal guys' girlfriends away from them—it just happens. He tells us it takes about twenty-five minutes for him to do his hair, and it always "comes out perfect." The Situation boasts about how ripped his abs are from his diligent workout routine, as he defines a Guido as "good looking, smooth, well dressed, Italian" and claims that girls love Guidos. Ronnie, who's built like the Terminator, says he just takes his shirt off and girls come to him, as

FIGURE 16.1.
A twenty-first century television superstar is born: Nicole "Snooki" Polizzi.

he notes metaphorically, "like a fly comes to shit." In the first episode, the camera shows the Situation packing a ton of hair gel and cologne to take to the Jersey Shore, and we see him putting on lip gloss as well.

Just as the "Guidos" incorporate an obsession with grooming practices and appearances into their bicep-centered version of masculinity, so do the "Guidettes" adopt a tough-talking, bellicose sexuality into their spin on femininity. Thus one of the program's fascinations is witnessing these hybrid gender forms that both violate mainstream conventions of acceptable gender performance and allow for multiple scenes in which the boundaries of these performances are completely violated. The first words we hear out of Snooki's mouth are "I'm goin' to Jersey Shore, bitch!" and she boasts to the camera that "you haven't seen anything until you see me at the Jersey fuckin' shore." Sammi tells us, "I am the sweetest bitch you'll ever meet, but do not fuck with me." She defines a Guidette as someone who knows how to "club it up, takes really good care of themselves, has pretty hair . . . tanned skin, wears the hottest heels and knows how to own it and rock it." JWoww proclaims, "If you don't know me, then you hate me, and you wish you were me," and adds that so many girls hate her because "whatever they are, they can't compare to me." In case only female viewers are intimidated by this, JWoww asserts that she is "like a praying mantis, after I have sex with a guy I will rip his head off." As we see her sticking her tongue out provocatively, and then dancing in a bar with her gigantic breasts just barely covered, she brags that she sends men "on a roller coaster ride to hell." Angelina, not to be outdone, emphasizes that she's "all natural," her boobs are hers, and asserts, "I'm hot." Whatever the advances (or not) of the women's movement, young women are not supposed to be this cocky and explicitly self-assured about their appearance and their ability to dominate men.

Jersey Shore takes the outrageous behaviors increasingly featured on *The Real World* and amps them up, combining the elements of melodrama, soap opera, soft-core pornography, professional wrestling, and farce. With its recurrent scenes of simulated sex on the dance floor, close-ups of tongues locking and one guy kissing two girls simultaneously, various couples "hooking up" or "smushing" (having sex), fist fights in bars and violent physical cat fights among various of the female housemates, and incessant fighting and screaming over nothing, *Jersey Shore* is a smorgasbord of voyeuristic titillation. It is a fantasy of the unregulated life, where you barely have to work, have minimal responsibilities, go out every night, and rarely have to monitor your own behaviors and emotions. One appeal for viewers, then, is to escape into this carefree yet intensified world, while condemning it at the same time.

Jersey Shore also draws from two enduring tropes from celebrity gossip magazines that media scholar Joke Hermes has labeled the "extended family repertoire" and the "repertoire of melodrama."[8] Indeed, one of the cast members' most repeated words is "drama," suggesting they have been coached to frame as many interactions as possible as melodramatic. Melodrama involves an exaggerated emphasis on heartbreak and betrayal, as well as on sensation, sentimentality, and heightened emotionality, and here the show does not disappoint. Screaming matches over what kinds of women the guys bring into the house, disputes over who should do the dishes, and hair-pulling fist fights between the girls have all been staples of different episodes. As such, we get pleasure from witnessing the absurd over-dramatization of everyday tensions, which may make us feel better not only about our own, hopefully less fraught lives, but also about our more controlled behaviors and maturity.

Working, oddly, in tandem with such melodrama is the extended family repertoire, which ties audiences to a larger community beyond their own, makes those ties intimate by providing detailed private information about those on the screen, and constructs an imagined extended family in which, despite everything, solidarity prevails. In one of the most notorious scenes from the first season, the group is in a bar where men whom Vinny describes as "typical fraternity college guy losers" begin to take drinks the group has bought for themselves. As Snooki screams at them at increasingly higher decibels, one of the "losers" punches her in the face. (We soon learn that the assailant was no college guy, but a high school gym teacher.) As the girls comfort Snooki, the guys vow to beat the pulp out of her attacker, but the police arrest him before they can have their revenge. The event provides one of many opportunities throughout the series for the cast members to assert that they are family and that nothing is more important than that family. Thus the excessive behaviors—the drunkenness, the casual hook-ups, the fights—nonetheless provide a forum for reinforcing some relatively traditional values of community and kinship.

By examining which activities the camera foregrounds, what the biggest fights are about, which language is the most inflammatory, and what the cast members comment on most frequently or passionately, it becomes clear that *Jersey Shore* is primarily about relationships and behavior, particularly the sexual behavior of young women. While the female housemates can easily be seen as promiscuous— Snooki, in the very first episode, strips down to her bra and a leopard thong in the hot tub and slithers up against the guys, and JWoww, with a boyfriend back home, nonetheless gets into bed with Pauly and admires his pierced penis—they condemn other young women from outside the house who behave similarly as "sluts," "whore bags," and "trashy skanks." Vinny helps viewers see the difference. If it takes a couple of meetings with girls before they'll hook up, then they aren't whores, and he distinguishes between girls who will just strip off and get into the Jacuzzi at a first meeting versus those you have to "treat like girls, human beings." So despite its libertine sensibility, the show reinforces the virgin-whore dichotomy and utterly justifies the objectification of some women more than others.

Because JWoww and Angelina have boyfriends back home, their storylines provide dramas about fidelity, cheating, and the missed sexual and romantic opportunities that remaining faithful forecloses. The show poses a central question: when you're young and surrounded by opportunity for lots of sex with multiple partners, is it better to be promiscuous and unfettered, or have a partner you can trust, rely on, and be intimate with, but who limits your options? The show repeatedly wavers on this question, and while the female cast members dance like strippers in the bars they frequent, make out with other women, and hook up with men, these behaviors are meant to titillate, shock, and provoke scandalized outrage from viewers. Thus, like so much of contemporary popular culture, the show is simultaneously prudish and pornographic, and urges viewers to calibrate what is appropriate sexual behavior along this spectrum.

The ignorance and stupidity of the cast members are both a source of humor and means for flattering the audience. In the first season, Pauly D is so dumb he puts charcoal in a gas grill, with the expected disastrous results. In anticipation of going to Florence, Snooki opines that when she thinks of it, "I think of *Lady and the Tramp*, you know, just beautiful." When they arrive, they note that the city is like the Disney movie *Beauty and the Beast* (which, of course, takes place in France); they expect people to lean out of their windows and start singing. For anyone with a modicum of cultural capital, it is impossible not to feel superior to these clueless narcissists whose main cultural references seem to come from cartoons.

As we stand back from a show addressed to young people at the height of the Great Recession, where connections and cultural capital matter more than ever in landing a job, where rampant acceleration pervades so many lines of work, and where class distinctions are becoming more acute, *Jersey Shore* is almost like a class and ethnic minstrel show, providing a place where young people can project (and release) their anxieties about not having the proper decorum or work ethic to succeed in today's job market. In addition, with so many contradictory expectations around gender roles and sexuality, where young women in particular are expected to look "hot" yet damned if they're "sluts," and constantly pitted against each other over appearance and sexual appeal, *Jersey Shore* stages parodies of female sexuality and aggression run amok. It simultaneously blasts and reinforces the sexual constraints imposed on women, a contradiction many young women confront every day.

It is these excesses that provide voyeuristic pleasures in watching irresponsible, even dangerous behaviors with no risk to ourselves. We are transported into a realm where we can try on identities unthinkable in our own lives and then vicariously test out our own ethical and sexual limits. The show is a fantasy about escaping from middle-class conformist strictures that govern success at work and acceptable codes of interpersonal behavior. It simultaneously reinforces exaggerated gender roles—muscled men and buxom women—while offering deviations—men who spend a half an hour on their hair, women who relish a good fist fight—in a way that reassures us about our own gender performances, however circumscribed they might be. In analyzing such "bad" television, paying attention to what behaviors are made salient, which gender norms are reinforced and violated, how class is performed, and how difference and solidarity are staged, can help us understand how a show as obviously and deliberately trashy as *Jersey Shore* can nonetheless be doing significant cultural and ideological work.

NOTES

1. I would like to thank Chaz Cox for his help with the research for this essay.

2. Robert Seidman, "The MTV 'Jerzday' Phenomenon Continues as 'Jersey Shore' Leads All Thursday Night Television," TV by the Numbers, http://tvbythenumbers.zap2it. com/2011/08/19/the-mtv-jerzday-phenomenon.

3. Frederic Jameson, "Reification and Utopia in Mass Culture," *Social Text* (Winter 1979), 130–48.

4. John Fiske, "The Cultural Economy of Fandom," in Lisa A. Lewis, ed., *The Adoring Audience: Fan Culture and Popular Media* (New York: Routledge, 1992), 37–38.

5. Joke Hermes, "Reading Gossip Magazines: The Imagined Communities of 'Gossip' and 'Camp,'" in P. David Marshall, ed., *The Celebrity Culture Reader* (New York: Routledge, 2006), 295.

6. This discussion draws from my book *The Rise of Enlightened Sexism: How Pop Culture Took Us from Girl Power to Girls Gone Wild* (New York: St. Martin's Griffin, 2010), 14–15.

7. See Stan Denski and David Sholle, "Metal Men and Glamour Boys: Gender Performance

in Heavy Metal," for an analysis of the incorporation of female traits into masculine performance in Steve Craig, ed., *Men, Masculinity and the Mass Media* (Newbury Park: Sage, 1999), 41-60.

8. Hermes, 297–99.

FURTHER READING

Douglas, Susan J. *The Rise of Enlightened Sexism: How Pop Culture Took Us from Girl Power to Girls Gone Wild.* New York: St. Martin's Griffin, 2010.

Hermes, Joke. *Reading Women's Magazines: An Analysis of Everyday Media Use.* London: Polity, 1995.

Gill, Rosalind. *Gender and the Media.* London: Polity, 2007.

Murray, Susan, and Laurie Ouellette, eds., *Reality TV: Remaking Television Culture.* New York: New York University Press, 2004.

III

TV Politics
Democracy, Nation, and the Public Interest

17

30 Days
Social Engagement

GEOFFREY BAYM AND COLBY GOTTERT

Abstract: While we often think of reality television as exploitative or sensational, this essay explores a reality show with an explicit agenda of social engagement and education: *30 Days*. By looking at the show's ties to documentary and reality television traditions as analyzed in an episode personifying the illegal immigration debate, we can see the possibilities and limitations of socially activist programming within a commercial television system.

In 2004, Morgan Spurlock's film *SuperSize Me* achieved a rare combination for a documentary film: commercial success and sociopolitical influence. The film became the fourth-highest grossing feature documentary ever at the time, earning over $10.5 million in ticket sales.[1] At the same time, it drew attention to the potential public health problems of fast-food consumption, and undoubtedly played a role in McDonald's subsequent decision to discontinue the "supersize" option from its menus.[2] Two years later, Spurlock would try to recreate on television what he had achieved with film, launching the reality TV show *30 Days* (FX, 2005–2008), through which he hoped to replicate both the commercial success and sociopolitical impact of *SuperSize Me*. Borrowing its operating concept from the film, each episode of the show would feature a person forced to confront different lifestyles or political attitudes for thirty days in order to educate the audience about an issue of public significance and perhaps transform their (and the featured character's) attitudes about that issue.

Using the form of reality TV to explore storylines intervening in social politics, *30 Days* differed from the majority of its genre, which borrows techniques from documentary film but generally privileges melodramatic narrative or staged competition over civic education and political engagement. While many critics consider reality TV a degradation of documentary form and intent, *30 Days* sought to harness the entertaining appeal of melodrama as a means of offering factual information and critical commentary about public affairs. In so doing, the show drew on ideals of the civic potential of documentary, a tradition often referred to as "Griersonian," in reference to the early British filmmaker John Grierson, who not only coined the term "documentary," but also argued for its necessary political significance. *30 Days* thus provides grounds for a unique case study in the Griersonian potential of reality TV, a sociopolitical function to which that genre rarely aspires.

For Grierson, the kind of film he labeled "documentary" could, and should, serve the function of civic education, helping to translate the complexities of social problems into readily understandable stories that citizens could contemplate and act upon. Grierson saw documentary as much a *sociological* project as an *aesthetic* one. "A dramatic apprehension of the modern scene," he suggested, "might solve the problem" of civic education, while the cinema could be an important tool in "the practice of government and the enjoyment of citizenship."[3] Grierson's work established the dominant approach to documentary as what film scholar Bill Nichols has called the "discourse of sobriety." As Nichols explains, documentary has a "kinship" with other "nonfictional systems" such as science, politics, education, and religion, which assume they have "instrumental power"— that is, they believe "they can and should alter the world" and "effect action and entail consequences."[4]

Such assumptions shaped the practice of broadcast journalism as well. During the heyday of U.S. network television news, for example, the legendary broadcast journalist Edward R. Murrow and his team at CBS produced the powerful film *Harvest of Shame*, which aired commercial-free on Thanksgiving Day, 1960, and exposed the plight of migrant farm workers. The film, now considered one of the most important works of twentieth-century journalism, both invoked empathy for the laborers and made a call to political action in an explicit request that the affluent audience "influence legislation" on behalf of those who "have no voice in legislative halls."

It may be hard to imagine such a television broadcast in today's hyper-commercialized media environment. Media scholar John Corner has suggested that documentary intended as civic inquiry largely has been replaced by a documentary of diversion.[5] Instead of the once-common public affairs documentary, we now have any number of "reality TV" shows that have adopted the formal techniques of documentary, but not its ideals. For most reality TV, stories about individual people's feelings and experiences have taken the place of civic engagement and social argument. For Corner, this transformation is consistent with wider cultural, political, and economic shifts between notions of citizenship and consumption. Emphasizing personal pleasure and private profit in place of public life, television producers have largely rejected serious documentaries and the language of belonging they depend on.

By contrast, television scholar Laurie Ouellette argues that Corner misreads the civic function of reality TV. She suggests that transformations in the structure of society have shifted the nature of citizenship and the responsibilities and needs of individual citizens. Reality TV, Ouellette says, may not divert audiences from public life, but rather instruct viewers on "navigating the changing expectations and demands of citizenship" in a neoliberal society.[6] Makeover, programs, life-skills shows, and other formats focused on individual transformations, she argues, may teach viewers techniques for successfully negotiating a pluralist, free-market society.

The civic function of Spurlock's *30 Days* falls somewhere in between those perspectives. As did the film that established the show's concept, *30 Days* sought to find the point of intersection between narratives of personal change and arguments about socio-political problems requiring structural solutions. Spurlock himself suggested his intent with *SuperSize Me* lay with individual life choices: "The one thing I had hoped that would happen with this movie," he says, "was it would make people start to think about how they eat, how they live."[7] Whether the film encouraged changes in individuals' eating habits is unclear. But it undoubtedly had *discursive* impact, influencing the national conversation about food.[8] It also had *material* impact, with McDonald's deciding to change its menu just months after the film's release.

Building on the success of *SuperSize Me*, *30 Days* was an experiment in the possibilities of reality TV: a show that each week would feature an individual's personal transformation, often in the context of public problems and sociopolitical controversies. The program averaged 2.4 million viewers per episode, a surprisingly large audience for a show that dealt with topics such as abortion, homophobia, gun control, and illegal immigration.[9] For his part, Spurlock said the explicit goal was to "shatter stereotypes" by inviting people with strong views to spend a month living with people representing the opposite side. Thus, for example, one episode paired an avid hunter with a committed member of People for the Ethical Treatment of Animals; another placed a man who was certain that all Muslims were terrorists with a suburban Islamic family. At the same time, Spurlock also envisioned an agenda reminiscent of Grierson or Murrow: "For me," he explained, "the goal is to reach an audience that may not know everything, and you're trying to give them the broad strokes that can get them engaged and get them into what you're talking about."[10]

30 Days tried to achieve the dual function of entertaining audiences through melodramatic narratives of conflict and personal change, while also addressing issues of public concern. To explore this dynamic, we look closely at one particular show: the premiere episode of the second season, which tackled illegal immigration (July 26, 2006). Produced in the midst of the debate over attempts to reform

FIGURE 17.1.
Documentary filmmaker
and *30 Days* host, Morgan
Spurlock.

national immigration policies, the episode featured the Cuban American Frank Jorge, a staunch anti-illegal immigration activist, who spent thirty days with a family of illegal immigrants from Mexico (given the pseudonym "Gonzalez") in their meager East Los Angeles home. The episode, we suggest, illustrates the program's wider form and function, as well as its possibilities and shortcomings.

In this episode, Frank and the Gonzalez family represent the two sides of the immigration debate. Frank stands for the law-and-order side, which sees undocumented immigrants as criminals who deserve legal penalty. The Gonzalez family represents the pro-immigrant side, which sees immigrants as people in search a better life and deserving of compassion.[11] These characterizations describe the opposing sides of the issue, but more importantly for the program, they establish the main characters of the melodrama. In the opening segment, Frank is positioned as the villain of the story: a "patriotic Minuteman vigilante," Spurlock explains in a voiceover, as we see images of Frank heavily arming himself to "patrol" the Arizona-Mexico border. Meanwhile, the Gonzalez family is introduced through the beautiful daughter Armida, the aspiring high-school senior who is identified as the heroine of the story in a montage of her preparing to play golf, putting on makeup, and donning a pink sweater. From there, the relationship between Frank and Armida drives the narrative, as tension builds and we wonder whether Frank will move beyond his brutish ideology to win Armida's (platonic) affection.

While establishing an archetypal beauty-and-the-beast melodrama, the show draws on multiple traditions of nonfiction TV. In part, it borrows from the "docusoap" strand of reality TV, a hybrid of the observational documentary and the soap opera, as it focuses on the evolving emotional relationships between the central characters.[12] Throughout, the producers orchestrate scenes designed to provoke emotional content, build character arcs, and drive the narrative forward. The show also includes the genre's now-familiar "confessional" interviews through which characters share their thoughts about the ongoing drama.

At the same time, the program also functions as a social experiment, creating artificial settings designed to test the limits of the character's attitudes.[13] Literally establishing the parameters of the experiment, Spurlock explains the "rules" that Frank must adhere to during his thirty days: "First, he will have to leave any and all personal identification behind. Second, he will have to move in with the whole family of illegal immigrants and share their tiny apartment. And third, he will be put to work as a day laborer." These rules define the experiment and create a series of obstructions that heighten the stakes of Frank's challenge. While the "rules of the game" enhance the melodrama, the social experiment also creates an unlikely situation through which the viewer can explore the immigration debate, a technique with roots in the *verité* tradition of documentary cinema. The pioneering filmmakers Jean Rouch and Edgar Morin practiced what they called *cinema verité* ("true cinema")—an approach exemplified by their seminal film *Chronique d'un Eté* (*Chronicle of a Summer*), in which people participated in staged situations designed to break through the "membrane that isolates each of us from others" and provoke people to reveal core truths about the human condition.[14] *30 Days* here achieves something similar, placing Frank in an artificial situation designed to challenge his prejudices and allow the viewer to observe the reconciliation of opposing political perspectives.

30 Days also draws on the Griersonian approach, placing the melodrama within the context of the national immigration debate. After the initial forty-second hook in which Spurlock introduces the characters and sets the stakes, he addresses the political dimensions of the episode through a one-minute introduction featuring direct address, voiceover, and video of immigration protests and congressional debates—all formal techniques long associated with public affairs documentaries. Here, Spurlock provides a brief historical summary of the issue, describes the current debate, and concludes with unusual fare for a reality TV show: soundbites from Arizona Senator John McCain and then-President George Bush.

Drawing on various nonfiction traditions ranging from public affairs to Rouchian cinema verité to docusoap, the episode—and *30 Days* more broadly—straddles the line between politics and melodrama, between narratives about individual attitudes and examinations of structural problems that require legislative solutions. In the illegal immigration episode, Spurlock explains the ongoing policy debate over whether to facilitate a path to citizenship for immigrants such as the Gonzalezes, while at the same time framing the show around the question of whether Frank will "hold on to his belief that illegal immigrants are a plague on the nation that needs to be removed" or will come to see the Gonzalezes "as equals who deserve to become Americans."

From there, the program proceeds on this dual track as Frank is sent on different missions that function simultaneously to deliver factual information and humanize the terms of the debate. For example, when Frank works as a day laborer with the father, Rigoberto, Spurlock explains the family survives on $15,000 a year, well under the U.S. poverty line. Frank and Rigoberto discuss questions of work and wages, with Rigoberto arguing that illegal immigrants don't take jobs from Americans, but do the work that Americans refuse to do, and that because of their illegal status, do so for far lower pay. Elsewhere, Frank accompanies the mother, Patti, as she collects recyclable cans to earn extra money. She makes five dollars, and explains to Frank that she is saving so that this year she can buy Christmas presents for the family, further humanizing her struggle, and tugging on the audience's heartstrings.

Seeking the point of intersection between empathy and ideology, the show also explores the dangers of polarization and incivility. In a scene certainly designed as provocation, Frank and the family go out to dinner with Armida's high school teacher to celebrate her upcoming graduation. The dinner devolves into heated argument between Frank and the teacher, during which the teacher scolds Frank for his intolerant and entirely impractical insistence that all illegals, the Gonzalezes included, be immediately deported. When the teacher condescendingly says of the Minutemen (of which Frank is a member) "Oh, those guys are idiots," Frank yells in response: "I am not an idiot!" The argument progresses and Frank becomes even more heated, screaming, "This goddamn government doesn't do what it's supposed to!" and "Their goddamn government in Mexico has let them down!" The scene reinforces the initial characterization of Frank as irrational hothead—we see Patti later saying she was frightened by Frank's anger—and advances the genre's melodramatic imperative. At the same time, however, it offers a metacommentary on political argument, suggesting the futility of debate shaped by closed-minded incivility (on both sides) rather than mutual respect.

Shifting between the political and the melodramatic, the episode returns to direct engagement with public affairs as the Senate prepares to vote on the issue. We see Armida showing Frank a newspaper story about the bill, which, to her dismay, prompts him to declare his opposition to any plan that would grant "amnesty" to illegals (Armida included). Frank and Armida then attend a pro-immigration rally. There, despite Armida's efforts to convince him that the rally participants want to be Americans, a highly uncomfortable Frank continues to compare the crowd to an invading army intent on overthrowing the U.S. government. Here, the emotional struggle between the two main characters is clearly placed within the broader political context. Soon after, however, Armida returns the focus to Frank's need for personal transformation. Speaking alone to the camera, she frames the remainder of the show: "Only he can change his mind. It's up to him . . . he has to see it and come up with his own conclusion."

The episode's climax occurs when Frank travels to Mexico to meet the extended Gonzalez family and visit the house where they used to live. The scene marks the awaited transformation, as Frank finally comes to understand the Gonzalezes' motivations. We see him pensively walking around the crumbling walls of the family's former house while emotional music plays in the background. He then proclaims: "This is a horrible place to live." With a hint of tears, he suggests, "Only someone who was homeless, which they were, would live in a place like this. You couldn't last very long." After he returns to Los Angeles to finish his thirty days, Frank reveals the impact of the trip. During a confessional interview he says, "Although I oppose, I understand. I can't blame them for seeking a better life." Frank's transformation from fear and anger to tolerance and compassion seems to be confirmed during the show's penultimate scene, when we see him golfing with Armida. "I never thought I would feel as warmly about this family as I am," he says. "First and foremost we are human beings." Armida also recognizes the change in Frank's character: "He really is changing and he doesn't feel as strong about his beliefs as he did before . . . it shows the transformation."

In the end, Frank's thirty days has taught him to be more tolerant of those he had previously judged, but lost in the emotionally satisfying conclusion is the question of *political* change. As he bids a tearful goodbye to the family—and we're left not quite clear about what will become of the Gonzalezes—Frank offers the narrative coda. Summarizing the episode, and perhaps the approach of the entire series, he explains, "There comes a time when you love people for who they are, all politics aside." Thus, at the end of the emotionally moving story, we are left with the thought that if we could only put "politics aside," we could find love for one another. While Murrow concluded *Harvest of Shame* with an explicit call for the audience to influence legislation on behalf of migrant workers, here *30 Days* ends by eliding the question of political engagement altogether.

30 Days distinguished itself from most reality TV shows by placing melodramatic narratives within the context of socio-political debates. A hybrid form of nonfiction public affairs television, it sought both to entertain viewers and to educate, if not outright influence, them. However, the show ultimately was constrained by the limits of the genre and its privileging of emotional melodrama and predictable personal transformation. Indeed, *every* episode ended with the requisite character change, to the point that such transformations became not only expected, but formulaic. By the end of the illegal immigration episode, we may be hopeful that individuals can soften their ideological stances and move toward greater compassion, but we are never asked nor expected to intervene in the actual policy debate.

Interestingly, the episode was not without material effect. Throughout the show, a subplot focuses on Armida's desire to attend college. We are sad to see her rejected by Princeton, but later happy when she is accepted to Santa Clara University. Unfortunately, however, we know she can't afford the tuition, a suspicion confirmed in a closing graphic that tells us she is taking classes at a local community college. Remarkably, individual viewers made donations online, ultimately enabling Armida to attend Santa Clara.[15] This, then, brings us to the crux of the question. As a result of an emotionally engaging narrative that humanized the struggles of one family, people were moved enough to give money to help improve the life of a single individual. This seems consistent with the argument that reality TV is calibrated to new, more entrepreneurial modes of citizenship. Yet the wider political, legal, and economic struggles facing all the other Armidas (including those who are less telegenic) remain unaddressed, except for a brief moment elided in an individualistic, consumer-based television landscape.

Within that landscape, however, *30 Days* presented a compelling approach to reality TV, attempting to use the popular appeal of melodrama to explore public issues. However, instead of using its position of influence to deliver a clear call for political engagement—either for those whose hearts go out to Armida or those who side with Frank—the show too often retracted into the comfortable, and predictable, zone of tolerance and compassion. While these are certainly not bad places for a television show to be, particularly in a format that generally urges us to "outwit, outplay, and outlast," the lessons of *30 Days* are twofold. On one hand, it shows us the difficulty of balancing the melodramatic imperative of reality TV with a Griersonian social ethos of documentary. On the other, with its brief success on (of all places) a Rupert Murdoch-owned channel, it suggests that the genre itself need not be confined to the consumerist arena of lifestyle and self-help, but instead can address issues once considered the domain of the traditional public affairs documentary and its increasingly obsolete discourse of sobriety.

NOTES

1. Geoffrey Kleinman, "Morgan Spurlock—*SuperSize Me*," www.dvdtalk.com/interviews/morgan_spurlock.html.
2. "McDonald's to Cut 'Super Size' Options," *Advertising Age*, March 8, 2004, 13.
3. John Grierson, *Grierson on Documentary* (New York: Praeger Publishers, 1971), 207.
4. Bill Nichols, *Representing Reality* (Bloomington: Indiana University Press, 1991), 3.
5. John Corner, "Performing the Real: Documentary Diversions," *Television & New Media* 3 (2002): 255–69.

6. Laurie Ouellette, "Reality TV Gives Back: On the Civic Functions of Reality Entertainment," *Journal of Popular Film & Television* 38 (2010): 68; see also Laurie Ouellette and James Hay, "Makeover Television, Governmentality, and the Good Citizen," *Continuum: Journal of Media & Cultural Studies* 22 (2008): 471–84.

7. Kleinman, "Morgan Spurlock—*SuperSize Me*."

8. Robert Gottlieb and Anupama Joshi, *Food Justice* (Cambridge, MA: MIT Press, 2010), 67.

9. FX Networks, "*30 Days*—About The Show," http://www.fxnetworks.com/shows/ originals/30days/about.php.

10. Talk Talk, "You Are What You Eat," www.talktalk.co.uk/entertainment/film/interviews/ morgan_spurlock.html.

11. Jodie Michelle Lawston and Ruben R. Murillo, "The Discursive Figuration of U.S. Supremacy in Narratives Sympathetic to Undocumented Immigrants," *Social Justice* 36 (2009): 38.

12. See Annette Hill, *Reality TV: Audiences and Popular Factual Television* (New York: Routledge, 2005); Carolina Dover, "'Crisis' in British Documentary Television: The End of a Genre?" *Journal of British Cinema & Television* 1 (2004): 242–59.

13. Hill, *Reality TV*.

14. Edgar Morin, quoted in Jean Rouch, *Cine-Ethnography* (Minneapolis, MN: University of Minnesota Press, 2003), 231.

15. Talk Talk, "You Are What You Eat."

FURTHER READING

Corner, John. "Performing the Real: Documentary Diversions." *Television & New Media* 3 (2002): 255–69.

Hill, Annette. *Reality TV: Audiences and Popular Factual Television.* New York: Routledge, 2005.

Ouellette, Laurie, and James Hay. *Better Living Through Reality TV: Television and Post-Welfare Citizenship.* Malden, MA: Wiley-Blackwell, 2008.

18

America's Next Top Model
Neoliberal Labor

LAURIE OUELLETTE

Abstract: Reality competitions have emerged as one of the most popular and prevalent formats on contemporary television, typified here by *America's Next Top Model*. Laurie Ouellette argues that through the lens of social theory, we can see how such programs enact a version of contemporary labor practices, helping to train viewers as workers within new economic realities.

America's Next Top Model (UPN, 2003–2006; CW, 2006–present) is a reality series in which ten to twelve young women take part in a "highly accelerated boot camp to see if they have what it takes to make it in the high-profile modeling industry."[1] Fusing the conventions of the televised makeover, the internship, and the talent competition, the show immerses the women in lessons, tests, and challenges deemed integral to their success in the competitive modeling business. This skill set includes posing for the camera, improvising and performing scripts, body management, self-stylizing, and emoting on command, as well as less obvious job requirements such as social networking, self-esteem, adaptability, and self-promotion. Stylists, former models, photographers, and other industry intermediaries coach and evaluate the aspiring models while the cameras roll, and a panel of judges led by former supermodel and *ANTM* creator Tyra Banks sends one contestant home each week until the winner is revealed.

The prize is a $100,000 contract with Cover Girl cosmetics, a referral to the Elite Model Management agency, and an appearance in *Seventeen* magazine. While there can be only one Top Model per "cycle," the series claims to help all the contestants by providing vocational training. Most, in fact, do not become professional models, and even the winners tend to fade from sight post-competition. Nonetheless, *ANTM* flourishes as a televised stage for learning to labor in a field that demands a high degree of "to-be-looked-at-ness," performativity, flexibility, and self-enterprise from its aspirants.[2] At a time when many workers are facing similar requirements, particularly in the service industries, its curriculum extends to TV viewers at home, even as we watch for entertainment purposes. Just as schools facilitated the social reproduction of the (mostly male) factory workers needed by industrial capitalism, reality games like *ANTM* help socialize today's post-industrial workforce, with the help of informal teachers including coaches, stylists, photographers, and business moguls. As a feminized "display" profession set in the cultural industries, modeling provides the perfect context for this schooling. Illustrating the dos and don'ts of the modeling profession, *ANTM* teaches us all to navigate the changing demands of twenty-first-century work.

This essay uses social theories to analyze *ANTM* as a case study of reality television's labor politics. I show how a television production about "real life" amateur models intersects with broader trends, including cheaper modes of production, the rise of aesthetic labor, the feminization of job skills in post-industrial societies, and the extent to which today's workers are encouraged to envision themselves as "entrepreneurs of the self" rather than relying on unions or long-term job security. While *ANTM* exploits the labor of unpaid female contestants who are often lower income and women of color, it also constitutes the young women as the ultimate beneficiaries of their own self-enterprising activities. In this version of a labor market without guarantees, the winner is never simply a passive beauty or an obedient worker—she is the contestant who transforms herself into her own best asset. She is cruelly subjected to others (producers, experts, cultural intermediaries, judges) who profit from her labor, but is also invited to "maximize" herself for her own gain. *ANTM* does not conceal the predicament of the aspiring model, as much as it uses her double experience to demonstrate the rules of the game.

To analyze *ANTM* requires a critical understanding of labor. We begin with *commodity fetishism*, defined by Marx as the erasure of labor power and the signs of production as the source of a commodity's value, or an elimination of "any trace of the grime of the factory, the mass molding of the machine, and most of all, the exploitation of the worker," as Laura Mulvey explains. The commodity is instead endowed with a "seductive sheen," competing to be desired on the market.[3] While reality television production shifts away from the traditional Fordist factory, its commercial "sheen" is similarly divorced from behind-the-scenes labor practices. Encouraged by media deregulation, the proliferation of channels, and a desire to minimize labor costs, the television industry has come to rely on unpaid amateur talent and on non-unionized and freelance production crews who can be denied routine benefits, long-term employment contracts, overtime wages, and residuals.[4] *ANTM* exemplifies these trends, and like most reality productions, it also avoids hiring professional writers on the grounds that the competition isn't written. When the mostly female staffers responsible for shaping characters and devising story arcs from hours of footage went on strike to obtain better pay, health coverage, and Writers Guild representation in 2006, they were fired and replaced by a new crop of workers.[5]

Just as the "erasure of the mechanics of production in Hollywood" constitutes a form of commodity fetishism, *ANTM* expunges the labor of camera operators, editors, and craft services workers from the "reality" captured on screen.[6] *ANTM* does however expose the mechanics of commercial image production, going behind the scenes of fashion modeling and advertising to witness the rehearsing, staging, direction, and reshooting that produces "desirable" women in magazines and TV commercials. *ANTM* demystifies the process whereby women are objectified, put on display, and fetishized for profit-making purposes. The female contestants not only resemble the commodity form—they literally are commodities. Indeed, the competition revolves around the market calculations of image-makers and the labor of the aspiring models, who must learn to create and perform salable versions of femininity.

Exposing the manufacture of the female object destroys some of the power and pleasure associated with the "male gaze." It is difficult to revel in a fantasy about the female body when the production of that fantasy is exposed, disrupting the dreamlike conditions of voyeurism. The labor required to produce femininity that sells—endless makeup and dieting, Brazilian waxes and hair extensions—is also made visible, disrupting the "sheen" of media representations and perhaps subverting femininity's perceived naturalness. But such possibilities are curtailed when female contestants are disciplined and shamed upon failing to produce the "right" images. We witness a policing of what counts as desirable femininity, as well as a hierarchical work structure marked by authoritative and sometimes abusive supervisory relationships. Far from showing a collective bargaining situation, however, this glimpse into the normally expunged labor of modeling is bound to an implied reward system in which the "boot camp" survivors earn the capacity to attract sponsors, command high fees, and market themselves in a cool (but highly competitive) industry. On *ANTM*, the labor involved in producing "model perfect" femininity is emphasized not to overcome problems of female objectification, but to encourage profiteering through self-fashioning.

Here the concept of *immaterial labor* is helpful. While early Marxists were mainly concerned with the industrial production of tangible goods (such as automobiles or cans of soup), the post-industrial economy hinges more on the commodification of feelings, images, attitudes, styles, identities, and expressions of social life. While professional intermediaries who make and sell knowledge and culture are crucial, we all perform degrees of immaterial labor. Our work is not limited to the labor we perform at the factory or the office for pay: what we do and feel outside the job can also be channeled into the profits of employers, sponsors, and capitalism at large, which autonomist Marxists call the "social factory."

The rise of fashion modeling anticipated the mainstreaming of such immaterial labor, emerging from a "post-industrial shift toward service work and consumerism, in which non-material goods such as services, ideas and images have become products of capitalist development and circulation." Modeling also served as a testing ground for collapsing boundaries between life and work. While the factory worker has a scheduled shift followed by a period of leisure, models are expected to work on their skills, connections, and appearance all the time. Similarly, *ANTM* contestants are expected to practice body maintenance, social networking, and other value-generating activities learned on the show during their "off hours," thereby participating in constructing modeling as less a contained job than a "way of life."[7] This effect is further accentuated by their appearing on reality television, where there literally are no off-hours.

Such a way of life is spreading to other parts of the workforce. As Angela McRobbie notes, aesthetic labor is on the rise, particularly in the growing retail and service industries, which now "expect its workforce to look especially attractive and stylish." The burgeoning culture of beauty treatments, fitness, and cosmetic surgery is simultaneously being marketed to provide "added values which can enhance performance in the workplace."[8] Similarly, if the job of the model is to generate "affective" consumer responses to her activities and images,[9] similar forms of affective labor are now required by most service sector jobs, from ice cream parlor barista to retail sales clerk.

Television scholars have analyzed reality productions as immaterial labor, showing how ordinary people create the images desired by producers and sponsors for free through self-commodification within a promotional framework.[10] Reality productions trade in stock personas (the troubled girl, the crazy bitch) that participants are encouraged to adopt and perform in the interests of "good" (profitable) television. On *ANTM*, the contestants, who share living quarters mired in melodramatic tensions, perform as docusoap characters as well as aspiring pitchwomen. While only a select few will win modeling contracts, all contestants perform immaterial labor by generating promotional images in the service of brands. In Cycle 14, the women are required to perform a thirty-second advertisement, broadcast live in Times Square, in which they "encapsulate the Cover Girl attitude through their actions"—the challenge is to generate a promotional text in which their unique "personality shines through" in ways that encourage "other girls find the tools to be the best they want to be" in the Cover Girl brand. This promotional image labor isn't limited to photo shoots and television commercial filming; rather, it is extended as contestants use and discuss Cover Girl cosmetics with stylists and among themselves. These scenes valorize the historically unrecognized labor of producing femininity, but only as a means to the affective ties to images and brands sought by corporations. As Tyra Banks boasted in an interview, "I see women in the mall or on the streets who look 10 times better than I do, but can they sell a product?"[11]

While Marxism helps us to see this seep of value production into social life, it cannot fully explain contemporary reality television's relationship to gender and work in the twenty-first century. Reality productions like *ANTM* also translate the "cruelty" of work in the neoliberal economy into ritualized games, suggests Nick Couldry. In this context, the term "neoliberal" refers to the concentration of wealth, the decline of job security, and the rollback of labor regulations and mandated protections such as pensions and the forty-hour work week. These changes coexist with the rising demands of aesthetic labor, emotional performance ("service with a smile"), and expectations of always being "on call" for work. Television "smuggles past" these intolerable conditions by translating the harshest realities of work into playful renditions of extended work time, declining job security, and the "deep acting of passion," so that we are more apt to accept these conditions without question.[12] In this sense, television performs "ideological work" in the lives and minds of audiences. Yet, reality games do more than this—they also play a productive role in guiding and shaping the ideal workers sought by the neoliberal economy. Shows like *ANTM* circulate the logics, practical techniques, and resources through which contestants and TV viewers alike become laboring subjects.

Here, theories of *enterprise culture* are useful. In the context of deregulation, privatization of government services, and the intensification of the free-market mentality, the role of the individual in managing his or her own well-being and future has accelerated. To assist, an expanded culture of for-profit self-help, motivational resources, DIY information, and informal schooling has emerged. Enterprise culture does not emphasize its utility to the neoliberal economy, but encourages a new "care of the self" as a personal enterprise. As an especially visible component of these trends, reality television perpetuates a culture in which "everyone is an expert on herself, responsible for managing her own human capital to maximum effect."[13] In an insecure labor market, the self becomes "a flexible commodity to be molded, packaged, managed and sold."[14] Games like *ANTM* teach contestants (and, vicariously, TV viewers) to envision themselves as human capital, so that the line between playing a role for television, navigating the conditions of work, and creating oneself as a marketable product is inextricably blurred.

Shows like *ANTM* may not be exactly what former Federal Reserve Chairman Alan Greenspan envisioned when he promoted "lifelong learning" to prepare workers for a changing economy that values innovation, flexible labor, and entrepreneurship, but reality television offers a complimentary version of vocational guidance and schooling. Cultural and lifestyle intermediaries are crucial to this schooling, offering endless instruction on entrepreneurial behavior and strategic self-fashioning.[15] *ANTM* translates the intersecting requirements of short-term labor, outsourcing, and a shift from industrial production to promotion and branding onto resources to expand people's capacities to conduct themselves as enterprising subjects. This is not to deny the exploitation of labor, but to point out that current structures of work encourage, and indeed require that we all play an active role in fashioning, managing, and promoting ourselves. Here, too, the setting is crucial. While modeling enjoys a glamorous reputation, it is ultimately freelance work done on a project basis. Models do not receive benefits, enjoy job security, or control their working conditions. Thus a television production about models has particular salience as a technology of the self through which we all fashion ourselves as workers in a neoliberal economy.

One of the things that *ANTM* teaches is that self-enterprise is similar to being female. The self-invention demanded of workers requires an entrepreneurial relationship to the self that has much in common with the desire to make and remake femininity. What has long been demanded of women—to be adaptable, flexible, desirable, presentable, and consumable—has arguably been intensified and extended to the entire postindustrial workforce.[16] *ANTM* presents skills and attributes associated with white middle-class femininity, from makeup application to exuberant personality building, as a form of self-enterprise. This reward system perpetuates social hierarchies, but also brings women traditionally excluded from capitalist production into the logic of enterprise culture. Learning to labor requires mastery of a promotional femininity rooted in normalized class privilege and whiteness, maximizing such marketable differences. Women of color are "doubly commodified for their eroticized physical attractiveness and for their marketable personal narratives of racial self-transformation," Amy Hasinoff observes. Difference is "hyper-visible" as an indication of a so-called post-racial society, as a "malleable" commodity and as a reminder that disadvantage "can be overcome."[17] When Tiffany, an African American contestant whose grandmother reportedly went without electricity to buy a swimsuit for the competition, was eliminated in Cycle 4, it was not due to racial or class discrimination or to lack of potential, but because, as an enraged Tyra Banks says in a fan-favorite clip, she failed to "take control of her destiny."

On *ANTM*, elements of internship and competition are crucial for constituting the makeover as a route to success through self-enterprise. If modeling epitomizes the idealized attributes of white Western femininity, it is also an industry built upon entrepreneurial labor that is historically coded as corporate and masculine.[18] Models (much like new media workers) can be considered the neoliberal economy's "shock workers," required not only to work long hours, but also to accept risks previously mediated by firms, such as business cycle fluctuations and market failures.[19] On *ANTM* these risks are born by the contestants, who participate in the production for free and invest unpaid hours in the hopes of winning

FIGURE 18.1.
A contestant is
photographed
making herself a
Greek salad, in
Greece.

the competition and finding success in a precarious field in which most fail. At a time when entrepreneurial labor is spreading throughout the media, cultural, and service industries, *ANTM* stitches the most common forms of risk-bearing—the unpaid internship and investment in a flexible, attractive, and marketable self—into the requirements and promised rewards of enterprise culture.

The *ANTM* competition rewards contestants' risk-taking and self-invention, but also requires adaptability and improvisation. Aspiring Top Models are trained to create a unique personality and "look" which must be constantly adapted and modified to project the right image for different sponsors and clients, even as their creativity is guided by intermediaries who teach them how to be sexy, wholesome, sultry, bold, passionate, or glamorous.[20] Similarly, the fast-paced nature of the competition, and the range of tasks and challenges it presents, immerses contestants (and TV viewers) in what Richard Sennett calls the new culture of capitalism. Sennett's research shows that workers across industries are increasingly required to migrate from "task to task, job to job, place to place," while retraining frequently and developing new abilities to compensate for diminished returns on fixed skill sets. The ideal worker today must also be able to switch gears at a moment's notice and mobilize a "self-consuming passion" to keep themselves mobile within the labor force.[21] Television's labor games magnify these demands and reward contestants who, in addition to developing themselves as promotional images and human capital, are adept at learning new skills quickly, orienting themselves to new demands, and performing well across a moving platform of situations and challenges. On *ANTM*, this can involve improvising a performance, putting together a new look in ten minutes, projecting a feeling or affective state on command, or switching gears midstream to cater to the desires of a particular sponsor.

While it would be implausible to suggest that *ANTM* has a direct causal influence, it is worth considering reality television's role in learning to labor. After all, it is the contestant "who passes all the tests" who wins the competition, Tyra Banks claims, and this motto applies well to contemporary educational and labor conditions. Likewise, we need to bring critical theories of labor more fully into television studies. Whose interests are served when feminine subjects are constituted as aesthetic and affective laborers, and workers are recast as risk-bearing self-enterprisers? What are the stakes of training individuals to imagine themselves as commodities with uncertain shelf lives? As Banks suggests, "your product just happens to be your physical self and a little bit of your personality too. When they don't want it anymore, don't feel discarded. Just know that your product is just not hot anymore. Know that you'll have to revamp that product or go into another field."[22] As making and selling femininity has become integral to the post-industrial neoliberal economy, *ANTM* brings the process full circle by modeling these conditions for TV viewers.

NOTES

1. Margena Christian, "Tyra Banks: Says 'It's a Lot More than Just Looks' to Become 'America's Next Top Model,'" *Jet*, May 26, 2003.

2. The phrase "learning to labor" is from the influential study *Learning to Labor: How Working Class Kids Get Working Class Jobs* by Paul Willis (New York: Columbia University Press, 1977).

3. Laura Mulvey, "Some Thoughts on Theories of Fetishism in the Context of Contemporary Culture," *October* 65 (Summer 1993): 10.

4. Chad Raphael, "The Political Economic Origins of Reali-TV," in *Reality TV: Remaking Television Culture*, 2nd ed., Susan Murray and Laurie Ouellette, eds. (New York: New York University Press, 2008), 123–41.

5. For more on the strike see Richard Verrier, "Next Top Model Writers Threaten Strike," *Los Angeles Times*, July 21, 2006, and Writers Guild of America West, "Writers at CW's America's Next Top Model Strike to Secure Fair WGA Contract," press release, n.d., http://www.wga.org/subpage_newsevents.aspx?id=2103. For video testimonial from one of the strikers, see http://www.youtube.com/watch?v=0kGwKQ72UNY.

6. Mulvey, "Some Thoughts," 12.

7. Elizabeth Wissinger, "Modeling a Way of Life: Immaterial and Affective Labour in Fashion Modeling," *Ephemera: Theory & Politics in Organization* 7, 1 (2007): 250–69.

8. Angela McRobbie, "From Holloway to Hollywood: Happiness at Work in the New Cultural Economy?" in *Cultural Economy: Cultural Analysis and Commercial Life*, Paul du Gay and Michael Pryke, eds. (London: Sage, 2002), 100.

9. Wissinger, "Modeling," 250.

10. Alison Hearn, "'John, a 20-year-old Boston Native with a Great Sense of Humour': On the Spectacularization of the 'Self' and the Incorporation of Identity in the Age of Reality Television," *International Journal of Media and Cultural Politics* 2, 2 (2006): 131–47; see also Alison Hearn, "Meat, Mask, Burden: Probing the Contours of the Branded Self," *Journal of Consumer Culture* 8 (2008): 197–217.

11. Tyra Banks quoted in Christian, "Tyra Banks."

12. Nick Couldry, "Reality TV, or The Secret Theater of Neoliberalism," *Review of Education, Pedagogy, and Cultural Studies* 30, 1 (2008): 3–13.

13. Nancy Fraser, "From Discipline to Flexibalization? Re-reading Foucault in the Shadow of Globalization," *Constellations* 10, 2 (2003): 168.

14. Laurie Ouellette and James Hay, *Better Living Through Reality TV: Television and Post-Welfare Citizenship* (Malden, MA: Blackwell, 2008), 6.

15. Tania Lewis, *Smart Living: Lifestyle Media and Popular Expertise* (New York: Peter Lang, 2008).

16. Valerie Walkerdine, "Reclassifying Upward Mobility: Femininity and the Neo-Liberal Subject," *Gender and Education* 15, 3 (September 2003): 240.

17. Amy Adele Hasinoff, "Fashioning Race for the Free Market on *America's Next Top Model*," *Critical Studies in Media Communication*, 25, 3 (2008): 324–43.

18. Jennifer Craik, *The Face of Fashion: Cultural Studies in Fashion* (London, Routledge, 1994).

19. Neff, Gina, Elizabeth Wissinger and Sharon Zukin, "Entrepreneurial Labor among Cultural Producers: 'Cool' Jobs in 'Hot' Industries," *Social Semiotics* 15, 3 (2005): 307–34.

20. Elizabeth Wissinger, "Modeling Consumption: Fashion Modeling Work in Contemporary Society," *Journal of Consumer Culture* 9 (2009): 273–96.

21. Richard Sennett, *The New Culture of Capitalism* (New Haven: Yale University Press, 2006), 9–10, 93.

22. Tyra Banks, quoted in Christianson, "Tyra Banks."

FURTHER READING

Couldry, Nick. "Reality TV, or The Secret Theater of Neoliberalism." *Review of Education, Pedagogy, and Cultural Studies* 30, 1 (2008): 3–13.

Hasinoff, Amy Adele. "Fashioning Race for the Free Market on *America's Next Top Model*." *Critical Studies in Media Communication* 25, 3 (2008): 324–43.

Hearn, Alison. "'John, a 20-year-old Boston Native with a Great Sense of Humour': On the Spectacularization of the 'Self' and the Incorporation of Identity in the Age of Reality Television." *International Journal of Media and Cultural Politics* 2, 2 (2006): 131-47.

Ouellette, Laurie, and James Hay. *Better Living Through Reality TV: Television and Post-Welfare Citizenship*. Malden, MA: Blackwell, 2008.

19

Family Guy
Undermining Satire

NICK MARX

Abstract: With its abrasive treatment of topics like race, religion, and gender, *Family Guy* runs afoul of critics but is defended by fans for "making fun of everything." Nick Marx examines how the program's rapid-fire stream of comic references caters to the tastes of TV's prized youth demographic, yet compromises its satiric potential.

The *Family Guy* episode "I Dream of Jesus" (October 5, 2008) begins with the type of scene familiar to many fans of the series. Peter and the Griffin family visit a 1950s-themed diner, one that accommodates a number of parodic references to pop culture of the era. In a winking acknowledgment of how *Family Guy* (FOX, 1999–2002, 2005–present) courts young adult viewers, Lois explains to the Griffin children that 1950s-themed diners were very popular in the 1980s, well before many of the program's targeted audience members were old enough to remember them. As the Griffins are seated, they observe several period celebrity lookalikes working as servers in the restaurant. Marilyn Monroe and Elvis pass through before the bit culminates with a cut to James Dean "after the accident," his head mangled and his clothes in bloodied tatters. But, in characteristic *Family Guy* narrative logic, the episode stuffs more comedic fodder into the premise. Cleveland Brown, the good-natured black character of the cohort, enters the restaurant only to be blasted away by police officers with a fire hose and attack dogs. "Oh, that takes me back," Cleveland flatly remarks after being expelled from the restaurant.

The scene works according to the comedic logic of the "rule of three," setting up the gag's structure with Marilyn Monroe, reinforcing it with Elvis, and, finally, breaking the pattern in an unexpected way with James Dean. At first glance, Cleveland would simply seem to be further elaboration of the original joke, an extra punchline characteristic of the show's edgy approach to humor. But one of these punchlines is not like the others. By trotting out Monroe, Elvis, and Dean—all of whom died ignominiously—*Family Guy* makes fun of the supposed virtuousness commonly seen in cultural hagiographies like Time-Life's *Rock & Roll Generation: Teen Life in the 50s* and *The American Dream: The 50's*. Cleveland's inclusion, however, jarringly places celebrity scandal alongside civil rights conflict in the scene's range of comedic targets, suggesting that both are safely part of a past about which it is now permissible to joke. This has become the show's modus operandi: everything from television sitcoms to advertising mascots to systemic social inequalities are lampooned within a rapid-fire feed of flashbacks, cutaways, and perfunctory plot events. But is it all equally funny?

This question pervades much of the popular dialogue about *Family Guy*. Fans defend scenes like the one described above as "just a joke," while interest groups like the Parents Television Council protest that the program goes too far all too often. But before rushing to judgment, careful analysis of the show's industrial and aesthetic contexts helps us better to account for the wide range of responses it elicits. The question, then, might not be "Is *Family Guy* funny?" but "How and for whom does *Family Guy* create humor?" In many ways, *Family Guy* reflects television's present proliferation of comedic modes of social engagement. Situation comedies continue to dominate reruns, *The Daily Show with Jon Stewart* filters the news through comedic satire, and even the appeal of many reality shows is based on taking a schadenfreude-like pleasure in seemingly "real" scenarios. The humor of *Family Guy* shares similarities with these comedies, but its differences from them point to shifts in the ways we watch and understand television.

Family Guy is emblematic of what might be called a growing "click culture," the aesthetic and industrial practices of comedy that are both creating and created by television networks' expansion online, increased user-control of television content, and the integration of that content into social networking practices. The television industry strives to create as many iterations of *Family Guy* as possible, allowing loyal viewers to interact with the show through merchandising, spin-offs, and web forums, as has become a standard practice for many shows today. Aesthetically, however, *Family Guy* departs from many of its generic brethren by structuring most of its humor and episode plots around the unpredictable, non-sequitur nature of click culture. The program's compulsive habit of targeting—through flashbacks, cutaways, and narrative digressions—elements outside the Quahog storyworld give it both a distinct comedic voice and a problematic mode of representing and reproducing power relations. Indeed, animated sitcoms from *The Flintstones* to *The Simpsons* to *South Park* have made strategic use of reflexivity and extra-textual references for satiric purposes, but none to *Family Guy*'s extent. And when the jokes pile up so quickly, the program's ability to create meaningful satire becomes compromised.

If we remain critically aware of this dynamic—if we recognize that there is a difference between joking about a celebrity death and joking about the violent racist oppression of millions of Americans—we see how *Family Guy* represents dominant views about new comedic tastes being cultivated by the technology and lifestyles available to young viewers today. As the television industry has moved away from courting broad audiences by programming shows with mass appeal, it has been increasingly willing to risk alienating certain audience segments in order to target others. In the contemporary era of digital convergence and trans-medial movement of television content, the most valuable target audience has become young men aged 18–34. In addition to discretionary spending and trend-setting powers, this demographic is seen as susceptible to the siren song of non-television media like video games and the Internet. These "lost boys," as *Wired* dubbed them in 2004, "hunger for 'authenticity,'" and "like things fresh, unpredictable, and uncensored."[1] Resistant to television mainstays like thirty-second advertisements and conventional sitcoms, these viewers instead seek content that flatters their media hyper literacy and (self-declared) hip sensibilities.

Accordingly, the television industry has made every effort to bring these "lost boys" back into the fold. Cable channels like G4 target young men with programs about Internet trends, while Spike has staged an annual awards show for video games since 2003. Broadcast networks package television spots with advertising opportunities across their web and cable holdings, acknowledging that viewers—particularly young men—increasingly consume media in a multiscreen environment. In the industrial practices of click culture, these trends have been particularly acute. Comedy Central's *Tosh.0* pairs viral videos with comedic commentary, accompanied by frequent exhortations from host Daniel Tosh to engage with the program in a variety of digital media and live performances. Cartoon Network and HBO have also developed comedic television programs from the Webby award-winning *Children's Hospital* and FunnyorDie. com, respectively.

The low development costs of many comedic formats, along with viewers' ability to consume them in bite-sized chunks, make them amenable to the transmedial strategies of distribution and consumption so prevalent today. *Family Guy* embraces these practices, having spawned a number of spin-offs and ancillary products in video games, merchandising, and home video. Moreover, comedy—from *The Simpsons* to *Beavis & Butt-Head* to *South Park*—has always articulated an "edgy" appeal directed at the young-male demo, but *Family Guy* has pushed this risqué sensibility to new limits. Before uncritically accepting the pairing of *Family Guy* and young male viewers as a successful strategy, however, we need to consider what this industrial practice leaves out. That is to say, not all males aged 18–34 (let alone viewers of *Family Guy* outside this age group) share the same racial, ethnic, or sexual identity, come from a similar socio-economic background, or even have equal access to the technologies driving transmedial mobility. The growing danger of click culture as seen in the aesthetic and industrial practices of *Family Guy* is that it can reinforce the social power of already powerful audience categories, further excluding historically marginalized viewers whose tastes might not match the industry's demographic assumptions. How exactly, then, does click culture function, and how does *Family Guy* articulate these practices?

Think of reading the rapid-fire stream of jokes in *Family Guy* in much the same way you do items in a Facebook or Twitter feed. At any given time of day, you might encounter a friend posting a link to a tawdry gossip column, immediately followed by another friend who posts a link to a petition asking for signatures in an upcoming recall election. The respective roles that these two items play in your life are not as different as you might like to think, and both are brought to you by an information delivery mechanism that presents the stories contiguously. But clicking through to engage further with them requires different, though not mutually exclusive, critical sensibilities. The gossip column might be something you quickly repost for friends to see; the recall petition might inspire you to contact your neighbors and join a local rally. Facebook and Twitter do little to distinguish between the two items, but each inspires a range of uses. Even when events from the two seemingly disparate domains of politics and pop culture collide—as they do whenever a politician is caught in a sex scandal—we implicitly understand that there is no necessary connection between them.

Instead of affording consumers a similar range of responses to information and entertainment discourses, *Family Guy* flattens their significance to the same level and naturalizes their meaning under the aegis of everything being "just a joke." Where social networking sites loosely organize disparate stories for users, *Family Guy* reproduces the aesthetic experience of newsfeed navigation and organizes it much more rigorously according to the logic that everything appearing onscreen is equally capable of being lampooned. This aesthetic is driven by contemporary television's economic imperative, one that (in the case of *Family Guy*) places more value on the commodity audience of 18–34-year-old males and thus prizes this group's presumed response more than that of other audiences. But the quick-hit aesthetics of click culture programs like *Family Guy* belie their industrial motivations, creating the illusion that all audiences can find everything equally funny and constructing a false sense of comedic pluralism that elides the power differentials among comedic targets and audiences. In doing so, *Family Guy* rarely trades in critical takedowns of the powerful by the powerless—the very goal of satire; instead, it tends to reaffirm the politics of the status quo.

In one example from the episode "No Meals on Wheels" (March 25, 2007), Peter is annoyed at Mort Goldman's requests to borrow his personal belongings, calling him a "bigger mooch than the Mexican Super Friends." The ensuing cutaway begins with an exterior shot of the "Mexican Hall of Justice," a parodic reiteration of the headquarters of the Saturday morning cartoon *Super Friends* (ABC, 1973–1986), a show perfectly in tune with *Family Guy's* fixation on the American television heritage. As the scene moves into the hall, we see dozens of anonymous Mexican characters dressed in superhero garb milling around, with "Mexican Superman" conspicuously lazing with a beer and his feet up. A white landlord enters and confronts him about the number of people living in the hall, initiating a short vignette in which he and "Mexican Batman" deceive the landlord and defuse a prospective eviction.

The ostensible gag of the cutaway, running just over thirty seconds, is that the *Super Friends'* Hall of Justice is as overcrowded as a typical Mexican home, and the bit evokes a number of commonly circulated stereotypes about Latino/a populations in the United States as indolent, duplicitous, and freeloading. Moreover, the images play with the longstanding representational tradition in Hollywood film and television of caricaturing Latino/as as stock types like the "bandido" and "Latin lover."[2] Whereas this tradition often placed caricatured representations of marginalized groups within the narrative—by having the white cowboy defeat the sneaky bandido, for example—*Family Guy* compulsively directs our attention beyond the narrative by recreating the aesthetic experience of newsfeed navigation that it presumes its "lost boy" audience enjoys. In our above example, the Mexican stereotypes are not contextualized, undermined, or reinforced with any clarity in the episode. Instead, they become one of any number of referents plucked from the pop cultural ether and placed alongside another one—the *Super Friends*—in the creation of a cutaway gag. This practice elides the history of the stereotypes and the vast power differentials between the two referents, suggesting instead that both are simply fodder for jokes. In doing so, *Family Guy* naturalizes the notion that its audience's everyday lived experience is one in which everyone and everything is capable of being made fun of.

Indeed, *Family Guy's* complexity as a site of analysis is the same trait that makes its popularity so problematic. On the one hand, the program's formal adventurousness has influenced everything from *30 Rock* to parody films like *Scary Movie*, *Date Movie*, and *Epic Movie*. One early notable gag that climaxed with the Kool-Aid man bursting through a courtroom wall, for example, had critics comparing the show to everything from *Pee-Wee's Playhouse* to the magical realism of Latin American authors like Gabriel García Márquez.[3] On the other hand, *Family Guy* foregrounds this formal adventurousness in a way that obfuscates its economic motivations and consequences. It appears to make the same accommodations of disparate discourses that social networking sites do, but it is more rigidly structured according to the transmedial pursuit of "lost boys," aping their (presumed) simultaneous consumption of everything from stereotypes to comics under the idea that

FIGURE 19.1.
An angry landlord con-
fronts the "Mexican
Superfriends."

they are all equally funny elements of a continuous comedic feed. Clearly, crucial differences exist between social networking sites and television programs.[4] But by toying with the conventions of the latter to look more like the former, *Family Guy* forecloses many of the powerful representational possibilities unique to television.

Family Guy's formal play manifests most prominently in its emphasis on seemingly extraneous material over conventional sitcom narratives driven by character and plot. Some episodes are more driven than others by characters' particular goals and plotting, but a common complaint of the show is that its Quahog storyworld and the characters that inhabit it exist as little more than jumping-off points for cutaways, flashbacks, and nonsensical extra-textual references. This critique found a particularly explicit articulation in *South Park*'s (Comedy Central, 1997–present) "Cartoon Wars" episodes (April 5 and 12, 2006). In them, bigoted firebrand Eric Cartman rails against the inexplicable narrative logic of *Family Guy*, upset that the other boys think he would like the show because it jibes with his raunchy sense of humor. But Cartman retorts: "Don't you ever, ever compare me to *Family Guy*! When I make jokes, they are inherent to a story—deep, situational, and emotional jokes based on what is relevant and has a point, not just one random, interchangeable joke after another!" *South Park* has long commented on current events by incorporating them into its storyworld, and the "Cartoon Wars" episodes go on to ridicule extremist rhetoric about the *Jyllands-Posten* Muhammad cartoon controversy by explicitly playing out *South Park*'s censorship battle with Comedy Central. The episodes climax when the *South Park* boys discover *Family Guy* is written by manatees that choose "idea balls" containing pop culture references and run them through a "joke combine," a process that results in a nonsensical cutaway gag about Muhammad delivering Peter a salmon atop a football helmet. *South Park*'s critique of *Family Guy* is thus less about its seemingly scattershot sense of humor than how that sensibility prevents *Family Guy* from engaging in dialogue with broader discourses in the contextualized manner that *South Park* strives for.

Perhaps the discourse *Family Guy* has engaged most explicitly and controversially in recent years is that of "post-racial America," the idea that issues of racial prejudice, persecution, and discrimination no longer matter as much as they once did. These talking points have been taken up by both ends of the political spectrum during the presidency of Barack Obama, and *Family Guy* has articulated them in feuds between the left-leaning Brian and the conservative pundit Rush Limbaugh ("Blue Harvest," September 23, 2007, and "Excellence in Broadcasting," October 3, 2010). The episodes hint at a *South Park*-like critique of hyperbolic political rhetoric, asserting that neither side can accurately claim the complex machinations of race relations for its own purposes. Yet representations of race, ethnicity, and religion—from Jews ("When You Wish Upon a Weinstein," November 9, 2003) to Arabs ("Quagmire's Baby," November 15, 2009) to the above-mentioned examples of African Americans and Mexicans—repeatedly undercut this reading. By equating the comedic value of racial/ethnic representations with that of other pop culture ephemera, *Family Guy* appropriates discourses of "post-racialness" more than it subverts them.

Creative personnel involved with the show have tried to discourage readings of its racial/ethnic humor as reinforcing the power of already dominant social groups. Instead, they claim, everyone is made to seem powerless because everyone is made fun of equally. Creator Seth MacFarlane has defended the show as an "equal-opportunity offender,"[5] a sentiment echoed by black voice actor for *The Cleveland Show,* Kevin Michael Richardson: "If it was just the blacks, we'd have a problem. But the fact that it offends everybody, I can laugh."[6] A public endorsement from a black actor affiliated with MacFarlane would seem to ameliorate the effects of offensive humor on *Family Guy*, yet it conflicts with how the show has been represented in other publicity materials. In 2010, for example, MacFarlane and company sent a brochure out to Emmy voters that featured Peter Griffin in a tableau parodying the overweight, black lead actress from the movie *Precious*.

At the time of this brochure, the film—an intense drama about a teenaged girl abused by her mother and impregnated by her father—had become something of a critical darling, going on to garner six Oscar nominations and two wins. At first glance, the mailer is mocking the tendency of awards institutions to laud "issue" films like *Precious*, ironically and reflexively commenting on *Family Guy*'s decidedly unserious take on matters of social import. But in typical *Family Guy* fashion, the mailer asks voters to celebrate the program's diversity, noting that it is "written by 8 WASPS, 6 Jews, 2 Asians and 1 Gay." This information presumably explains the tagline at the bottom of the mailer, "Vote for us or you're racist."

FIGURE 19.2.

A brochure sent to Emmy voters invokes diversity in a parodic (and problematic) plea for recognition.

Many comedic traditions have a history of appropriating racial/ethnic imagery and using it to satirize, among other things, the politics of representation. But the mailer effectively neuters this broader critique by reducing both *Family Guy* and *Precious* to the racial/ethnic/sexual identities of their respective creators. Indeed, part of the joke is pointing to how Oscar voters might be conflating their own white guilt with the artistic value of a film by black creators. But in equating its own diversity to that of *Precious*, *Family Guy* overlooks the differences in power relations between them, as if to say that both exist in a moment when equality is no longer a concern. In other words, if the racial identities in *Precious* are enough to garner critical acclaim, the same should go for other "diverse" media like *Family Guy*; if race is not the basis for the awards-show success of *Precious*, then diversity should not be an issue at all. The mailer strives to satirize "post-racial" discourses, yet overlooks their complexities in the name of humor, as well as unwittingly positing the show as existing in a "post-racial" moment. In doing so, it risks replacing the real world efficacies of diversity efforts with a sense that they no longer matter.

Of course, racial categories, televisual representations of race, and social structures built upon racial/ethnic identities still matter. But their importance does not preclude the possibility of finding humor in the way that we talk about and live racialized experiences in America. Indeed, humor can be a very powerful element of racial discourses. Yet it is important to recognize the complex nature of this power and bear in mind that it is not uniform across all forms of humor. Humor manifests in a range of comedic formats on television, some that speak from positions of the already powerful, others that elevate marginalized voices to take down the powerful, and many that fall somewhere in between. *Family Guy* flattens this range of power relations and elides differences among them, all in the name of "making fun of everything." It privileges this seemingly equalizing use of humor, just as the contemporary television industry privileges the "lost boy" audience. But it is up to viewers from all audience categories to maintain a critical sensibility toward click culture in a way that acknowledges the already powerful, heeds the marginalized voices, and strives for an engagement with television that closes the gap between the two groups.

NOTES

1. Frank Rose, "The Lost Boys." *Wired*, (August 2004), http://www.wired.com/wired/archive/12.08/lostboys.html.
2. See Charles Ramírez Berg, *Latino Images in Film: Stereotypes, Subversion, Resistance* (Austin: University of Texas Press, 2002), 66–86.
3. See Alison Crawford, "Oh Yeah!': *Family Guy* as Magical Realism?" *Journal of Film and Video* 61, 2 (Summer 2009): 52–69.
4. For a fuller discussion of click culture, *Family Guy*, and representational strategies, see Matt Sienkiewicz and Nick Marx, "Click Culture: The Perils and Possibilities of *Family Guy* and Convergence Era Television," under review.
5. Maria Elena Fernandez, "Sarah Palin vs. 'Family Guy': Seth MacFarlane responds (sort of)," *Los Angeles Times*, February 16, 2010, http://latimesblogs.latimes.com/showtracker/2010/02/sarah-palin-v-family-guy.html.
6. Dave Itzkoff, "Spinning Off Into Uncharted Cartoon Territory," *New York Times*, August 17, 2009, http://www.nytimes.com/2009/08/30/arts/television/30itzk.html

FURTHER READING

Crawford, Alison. "Oh Yeah!': *Family Guy* as Magical Realism?" *Journal of Film and Video* 61, 2 (Summer 2009): 52–69.
Dobson, Hugo. "Mister Sparkle Meets the Yakuza: Depictions of Japan in *The Simpsons*." *Journal of Popular Culture* 39 (February 2006): 1.
Sienkiewicz, Matt, and Nick Marx. "Beyond a Cutout World: Ethnic Humor and Discursive Integration in *South Park*." *The Journal of Film and Video* 61, 2 (Summer 2009): 5–18.

20

Fox & Friends
Political Talk

JEFFREY P. JONES

Abstract: That Fox News is slanted conservative has passed from criticism into truism and branding strategy. However, there is danger in simply accepting this view and neglecting critical analysis of what continues to be the most highly rated cable news network. Jeffrey P. Jones shows how the long-running *Fox & Friends* turns the morning talk format on its head, performing an "ideological, often hysterical view of the world" that, he argues, impacts and transforms our world in the process.

It just feels like high school all over again. There's the intellectually challenged and dim-witted jock wannabe, the guy who still refers to women as "babes" and "skirts," yet who is clearly outclassed by all the women around him.[1] Then there's the popular and attractive mean-girl who thinks she needs to show her legs first and her smarts second, whose viciousness and bitchiness are exceeded only by her ambition.[2] And then there's the gay guy, always exhibiting a smirk wrapped in smarm, the go-to guy for the group's requisite mean-spirited put-down or latest innuendo and salacious rumour. Brian Kilmeade, Gretchen Carlson, and Steve Doocy form the trio of hosts for the Fox News Channel's morning talk show, *Fox & Friends* (1996–present).[3] And whereas the broadcast networks' morning talk shows—*The Today Show, Good Morning America, The Early Show*—have historically offered an ensemble of hosts designed to invoke the feeling of a happy family (the trustworthy brother, the cute sister, the wacky uncle, etc.), *Fox & Friends* is more akin to a trip back to the high school homeroom. Fox has staged the show in this way not just to stand out from the competition through a different look and feel, but also to create the necessary discursive setting for furthering the channel's ideological goals and agenda.

While this formulation is overly reductive and dismissive—much like the discourse on the show itself—these pejorative descriptions only begin to capture what Fox is crafting in its popular morning talk vehicle. Fox has assembled a group of distinct personality types whose job is to ruminate collectively over the previous day's events, including political ones. Yet unlike Fox News's primetime hosts, who assemble a group of yes-people to confirm and reify what the stars such as Bill O'Reilly and Sean Hannity proclaim, the morning crew has no stand-out star talent around which to build a show. But then that isn't the objective. Instead, the show is designed to thrust the viewer into the world of common-sense groupthink, complete with all the rumours, smears, innuendo, fear-mongering, thinly veiled ad hominem attacks, and lack of rational discourse they can muster—you know, just like high school. Indeed, the function of the program is to begin the broadcast day with cavalier discussions of political matters—to trot out all manner of conspiracy theories, catchphrases, and buzz words that can prime the audience, both cognitively and semiotically, for similar narratives derived from contemporary right-wing conservative ideology which they will encounter throughout Fox's schedule.[4]

In general, narratives play an important role in shaping public opinion about national politics. Most citizens may not understand the intricacies of or competing ideas and debates about issues of governance such as economic policy, regulatory structures, or international diplomacy, but they certainly understand stories. And stories are what media are in the business of providing—tales that continuously contribute to and often shape what politics *mean*. Trade imbalances, national security policies, Supreme Court rulings, Medicare solvency—none of these things make any *sense* unless they are explained, contextualized, and judged as good, bad, or indifferent to the daily lives of citizens. Competing political narratives thus abound and, indeed, are part of the battleground in currying favor with voters and viewers. But competing news narratives are especially powerful in the cable era, and nowhere more starkly asserted than on Fox News. Fox has proven itself a strong rhetorical force in crafting political narratives that oppose whatever political "reality" liberals or Democratic politicians might construct on a given day. This is true as well on *Fox & Friends*, where such narratives are performed through a genre and program perfectly cast to achieve such political and ideological ends.

That Fox News is conservative in its programming is an undeniable point, despite the channel's own denials. Scholars and media watchdog groups have provided detailed and copious evidence of Fox's overtly ideological narratives in both its news and opinion programs.[5] Audiences also recognize Fox as conservative, as demonstrated in both their opinions of the channel and their viewing behaviors: notably, self-defined conservative viewers overwhelmingly flock to Fox News over any other television news source.[6] Arguments over whether Fox is or isn't conservative, or that its ideology is noticeable only because all other media are liberal, are diversionary, at best—a rhetorical move that allows Fox and its supporters to shift the focus from its questionable rhetorical practices that hide behind the veil of "news" to the chimera of supposed bias in traditional journalism outlets and established reporting practices.

Political intentionality aside, conservative ideology is how the channel has branded itself, making it distinctive from its competition as a commercial product that consumers can depend on to deliver predictable or reliable results. With three competing cable news channels needing to fill twenty-four programming hours each day (as opposed to the thirty minutes of national news in the broadcast network era), markers of distinction are significant in attracting and retaining niche audiences. But as with all brands, that distinct image has to be constructed through a consistent set of practices or offerings that reiterate the brand's identity. That is to say, it must be *performed* regularly.

It is here, in the realm of performance, that we should look to understand how and why *Fox & Friends* not only differs so much from its morning talk show competition, but also serves a particular role in branding Fox News as conservative. There are two distinct aspects of "performance" at play here: performance as *aesthetic expression*, or the stylistics or poetics that dramatize, in this instance, ideological thinking; and what theorists of language describe as *performativity*, or how speech acts or utterances don't just report or describe something, but actually bring that thing into *being* through the act of speaking.[7] A classic example of a performative speech act is a wedding official pronouncing a man and woman "husband and wife," changing material reality through speech. Accordingly, this analysis will examine both how *Fox & Friends* routinely brings ideology to life through its dramatic performances and how it crafts reality—literally making things performatively "real"—through its repeated rhetorical assertions.

Let's first look at the broadcast networks' morning talk shows, though, for a rough sketch of how the genre has traditionally operated, using NBC's *Today* show (1952–present), the historical standard bearer and ratings leader, as the genre definer. The *Today* show's cast is designed to mesh with the waking family having breakfast or preparing for work and school, offering friendly faces that can easily blend with the family unit. Thus, its content steers clear of the politically controversial, offering instead light fare comprised of a smattering of news headlines, weather updates, and interviews with newsmakers, typically foregrounding the human-interest side of news. Primarily, though, the show is geared toward women viewers who are fashioned as mothers/homemakers and treated as the primary household consumer, with a majority of content focused largely on entertainment, cooking and food, parenting, fashion and beauty, relationships, travel, money, and health. These aspects of the show are performed when experts discuss child rearing, for instance, or the latest fashion trends are highlighted, chefs offer cooking demonstrations, or guest musical performances are put on. In the digital era, the show has also attempted to foster a feeling of community among fellow female viewers and the show, its hosts, its online content, and other offerings in the NBC television family.[8]

Fox & Friends also attempts to craft a feeling of community, but not in terms of gender or consumption interests. Rather, conservative ideology serves as the crucial mechanism linking Fox viewers to each other and to the channel. As with much of Fox's programming, the narratives on the morning show are comprised of a discourse that embraces what has become standard ideological tenets of contemporary conservatism—militaristic patriotism, patriarchal gender norms, conservative cultural "values," Christian religiosity, Second Amendment rights, and free-market capitalism, while also castigating and villainizing government, immigrants, liberals, labor unions, and non-Christian religions (especially Islam). Importantly, this discourse is repeatedly wrapped in expressions of celebration and triumph or, more typically, fear and anxiety as manifested through a tone of anger and disgust, a rhetoric of victimization, and a posture of defiance.[9]

Take, for example, *Fox & Friends'* soft-news program segments. The show welcomes the winter holiday season not just with features on food or shopping trends, but also with a barrage of stories they have manufactured called the "War on Christmas." This made-up war arises from the belief that secular society is removing the Christ from Christmas, and then becomes the occasion to demonstrate this "fundamental attack on American values" through repeated anecdotal evidence.[10] In 2011, for instance, *F&F* repeatedly ran stories under the "War on Christmas" segment graphic with such topics as "Are Christians the Only Ones Being Forced to be Tolerant?" and "FL City Bans Christmas Trees and Menorahs," as well as several stories attacking Rhode Island Governor Lincoln Chafee for calling the Christmas tree in the capitol a "holiday tree" (even posting the governor's phone number on screen while encouraging viewers to call him to express their outrage). That *F&F* manufactures this supposed "war" is seen in this last instance, in which the hosts castigate the governor for his invitation to a "holiday tree lighting" ceremony, even though the previous Republican governor had produced exactly the same invitation two years earlier.

Yet nothing riles up the hosts' hatred and full-throated high school smears quite like President Barack Obama. *F&F* has become a favored location on Fox to entertain an array of right-wing conspiracy theories, from claims that Obama was "educated in a madrassa" and "raised as a Muslim," to his not being a natural born citizen of the United States to the accusation that Obama's first book was written by former 1960s radical Bill Ayers.[11] But the high school-ishness of it all is perhaps best seen in two petty attacks, the first being a segment that debated

FIGURE 20.1.
Hosts Doocy and Carlson express their daily dose of outrage and emotional intensity over the latest news.

whether it was appropriate for President Obama to wear flip-flops while he was on vacation.[12] The other occurred when, during a period of persistent U.S. unemployment hovering above 9 percent, Obama introduced a jobs bill in a White House ceremony. Steve Doocy felt it proper to attack the choice of paper clip that Obama used in holding up the proposed legislation to the public! Graphically highlighting the supposedly unseemly nature of the offending clip, Doocy exclaimed, "President Obama's jobs bill, hot off the presses—at Kinko's? Hundreds of billions in tax hikes and new spending bound together with a chintzy clip. Look at that thing."[13]

Another technique for attacking its villains while supporting its ideological performances involves attributing a critique or counterclaim to unnamed sources by simply saying, "some would say." For instance, in attempting to blame a poor economy on labor unions, Gretchen Carlson offered, "Some would say that it's the unions that have crippled the U.S. economy and led to the United States' debt." As Media Matters notes, the "some" referred to in the formulation are often simply other Fox News hosts, as opposed to experts such as, in this instance, economists.[14] In other instances, the show's anchors use the saying as a rhetorical set-up to introduce guests, yet in the process establish the key attack as an unproblematic reality. "So is this a continuation of the president's plan to promote class warfare, [as] some are suggesting? Joining us now is Fox News legal analyst Peter Johnson," went one analysis of an Obama speech. A similar rhetorical move occurs in guest introductions where the host makes an extreme assertion, yet poses it as an "innocent" question. For instance, Steve Doocy introduced one guest by asking, "Could President Obama be running the most destructive administration in our history?" Such loaded phrases are simply not found in the language of other morning shows or newscasts. The fact that these instances happen repeatedly and with such venom and vigour marks the program as both ideologically and generically distinctive.

What is also noteworthy in these two examples is how *F&F* features guests to perform the argument the hosts want to make, while arranging for the guests to be directly responsible for making the claim, in such a way that the hosts' comments are effectively insulated from charges of bias. As we will see below, guests are also used to demonstrate villainy in their "us versus them" formulation, thereby establishing "the Other" while supposedly demonstrating that Fox is "fair and balanced" by giving the other side an opportunity to be heard.

We must look not just at the ways ideology is encoded in their performances, but also at the ways in which the language employed may bring certain "realities" into being. As noted above, understanding language as *performative* involves a recognition that language often produces, not just reflects upon, that which it names.[15] Performativity theory highlights how words can be "actions in themselves"—they bring into being that which is spoken.[16] The "War on Christmas" is one example, for no "war" exists outside that which Fox has constructed and brought into being. Similarly, Fox News's speech acts may name something—for instance, labelling a proposed Islamic community center in the lower Manhattan neighborhood near the former World Trade Center a "Ground Zero Mosque"—but the utterance also warns citizens of a supposed threat to American values and honor, perhaps even mobilizing people to vote in the midterm congressional elections for candidates voicing opposition to such a "mosque." Thus the repeated iteration of such utterances not only creates realities—"mosque," not community center, becomes the standard usage on other news channels—but now has the potential to mobilize concrete political actions through their performative power.

Fox & Friends was at the forefront of the "Ground Zero Mosque" event, repeatedly running segments on the Park 51 project (as it was officially called) that stoked the flames of fear, paranoia, revenge, hatred, racism, and whatever else could be mustered three months before the midterm congressional elections.[17] Not only did the hosts pick sides, but through repeated invocation, they literally brought a proposed "mosque" into being—as a religious center, as a "command center" for terrorists, as a slap in the face of Americans, as a threat, as evil, as a *controversy* that did not exist in the early stages of the project.[18] Despite the facts that an actual mosque existed in the former World Trade Center prior to 9/11, and that one still exists today in the Pentagon, Fox saw an opportunity to link the 9/11 terrorist attacks to the project, transforming a place of community gathering and worship into an imagined terrorist threat with alleged ties to radical Islamic terrorist groups worldwide.

Here again, guests on *F&F* played a crucial role. In one segment, the program hosted Imam Feisal Abdul Rauf, the project's organizer. But instead of interviewing him directly, the hosts literally pitted him against a 9/11 firefighter who was opposed to the project, featuring the firefighter as the lead guest. Despite the fact that the Imam and firefighter sat together on the same couch, *F&F* chose to frame the two men in picture boxes—allowing viewers to see them not just as rhetorically opposed, but visually as well, thus crafting a cognitive tool to posit key dichotomies to further its rhetorical ends: good versus bad, white person versus person of color, Christian versus Muslim, 9/11 victim versus 9/11 perpetrator.[19] Given the way this visual framing routinely occurs on the show, we might refer to the technique as "Boxes of Discord and Empathy." In a different episode, the show featured another 9/11 firefighter who was suing the "mosque's" developers for $350 million. As the firefighter and his lawyer discussed their reasons for entering the suit, the firefighter was framed in a picture box, but this time counterpoised with images of the attack on the World Trade Center and its smoky aftermath.[20] In both instances, the guests help perform the ideological function—visually and representationally, as much as anything they have to say—of constructing clear heroes and villains, threats and sacred objects.

In sum, *Fox & Friends* has played a central role in constructing a specific "reality," a threat made tangible and real through its ability to mobilize emotion. That reality is brought into existence through its repeated performance, as well as being brought to life through the dramatic presentations that the format of the talk show encourages and allows. What repeated viewing of the program also demonstrates is how emotion and drama feed off each other, as the program's repeated installments of a "War on Christmas" or "Ground Zero Mosque" become, in essence, hysterical. And as with all hysterical performances in American history—Puritan witch hunts, early twentieth-century temperance movements, hearings seeking post-war Communists in the military, claims of secret Muslims in the White House—those who participate in them generally come to believe they have "found" what they have created through their performances. In short, *Fox & Friends* performs an ideological, often hysterical view of the world, and in the process, transforms that world through its dramatic rendering.

By branding itself conservative, and performing that ideology twenty-four hours daily within an array of programming types, Fox has now become a central rhetorical force in articulating and asserting a conservative ideological worldview. But *Fox & Friends* is more than just another programming venue for the channel's ideological appeals. The program has radically altered the morning talk genre in significant ways, in particular the important role the genre has traditionally played in offering viewers some degree of what Roger Silverstone calls "ontological security," or the feeling of trust—often achieved through habits and rituals such as watching television—that the chaotic world is not a direct threat to one's self-identity or to one's family.[21] Morning talk shows typically offer a relief of anxieties by integrating the family unit into the broader world of politics and consumption through its soft-news features, and vice versa, by taking the threats of the world and domesticating them through nonthreatening and noncontroversial performances of normality.

Fox & Friends offers ontological security, but not through normalizing the chaotic world. Quite the opposite, *F&F* destabilizes the world by presenting most of it as a threat to the viewers' values and ways of life. The show then provides the security found in an ideological worldview that aggressively and defiantly challenges those threats—all of which is normalized through the banter and group-think of the trio of hosts. Trust is achieved and equilibrium restored by speaking a language that everyone understands—not the elitist language of the learned, but the base level of smears, innuendo, and aggressive attacks on that which seems threatening. You know, just like in high school.

NOTES

1. See media watchdog Media Matters for an extensive history of Kilmead's sexism: http://mediamatters.org/mmtv/201111210001.
2. Carlson is a former Miss America pageant winner whom *The Daily Show with Jon Stewart* has critiqued for intentionally dumbing-down her on-screen persona to appease Fox viewers. See http://www.thedailyshow.com/watch/tue-december-8-2009/gretchen-carlson-dumbs-down.
3. These are the hosts for the weekday versions of the program, with alternate hosts serving weekend duties.
4. As one investigative journalist reported, "According to insiders, the morning show's anchors, who appear to be chatting ad-lib, are actually working from daily, structured talking points that come straight from the top. 'Prior to broadcast, Steve Doocy, Gretchen Carlson—that gang—they meet with [Fox President] Roger [Ailes],' says a former Fox deputy. 'And Roger gives them the spin.'" See Tim Dickinson, "How Roger Ailes Built the Fox News Fear Factory," *Rolling Stone*, May 25, 2011.
5. See Kathleen Hall Jamieson and Joseph N. Cappella, *Echo Chamber: Rush Limbaugh and the Conservative Media Establishment* (New York: Oxford University Press, 2008). See also Media Matters for America (http://mediamatters.org), a watchdog group dedicated to monitoring and reporting on right-wing media (in particular Fox).
6. "Fox News Viewed as Most Ideological Network," Pew Research Center for the People and the Press, October 29, 2009, http://www.people-press.org/2009/10/29/fox-news-viewed-as-most-ideological-network/.
7. James Loxley, *Performativity* (London: Routledge, 2007).
8. Jeffrey P. Jones, "I Want My Talk TV: Network Talk Shows in the Digital Universe," in

Beyond Prime Time: Television Programming in the Post-Network Era, Amanda Lotz ed. (New York: Routledge, 2009), 14–35.

9. For an account of the correlation between the rhetoric of fear in Fox's programming to that being sold by Fox's advertisers, see Mark Andrejevic, "Fox News: 'Don't Worry, Be Anxious,'" *In Media Res* (blog), April 2, 2007, http://mediacommons.futureofthebook.org/imr/2007/04/02/fox-news-dont-worry-be-anxious.

10. Media Matters dates Fox's creation of this "War on Christmas" to 2004, and notes that the organization has accumulated nearly 250 instances in Fox's programming. See http://mediamatters.org/blog/201112090008.

11. http://mediamatters.org/research/201103290023.

12. http://mediamatters.org/blog/201101050012.

13. http://mediamatters.org/blog/201109130010.

14. http://mediamatters.org/research/201112020017.

15. For the original formulation of the theory, see J. L. Austin, *How to Do Things with Words*, 2nd ed., J. O. Urmson and Marina Sbisa, eds. (Cambridge, MA: Harvard University Press, 1975). For a summary of performativity theory, including its relationship to other theories of performance, see Elizabeth Bell, *Theories of Performance* (Los Angeles: Sage, 2008).

16. Loxley, *Performativity*, 2.

17. The issue mysteriously and suddenly disappeared from Fox News after the election.

18. Less than a year earlier, a Fox News host publicly supported the project. See http://www.thedailyshow.com/watch/thu-august-19-2010/extremist-makeover---homeland-edition.

19. http://www.youtube.com/watch?v=1gMHP-OY5xs.

20. http://www.youtube.com/watch?v=fu4oMK8FQ2A. For similar visual framing using picture boxes to create visual cues of identification and discord, see http://www.youtube.com/watch?v=BqJj5nOPmWY.

21. Roger Silverstone, *Why Study the Media?* (Los Angeles: Sage, 1999), 118–19.

FURTHER READING

Auletta, Ken. "The Dawn Patrol: The Curious Rise of Morning Television, and the Future of Network News." *New Yorker*, August 8, 2005.

Bell, Elizabeth. *Theories of Performance*. Los Angeles: Sage, 2008.

Dickinson, Tim. "How Roger Ailes Built the Fox News Fear Factory." *Rolling Stone*, May 25, 2011.

Greenwald, Robert, and Alexandra Kitty. *Outfoxed: Rupert Murdoch's War on Journalism*. New York: The Disinformation Company, 2005.

Jamieson, Kathleen Hall, Jamieson and Joseph N. Cappella. *Echo Chamber: Rush Limbaugh and the Conservative Media Establishment*. New York: Oxford University Press, 2008)

Swint, Kerwin. *Dark Genius: The Influential Career of Legendary Political Operative and Fox News Founder Roger Ailes*. New York: Union Square Press, 2008.

21

M*A*S*H
Socially Relevant Comedy

NOEL MURRAY

Abstract: Long hailed as one of the most groundbreaking and politically engaged sitcoms, *M*A*S*H* is a key text from 1970s television's "turn toward relevance." Noel Murray, writing in a journalistic style for the popular online criticism site *The A. V. Club*, discusses a distinctive episode from the series to highlight how the show used the past to talk about the present, and how we might look at the program's legacy on the rising culture wars of the 1980s.

Though we hold the ideal of the free press as sacrosanct in the United States, the supremacy of the First Amendment is sometimes challenged when it comes to television. Music, movies, fine art, and printed material can be produced and distributed independently by anyone who has the means, but there are only so many notches on a television dial and so much space on the broadcasting spectrum, which means that the major broadcasting conglomerates have to be licensed by governmental agencies with the authority to squelch broadcasting they find offensive or seditious—or at least to apply enough pressure that the networks make changes "voluntarily." The nature of the fight over who has the right (or privilege) to air his or her opinion has changed over the decades, but the fight itself still rages.

Case in point: in 1967, the *San Francisco Chronicle* and CBS Television commissioned a documentary called *Inside North Vietnam*, made by British journalist Felix Greene, which showed the North Vietnamese as bloody but unbowed, and depicted them in a far more human light than any report that was coming out of the U.S. State Department at the time. CBS declined to air the film, but licensed it to the National Educational Television network, the forerunner of PBS. When news leaked that *Inside North Vietnam* was going to be broadcast, a group of congressmen drafted a letter of protest to NET president John White, suggesting that his decision to air "Communist propaganda" made him unfit to serve in a post funded by tax dollars.

Yet even with congressmen threatening legislation, television still began to question the United States' involvement in Vietnam in the late 1960s and early 1970s—first with detached skepticism, then with outright hostility. By the time U.S. troops drew down in 1975, it would have been hard to find anyone on primetime TV who openly supported the war, outside of maybe Bob Hope. The CBS sitcom *M*A*S*H* (1972–1983) wasn't explicitly about Vietnam, though like the movie that inspired the show (and the novel that inspired the movie), it did debut while the war was in full swing. *M*A*S*H* used the Korean War as a stage from which to comment on the futility of *all* war, and the inherent madness of military life no matter the era or specific conflict.

The *M*A*S*H* episode "The Interview" (February 24, 1976), which aired at the tail end of the series' fourth season, confronted the question of whether war has any value head on, via direct-to-the-camera addresses by the show's main characters framed by a fictional journalist making a wartime documentary. At one point in "The Interview," the men of the 4077th M*A*S*H unit in Korea are asked whether any kind of special medical or technical developments are coming out of the war. Here are their replies:

> COLONEL SHERMAN T. POTTER: Oh, there are some things that get a practical trying out here that maybe wouldn't with the same speed back home, but when you counterbalance that with the frightful expense, the frightful destruction and loss of life, I don't think it's an equal balance.
>
> MAJOR FRANK BURNS: Korea will become a shining example of the American policy of benign military intervention.
>
> CORPORAL MAX KLINGER: I think it's the most stupidest thing in the world. You call it a police action back home, right? Over here it's a war! Police action sounds like we're over here arresting people. Handing out parking tickets. War is just killin', that's all.

As a follow-up, when Colonel Potter is asked if he sees *anything* good coming out of the war, he snaps, "Not a damn thing," then glances at the camera, not sure whether he should apologize for swearing.

Though "The Interview" is based on an episode of *See It Now* (CBS, 1951–1958) in which Edward R. Murrow interviewed Marines in Korea at Christmastime, it has more in common with the cinema verité documentaries that emerged in the 1960s and 1970s. The use of jump cuts, the relaxed tone of the interviewees, and the frankness all convey "1976" more than they convey the early 1950s. "The Interview" would feel right at home on television today, in the age of the mockumentary format. The old colonel's awkward glance at the camera when he slips and says "damn" is like something out of *The Office*.

Also, while "The Interview" is an atypical *M*A*S*H* episode, it's still very *M*A*S*H*-like. After the opening credits, a voice informs us that the show will be in black-and-white; oddly, barely fifteen years after color became common-place on television, an episode in black-and-white was considered an event. Then Clete Roberts—a veteran broadcaster who was an actual war correspondent in the early 1950s—introduces the concept of the mobile surgical hospital and ex-plains that he's going to share with us his conversations with some of the person-nel, while warning that their saltier language might be bleeped. That's a curious warning on a meta level, given that in nearly every other episode of *M*A*S*H* viewers have seen these people in much more stressful situations than a television interview, and yet they've never said anything that had to be bleeped. Even more meta: while the interviewee's answers are meant to be off the cuff, many of their replies sound unusually quippy, as though they were scripted by a comedy writer.

And the kinds of questions that Clete Roberts asks in "The Interview" aren't so much the kinds of questions that a Korean War correspondent would ask a *M*A*S*H* unit as they are the kinds of questions that a fan of *M*A*S*H* would ask the show's characters. Writer-director Larry Gelbart, who helped develop the series and worked on it for the final time with "The Interview," built the episode through a combination of improvisation and scripting, letting the actors answer questions based on what they thought their characters would say. There's a dis-tinction between what Harry Morgan would say as Colonel Sherman T. Potter on the TV sitcom *M*A*S*H* in 1976 and what an actual commanding officer of a field hospital in Korea in 1951 would have said during the actual war—es-pecially to a TV reporter. The Korean War was a fascinating conflict: a foreign policy overreach on the part of an America so confident after the triumphs of World War II that its leaders failed to take into account how much they'd drained the military's resources in the years that immediately followed the surrenders of Germany and Japan. But outside of the occasional regional or historical refer-ence, *M*A*S*H* was never all that concerned with telling true-to-life stories about fighting and doctoring in Korea. After all, this was a show that took eleven years to depict a war that ended in three. So "The Korean War" on *M*A*S*H* became something existential and metaphorical, not actual.

None of the above is meant to denigrate *M*A*S*H*, "The Interview," or the work of Larry Gelbart—all of which are estimable. It's only to note that *M*A*S*H* had a different agenda than historical accuracy. It was about skewering authori-tarianism, advocating for simple human decency, and exploring the changing roles of women and men, all as seen from the perspective of its own time in the 1970s, not the 1950s.

What also made *M*A*S*H* special was that it had a look and feel unlike any of the other mature sitcoms that became popular in the early 1970s. It wasn't as warm

FIGURE 21.1.

War correspondent Clete Roberts introduces TV audiences to the 4077th in the documentary-style episode "The Interview."

and wry as *The Mary Tyler Moore Show* (CBS, 1970–1977) or *The Bob Newhart Show* (CBS, 1972–1978), and it wasn't as intense as the Norman Lear family of sitcoms such as *All in the Family* (CBS, 1971–1979) and *Maude* (CBS, 1972–1978). *M*A*S*H* was shot on a film studio lot, with no audience, and using a single-camera set-up, more like a feature film. It had a laugh track that the producers often fought to diminish or eliminate—notably, there's no laugh track in "The Interview." And while Robert Altman's 1970 movie featured naturalistic, overlapping dialogue, Gelbart—who honed his chops working for Sid Caesar during TV's first decade—was more classically showbiz, favoring gags and punchlines.

The cast of *M*A*S*H* was a mix of old Hollywood types and actors who fit more with the 1970s "New Hollywood." Loretta Swit was off doing a play when this episode was shot, but "The Interview" features the rest of the show's core players. Alan Alda as surgeon Benjamin "Hawkeye" Pierce became known as the quintessential "sensitive man" in the touchy-feely 1970s, even though his most famous character is a womanizer, and a bit of a jerk. Mike Farrell is much more sensitive as the soft-hearted surgeon B. J. Hunnicutt, self-described in "The Interview" as "a temporarily mis-assigned civilian." Harry Morgan had been playing grizzled characters for decades in Hollywood genre movies (and on TV's *Dragnet*) before he took on Colonel Potter, and he positioned the CO as a jaded paternal type, as though he'd wandered in from some old war movie. Larry Linville as Major Burns spoofed paternalistic arrogance, showing how people who are convinced they're right about everything have been insufferable in every era. William Christopher and Jamie Farr were both steadily employed character actors in the 1960s on television and in movies, and didn't venture too far from their types as Father Mulcahy and Corporal Klinger—the former meek and kind, the latter brash and earthy. And Gary Burghoff as company clerk Radar O'Reilly was the lone *M*A*S*H* regular who also appeared in the movie, and had the kind of low-key, quirky presence that Altman loved.

Here are Linville, Alda, Morgan, Farrell, and Burghoff at work, answering on behalf of their characters the question, "What do you miss most from home?"

> MAJOR BURNS: [Long pause.] Well, my family of course. My wife, my chil-
> dren. . . . They're my strength! I'm one of those that feels that marriage is
> the headstone of American society.
>
> CAPTAIN PIERCE: Pistachio ice cream . . . and bananas. And pancakes, I miss.
> And bacon frying. I miss the smell of bacon in the morning, waking up to
> that. It's a long time since I smelled that.
>
> COLONEL POTTER: I miss my wife, of course. I miss my son, my daughter-in-
> law. I have a new baby grandchild, I haven't seen her, I'd like to. But one
> of the things I miss the most is people my own age for companionship.
> I'm old enough to be the father of almost everyone around here, and then
> some. You just miss being able to sit around and chew the fat with some-
> body your own age, somebody with your own background. Well, not back-
> ground, but your own experiences.
>
> CAPTAIN HUNNICUTT: I've got a lot of lost time to make up to my family.
> The Bay area, San Francisco, specifically Mill Valley, is where I live. That's
> where Peg is, and my daughter, Erin. She's lovely. She squeezes your nose.
>
> CORPORAL O'REILLY: Well, first thing I want to do is see my mom. And then
> I got this '49 Chevy that I'm fixin' up. A neighbor swapped me it for one of
> my pregnant sows, y'know. . . . Ottumwa, Iowa. Nobody famous ever came
> from there, except once Eleanor Roosevelt's car got stalled at our train
> crossing. Some people heard the screaming and they said, "That sounds
> just like Eleanor Roosevelt!"

The way Burghoff delivers the punchline of his story ("That sounds just like El-eanor Roosevelt!") differs from how Linville delivers his ("I'm one of those that feels that marriage is the headstone of American society"). One *sounds* like a punchline; the other sounds more natural and whimsical. Neither is preferable, necessarily, just different. But Burghoff's performance—or maybe just the way his character was written—gives him the flexibility to make a joke elsewhere in "The Interview" about how whenever the wooden latrines give him slivers, "you really find out who your friends are," and then later to deliver a heartbreaking mono-logue about turning away Korean orphans who need medicine and food. In that monologue, Burghoff as Radar also says, "That's where it's really at, y'know?"—a bit of slang which adds to the feeling that *M*A*S*H* has its head more in the 1970s than the 1950s.

FIGURE 21.2.
Off-the-cuff comments from Alan Alda's "Hawkeye" Pierce articulate 1970s attitudes about war and military life more so than those of the 1950s.

"The Interview" offers a mix of those poignant monologues and quickie one-liners, all allowing Gelbart to deliver his last *M*A*S*H* thoughts on war in general and these characters in particular. Klinger gets to give one more shout-out to Tony Packo's in Toledo, home of "the greatest Hungarian hot dogs." Hunnicutt gets to express his admiration for the nurses for doing "man's work" and to describe how on his first day at the 4077th, he performed three amputations before he had his first breakfast. Potter gets to say that his heroes are Abe Lincoln and Harry Truman, and that he won't take advantage of the opportunity to say hello to his wife and family because "it's not dignified." And Father Mulcahy gets to say that he's looking forward to going home someday to "run the CYO." He also gets to deliver one of the most memorable speeches in *M*A*S*H* history:

> "When the doctors cut into a patient, and it's cold, y'know, the way it is now, today . . . steam rises from the body. And the doctor will . . . will warm himself, over the open wound. Could anyone look on that and not feel changed?"

Mulcahy's talking about doctors warming themselves over open wounds complicates some of the main questions often asked about *M*A*S*H*, then and now: Is the show harsh enough when it comes to the realities of war? Is it *too* harsh? Robert Altman used to complain that the TV series had sanitized and cuted-up his more anarchic film. (Of course, Altman was also annoyed that his son Mike made more money for writing the show's theme song "Suicide Is Painless" than Altman ever made for directing the movie.) Sam Fuller, meanwhile, used to say that it was impossible to make any movie or TV show that was truly anti-war, because even the most raw-looking production would become "another goddamn recruitment film" to young men who wanted to prove they could handle the mayhem. And yet Mulcahy's speech defies the conventional wisdom about anti-war statements. It's so matter-of-fact, and melancholy, and not in the least bit attractive or soft.

At one point in "The Interview," Roberts asks the people of the 4077th if war was ever glamorous to them, and Hawkeye responds that his experiences have shaken him so much that he can't read Hemingway any more. But Hawkeye also gives a reason why war might have some lasting value when he describes his colleagues as the "finest kind" (a Hawkeye-ism held over from Richard Hooker's original novel, as well as the movie). And when B.J. is asked whether he's planning to maintain any of his 4077th friendships once he leaves Korea, he says he's torn between honoring those relationships and forgetting this whole chapter of his life.

Regular *M*A*S*H* viewers felt at home at the 4077th, no matter how miserable the characters were. Fans knew every character's hometown, and may have pined right along with them when they waxed rhapsodic about Ottumwa or Crabapple Cove, even though those same fans were perfectly happy to spend time in Uijeongbu week after week—or even night after night once the show was sold into syndication. That reinforces what Hawkeye says in the closing montage of "The Interview":

A war is like when it rains in New York, and everybody crowds into doorways, y'know? And they all get chummy together. Perfect strangers. The only difference of course is in a war it's also raining on the other side of the street and the people who are chummy over there are trying to kill the people over here who are chums.

Did *M*A*S*H* make military life look both glorious and familial, or was the series so irreverent that it bordered on the unpatriotic? It's worth comparing "The Interview" to the *See It Now* episode that inspired it, in which Murrow tries once or twice to get the troops to say that their work in Korea is wasteful and pointless, though Murrow never pushes too hard and the Marines never stray off-message. In "The Interview," by contrast, Hawkeye talks about writing a sexually suggestive letter to Bess Truman, and complains that in the Army "the clothes are green, the food is green . . . except the vegetables," and says that in a war, to stay sane, "One thing you can do is to get out in the road when the jeeps are coming by and everybody sticks their foot out in front of the jeeps, and the last one to pull his foot in is the sane one." The character's contempt is palpable.

After Gelbart left *M*A*S*H*, the show maintained its excellence by and large, though there were times when the writers couldn't tell the difference between sophisticated storytelling and smug preachiness, and Alda's alternately sullen and snappish portrayal of Hawkeye did become distractingly rooted in Me Decade pop-psychology. And every time the show lost a character and added a new one, it tended to move further away from the farcical elements and broad comedy that Gelbart and his co-producer Gene Reynolds had used in the early seasons to balance the earnestness. (The quips, however, remained. The show was practically a punchline factory in its later years.)

And though M*A*S*H became a huge hit and an enduring favorite of TV fans and critics alike, there were times when its continued existence was as precarious as that of *Inside North Vietnam*. In 1974, FCC chairman Richard Wiley, in collaboration with the heads of the major networks, decided to forestall threatened action against the increasing maturity of TV content by drafting an industry-wide policy creating a "family hour" from 8 to 9 p.m. eastern time. The Writers Guild Of America filed a lawsuit, and at trial, Larry Gelbart testified that the "family hour" policy had produced a chilling effect on TV series with adult themes, and that he'd already had four previously approved M*A*S*H story proposals sent back for retooling by CBS. The judge on the case ultimately ruled that the "family hour" was a violation of the First Amendment, and was especially appalled when a network executive explained that the policy wasn't so much designed to safeguard children as it was to protect parents from being embarrassed when they watched these shows with their kids.

So the major TV creators of the 1970s, like Gelbart and Lear, remained free to keep exploring mature themes, and to express a political point of view that was unapologetically leftist, or at least flippant about traditional conservative American values. Their sensibility dominated television in the 1970s, and on into the decades that followed in syndication, and it was so pervasive that an entire generation of right-leaning people grew up feeling marginalized. Subsequent Republican politicians fought back by changing the media market, allowing individuals and corporations to increase their media holdings, and thus making rocking the boat less of a priority.

If Gelbart's intention was to advance a liberal message via popular entertainment, he succeeded, inasmuch as M*A*S*H became a long-running and beloved TV hit. The anti-authoritarian side won key battles in the 1960s and 1970s, not just politically, but in the court of public opinion, where progressive attitudes toward race relations, pacifism, feminism, and charity became entrenched as "the norm," with anyone standing in opposition automatically cast as a villain or a relic. But once the Vietnam War was over, the Culture War intensified. Gelbart, Lear, and their peers were helped some in their time by the perception that they were the underdogs, speaking out despite government-sponsored attempts to silence them. But massive success changed that perception. Subsequently, conservatives could claim the mantle of the righteously aggrieved, as they saw themselves portrayed as mean-spirited buffoons (and in primetime, no less). And so, just as they had in the 1950s, the Right pushed back, reopening a discussion on right and wrong that shows like *All In The Family* and *M*A*S*H* seemed to have settled. In the early days of television, the Right exerted pressure through legislation and oversight. More recently, they've emphasized the fundamental American sense of "fairness," arguing—rightly or wrongly—that the Hawkeyes have had their say, and that now it's time pass the microphone to Frank Burns.

FURTHER READING

Barker, David. "Television Production Techniques as Communication." *Television: The Critical View,* 6th ed. Horace Newcomb, ed. New York: Oxford University Press, 2000.

Barnouw, Erik. *Tube of Plenty: The Evolution of American Television,* 2nd ed. New York: Oxford University Press, 1990.

Diffrient, David Scott. *M*A*S*H.* Detroit, MI: Wayne State University Press, 2008.

Thompson, Ethan. "Comedy Verité? The Observational Documentary Meets the Televisual Sitcom." *The Velvet Light Trap* 60 (Fall 2007).

Wittebols, James H. *Watching M*A*S*H, Watching America: A Social History of the 1972–1983 Television Series.* Jefferson, NC: McFarland and Company, 1998.

22

Parks and Recreation
The Cultural Forum

HEATHER HENDERSHOT

Abstract: Throughout its history as a mass medium, network television strove for wide appeal, while also occasionally courting controversy. In this look at contemporary sitcom *Parks and Recreation*, Heather Hendershot considers how television might still function as a site for negotiating controversial topics and modeling civic engagement, even in an era of niche programming when there seems to be less and less shared culture.

In their landmark 1983 essay "Television as a Cultural Forum," Horace Newcomb and Paul M. Hirsch argue that television provides a space to express collective cultural concerns. To put it simply, TV's stories gravitate to issues in which we are all interested. This "we" might at first sound a bit fishy to someone reading the essay today. After all, in a fragmented, post-network environment, most TV targets rather specific, narrow interests: cooking, travel, pets, home improvement, classic films, and so on. But in the pre-cable days, programs did generally seek out large groups of viewers, not atomized constituencies. The American audience had a sense of collectivity insofar as "we" all saw the same shows. Whether or not you liked the miniseries *Roots* (ABC, 1977), it was a major phenomenon, and you might watch it just to be in the loop. And if the president made a speech, it was on all three channels; you could only escape it if you turned off the tube. Watching TV by no means guaranteed that we were better citizens, but it did make us feel like we were, to some extent, all on the same page, even if we disagreed about what belonged on that page or what the page meant.

Newcomb and Hirsch explain that a single program might be of interest to viewers holding a wide range of political perspectives. Feminists watching *Charlie's Angels* (ABC, 1976–1981) upon its initial release might have disparaged the show's display of jiggle and its silly sexual banter, while more conservative viewers might have reacted negatively to exactly the same factors, albeit for different reasons. Rather than imperiously declaring the program "really" to be liberal, conservative, or simply exploitative, the authors find it more interesting to observe that different viewers made their own meanings of a text that tapped into an issue of general interest—namely, the rise of the working woman.

In discussing an episode of *Father Knows Best* (CBS, 1954, 1958–1960; NBC, 1955–1958) that seems to support the notion that women should work in traditionally male professions (daughter Betty wants to be an engineer), only to backtrack with a disappointing heteronormative conclusion (Betty decides to date an engineer instead), Newcomb and Hirsch wonder to what extent the cursory ending actually cancels out the preceding twenty-five minutes. (In fact, years later the author of the script for that episode, Roz Rogers, said that the ending, which had been tacked on in order to reach a quick resolution, "did not ring true" for him.[1]) Certainly, individual viewers will make what they will of the episode's conservative conclusion. The truly interesting thing, then, is not whether the show is actually pro- or anti-feminist, but, rather, the fact that a putatively "innocuous" show even debates the issue of gender roles.

Newcomb and Hirsch's essay still contains much of value for contemporary readers, especially for the historically minded. Particularly interesting is the authors' turn to discussing activists: "In forming special interest groups, or in using such groups to speak about television, citizens actually enter the [cultural] forum. Television shoves them toward action, toward expression of ideas and values."[2] The very idea of reformers seeking to improve television is one of the most dated aspects of the essay, and it is precisely this datedness that is fascinating. A wide range of citizen-reformers—African Americans, gays and lesbians, antiabortion advocates, pro-choice advocates, fundamentalist Christians—sought to influence network programming throughout the 1960s, 1970s, and 1980s.[3] While one should not romanticize or overvalue such activism—it was hardly "typical" viewer behavior—it is important to remind ourselves, in this age of obsessive presentism and futurism, that very different approaches to interacting with media existed in the past, and that in the days of only three networks it was easy to spot controversy and to feel personally invested in the outcome. Was your favorite show in danger of cancellation because of pressure group activism? Was that show really immoral, racist, sexist, homophobic, or whatever was being claimed by irate protestors?

Today, with hundreds of channels on offer, it is difficult for a program to generate high-profile controversy, and viewers may find that politically challenging series are easy to ignore.[4] Previously, as Newcomb put it in an interview in 2007, TV made you "confront your beliefs." Such confrontation was central to the cultural forum model and, thus, specific to the network era; in a niche-viewing environment, however, viewers tend to gravitate to content that matches their preexisting interests. Narrowly targeted niche TV thus provides "self-confirmation," leaving little room for the old cultural forum ideal of ideas in conflict.[5]

What place, then, might programs with potentially "controversial" political aspirations have in today's televisual environment? Can programs hope to address—or even confront, challenge, or offend—a "mass" rather than a "niche" audience, or does our narrowcasting environment ensure that politically ambitious programs preach to the choir? If the old cultural forum idea truly fizzled out with the decline of the dominance of the Big Three networks, would any series dare to speak to a heterogeneous audience? There is at least one program that strives to do exactly this: *Parks and Recreation* (NBC, 2009–present). Celebrating the virtues of local government and staking a claim for the value of civic engagement and the possibility of collaboration—or at least peaceful coexistence—between different political camps, *Parks and Recreation* offers a liberal pluralist response to the fragmented post–cultural forum environment.

Appearing at a moment of right-wing resurgence—with Tea Partiers calling for the elimination of social welfare programs, extolling the virtues of gun ownership, and opposing gay marriage—*Parks and Recreation* offers a retort to the Right by insisting that government is a positive force that provides necessary, basic services. In advancing its argument, the show makes a few interesting maneuvers. First, it avoids direct confrontation with highly polarizing issues like abortion and focuses instead on municipal rather than state or federal government issues. Second, it insists that local government should be politically neutral; providing services does not count as "liberalism," per se, the show insists. Third, through its characters of varying political stripes, the program conveys the basic goodness of public servants. Fourth, it celebrates the virtues of the public sphere, a utopian space where even irrational debate can produce social harmony, or at least the kinds of *truces* that enable society to function. Two episodes in particular, "Pawnee Zoo" and "Time Capsule," illustrate how *Parks and Recreation* gently conveys a liberal perspective without ever naming it as such.

Before turning to these episodes, it will be helpful to discuss the two characters at the political heart of the program, Leslie Knope and Ron Swanson. Leslie, the deputy director of the Parks and Recreation Department in Pawnee, Indiana, does not overtly identify herself as a liberal, claiming that Pawnee's public servants are expected to be neutral (a local garbage collector, she notes, was suspended for wearing an anti-cancer Livestrong bracelet). Her office is decorated with photos of powerful women, from left, right, and center—Bella Abzug, Madeleine Albright, Condoleezza Rice, Hillary Clinton, Nancy Pelosi. Leslie's love for her job and bottomless optimism are virtually unmatched on TV; only SpongeBob SquarePants out-enthuses Leslie Knope. Leslie's work ethic, I would argue, is a crucial "conservative" aspect of her character; liberals don't devalue hard work, but the celebration of individual achievement and meritocratic rewards is certainly a cornerstone of contemporary conservative values. Today's televisual landscape is littered with cynical characters who hate their jobs, with housewives (real, desperate, or otherwise) lacking career objectives, and with drunken, fornicating twenty-somethings with no visible source of income. In Leslie, by contrast, we find a character who earnestly embraces a can-do work ethic and keeps her sex life relatively private. So, on the one hand, Leslie resonates with certain conservative values, and *Parks and Recreation* as a whole is distinctive for its emphasis on the civic virtue of hard work. On the other hand, Leslie's cheerful understanding of government as a public good can only be construed as liberal in the current political climate. Conservatives will find in Leslie someone who sees hard work as the cornerstone of happiness, yet who works for "the enemy," the government.

While it would be reductive to construe *Parks and Recreation* only as a response to the current surge in right-wing anti-government sentiment, this clearly must be understood as one key aspect of the program, and Ron Swanson, Leslie's boss, is the linchpin of that response. Director of Pawnee's Parks and Recreation Department, Ron works for the government but is explicitly anti-government. In fact, he favors privatizing parks and having corporations run them, citing Chuck E. Cheese's as a business model. His drive for privatization is portrayed as flawed, yet the series works hard to keep the character likeable; Ron is not vilified for his beliefs. Indeed, while Ron is consistently "masculine" (sexy, if you will), he is never misogynist; drawn to powerful women, he goes to "an inordinate number of WNBA games." He and Leslie disagree about many things, but he is more often her ally than her foil.

Ron can be understood as a Tea Partier—though he is never named as such—insofar as he echoes and satirizes many of their positions ("child labor laws are ruining this country"), but one must also bear in mind that the Tea Party is a disjointed movement, not a centralized organization with a strictly coherent platform. Movement participants range from libertarians on one end to evangelical Christians on the other. While these two contingents likely agree about taxation and gun control, they may strongly disagree about abortion and gay marriage. *Parks and Recreation* pulls its punches, clearly, by establishing Ron as a libertarian, not a social/religious conservative, and by allowing him to attack taxation and celebrate gun-ownership without ever mentioning issues such as reproductive rights. However, though such issues remain unspoken, it is hard to imagine Ron meddling in the personal decisions of others, as he is strictly concerned with individual liberties. Pawnee is the fourth most obese city in America, but for the local government to encourage good health, he contends, would be wrong: "The whole point of this country is if you want to eat garbage, balloon up to six hundred pounds and die of a heart attack at forty-three, you can. You are free to do so. To me, that's beautiful" ("Sweetums," February 4, 2010).

Thus, Ron and Leslie offer something to both conservative and liberal viewers, even if the show ultimately lampoons the conservative-libertarian perspective and privileges a liberal one. It is important to stress that what we find here is not the "balanced" approach that was typical of the network era, when a conservative character would be countered by the presence of a liberal character. Nor do we find the common post-network "something for everyone" approach in which shows assemble a heterogeneous crew of characters to attempt to appeal to a wide range of viewers. One reason that programs such as *Heroes* and *Lost* use highly diverse ensemble casts is to lure a post-network version of the "mass" audience. As *Heroes* writer Jesse Alexander puts it, "if you don't like the cheerleader, you'll like someone else."[6] The hope is that a diverse cast will appeal to numerous demographics, with one "mass" show theoretically providing "niche"-like self-confirmation. *Parks and Recreation*, by contrast, does not simply use Leslie to appeal to the Left and Ron to appeal to the Right. Rather, it shows how opposing factions can communicate and collaborate.

If Ron and Leslie embody the program's dialectical political aspirations, season 2's "Pawnee Zoo" (September 17, 2009) is perhaps the episode that most specifically encapsulates the show's political perspective. The episode opens with Leslie choreographing a "cute" event to create publicity for the zoo: she officiates at the wedding of two penguins, Tux and Flipper. The birds consummate their marriage *immediately* upon being pronounced "husband and wife," and one of the children in the crowd of onlookers asks the zookeeper if they are making a baby. He responds that, no, these are two *male* penguins, so they really should have been pronounced "husband and husband." Having accidentally performed Pawnee's first gay marriage, Leslie is celebrated by the local gay community, while the local conservative evangelicals from the Society for Family Stability Foundation attack her, explaining that "when gay people get married, it ruins it for the rest of us." Leslie had not intended to do anything controversial, having assumed that the penguins were male and female, and she tries to decline the celebration held for her at a gay bar, but she finds herself swept away by the drinking and dancing. Meanwhile, the pro-family activists demand that she both annul the penguin marriage and resign from her job. Leslie stands up for herself on the local talk show, *Pawnee Today*, and the episode ends with Leslie delivering Flipper and Tux to a zoo in Iowa, where gay marriage is legal.

"Pawnee Zoo" is clearly a product of the post-network era insofar as the program raises a "controversial issue" without neatly resolving it. When overtly addressing controversial issues, network era programs tended to insist that each side (there were generally only *two* sides) had to "learn a valuable lesson" from

FIGURE 22.1.
Leslie visits the
penguins at the zoo,
where anti-gay activ-
ists have proclaimed,
"It's Flipper and
Eve, not Flipper and
Steve!"

the other. Leslie and the anti-gay marriage activists don't exchange ideas in order to become better people, as per the formula of earlier shows. Notably, though, Leslie does learn a lesson from Flipper and Tux that she can apply to her own life: her would-be lover Mark is not her "gay penguin" (penguins mate for life), but maybe Mark is destined to be her friend Ann's "gay penguin," so Leslie realizes she must relax about her friends dating each other. It's all a bit silly—this is a comedy after all—but it's also quite smart. Rather than jumping up on a soapbox and speechifying in favor of gay marriage, Leslie simply respects the right of two penguins to be in love, and she extends this respect to others. This sort of character improvement evokes the old days of network TV, reminding us that *Parks and Recreation* may not actually reach a huge mass audience, but it *is* on NBC, where advertising stakes are higher than they would be elsewhere and where even a rather unusual show like *Parks and Recreation* is unlikely to be too "edgy."

Notably, the protest that might have arisen in the network era is worked into "Pawnee Zoo" itself, with the Society for Family Stability Foundation's humorless spokesperson Marcia Langman standing in for the angry activist groups that used to come out of the woodwork when a program dared to address gay issues. "Pawnee Zoo" doesn't expect the Moral Majority to rise from the grave to attack it; but by representing right-wing protest within its fictional world, it conveys the notion that if the Christian Right would actually *notice* this gutsy show, they might reasonably be provoked.

Sadly, although both the Gay and Lesbian Alliance Against Defamation and TV critics praised "Pawnee Zoo," almost no one else noticed the Flipper and Tux affair. In fact, the ratings for *Parks and Recreation* have been consistently poor. "Pawnee Zoo" would seem to raise issues of wide interest—the old cultural forum idea—and years ago the Religious Right would have jumped on it, just as they jumped on *Soap*'s gay character in 1977 and, later, on the lesbian kiss on

Roseanne in 1994. But why attack "Pawnee Zoo," an episode that appears to have made so little impact? We end up with the old "if a tree falls in the woods . . . " koan: if a program raises important issues, but no one is watching, does it matter? Provisionally, I would argue that in a multichannel and multiplatform age of widely dispersed content, programs often find their audiences gradually over time. Given that many people now watch programs whenever and wherever they want, ratings are simply no longer a very useful gauge (if they ever truly were) for determining the impact of a program. Viewers looking for smart, funny TV will make their way to *Parks and Recreation* eventually—if not soon enough to guarantee the show a long life on NBC. Setting aside such speculation, it is worth marveling at the episode's efforts to humorously portray the collision of liberals and conservatives around the gay marriage issue, and to do so without bitterness. Though siding with gay rights, the program does not hate "the other side." Rather, it contends that some differences are probably irreconcilable; we simply have to find a way to get along, even if we cannot change each other's minds.

"Time Capsule" (February 3, 2011) is a more didactic episode. Leslie is gathering items for a time capsule representing the Pawnee of 2011, and a local citizen suggests that she include a copy of Stephanie Meyer's *Twilight*. Leslie counters that *Twilight* is not really about Pawnee, but the insistent citizen will not give up. To resolve the question of what belongs in the capsule, Leslie calls a public forum—or, as Ron describes it, a "crackpot convention"—to debate the issue. In the process, the episode presents a comic version of the public sphere as conceptualized by social theorist Jürgen Habermas, who proposed that rational discussion and debate enables democracy to function. Critics of the Habermasian ideal have noted its limits: members of "the public" who speak from a position of privilege are more likely to be heard than those who speak from a disempowered position. In other words, the public sphere should be a level playing field, but it rarely is.[7]

In the would-be utopia of Pawnee, though, everyone's voice is heard. Indeed, Leslie considers listening to her constituents' complaints to be a highlight of her job. Predictably enough, sourpuss Marcia Langman reappears and complains that *Twilight* is anti-Christian and contains "strong sexual overtones" and a "tremendous amount of quivering." A ticked-off member of the National Civil Liberties Association, conversely, complains about the book's "overt Christian themes." Leslie's first solution to the time capsule crisis—acquiesce to everyone's demands and create multiple capsules to hold the Bible, urns containing ashes of beloved pets, the Bill of Rights, baseball cards, and *Crazy from the Heat* (the David Lee Roth story)—is not practical. A colleague tells Leslie that he finds the whole discussion "kind of impressive. I've been to a lot of towns, and usually people don't care about anything. I mean, don't get me wrong, these people are weirdoes, but they're weirdoes who care." This inspires Leslie to put only one item in the time capsule, a video recording of the public forum. In a speech addressed to those opening the capsule in the future, Leslie explains that "This is truly what life was like. A lot of people, with a lot of opinions, arguing passionately for what they believed in." She thus acknowledges that it is *conversation* (rational or not, loud or soft) that keeps democracy alive. Ultimately, the episode offers a humorous civics lesson in what a public sphere could look like.[8]

The televisual cultural forum that Newcomb and Hirsch identified so long ago may not exist today, but *Parks and Recreation* suggests that we *should* respond to the issues it raises. In effect, the show models how controversy and debate can function in a democracy. The message is a decidedly centrist one: extremes of both left and right can coexist, but only a moderate approach can resolve our problems. While one might argue that *Parks and Recreation* lessens its political efficacy by advocating "middle of the road" solutions, it is precisely its insistence upon keeping its politics understated, coupled with its insistence upon the humorousness of extremism (and the humorlessness of extremists), that makes *Parks and Recreation* work particularly well as a retort to the rising tide of right-wing, anti-government sentiment. The lesson offered, as Leslie might declare with naive optimism, is that liberals and conservatives can work together within local government—perhaps even sharing a plate of waffles—in order to make the world a better place.

Thirty years ago, Newcomb and Hirsch sought to transcend conventional left-right debates over TV, where one side argued that the medium was one of indoctrination into hegemonic beliefs, and the other argued that TV undercut traditional values. They shifted the discussion to claim that TV's emphasis was on "process rather than product, on discussion rather than indoctrination, on contradiction and confusion rather than coherence."[9] This was the essence of their conception of television as a cultural forum. And this is the essence of *Parks and Recreation*'s vision of a healthy democratic society.

NOTES

1. Rogers cited in Nina C. Leibman, *Living Room Lectures: The Fifties Family in Film and Television* (Austin: University of Texas Press, 1995), 49.

2. Horace Newcomb and Paul M. Hirsch, "TV as a Cultural Forum," in Horace Newcomb, ed. *Television: The Critical View,* 6th ed. (New York: Oxford University Press, 2000), 570.

3. Kathryn C. Montgomery, *Target: Prime Time: Advocacy Groups and the Struggle over Entertainment Television* (New York: Oxford University Press, 1990).

4. Heather Hendershot, "'You Know How It is with Nuns': Religion and Television's Sacred/Secular Fetuses," in Diane Winston, ed. *Small Screen, Big Picture: Television and Lived Religion* (Baylor, TX: Baylor University Press, 2009). The Parents Television Council (PTC)

and the Gay and Lesbian Alliance Against Defamation (GLAAD) are the only high-profile advocacy groups currently stoking audience protest. PTC encourages citizens to submit complaints about explicit sexual material to the FCC, while GLAAD protests negative images of gays, but also strives for a non-censorious image by honoring programs that offer positive gay/lesbian stories and characters.

5. "Horace Newcomb in Conversation with Tara McPherson," *e-media studies* 1, 1 (2007), http://journals.dartmouth.edu/cgi-bin/WebObjects/Journals.woa/2/xmlpage/4/article/320.

6. Jesse Alexander, "Cult Media" panel, Futures of Entertainment 2, MIT conference, November 16–17, 2007.

7. Craig Calhoun, ed. *Habermas and the Public Sphere* (Cambridge, MA: MIT Press, 1993).

8. One might argue that this episode problematically implies that the civically engaged are kooks who must be kept in line by officials. I read the community meeting more as a send-up of how difficult it is for opinionated people to get things done. Anyone who has ever attended a contentious faculty meeting should be able to able to identify with Leslie's frustration. Further, season 4's campaign manager, Jennifer Barkley, drives home a key theme: passionate people may be nutty, but it is the dispassionate we should most fear when it comes to politics. Leslie runs for office because she believes in something; for Barkley, politics is just a job.

9. Newcomb and Hirsch, "TV as a Cultural Forum," 564.

FURTHER READING

Cowan, Geoffrey. *See No Evil: The Backstage Battle over Sex and Violence in Television.* New York: Touchstone, 1980.

Gitlin, Todd. "Prime Time Ideology: The Hegemonic Process in Television Entertainment." In Horace Newcomb, ed. *Television: The Critical View,* 6th ed. New York: Oxford University Press, 2000).

Levine, Elana. *Wallowing in Sex: The New Sexual Culture of 1970s American Television.* Durham, NC: Duke University Press, 2006.

23

Star Trek
Serialized Ideology

ROBERTA PEARSON

Abstract: Fictional television, especially from the allegorical genre of science fiction, frequently offers commentary on contemporary events, inviting us to read a single episode as a critique of current affairs. However, Roberta Pearson cautions us not to decontextualize an episode from the larger scope of a series and its established characters and relationships by using two episodes from the *Star Trek* franchise to offer nuanced analyses of the program's ideological commentary.

From the very beginning, the *Star Trek* television franchise—*Star Trek: The Original Series* (NBC, 1966–1969), *Star Trek: The Next Generation* (syndicated, 1987–1994), *Star Trek: Deep Space Nine* (syndicated, 1993–2000), *Star Trek: Voyager* (UPN, 1995–2002), and *Star Trek: Enterprise* (UPN, 2001–2005)—addressed some of the major social and cultural issues of the times, ranging from race and gender to war and terrorism. For example, *The Original Se*ries featured the first interracial kiss on network television ("Plato's Stepchildren," November 15, 1968) as well as a racial conflict that destroyed an entire civilization ("Let That Be Your Last Battlefield," January 10, 1969), while *Deep Space Nine* and *Voyager* broke ground with a black and female captain respectively. Yet scholars writing about the social and cultural meanings of *Star Trek* have frequently viewed the programs as complicit with patriarchy, American imperialism, and other practices benefitting the society's most powerful elements.[1] For the most part, these scholars have operated on the basis of what we might term the "reflection paradigm," assuming that a program originating from a particular society will automatically reflect that society's dominant assumptions. The reflection paradigm presupposes a direct connection between the society and the text, but fails to take into account the ways in which the specific characteristics of a fictional text can refract rather than directly reflect dominant assumptions.

As Horace Newcomb and Paul M. Hirsch argue in their article "Television as a Cultural Forum," television drama debates rather than reproduces a culture's dominant assumptions:

> The conflicts we see in television drama, embedded in familiar and nonthreatening frames, are conflicts ongoing in American social experience and cultural history. In a few cases we might see strong perspectives that argue for the absolute correctness of one point of view or another. But for the most part the rhetoric of television drama is the rhetoric of discussion. . . . We see statements about the issues and it should be clear that ideological positions can be balanced within the forum by others from a different perspective.[2]

Television drama's storytelling mode lends itself to the presentation of multiple perspectives on social and cultural issues. By contrast with most cinema, television drama features recurring characters whose personalities become familiar to viewers watching them over the course of a season or over several years. And by contrast with most cinema's single protagonists, television drama features ensemble casts composed of characters who, to provide maximum dramatic potential, tend to be quite distinct from each other. A diverse and varied crew has been a *Star Trek* hallmark since *The Original Series*, with demographic oppositions of male and female, youth and maturity, human and non-human, and white and non-white. Emotional oppositions also structure the crew's makeup: Spock's cool logic versus McCoy's warm compassion; Picard's reserve versus Riker's easy charm; Data's rationality versus Worf's hotheadedness; Odo's integrity versus Quark's lack of scruples. When an episode tackles a controversial social issue, the diverse range of characters in each of the *Trek* series can voice a diverse range of views rather than simply reflecting the society's dominant assumptions. And since these diverse and sometimes controversial opinions are voiced by familiar and even beloved characters, viewers may be more inclined to consider positions differing from their own. From an analytic perspective, this means that television episodes cannot be considered in isolation from the broader series into which they accumulate. Rather than selecting single episodes most likely to conform to the ideological reflection paradigm, critics should understand how a single episode fits into a cumulative storyworld.

The rest of this essay illustrates the ways in which television drama's ensemble casts debate rather than reproduce dominant social assumptions by focusing on two *Star Trek* episodes which were created during different historical periods and concern particularly sensitive social issues: "A Private Little War" (*The Original Series* [*TOS*], February 2, 1968), dealing with the Vietnam War, and "The High Ground" (*The Next Generation* [*TNG*], January 29, 1990), tackling terrorism. "A

Private Little War" is one of *TOS*'s most direct engagements with contemporary political debates, with the central Federation/Klingon confrontation representing a very thinly disguised Vietnam War metaphor.[3] In the episode, Kirk returns to a primitive planet that he first visited thirteen years ago as a young lieutenant. He discovers an ongoing conflict between the planet's inhabitants, the villagers and the hill people, the former armed with flintlocks given to them by the Klingons. The Klingons have disturbed a Garden of Eden, which, Kirk argues, would have developed into a remarkably civilized culture if not for their intrusion into planetary politics. Kirk articulates the contemporary dominant rational for the U.S. presence in Vietnam: Americans were not embroiling themselves in a civil war but fighting Communist outsiders to restore stability. Kirk decides to re-establish the balance of power by giving the hill people their own flintlocks, his strategy clearly linked to the Cold War policy of brinksmanship and mutually assured destruction. McCoy vehemently contests this decision. The emotional and compassionate doctor opposes the pragmatic captain as they debate Federation intervention on the planet (and metaphorically American intervention in Vietnam):

K: We must equalize both sides again.

M: You're condemning the whole planet to a war that may never end.

K: Do you remember the 20th century brush wars on the Asian continent? Two great powers involved, not unlike the Klingons and ourselves. Neither side felt they could pull out.

M: I remember it well. It went on year after bloody year.

K: But what would you have suggested? That one side arm its friends with an overpowering weapon? Mankind would never have lived to travel space if they had. No, the only solution is what happened back then. Balance of power. The trickiest, dirtiest game of them all, but the only one that preserves both sides.

In spite of this argument, the captain is seen to have lingering reservations when at episode's end he orders Scotty to make a hundred flintlocks—"serpents for the Garden of Eden." "A Private Little War" offers opposing viewpoints on the planetary conflict (and by implication on the Vietnam conflict), but seems constrained by a contemporary political climate in which the anti-war movement had yet to make a significant impact upon politicians or the public.

The inclusion of the cool and rational Spock, exiled to sickbay at the episode's beginning by a shot from one of the villager's muskets, might have resulted in a more vigorous debate of the society's dominant assumption concerning American involvement in Vietnam. The episode fails to take full advantage of the well-established relationship among the program's three central characters, with

FIGURE 23.1.
Deciding to intervene
in a conflict on a primi-
tive planet, Kirk teaches a
group of hill people how to
fire a flintlock.

McCoy's emotional and Spock's logical perspectives mediating Kirk's frequent tendency to kick ass first and ask questions later. The two-sided exchange between Kirk and McCoy tips the balance in favor of the captain. Kirk, in keeping with his pre-established tendencies toward military rather than diplomatic solutions, at least offers a resolution to the planetary conflict, however unsatisfactory it may be. In keeping with his pre-established traits of caring and compassion, McCoy laments condemning the planet to an eternal war but offers no alternative plan. Spock's sidelining simplifies the murky politics of the fictional world (and of the real world as well), as the two-sided debate between the militaristic Kirk and the soft-hearted McCoy resonates with the contemporary binary opposition between hard-headed hawks and bleeding-heart liberals. "A Private Little War" gestures towards television drama's capacity for debate, but does not fully embrace it.

More than twenty years later, in 1990, "The High Ground" explores the morality of terrorism, the writers perhaps less constrained by contemporary dominant opinions than their *TOS* counterparts since they were addressing an issue not then as high on the American political agenda as it has become since 2001. In the episode, the *Enterprise* delivers medical supplies to Rutia 4, a planet torn by conflict between the Rutians and the Ansata. The Ansata are carrying out continuous attacks on the Rutian populace to persuade the government to give them control of the western continent that they see as rightfully theirs. Seeking to involve the Federation in the conflict, the "terrorists" and their leader, Finn, kidnap first Dr. Crusher, then Captain Picard and then attempt to blow up the *Enterprise*. At episode's end, Commander Riker and the head of the Rutian security services,

Alexana Devos, rescue the Starfleet personnel. Finn, still hoping for Federation intervention, threatens to kill Picard, and Alexana shoots him dead.

Kent A. Ono, in a typical ideological critique, argues that *TNG* in general, and "The High Ground" in particular, unproblematically support American interests, with nationalism and "military authority as mechanisms for achieving the ultimate good" and Federation (for which read "American") logic reigning supreme.[4] But Ono has clearly selected an episode that he thinks most likely to support his argument, a mistake he then compounds by analyzing the episode in isolation from the *TNG* storyworld, most particularly the characters' relationships and backstories. This leads him to ignore the ways in which the ensemble cast voices various and opposing viewpoints, as well as the ways in which viewer familiarity with the characters might inflect interpretations. Ono argues that Captain Picard acts throughout the episode and, indeed throughout all of *TNG*, as the upholder of Federation (and American) patriarchy and imperialism. But in "The High Ground," Picard is not the hero—there isn't one, which is rather the point. "The High Ground" is the twelfth episode of *TNG*'s third season: the previous fifty-nine episodes had established the Picard character as the consummate, cultivated, and intellectual European, a man who highly values reason and civility. Picard's consistent and accumulated choices of action over these episodes had revealed him as a man of courage, integrity, compassion, courtesy, and rigid self-control. The captain serves as mentor to several of his crew: the ambitious Riker, who is learning the ways of command; the boy Wesley, who is learning to be a man; the caught-between-cultures Worf, who is learning to reconcile his Klingon inheritance with his human upbringing; and the android Data, who is learning to be human. These relationships highlight Picard's sensitivity and compassion, reinforcing his position as the crew's moral compass, the man to whom all the others look for orders and for guidance. In "The High Ground," however, the captain's resentment at the Ansata's kidnapping of Doctor Crusher and their threats to his ship cause him occasionally to act uncharacteristically; for the viewer familiar with the character from the previous episodes, this deviation from his pre-established behavior may undermine his interpretive authority.

The episode most directly questions Picard's objectivity in an interchange between him and Dr. Crusher. When Picard is captured and imprisoned with Crusher, she apologizes for refusing his order to abandon a victim of an Ansata attack and beam back to the ship, her disobedience leading directly to her capture:

> c: I'm sorry. If only I'd gone back to the ship.
> p: I should have beamed you up.
> c: You wouldn't dare.
> p: Oh yes, I would and should.

c: Without my permission?

p: If you don't follow orders.

c: If you'd give reasonable orders I'd obey.

p: Doctor, I'll be the judge of what is reasonable.

Ono asserts that Picard uses his patriarchal authority to dismiss Dr. Crusher's opposing views. Taken in isolation, Picard's last line could, as Ono argues, be seen as an imposition of male rationality on female irrationality. But for a viewer who knows the two characters and their relationship, the line takes on a different meaning. This viewer knows that Crusher has a fiery temper and that Picard has difficulty dealing with emotion; that Crusher, the widow of Picard's deceased best friend, knew him prior to her posting to the *Enterprise*; and that sexual tension underlies the Picard/Crusher relationship. To our hypothetical viewer the "no, you wouldn't; yes, I would" dispute may read as an argument between very close old friends or even a lover's spat. In this light, Picard's use of Crusher's official title and his "I'll be the judge" seem more a frustrated man's desperate claim than a captain's affirmation of the chain of command—an interpretation given credence by Patrick Stewart's acting. After proclaiming that he'll judge what's reasonable, Picard glances around the chamber that holds them captive, clearly realizing the silliness of the argument in their current predicament.

By contrast, Picard's interactions with the android Data are in keeping with both the captain's pre-established behavior and the two characters' ongoing relationship. The following dialogue between Picard and the android Data sets up the episode's central problematic: is violence ever a suitable means to a political end?

d: I have been reviewing the history of armed rebellion and it appears that terrorism is an effective way to promote political change.

p: Yes it can be, but I have never subscribed to the theory that political power flows from the barrel of a gun.

d: Yet there are numerous examples when it was successful: the independence of the Mexican state from Spain, the Irish unification of 2024, and the Kensey rebellion.

p: Yes, I am aware of them.

d: Then would it be accurate to say that terrorism is acceptable when all options for peaceful settlement have been foreclosed?

p: Data, these are questions that mankind has been struggling with throughout history. Your confusion is only human.

Ono asserts that Picard simply discounts Data's difficult questions: "Picard, through characteristic frustration with Data's obsession with rationality, dismisses

FIGURE 23.2.
Kidnapped by the Ansata,
Dr. Crusher discusses the
history and the morality
of terrorism with their
leader, Finn.

Data's potentially narrative-threatening logic and reminds him of his honorary 'human' status."[5] But a viewer familiar with *TNG* would interpret the exchange through knowledge of the characters' previous interactions. Ono is correct to say that Picard had previously expressed "frustration with Data's obsession with rationality," although such frustration was often played to comic effect. But implying that reminding Data of his honorary human status constitutes a veiled threat overlooks a major element of the characters' backstory established most clearly in the classic second-season episode "Measure of a Man" (February 13, 1989). In this episode, Commander Bruce Maddox wishes to dissemble Data in order to recreate the technology and provide the Federation with an army of androids. Data refuses, fearing damage to his delicate circuitry, but Maddox insists that Data, as the property of Starfleet, has no right to self-determination. A hearing ensues, in which Picard successfully establishes that Data is a sentient being entitled to the rights accorded all citizens of the Federation. While Ono correctly states that Picard occasionally finds Data's extremely logical behavior frustrating, a viewer familiar with "Measure of a Man" and other previous episodes would know that the android looks to the captain as his tutor in the humanities and humanity. For this competent viewer, Picard's reminding Data of his honorary human status gives legitimacy to Data's questions, rather than dismissing them. Ono, however, either unfamiliar with or ignoring the characters' backstory, produces a reading of the scene that upholds his ideological critique.

Exchanges between other characters, most notably Crusher/Finn and Riker/ Alexana, add to a diverse chorus in which some voices challenge and others support the dominant rejection of violent terrorist tactics as irrational and unjustifiable. In Crusher's dialogues with the Ansata leader, Finn makes a strong case against the Federation's, and by implication, the United States', claims to the moral high ground.

> F: Yes, I've read your history books. This is a war for independence, and I'm no different than your own George Washington.
> c: Washington was a military general, not a terrorist.
> F: The difference between generals and terrorists, Doctor, is only the difference between winners and losers. You win, you're called a general; you lose . . .
> c: You are killing innocent people. Can't you see the immorality of what you're doing, or have you killed so much you've become blind to it?
> F: How much innocent blood has been spilled for the cause of freedom in the history of your Federation, Doctor? How many good and noble societies have bombed civilians in war, have wiped out whole cities, and now that you enjoy the comfort that has come from their battles, their killings, you frown on my immorality? I'm willing to die for my freedom, Doctor. And in the finest tradition of your own great civilization, I'm willing to kill for it.

If, as Ono asserts, the Federation is the metaphoric equivalent of the United States, Finn's exchange with Crusher metaphorically criticizes rather than upholds American authority. This critique is given further weight when in a later exchange with Picard, Crusher refuses to dismiss Finn's argument completely.

The conversations that Alexana, the Rutian security chief, has with first officer Commander Riker, charged with liaising with Rutian security, counterpoint Finn's conversations with Crusher; Alexana's viewpoint that terrorism is always unacceptable counterbalances Finn's defense of his terrorist tactics. Alexana first appears as an inflexible ideologue. In a meeting with Picard and Riker soon after Crusher's kidnapping, she tells them, "These are not people we're dealing with here; they're animals, fanatics who kill without remorse or conscience, who think nothing of murdering innocent people." When Picard wonders why they captured Crusher rather than killing her, Alexana responds, "Don't ask me to explain them. I can't." In her next scene, she tells Riker that before becoming security chief she'd considered herself a moderate. He asks what changed her mind. She says: "The event that really opened my eyes took place only a few days after my arrival. A terrorist bomb destroyed a shuttle bus. Sixty school children. . . . That day I vowed that I would put an end to terrorism in this city and I will." In a later scene in the central square, Riker and Alexana watch the security forces rounding up Ansata suspects. Alexana tells Riker that her assassinated predecessor had operated even more repressively. "Suspects would be brought into police headquarters and would vanish. I put a stop to that." The inflexible ideologue, it turns out, has some regard for human rights. Like Finn, she also has good reasons for her actions. Seeing a young child arrested, Riker asks, "You mean to tell me that little boy is a threat?" She tells him that it was a teenager who blew up the school bus. "In a world where children blow up children, everyone's a threat." Her penultimate scene reveals that, in her own way, she is just as much a victim as Finn. She tells Riker, "I want to go home, back to my own country, to leave behind the roundups, the interrogations, the bodies lying in the streets, to be able to walk without the bodyguards. That's what I want."

At episode's end, after Alexana shoots Finn dead, a young boy, with whom Beverly has previously bonded, aims a phaser at Alexana. Beverly says to him, "No more killing." After a tense moment, he lowers his weapon. Alexana reads his actions from her hegemonic perspective. "Already another one to take his place. It never ends." Riker responds, "He could have killed you. He didn't. Maybe the end begins with one boy putting down his gun." The episode ends on an unresolved chord, rather than imposing a dominant viewpoint upon the exchange of diverse views that has gone before.

"The High Ground," together with "A Private Little War," show that rather than simply reflecting dominant assumptions, television drama frequently debates and sometimes challenges them. But a critic wishing to understand and illuminate these debates and challenges must be as familiar with the program's storyworld as the most loyal of viewers. This essay contests Kent Ono's interpretation of "The High Ground" because it illustrates a fairly common methodological failure in television studies: the isolation of a single episode of an ongoing series from the storyworld and character relationships established in previous episodes. By contrast with the ideological criticism of film, which has to account for only a single text, ideological criticism of a television program must place any episode in context among the tens or even hundreds of episodes that constitute a series.

NOTES

1. See for example, Taylor Harrison, Sarah Projansky, Kent A. Ono, and Elyce Rae Helford, *Enterprise Zones: Critical Positions on Star Trek* (Boulder, Colorado: Westview Press, 1996) and Daniel Bernardi, *Star Trek and History: Race-ing toward a White Future* (New Brunswick, NJ: Rutgers University Press, 1998).

2. Horace Newcomb and Paul M. Hirsch, "Television as a Cultural Forum," in *Television: The Critical View*, 6th ed., Horace Newcomb, ed. (Oxford: Oxford University Press, 2000), 566.

3. For more on *TOS*'s Cold War context, see Rick Worland, "From the New Frontier to the Final Frontier: *Star Trek* From Kennedy to Gorbachev," *Film & History* 24, 1–2 (1994): 19–35.

4. Kent A. Ono, "Domesticating Terrorism: A Neocolonial Economy of Différance," in Taylor

Harrison, Sarah Projansky, Kent A. Ono, and Elyce Rae Helford, *Enterprise Zones: Critical Positions on Star Trek* (Boulder, CO: Westview Press, 1996), 159.

5. Ibid., 166.

FURTHER READING

Bernardi, Daniel. *Star Trek and History: Race-ing toward a White Future.* New Brunswick, NJ: Rutgers University Press, 1998.

Harrison, Taylor, Sarah Projansky, Kent A. Ono, and Elyce Rae Helford, eds., *Enterprise Zones: Critical Positions on Star Trek.* Boulder, CO: Westview Press, 1996.

Pearson, Roberta, and Máire Messenger-Davies. "The Little Program That Could: The Relationship between NBC and *Star Trek.*" In *NBC: America's Network,* Michele Hilmes, ed., Berkeley: University of California Press, 2007.

———. "You're Not Going to See that on TV: *Star Trek: The Next Generation* in Film and Television." In *Quality Popular Television: Cult TV, the Industry and Fans,* Mark Jancovich and James Lyons, eds. London: British Film Institute, 2003.

Sarantakes, Nicholas Evan. "Cold War Pop Culture and the Image of U.S. Foreign Policy: The Perspective of the Original *Star Trek* Series." *Journal of Cold War Studies* 7, 4 (2005): 74–103.

24

The Wonder Years
Televised Nostalgia

DANIEL MARCUS

Abstract: One of the cultural functions of television is to serve as a site of social memory, constructing visions of the past for multiple generations. Daniel Marcus analyzes how the popular 1980s sitcom *The Wonder Years* remembers the 1960s, creating both nostalgia for and political commentary about a formative and controversial moment in American history.

The Wonder Years (ABC, 1988–1993) recounts the adolescence of Kevin Arnold and his friends as they confront school bullies, early romance, and social tumult in middle-class suburbia of the late 1960s and early 1970s.[1] The intermittently serious comedy was part of a reevaluation of "the Sixties" that occurred after the conservative electoral success of the Reagan era and its call for a return to "Fifties" values.[2] The production was the first television series to find popularity by reaching back to the late 1960s as a historical touchstone and relied on viewers' knowledge of events of that time in telling its stories. *The Wonder Years* can be seen as part of a generational effort to understand the relationship between two controversial eras in recent American history, the late 1960s and the 1980s, presented from the perspective of a fictional secondary participant in the social changes of the 1960s. Developing parallels between the shock of adolescence and the trauma of the Vietnam War and rapid social change, the shows brings these strands together in its portrayals of the generation gap and family loss.

The vivid 1960s popular culture, however, also provides a context for personal experimentation and growth for its young characters. The series illustrates the various ways that entertainment media invoke, adapt, and organize memories and images of the past, creating fictional archives for public commemoration and discussion. By depicting private lives embroiled in the public issues of a controversial era, *The Wonder Years* uses nostalgia for childhood experiences to appeal to key demographic groups, even as it universalizes situations specific to a time and place to forge a wider-ranging audience.

By locating its story in early adolescence, the series can appeal to viewers whose childhood occurred during the depicted era, and to a younger generation of audience members grappling with issues of youth in the 1980s. This construction of a shared perspective on the Sixties as a time of adolescent development created a large enough audience to make *The Wonder Years* commercially viable, and its nostalgic framing defused some of the controversy surrounding highly charged historical events. The series' sentimental, appreciative, and mainly comic vision of the era confronted more critical evaluations made by political and cultural conservatives. The perspective on the recent past asserted by the producers, shaped by industry needs, and affirmed by commercial popularity, competed to become the dominant cultural memory of the Sixties in American society.

American culture experienced a succession of nostalgia waves beginning in the late 1960s. Nostalgia is an emotion triggered by a sense of loss from changes in location or the passage of time. In temporal nostalgia, feelings of longing are triggered by the impossibility of going back to the past, except through fantasies purveyed in entertainment or politics, or the consumption of unchanged media from the previous era. Fans of nostalgic entertainment wish to look back to previous eras for what they have since lost, either personally or as members of a group. Nostalgia can be for a particular period in one's own life, such as early childhood or the senior year of high school, or for a historical period like the 1950s, or 1960s, or 1980s. Because these eras are documented in media and discussed through the recollections of participants, even individuals who were not alive during these times may want to "go back" to a previous era. When media productions invoke a nostalgia that speaks to both individual and collective loss or dislocation, they have the potential to have both deep and broad appeal.[3]

In the late 1960s, during a time widely perceived as experiencing rapid and sometimes traumatic social change, the youth counterculture embraced a re-appreciation for Fifties youth culture, from early rock and roll to such TV figures as Howdy Doody (a puppet who starred on a children's show.) This renewed embrace of Fifties themes spread to other segments of society in the 1970s and found expression in films such as *American Graffiti* (1973) and *Grease* (1978), and the television series *Happy Days* (ABC, 1974–1984). With the ascendancy of Ronald Reagan and the conservative movement in 1980, nostalgia for the period moved from the cultural realm to the political one. Conservatives touted the 1950s as a time of stable family structures, American military strength, and economic growth. Correspondingly, they criticized the 1960s, particularly the late 1960s, as a time of social chaos and violence, attacks on American patriotism, and increasing threats to the nuclear family which ranged from teenage drug use to feminism. Reagan and other conservatives proclaimed the 1980s as a time to re-turn to American greatness, calling for repeal or reduction of many of the social programs created or expanded in the 1960s, and suppressing the demands made by groups associated with the era, such as civil rights and feminist organizations. Those whose memories corresponded to this constructed conservative narrative of greatness, decline, and renewal could place themselves on the right side of his-tory; those whose recollections clashed with the conservative vision were defined as out of step with mainstream thought.[4]

While 1980s Democrats provided no answer to the political narrative of nos-talgia for the 1950s and condemnation of the 1960s, cultural producers did try to counter the conservative offensive. Television responded in the late 1980s with *thirtysomething* (ABC, 1987–1991), about 1980s yuppies haunted by the less ma-terialistic values of the Sixties, and *The Wonder Years*, which retold the story of 1960s youth by focusing on the younger siblings and cousins of the famous hip-pies and anti–Vietnam War protesters of myth and lore. *The Wonder Years* chose to highlight facets of 1960s experience through newly adolescent eyes, a perspec-tive that had previously been ignored in the culture wars over the significance of the Sixties.

The show's key themes can be seen in the pilot episode (January 31, 1988). While the series shifted a bit when it changed showrunners in 1989, moving to a greater emphasis on the characters' dating lives and adopting an even more sen-timental tone, the dynamics of memory and nostalgia are quite evident from the start. The series begins the summer before Kevin Arnold starts junior high, in what is depicted as a typical American middle-class suburb of 1968. As Kevin moves into adolescence, he must grapple with the challenges of encroaching adulthood, which include establishing a masculine identity to attract girls and re-pel bullies, evade or stand up to hostile authority figures in his family and school, and negotiate an increasingly complex social scene based on group identity and personal style. He displays ambivalence in meeting all of these challenges, mix-ing bravado with cowardice, self-confidence with self-deprecation, and sensitivity with cluelessness. The series is a record of his halting steps toward maturity and wisdom, as explicitly framed by a voiceover narration supplied by the adult Kevin of the present day.

From the show's very beginning, the producers offer a specific historical con-text for Kevin's experiences, even as they present the lessons he learns as almost universally applicable to childhoods across the ages. The opening credits show what looks like home movie footage of Kevin's suburban nuclear family and im-portant friends, playing ball and enjoying cookouts. The next sequence features newsreel footage of some of the momentous public events of 1968, such civil rights marches, anti-war protests, astronaut space walks, and familiar figures

Martin Luther King, Jr., and Robert Kennedy, each assassinated that year. Right from the start, the series takes advantage of memories of the specific era in framing its story, using the visual (and musical) archives of the time to stir media memories among its audience.

Just as the family movies in the credits make way for news clips of the great issues of the day, Kevin's entrance into adolescence features the growing encroachment of the larger world into his childhood idyll. After leaving the banally named Hillcrest Elementary School, Kevin enters the seventh grade at the newly renamed Robert F. Kennedy Junior High. The adult Kevin mentions that schools all over the country were being similarly renamed that fall, without explicitly explaining that it was in tribute to the recently slain senator and presidential candidate. The show presumes that viewers will understand the timing, twenty years after the fact. This presumption marks Kennedy's death as a significant event in U.S. history, something that all adult viewers would recognize, and perhaps younger viewers as well. Such offhand references to larger events can flatter viewers by paying tribute to their knowledge of the depicted era, and continue Baby Boomer self-identification with the traumatic events of their childhood—a generation brought together by the shared memory of how they heard that John F. Kennedy had been shot, and experiencing the further dislocations of the King and Robert Kennedy assassinations.

The pilot addresses more than just the political history of 1968. The closer-to-home theme of the generation gap, changes in music, clothing, and language, and the introduction of drugs into suburbia are all depicted in the episode. Kevin's older sister identifies with the youth counterculture, wears hippie-ish clothes, greets her mother with "Peace, Mom, OK," advises her against "bad karma," and announces at the dinner table that she wants to start using birth control, to her parents' dismay. Kevin's own foray into countercultural behavior is characteristically milder, amounting to wanting to wear a psychedelic shirt and flared pants to the first day of junior high, before his mother asserts her authority and he ends up with a more staid and boyish ensemble. Meanwhile, as the family gathers together for dinner and their nightly dose of low-intensity antagonism, televised news reports from Vietnam play in the background.

The personal and the political are conflated in these family scenes, which mix perennial issues of parent-child relations with the specificities of the Sixties generation gap. This combination continues in school scenes, in which teachers and administrators are portrayed as stupid, uptight authority figures who cannot understand the stresses of adolescent life in ways that are in keeping with the verities of both 1980s youth-themed entertainment and Sixties ideology. Kevin rebels by deliberately flouting cafeteria rules in a misguided attempt to impress his peers, and justifies his doing so by claiming the school "had played power games with me," in an echo of the student protests against administrator prerogatives occurring on college and high school campuses at the time.

Through this continual, mutual reflection between the private, individual travails of childhood and the larger, public controversies of the era, the show appeals to a mix of audiences. Younger viewers can enjoy tracing the changes in American life brought up by the airing of the series, and form their own takes, whether nostalgic or condescending, on both childhood and the famous Sixties. Children uninterested in the issues of that era can be entertained by the dramatization of timeless adolescent experiences—the first day at a new school, facing bullies and antagonistic siblings, getting into trouble with authority figures, and coping with a burgeoning interest in sex.

Their parents and other Baby Boomers can be flattered that an era that marked them with a generational identity is being recapitulated twenty years later, and can compare their youthful perspectives from the time with a more mature take on its issues and crises, both personal and political. Their perspectives as adults are reaffirmed by the narration, as the adult Kevin sometimes draws these comparisons as well, while mostly explaining the thoughts of the younger Kevin with a combination of empathy and irony. All viewers can share the narrator's superior knowledge of looking back on the past from the vantage point of the 1980s—they know how the story of the nation, if not of Kevin personally, turns out. Indeed, viewers of all ages can enjoy trying to deduce the facts of Kevin's post-1960s life (which are disclosed only late in the series) while maintaining a more knowing historical position than the young Kevin on the screen. Shared enjoyment of the series can comfort viewers that the infamous generation gap of the Sixties has been bridged in the 1980s, while constructing a family hour audience for ABC.

In contemporary society, personal memories mix with media representations to create collective senses of the past, because so much of what we learn and know about the world comes through contact with media. For younger viewers curious about the Sixties, *The Wonder Years* can function as an accessible archive of the era. The series not only provides information about the 1960s; it also prompts those with memories counter to the conservative interpretation of the era to reactivate their feelings about the period. In 1988, a wave of articles appeared in the media comparing the present with the late 1960s, as the twentieth anniversaries of King's and Robert Kennedy's deaths inspired writers to wonder how the martyrs' visions of the direction of the country contrasted with the Reagan America of the 1980s. The felt difference between the 1960s, often seen as dominated by developments on the political and cultural left, and the conservative 1980s, led to discussions of the vagaries of history and the trajectory of American history. *The Wonder Years* could contribute to the effort to trace the changes in society without agreeing to the conservative narrative of greatness, decline, and renewal.

Nostalgia is often seen as inherently conservative, in wanting to reverse the progress of history. In an era permeated by conservative nostalgia for the Fifties, however, nostalgia for the Sixties could serve as a rallying point for opponents of the conservative movement. For some fans, the series may have been just a comforting fantasy of the way things used to be; for others, however, it could be the basis for reclaiming earlier ideals, especially as Americans started to re-examine Reagan's policies in light of scandals and policy failures. Progressives who regretted some of the missteps of the Left in the 1960s could adopt the series' attitude toward its hero's youthful mistakes—admitting to imperfection while asserting that their experiences and attitudes could serve as a foundation for future insight and success, rather than be simply rejected as worthless or too damaging.

The pilot episode culminates with the ultimate convergence of the personal and political in the series. Winnie Cooper, Kevin's old neighborhood pal and newfound romantic interest, loses her older brother in Vietnam, and while Kevin comforts her, they each experience their first kiss. The scene is constructed to show Kevin's first major step toward adulthood, as he takes on the role of comforter and romantic partner—as someone who can grasp, however fumblingly, human tragedy and loss and respond appropriately. The national and personal trauma of the era becomes the catalyst for Kevin's maturation. Throughout the episode, the adult Kevin has ruefully argued that, despite appearances, the conformist suburbs of the American middle-class contain stories of real value and depth, and this final, wrenching, but momentous scene confirms his view, as he reflects that his suburban childhood was replete with such "moments . . . of sorrow and wonder."

The Wonder Years' depiction of the traumas of the late 1960s through the experiences of the relatively innocent Kevin works to redefine the era away from the conservatives' vision of it as the nadir of American history and the source of most of the nation's contemporary problems. Baby Boomers were closely identified with Sixties politics and culture, but it was the older Boomers, born in the 1940s and early 1950s, who were seen as full participants in its tumult, from fighting in Vietnam to protesting the war at home. In *The Wonder Years*, the Baby Boomer frame shifts from the perspectives of the early Boomers to the viewpoints of those born from the mid-1950s to the early 1960s—thus to those who were more witnesses than participants in the issues of the time, and consequently had less directly at stake.

The series does not shy away from society's convulsions. Rather, it does so in a convincingly comic mode, as the adult Kevin expresses his appreciation for what he gained through his intermittently painful experiences. Indeed, the late 1960s seems to have prepared him well for life in later periods. The series invokes the

FIGURE 24.1.
While comforting Winnie
after her brother's death
in Vietnam, Kevin experi-
ences his first kiss.

memories of middle-class, suburban late Boomers to answer the conservative de-monization of the time and the denunciation of the youth culture that was its most colorful artifact. In doing so, these memories bid to become a central com-ponent of the nation's shared memory of the 1960s, partially displacing though not wholly replacing the more traumatic memories of other groups. Nostalgic feelings for childhood are affixed to an era that had been defined as antithetical to fond remembrance or feelings of longing by the dominant political movement of the 1980s.

The adult figure of Kevin is the program's crucial reappraiser of Sixties experi-ence, and shares general narrative authority with the camera. Occasionally, the camera will show that Kevin's memories are not perfect—he tries to convince viewers that he was a good athlete as a kid, when evidence to the contrary is presented right up on the screen. Mostly, however, the adult Kevin is presented as a reliable and trustworthy narrator, embodying the show's narrative power. It is adult Kevin's choice of memories to share that determines the shape of each episode. Within each scene, the camera is the ultimate denotative authority, pre-senting irrefutable surface facts, but Kevin's voiceover is the ultimate connotative authority, the definer of the deeper meaning of what viewers see. Whether rueful, nostalgic, bemused, or pedantic, Kevin's voice provides social and historical con-text, emotional valence, and psychological insight to the scenes that the camera dispassionately reveals.

The heard but unseen adult Kevin comes off as a sensitive man comfortably in touch with his feelings and those of others. The Reagan era had seen a series of hyper-masculine heroes, particularly in spectacular action films, who responded to feminist and international challenges to masculine American prerogatives with macho attitudes, steroidal physiques, and hyperbolic firepower. The defenders of Sixties values who created *The Wonder Years* and *thirtysomething* posited a different sort of male hero, one who tries to understand his own emotional needs and weaknesses while struggling to create egalitarian relationships with women. These figures served as precursors to the new model of masculinity that Bill Clinton brought to the presidency in 1993; as a child of the Sixties, married to a feminist, Clinton would well up in tears as he felt others' pain. The adult Kevin of *The Wonder Years* is openly sentimental, and implicitly locates his sense of masculinity in his eventual ability to relate to women (along with fantasies about being good at sports). The show presents one legacy of the Sixties as an increased male emotional intelligence and maturity emerging from an earlier masculine archetype of bluster and insensitivity, personified by Kevin's father, who loves his family but rarely understands how to show it.

This move to rewrite history according to the dual perspectives of a twelve-year-old middle-class white boy in 1968 and a seemingly well-adjusted adult man in 1988 may have been crucial for *The Wonder Years'* commercial success, not just in terms of its appeal to progressive audiences, but also in its usually keeping the most controversial or depressing aspects of the late 1960s at arm's-length and thereby attracting a more variegated viewership. Other series that used children as the entry point for discussion of the Sixties, such as *Any Day Now* (Lifetime, 1998–2002) and *American Dreams* (NBC, 2002–2005), achieved some success, particularly when depicting the events of the early 1960s, around which a national consensus supporting John Kennedy and desegregation had developed by the 1980s.[5] Series that attempted to portray the latter half of the decade or used adult experience as their focus, such as *Almost Grown* (CBS, 1988–1989) and *I'll Fly Away* (ABC, 1991–1993), failed to find consistent audiences. Vietnam-themed series, such as *China Beach* (ABC, 1988–1991) and *Tour of Duty* (CBS, 1987–1990), did find some commercial success, but no series that has depicted the American homefront and late 1960s domestic issues from the point of view of anyone older than Kevin Arnold has survived on network television.[6]

The Wonder Years depicts one of the most polarizing periods of modern American history through frames of memory and nostalgia, offering multiple avenues for identification by its potential audiences. Providing viewers with a new media representation of the late 1960s, the series traverses the felt distance between past and present in both individual lives and the perceived life of the nation. By redefining the late 1960s through the experiences and memories of later Baby Boomers, the series provides a significant if muted response to conservative narratives of decline and trauma. While acknowledging the tragedies and difficulties of the period, the series presents it as a time of cultural vitality and innovation, personal growth, and worthwhile challenges to an emotionally constrained status quo, and does so in a way that counters conservative views of the era. The show combines universalized themes with the stylistic and political specificities of the time, and in doing so, created the most commercially successful historical treatment of the late 1960s on American television.

NOTES

1. The author wishes to thank Jason Loviglio, Alex Russo, and Sonja Williams for comments on a draft of this essay.
2. I use the terms "1950s" and "1960s" to denote the actual years of these decades, and "the Fifties" and "the Sixties" to denote the combinations of cultural elements, political meanings, and other associations that have come to be attached to the temporal periods.
3. For more on cultural nostalgia, see Fred Davis, *Yearning for Yesterday: A Sociology of Nostalgia* (New York: Free Press, 1979).
4. Daniel Marcus, *Happy Days and Wonder Years: The Fifties and the Sixties in Contemporary Cultural Politics* (New Brunswick, NJ: Rutgers University Press, 2004).
5. See Faye Woods, "Nostalgia, Music, and the Television Past Revisited in *American Dreams*," *Music, Sound, and the Moving Image* 2 (2008): 27–50; and Jennifer Fuller, "Debating the Past through the Present: Representations of the Civil Rights Movement in the 1990s," in *The Civil Rights Movement in American Memory*, Renee Christine Romano and Leigh Raiford, eds. (Athens: University of Georgia Press, 2006): 167–96.
6. See Albert Auster, "'Recollections of the Way Life Used to Be': *Tour of Duty, China Beach*, and the Memory of the Sixties," *Television Quarterly* 24 (1990): 61–69; Daniel Miller, "Primetime Television's *Tour of Duty*," and Carolyn Reed Vartanian, "Women Next Door to War," in *Inventing Vietnam: The War in Film and Television*, Michael Anderegg, ed., (Philadelphia: Temple University Press, 1991): 166–89 and 190–203, respectively; and Sasha Torres, "War and Remembrance: Televisual Narrative, National Memory, and *China Beach*," *Camera Obscura* 33–34 (1995): 147–65.

FURTHER READING

Anderegg, Michael, ed. *Inventing Vietnam: The War in Film and Television*. Philadelphia: Temple University Press, 1991.

Edgerton, Gary R., and Peter C. Rollins, eds. *Television Histories: Shaping Collective Memory in the Media Age*. Lexington, KY: University Press of Kentucky, 2001.

Marcus, Daniel. *Happy Days and Wonder Years: The Fifties and the Sixties in Contemporary Cultural Politics*. New Brunswick, NJ: Rutgers University Press, 2004.

IV

TV Industry
Industrial Practices and Structures

25

Entertainment Tonight
Tabloid News

ANNE HELEN PETERSEN

Abstract: Much of the television schedule is taken up by programs that seem like "filler" to many critics, but here Anne Helen Petersen shines a light on the often-ignored realm of tabloid news via the influential and still-popular landmark *Entertainment Tonight*. Petersen's account highlights how scheduling practices, regulation, and ownership can all have powerful impacts on a wide range of media content.

Until the early 1980s, "first-run" syndicated programming—that is, programming created for initial airing in syndication, not reruns—was limited to a "ghetto of game shows, talk shows and cartoons."[1] *Entertainment Tonight* (syndicated, 1981–present) gentrified that ghetto, changing the way that both television producers and stations conceived of first-run syndication and its potential profitability. Indeed, if you flipped through the channels between the evening news and the beginning of primetime during the 1980s, you would almost certainly happen upon a now-familiar sight: the wholesome face of Mary Hart, reporting on the latest happenings in Hollywood. As the host of *Entertainment Tonight*, Hart helped popularize a new mode of celebrity gossip in which stories on the private lives of stars and celebrities comingled with reportage of box office receipts and on-set exclusives.

Since its debut, *ET* has become one of the longest running, most consistently profitable programs on the air. In the 1980s, it readied the way for a profusion of entertainment news programs and venues that now form a major node in the media landscape, from E! to *Entertainment Weekly*. Yet *Entertainment Tonight's* success must be situated amidst a constellation of technological and regulatory changes, from the spread of cable and satellite technology to the gradual repeal of the Financial and Syndication Rules and other anti-monopoly regulations. This essay positions *ET* within the greater industrial climate of the 1980s, underlining the ways in which the program's unmitigated success fundamentally altered the landscape of first-run syndication.

Beginning in the days of early radio, the Federal Communications Committee (FCC) blocked Hollywood studios from entering into broadcasting, fearing the consolidation of entertainment media into the hands of few. This practice continued when broadcasting expanded from radio to television, as the FCC blocked film studio attempts at entering into television, station ownership, cultivating "Pay-TV" options, or starting their own networks. At the same time, the FCC was wary of the existing networks, their growing power, and their apparent negligence of the mandate to use the airwaves for the public good. By the end of the 1950s, ABC, CBS, and NBC relied on programming which they owned or had invested in—a practice that may have streamlined profits, but also resulted in a schedule replete with derivative game shows and Westerns.[2]

The resultant crop of programming, famously deemed a "vast wasteland" by FCC chairman Newton Minow in 1961, encouraged FCC passage of the Financial Interest and Syndication Rules, otherwise known as Fin-Syn, in 1971. Fin-Syn prohibited the networks from securing financial interest in independently produced programming and syndicating off-network programming. Coupled with the Prime Time Access Rule (PTAR), Fin-Syn also limited the amount of programming that each network could produce for itself (such as news) and freed a portion of primetime from network control. The resultant time slots, dubbed "prime access," would allow affiliates to program independently, hopefully with shows serving the local interest.

In short, the FCC blocked the networks' attempt to vertically integrate, barring them from *producing* the content they *distributed*. With the passage of Fin-Syn and PTAR, the FCC also hoped to free broadcast hours from network-induced repeats, opening the airwaves to local interests and concerns. In several crucial ways, these regulations served that purpose, but failed to encourage local programming. When tasked with filling the hours vacated by PTAR, local stations usually opted for syndicated offerings from studios or independent production companies, which not only cost less, but brought in higher ad revenue.[3] Without Fin-Syn and PTAR, *Entertainment Tonight*—a show produced by a major studio (Paramount) and broadcast during prime access—would not have been possible.

Entertainment Tonight was conceived by Alfred M. Masini, a former advertising executive and the creative force behind the hit music program *Solid Gold*. Masini came up with the idea for *ET* by studying what was *not* on the air—no one was providing "entertainment news" in the form of information on box office receipts, upcoming projects, Nielsen ratings, gossip, and personality profiles.[4] But the particular brand of "news" that *ET* was prepared to offer was a commodity that consumers had no idea they were supposed to desire. Indeed, before 1981, "almost no one, outside of pencil pushers in the business, had heard of television's upfront ad-selling season" let alone attendance figures, production deals, and industry machinations.[5]

But if *ET* provided that news, Masini hypothesized, audiences would watch. As longtime *ET* host Mary Hart recalled, "Do people really want to learn all these details—the weekly TV show ratings, the top-grossing movies? If we present it concisely and regularly, the answer is yes, people do want to learn."[6] Hart's rhetoric reproduced the implicit message of the program, which suggested that entertainment news, when offered concisely on a daily basis, accrues gravity and importance. In other words, *ET* supplied entertainment news and figures with such regularity that such information no longer appeared superfluous but *necessary* to make sense of the entertainment world.[7]

While *Entertainment Tonight* was introducing a new genre of programming, it was also proposing a novel model of distribution. *ET*, like Maisani's other hits, was syndicated. For the previous thirty years, syndicated programs had been "bicycled" from station to station, airing in one market, then sent, via the mail, to another. As a result, the lag-time between production and airing could be weeks—unacceptable for a program promising up-to-date Hollywood news. Paramount offered a solution in the form of satellite technology. In exchange for control of the show, Paramount offered to install and lease dishes to any station willing to air *ET*.[8] The offer resulted in a collection of 100 local stations equipped to receive the *ET* feed and a reach unthinkable without Paramount's infusion of capital.[9]

Satellite distribution also allowed *Entertainment Tonight* "day and date" transmission, meaning the show could be aired the same day it was filmed. This promise of immediacy would prove quintessential to *ET*'s image. In the early 1980s, the weekend's box office figures came in at noon on Monday. *ET* would tape its segment at 1:30 p.m., and the finished product would be seen across the nation within hours.[10] As a result, *ET* even beat the long-established Hollywood trade papers *Variety* and *Hollywood Reporter* in announcing figures crucial to the industry. In truth, such immediacy mattered little to *ET*'s audience, the vast majority of whom had no fiscal investment in the media industry. But the distinction of *ET* as the "first in entertainment news" bestowed its viewers with the status of insiders and experts and, by extension, encouraged dedicated viewership.

ET's cost and market penetration were unprecedented. Three months before it aired, *ET* had already been cleared in 100+ markets, reaching 77 percent of U.S. homes with all advertising spots sold for the year.[11] In its first week on the air, *ET* made good on its promises to affiliates, earning a 12.6 national rating—enough to make it the highest-rated national newscast.[12] But early reviews were not kind. The hosts were "dreadful"; the news was "so soft it squishes"; it was "*People Magazine* without that fine publication's depth."[13] One critic deemed it a "press agent's

FIGURE 25.1.
Host Mary Hart, for many
years the face of entertainment news.

dream," calling out a recent on-set visit to Paramount-produced *Grease II* as pure promotional propaganda.[14] In decrying *ET*'s intimacy with the industry, critics were in fact criticizing the designed cooperation between the production cultures at *ET* and the studios. In other words, *ET* was *intended* to be a press agent's dream and serve as a promotional vehicle for Paramount, not an independent journalistic outsider. These functions were not intended to be visible to the average viewer, only the savviest of whom would even realize that the show was produced by the same corporation as *Grease II*.

Over the next decade, critics would continue to criticize *ET*'s relationship with Hollywood. According to one *Time* reviewer, "*ET* is a part of the phenomenon it covers, another wheel in the publicity machine it seeks to explain."[15] *ET* has built a "cozy, symbiotic relationship" with celebrities, and "[t]he show has dropped almost all pretense of being anything but an arm of the Hollywood publicity machine," filled with "fluff indistinguishable from advertising."[16] Such assessments were not inaccurate, but perhaps missed the point, as *ET* had never aspired to function as a source for hard news or investigative journalism. From the start, *ET*'s tone has mirrored that of a traditional fan magazine, offering fawning, flattering portraits of the stars and Hollywood delivered by Hart and her various co-anchors in a bright, cheery fashion. While *ET* would not shy away from reporting on an existing celebrity controversy or scandal, the tone was never derogatory or denigrating. Most importantly, *ET* did not break such stories itself, lest it risk alienating a celebrity or publicist. The addition of entertainment news and figures helped *ET* gain credibility and attract a broader demographic, but it did not change the character of the relationship between the program and its subjects.

That relationship, however, was one of *ET*'s biggest assets. As *Variety* observed, the program is "a big wet kiss in terms of promotion of projects." A single appearance on *ET* could reach double, even triple the audience of a network morning show or late-night talk show.[17] Such reach gave *ET* tremendous leverage, especially over publicists eager to place celebrity clients on the show. *ET* producers exploited this leverage to exact a host of demands, including exclusive footage, access to stars, and the right to air a film trailer before any other outlet.[18] But *ET* needed celebrities and their publicists as much as they needed *ET*. "The reality is that we're all in bed with each other," said one top talent manager. "So nobody can tell anyone off. I need them. They need me."[19]

ET attempted to make up for lack of hard content with snappy editing, musical accompaniment, and fast-paced storytelling. Producers livened up its otherwise soft approach with flashy graphics, sound effects, and quick cuts that add "portent" and attract audience members who are "video fluent," thus manifesting a graphic mode that John T. Caldwell has termed "exhibitionism," in which stylization and activity take precedence.[20] In 1983, a typical program began with seven to eight minutes of industry news, delivered in the style of a nightly news program, followed by a "Spotlight" on celebrity and an on-set exclusive (a "Never-Before-Seen glimpse behind Johnny Carson's desk!"). The show generally closed with an "in-depth" report on style, an industry trend, or "a look backward at entertainment of the past."[21]

From time to time, a longer, more investigative piece or multi-part series would replace the final section. Because *ET* was shot on video, producers could easily and cheaply manipulate graphics and other visual framing devices (bumpers heading to and from commercials, "Next On" previews, logos). The cluttered aesthetic compensated for the otherwise "low" production values and, more importantly, guided viewer response and discouraged viewers from changing channels. The carefully orchestrated mix of content, oscillating between headlines and statistics, eye-catching imagery, and slightly longer interviews and features likewise prevented viewer fatigue with a particular segment.

Over the course of the 1980s, *ET* continued to grow. By September 1983, it trailed only *Solid Gold* (1980–1988) and *Family Feud* (1977–1985; 1988–1995; 1999–present) among syndicated programming with an 8.9 weekly rating, while its weekend show, *Entertainment this Week*, earned a 14.4.[22] By the end of the decade, *ET* had established itself, in the words of one Hollywood observer, as "such an important component in the way the industry is covered by press and television that it would be difficult to imagine its absence."[23] According to Ron Miller, a journalist for the Knight-Ridder newspaper chain, *ET*'s concept had "revolutionized the TV syndication business and proved that expensive, original non-network programming can be profitable to everyone."[24] *ET* prided itself on its success, collecting both of the above quotes for a full-page *Variety* advertisement that trumpeted the program's success. With its placement in the leading

Hollywood trade, *ET* was effectively advising other Hollywood entities that the program had taken on a crucial promotional role within the industry and could not be ignored.

With the potential and profitability of the genre firmly established, imitators followed. Between 1981 and 1990, more than a dozen shows and pilots attempted to emulate the *ET* formula, including Metromedia's *All About US* (1984); Paramount's *America* (1985); King World's *Photoplay* (1986); Tribune Entertainment's *Public People, Private Lives* (1988–1989); TPE's *Preview* (1990); Twentieth's *Entertainment Daily Journal* (1990–1992); and Viacom's *TV Star* (1980), *Entertainment Coast to Coast* (1986), *Exclusive* (1988), and *America's Hit List* (1990). Some shows, such as the pilot for *All About US*, were clear attempts to create cross-media promotion for print publications, while others, such as Twentieth's *Entertainment Daily Journal*, attempted to provide promotion for parent companies, in this case Fox/News Corporation.

Imitators also struggled for a reason that had little to do with *Entertainment Tonight*. *ET* was innovative and addictive, but its initial clearances and subsequent growth took place during a period of high demand for syndicated programming. As the number of independent stations was growing (from 106 to 215 between 1980 and 1985), the number of shows being sold into "off-network" syndication (commonly known as reruns) was decreasing.[25] The networks had become increasingly quick to cancel high-budget shows with mediocre ratings, and without at least a season or two already produced, a program could not be profitably sold into syndication. The lack of rerun material thus bolstered the first-run syndication market, which included shows like *ET*, *Solid Gold*, and a raft of game shows such as *Family Feud* and *Wheel of Fortune* 1983–present).[26] *ET* and the game shows were joined in the late 1980s by televised tabloids— *A Current Affair* (1986–2005), *Hard Copy* (1989–1999), and *Inside Edition* (1988–present)— that distinguished themselves through interest in the weird, the tawdry, and other sensational subjects otherwise at home in tabloid journalism.[27]

Each station's schedule had a finite amount of "prime access" space between the evening news and primetime. Depending on the time zone and the length of the local news, a station had room for two, three, or maybe four half-hour "strips" at most. By the end of the 1980s, *ET*, *Wheel of Fortune*, *Jeopardy!* (1984–present), *A Current Affair* and *Inside Edition* had claims on all of the quality access time periods.[28] A program might settle for a moderate number of access clearances, slowly building its audience. Yet any program attempting to emulate the *ET* formula needed to expend a similar amount of capital, which, by 1988, was $21 million per year, or $400,000 a week. In order to turn a profit, a new program required prime access clearance in a similar number of markets, generally upwards of 100. With so few access spots available, competitors faced nearly insurmountable odds. *Entertainment Tonight's* success throughout the 1980s was thus a result of its novelty, innovations, and the ruling logic of the conglomerate media industry.

In 2011, Mary Hart stepped down from *Entertainment Tonight* after twenty-nine years as co-host. While the show goes on, Hart's exit signaled, however un-officially, the end of an era. The mode and speed with which *ET* disseminated "entertainment news" for the majority of Hart's tenure was a thing of the past, replaced by online video, breaking news sent to mobile phones, and celebrity Twitter updates. The transformation was gradual: over the course of the 1990s, a raft of similarly-themed programming (*Extra, Access Hollywood,* the entire E! channel), all with backing from major media conglomerates, cut into *ET's* market share. In the mid-2000s, the rise of gossip blogs further compromised *ET's* hold. These early blogs—*Perez Hilton, Gawker, Just Jared, The Superficial,* and dozens of others—offered immediacy, a markedly snarky attitude, and a distinctly new me-dia style of breaking and proliferating content that attracted millions of visitors.[29] In contrast, despite a content-sharing partnership with Yahoo, *ET's* web presence was negligible, attracting a mere 609,000 visitors in July 2007.[30] Of course, *ET* has historically catered to a different (older, less technologically savvy) demographic, and most viewers were content with a self-contained, twenty-two-minute televi-sion program.[31]

But in 2007, *TMZ on TV* expanded the parameters of the market. As the televised extension of *TMZ.com,* then garnering over 10 million unique visi-tors a month, *TMZ on TV* enjoyed a massive built-in audience, backing from Time Warner–owned Telepictures and AOL, and a clearance deal with FOX sta-tions across the country.[32] After one year on the air, it was available in 90 percent of American households, garnering an average Nielsen rating of 2.3. *TMZ* still trailed *ET,* but it brought in viewers who were both younger and male, and thus more valuable to advertisers.[33] Most importantly, *TMZ* modeled a form of con-vergence in which content transitioned seamlessly from the web to the airwaves, edited to fit the specifics of each medium and its audience.

ET had to change its attitude towards breaking news and digital content lest it be left in *TMZ's* dust. Between 2007 and 2010, it began broadcasting in HD, ex-panded to partner with *MSN.com,* and significantly updated its website to include many of the features found on *TMZ,* including streaming video, breaking news, photo galleries, Twitter updates, and the ability for users to share stories through social media.

While *ET* no longer enjoys the uncontested dominance that characterized its rein in the 1980s, perhaps we can gauge its importance somewhat differently. In 2011, *ET* maintained an average of 5.9 million viewers (more than the *CBS Nightly News*) and *ET*-style reporting on celebrity couples, movie grosses, and industry deals now infuses everything from *The Huffington Post* to CNN.[34] With Hart's departure and the continued surge of web-based content, including "intimate" access to celebrities via social media, *ET* may decline. Or it may endure, catering to those who like their celebrity coverage cheery and fawning, working to adapt to the increasingly convergent media culture. Regardless of its eventual fate, it is clear that *Entertainment Tonight* fundamentally altered the landscape of first-run syndication, paving the path not only for *Extra, Access Hollywood,* and *TMZ*, but the infusion of "entertainment news" in all its various manifestations across the contemporary mediascape.

NOTES

1. Aljean Harmetz, "TV Producers Discover New Path to Prime Time," *New York Times*, July 5, 1988, C16.

2. See Michele Hilmes, ed., *NBC: America's Network* (Berkeley: University of California Press, 2007); Janet Wasko, "Hollywood and Television in the 1950s: The Roots of Diversification," in *The Fifties: Transforming the Screen, 1950–1959*, Peter Lev, ed. (Berkeley: University of California Press, 2003), 135–46.

3. Marilyn J. Matelski, "Jerry Springer and the Wages of Fin-Syn: The Rise of Deregulation and the Decline of TV Talk," *Journal of Popular Culture* 33 (2000), 64–65.

4. Peter Funt, "One Man's Formula for Sure-Fire Hits," *New York Times*, April 6, 1986, 14.

5. Kevin Downey, "*ET*: It Changed Show Biz and Changed the Syndie Biz as Well," *Broadcasting and Cable*, November 17, 2003, 22.

6. Michael E. Hill, "*Entertainment Tonight*: On the Air Fan Magazine," *Washington Post*, May 27, 1984, 5.

7. See Michael Joseph Gross, "Famous for Tracking the Famous," *New York Times*, June 23, 2002, A1.

8. The show's ownership was a "patchwork" of production companies and cable providers: Paramount owned 40 percent, Cox Broadcasting-owned Telerep held 40 percent and Taft Broadcasting had the remaining 20 percent. Paramount was viewed as "the principal production entity," in part due to its role in funding the installation of the satellite network.

9. Funt, "One Man's Formula," 14.

10. Rick Kissell, "*ET* Innovations Now Taken For Granted," *Variety*, September 8, 2000, A6.

11. *Entertainment Tonight* Advertisement, *Variety*, June 24 1981, 57; Morrie Gelman, "Par TV's *Entertainment Tonight* Marks a Major Step in Networking," *Daily Variety*, June 23, 1981, 10.

12. "*Entertainment Tonight* Wins Big-Par TV," *Daily Variety*, October 6, 1981, 12.

13. James Brown, "All the Fluff That's Fit to Air," *Los Angeles Times*, September 24, 1981.

14. Howard Rosenberg, "Relentless Pursuit of Fluff," *Los Angeles Times*, March 10, 1982, G1.

15. Richard Stengel, "Turning Show Biz into News," *Time*, July 4, 1983, 72.

16. Gross, "Famous for Tracking the Famous," A1; Richard Zoglin and Tara Weingarten, "That's Entertainment?" *Time*, October 3, 1994, 85.

17. John Brodie, "*ET*'s New Competitor Sets Flack a-Flutter," *Variety*, July 25, 1994, 1.

18. Ibid.

19. Susanne Ault, "*ET*: The Business Behind the Buzz," *Broadcasting & Cable*, July 2, 2001, 14.

20. Gross, "Famous for Tracking the Famous," A1; Peter W. Kaplan, "TV News Magazines Aim at Diverse Viewers," *New York Times*, August 1, 1985, C18. John Thornton Caldwell, "Excessive Style: The Crisis of Network Television," in *Television: The Critical View*, 6th ed., Horace Newcomb, ed. (New York: Oxford, 2000), 652.

21. Stengel, "Turning Show Biz into News," 72.

22. "First Run Syndication Leader," *Variety*, September 21, 1983, 82.

23. Ibid.; David Gritten, quote attributed to *Los Angeles Herald-Examiner*. See *Entertainment Tonight* Advertisement, *Variety*, February 1, 1984, 67.

24. See *Entertainment Tonight* Advertisement, *Variety*, February 1, 1984, 67.

25. Michael Schrage, "TV Producers Woo the Networks," *Washington Post*, January 15, 1985, E5.

26. Ibid.

27. See Kevin Glynn, *Tabloid Culture: Trash Taste, Popular Power, and the Transformation of American Television* (Durham, NC: Duke University Press, 2000).

28. "*Entertainment Tonight* turns 3,000," *Broadcasting & Cable*, March 8, 1993, 30.

29. See Anne Helen Petersen, "Celebrity Juice, Not From Concentrate: Perez Hilton, Gossip Blogging, and the New Star Production," *Jump Cut*, 2007, http://www.ejumpcut.org/archive/jc49.2007/PerezHilton/index.html.

30. Paige Albiniak, "New, Improved Access," *Broadcasting & Cable*, September 10, 2007, 9.

31. While numbers for all television viewing had steadily declined with the expansion of cable and new media, *ET* still earned a 5.4 Nielsen rating in January 2006. Ben Grossman, "Entertainment Mags Rock," *Broadcasting & Cable*, January 23, 2006, 17.

32. For more on TMZ, see Petersen, "Smut Goes Corporate."

33. Paige Albiniak, "*TMZ* Stays in the News," *Broadcasting & Cable*, November 26, 2007, 12.

34. Brooks Barnes, "After Hart, a Deluge of Meaner Celebrity TV?" *New York Times*, May 19, 2011, C1.

FURTHER READING

Caldwell, John Thornton. *Televisuality: Style, Crisis and Authority in American Television*. New Brunswick, NJ: Rutgers University Press, 1995.

Glynn, Kevin. *Tabloid Culture: Trash Taste, Popular Power, and the Transformation of American Television*. Durham, NC: Duke University Press, 2000.

Petersen, Anne Helen. "Smut Goes Corporate: *TMZ* and the Conglomerate, Convergent Face of Celebrity Gossip." *Television & New Media* 11, 1 (2009): 62–81.

26

I Love Lucy
The Writer-Producer

MIRANDA J. BANKS

Abstract: Often hailed as a landmark series for a range of innovations, *I Love Lucy* can also be seen as groundbreaking for how it assembled its production staff and established the vital role of television's writer-producer. Miranda Banks explores the history of *Lucy*'s production and creative personnel, connecting it with key moments in establishing labor practices and production norms in the early days of television.

In 1953, Lucille Ball made history by giving birth to two boys in one night, 3,000 miles apart. One, Desiderio Arnaz, arrived by Caesarean section in Los Angeles; the other, Little Ricky Ricardo, was the first child to arrive via television airwaves into homes across the country from a fictional New York. By celebrating rather than shying away from showing the first pregnant woman on television, *I Love Lucy* (CBS, 1951–1957) and the arrival of little Ricky secured the Ricardos as a television family.[1] The series was globally adored for its comedy and its star—although *I Love Lucy* was not just a hit, but also a TV milestone. *Lucy* was a major force for ushering in certain changes that would ultimately define American commercial television. In the annals of television history, *I Love Lucy* is most often celebrated for five things: 1. Lucy and Ricky's position as the first interracial couple on television; 2. cinematographer Karl Freund's use of a multi-camera system to record the series on film in front of a live audience; 3. the announced arrival of Little Ricky; 4. making its stars, Lucille Ball and Desi Arnaz, the first television millionaires; and 5. being one of the series that convinced networks and studios that telefilm production in Hollywood would become the future of the industry. Less well-known is how *I Love Lucy* also, in a manner of speaking, gave birth to a role in television production that, while commonplace in Hollywood today, was surprisingly controversial at the time: the "hyphenate" writer-producer.

I Love Lucy was technically, culturally, industrially, and aesthetically ground-breaking; its significance as a single series within the history of the medium is virtually without rival. If *Lucy* was a contemporary series, it is quite likely we would be ascribing its success to a particular person: the series showrunner, heralding this person (or in some instances, persons) as a brilliant leader, technician, author, and, perhaps, creator. "Showrunner," a relatively new term that began appearing only in 1990 in the trade press, provides an easy road map to assigning credit that heretofore had been somewhat less decipherable.

"Showrunner" is not an official credit, per se. Without some knowledge beyond the credits listed onscreen or on IMDB.com, deciphering who is "in charge" of a television series is often a difficult task. Rather than the screen credit of "executive producer" or the older trade term of "head writer," the showrunner is someone who gives a series—and just as importantly, those who work for the series—a sense of structure and direction. The showrunner is in charge of the production and the creative content of a television show. The job demands the skills of a visionary: someone who can hold the entire narrative of the series in their head; who is the gatekeeper of language, tone, and aesthetics on the set and behind the scenes; who knows where the series has been and a sense, if not a plan, for its future. So, then, how did a television series that was such an overwhelming success "run" without a showrunner? Or was there a showrunner who was never celebrated as such? And if there was, who then deserves credit for *I Love Lucy*?

The easy answer would be to point to star Lucille Ball. From the show's first run in the 1950s to the present day, in the United States and around the globe, audiences have been enchanted with the unruly housewife who attempts to escape the confines of her apartment, only to find herself in the most outrageous of situations each week: stomping on grapes for an Italian film shoot ("Lucy's Italian Movie"), shoving chocolates into her mouth trying to keep up with her job on a conveyor belt at a candy factory ("Job Switching"), peddling Ricky's sponsor Vitameatavegamin on his TV show ("Lucy Does a Commercial"). These scenes are regularly celebrated as some of the finest performances in television comedy. It was Ball and her signature character that made the series the most popular show on television for four of its six seasons. However, while the show was entirely centered on its heroine, and she was one of the owners of Desilu Studio that produced the series, Lucille Ball was neither a manager nor was she responsible for running the series.

On further reflection, the answer to who is responsible for *Lucy* is not as easy as one might think. Desi Arnaz, as the head of Desilu, was like the best of studio moguls of the Hollywood era, assembling the most talented workers available. In this way, Arnaz himself could arguably be seen as the man in charge, especially since television corporations at the time were regularly considered more

FIGURE 26.1.

In this famous "Vitameatavegamin" scene, audiences are treated to a brilliant comic performance by Lucille Ball. Today, we would say the "showrunner" responsible for the episode was Jess Oppenheimer.

powerful—and more like media authors—than any individual.[2] Arnaz loved the attention pointed toward him as the series shot up in the ratings, and he gave himself an executive producer credit even though his role—at least in the early years of the series—was much more in line with actor and studio head.

Ball was the centerpiece of the series, and Arnaz was a young mogul who had a gift for locating the best person for each job on the Desilu set. The talent collected to make *I Love Lucy* run was some of the best TV would ever see. In many ways the series highlighted how collaborative the new medium could be. The crew that assembled was new to television—but each of them arrived with years of experience working in other media. Every one of these craftspeople brought with them knowledge and experience in entertainment, but arguably it was the mix of knowledge that led to the genius of the production. Writer Madeline Pugh Davis explained how the makers themselves were delighted by the diversity of the cast's and crew's talents, skills, and experiences: "Danny Cahn, who edited the first show . . . said the writers were from radio, Karl Freund was from the movies, Desi was from the theater and the stage, Lucy was from the movies, and everybody got together and put in their two cents and made it work . . . It was like inventing the wheel, as it all turned out rather well."[3]

The success of *Lucy* was a rare story, but it did mirror the general success of television: audiences craved great storytelling, and these makers of all different forms of popular entertainment—radio, film, and theater—who had been so talented in their original medium, turned their attention to television and together developed content that appealed to the new, and rapidly increasing, television audience. With all of this talent behind the scenes and in the front office, one moves on to ask who first "created" *I Love Lucy*.

Nowadays when we think about the author of a narrative television series, we assign a privileged role to its creator. The creator provides the original story, building a storyworld that an ensemble cast inhabits, and often has a continuing role as head writer-producer. The head writer is—at best—a benevolent dictator who provides a consistency of voice from episode to episode, runs the writers' room, works on set with the director, actors, cinematographer, and designers ensuring that the words on the page translate to the screen, and often sits in the editing room helping the editor craft a story. One could easily assume that it was Lucille Ball and Desi Arnaz who were the show's creators, but they were not. *Lucy*'s creator was a man whose name is barely remembered and rarely mentioned: Jess Oppenheimer.

Oppenheimer was a young radio writer, director, and producer on a number of hit series including Fanny Brice's *The Baby Snooks Show* (CBS, 1944–1950). This hyphenate role that Oppenheimer played in the series, in fact, had its roots in radio soaps and later in other celebrated popular series. He was brought in to run Lucille Ball's radio series *My Favorite Husband* (CBS, 1948–1951). When CBS and Desilu began conversations about creating a television series, Oppenheimer worked with stars Ball and Arnaz, his two co-writers on *My Favorite Husband*, Madeline Pugh and Bob Carroll, Jr., and the Milton Biow advertising agency. Out of this emerged a one-page treatment outlining the basic plot idea.

> He is a Latin-American orchestra leader and singer. She is his wife. They're happily married and in love. The only bone of contention between them is her desire to get into show business, and his equally strong desire to keep her out of it. To Lucy, who was brought up in the humdrum sphere of a moderate, well-to-do middle western, mercantile family, show business is the most glamorous field in the world. But Ricky, who was raised in show business, sees none of its glamour, only its deficiencies, and yearns to be an ordinary citizen, keeping regular hours and living a normal life.[4]

Then Desilu created a pilot episode. Somewhere along the way, Oppenheimer realized he needed to protect his idea, and with a single dollar bill and one slip of paper, he registered his premise for *I Love Lucy* with the Screen Writers Guild.

The hyphenated role of both writer and producer that Oppenheimer played on the set was something new. His interest and focus on storytelling provided consistency of narrative and voice that was helpful to the writers and guided the direction of the series. To Ball, Oppenheimer was known as "the brains" behind the show. Director William Asher called him "the field general." While the title had yet to be invented, this language of managerial control and creative authority is echoed in the descriptions used for today's showrunner. In an interview, writers Bob Schiller and Bob Weiskopf described Oppenheimer as a "stern taskmaster" and the best producer they ever worked for. He was the only producer they had ever written under who turned the radio off, who cut the phone to the writers' room, who refused to be distracted by concerns about casting, costumes, and make-up. The writers' room was broken into two writing partnerships: Pugh and Carroll, and Schiller and Weiskopf. After a day spent working as a team of five, Schiller and Weiskopf would take a first pass at writing a draft. Oppenheimer would make comments and then Pugh and Carroll would do a second draft. Finally, Oppenheimer came in to do a final draft. No script would ever reach the set without Oppenheimer's final pass. As he said:

> I made it a point, no matter how good their draft was, to re-dictate the entire thing from beginning to end, because that way each of the characters consistently spoke the same way each week. It didn't have to be *me*, necessarily, as long as it was filtered through one person's sense. But I felt that I knew best the mood and feel of our previous shows, and that I could bring it all into line so that nothing sounded too different or out of character. . . . The more consistency there is, the more comfortable [the audience is], and the more you can enjoy everything that happens. So, rightly or wrongly, the show sounded the same each time because it funneled through me.[5]

This language is quite common now, as staff writers on television series often talk about the need for consistency of voice from episode to episode. Writers even talk about needing the skill of a mimic, as they learn to write like the head writer. As both a writer and a producer, Oppenheimer had the vision, the skill, and the authority to create regularity in the series from episode to episode, season to season. This skill was unnecessary for film writers, as aside from serial shorts or the occasional film series, film writers need only be concerned with consistency of narrative within a single 75–160 minute window.

So was this successful and talented writer, rising to the top of this newly formed industry, venerated in Hollywood as the first of a new breed of writer? One might assume that though his name might not be known by audiences, people within the industry would know him as one of the brains behind bringing Hollywood writers new business in the form of the telefilm. The answer, though, is quite the opposite: Oppenheimer's role as both a writer and a producer proved extremely threatening to a community of writers who saw producers as management, and therefore their adversaries in contract and labor negotiations. Although Oppenheimer was a dues-paying member of the Screen Writers Guild as well as the newly formed Television Writers of America, his position as a producer overshadowed his work as a writer. Hollywood writers' agitation regarding Oppenheimer's hyphenated role ultimately played itself out in a National Labor Relations Board hearing.

In May 1953, two years after the premiere of *Lucy*, and its second year at the top of the television ratings, Oppenheimer—creator, head writer, and producer of

I Love Lucy—was called in front of the board that was placed in the middle of a battle between the Television Writers of America (TWA) and the Screen Writers Guild (SWG) regarding jurisdiction over television.[6] Testimony that day related to Oppenheimer's disparate roles: as a producer working for Desilu, as Vice President of the Television Writers of America, and as head writer of *Lucy*. The attorney for the SWG insisted that as a prestigious producer and a potential employer of writers, Oppenheimer was exercising an undue amount of influence recruiting writers to join the Television Writers Guild.[7] The Screen Writers Guild could not see how Oppenheimer, as both a producer and a writer—and thus, both as management and employee—should have any power to decide which trade organization would represent him, let alone have the potential to strong-arm his fellow writers to follow suit with whichever organization he preferred. Oppenheimer in his role as a writer-producer was a shocking new force in the history of relations between writers and producers. The Screen Writers Guild was in the business of representing writers in negotiations and disputes against management. And as of late, relations between the two were difficult at best. Just five years before the premiere of *I Love Lucy*, the Hollywood Ten (eight of them writers) were sent to jail for refusing to testify about accused Communist sympathies. Dozens of screenwriters had been blacklisted and lost their contracts with the studios. On this stage arrived Oppenheimer, and thus the Screen Writers Guild could see only the danger in this new role of writer-producer. Little could they foresee the power that hyphenates would soon carry in this new medium—power that ultimately would help not just television writers, but screenwriters as well.

Nowadays it seems absurd that a showrunner would be seen as a threat to his or her own series in negotiations between labor and management. The names of showrunners are venerated within the television community as powerful voices on series as well as for the rights of writers: Matt Weiner (*Mad Men*), Joss Whedon (*Buffy the Vampire Slayer, Angel, Firefly*), and Norman Lear (*All in the Family, Maude, The Jeffersons*) have all walked picket lines as Writers Guild members. But in the 1950s, the landscape of Hollywood looked quite different. After twenty years of battling against management, the Screen Writers Guild could not fathom the idea that a writer could balance his own interests as a producer and as a writer. Thus, they viewed the hyphenate role of a writer-producer as a powerful new threat and a potential infiltrator into the union.

There were at the time a number of other hyphenate writer-producers who were blazing a trail for a new role for writers in this new medium. One of them, in particular, was far more powerful than Oppenheimer ever could be. The role (if not the term) of the hyphenate writer-producer stems back to the earliest days of episodic television, even before *I Love Lucy*. Gertrude Berg, star of the early radio-cum-television series *The Goldbergs* (CBS, 1949–1951), is arguably the first and foremost example of what a television showrunner would become in the contemporary era. Berg embodied the hyphenate as a television pioneer: she was a writer, producer, and actor, and true show-woman. She was, unquestionably, a showrunner forty years before the term was ever conceived.

While there were examples of television writers beyond Oppenheimer and Berg who served as producers, the hyphenate truly emerged in the mid-1950s, when television production moved primarily to Los Angeles. Ultimately, the TWA dissolved in 1954, and all writers of scripted entertainment for film, television, and radio gathered under the umbrella of the Writers Guild of America. But it was on account of writers for shows like *Lucy*, who first claimed credit as writers and as producers, that conflicting notions of authorship and ownership came to a head for the guilds that represented these media workers. With the ascension of the hyphenate, a significant number of writers were placed in a position of power and authority previously unseen within the industry. Hyphenates had significantly more creative control of their series than screenwriters ever held on film sets. While screenwriters often had more cultural and financial capital, their loss of rights of authorship weighed heavily on many of them and gave television writers good reason to appreciate their lot.

In 1960, film and television writers walked the picket line together as the Writers Guild of America, demanding radical shifts in payment and benefits structures. With the rise of the Hollywood telefilm, as well as the airing of motion pictures on television networks, writers argued that compensation should be extended to cross-media exhibition and the rerun. Negotiations finally established a system of royalties, and years later the residual system, which has since ensured writers would see a profit from each replay of films and television series, as well as required payment by the studios and networks into member's pension and health benefits. Though at first the WGA was an uncomfortable marriage of film, television, and radio writers who had literally taken each other to court, by 1960 its members had realized that this alliance could emerge as a powerful labor force and as a strong voice for creative workers within the American media industries.

So the question of who deserves credit for *I Love Lucy* is partly only rhetorical: there was no singular showrunner, in name at least, and yet without someone leading a brilliant cast and crew of dozens through the rigorous filming schedule demanded in the early days of television, the series could have easily fallen apart. Nowadays, the person in charge of a television series is always listed as a producer—as was Jess Oppenheimer even in those early days—and rarely is the role of producer his or her only title. Sometimes the hyphenated role the person carries is that of director, as with Bruce Paltrow in *St. Elsewhere*. Sometimes that person has multiple roles in front of and behind the camera, as does *30 Rock* star, actor, writer, and producer Tina Fey.

Lucy taught television about its potential as a medium. When we flip our way around the dial and find a show that is truly exceptional, we have a natural inclination to assign credit to creative genius. We see something funny, thoughtful, wise, beautiful, or compelling, and we want to believe that such brilliance can emerge out of hard work and ingenuity. Creativity is often defined as a singular vision: so how can such singularity of mind come from a collection of, arguably, dozens of people? And yet, sometimes if it's the right collection of media makers, the results can turn into the best television has, and perhaps ever will, offer.

NOTES

1. See Mary Desjardins, "Lucy and Desi: Sexuality, Ethnicity, and TV's First Family," *Television, History, and American Culture: Feminist Critical Essays,* Mary Beth Harolovich and Lauren Rabinovitz, eds. (Durham, NC: Duke University Press, 2001), 56–74.

2. See Alisa Perren and Ian Peters, "Showrunners," *The Sage Handbook of Television Studies.* Manuel Alvarado, Milly Buonanno, Herman Gray, and Toby Miller, eds. (Thousand Oaks, CA: Sage, forthcoming).

3. Interview, Archive of American Television, November 24, 1997, Academy of Television Arts & Sciences Foundation, http://www.emmytvlegends.org/interviews/people/madelyn-pugh-davis.

4. Jess Oppenheimer with Greg Oppenheimer, *Laughs, Luck and Lucy: How I Came to Create the Most Popular Sitcom of All Time* (Syracuse, NY: Syracuse University Press, 1996) 139.

5. Ibid., 189.

6. In 1952, thirty-five television writers gathered together to form the Television Writers of America (TWA), a branch of the Authors League of America. The TWA had two primary concerns: that they were receiving low pay and that they had no benefits. They turned to the National Labor Relations Board for certification and to be officially named bargaining agents for television writers. Jess Oppenheimer was named vice president. Almost immediately, the Screen Writers Guild filed a complaint with the NLRB and demanded a hearing against the TWA.

7. "New Desilu Hearing Completed," *The Television Writer*, 2, 2 (May 1953): 2.

FURTHER READING

Banks, Miranda. *Scripted Labor: A History of American Screen Writing and the Writers Guild.* New Brunswick, NJ: Rutgers University Press, forthcoming.

Henderson, Felicia D. "The Culture Behind Closed Doors: Issues of Gender and Race in the Writers' Room." *Cinema Journal* 50, 20 (Winter 2011): 145–52.

Landay, Lori. *I Love Lucy.* Detroit, MI: Wayne State University Press, 2010.

Newman, Michael Z., and Elana Levine. *Legitimating Television: Media Convergence and Cultural Status.* New York: Routledge, 2011.

Perren, Alisa, and Ian Peters. "Showrunners." In *The Sage Handbook of Television Studies.* Manuel Alvarado, Milly Buonanno, Herman Gray, and Toby Miller, eds. Thousand Oaks, CA: Sage, forthcoming.

27

Modern Family
Product Placement

KEVIN SANDLER

Abstract: Although television is overwhelmingly a commercial medium, audiences still expect boundaries between commercials and program content, particularly in narrative programming. Kevin Sandler examines an interesting case of product integration: the controversy that surrounded an episode of the hit sitcom *Modern Family*, the narrative of which conspicuously centered on Apple's iPad just days before that device became available for purchase.

"Game Changer," a first season episode of ABC's *Modern Family* (2009–present), begins with Phil Dunphy all set to wake up early the next day—his birthday—and get in line at 6 a.m. at the Apple Store to buy an iPad. "It's like Steve Jobs and God got together to make this the best birthday ever!" he says. His wife Claire, thrilled to have a handle on what her husband Phil actually wants for his birthday (her previous idea was light-up barbecue tongs), offers to camp out at the Apple store to get him the iPad. Alas, she falls asleep on the couch, and the iPad is sold out before she arrives. Claire subsequently enlists her two daughters, Haley and Alex, to "Facebook, chat, buzz, bling" their way to an "iPad thingy." In the meantime, Claire hears about a new shipment of iPads at the Apple Store, only to get thrown out of line with her brother Mitchell (who retrieved her wallet from home) for fighting with a man who cut in front of them. Ultimately, though, Phil's son Luke obtains an iPad by emailing all of his father's "geek friends," claiming that Phil is dying and his final wish is to get an iPad. The episode concludes with Phil getting his iPad and celebrating his birthday with his family. Happy ending achieved, narrative equilibrium restored.

Prior to the airing of "Game Changer" (March 31, 2010), *Modern Family* had received nearly universal acclaim from critics and fans since its debut in September 2009. The show was the highest-rated new comedy of the broadcast season, and eventually won the Emmy Award for Best Comedy Series later that August. By its second season, *Modern Family* had become the most watched scripted broadcast series in the 18–49 demographic.[1] In fact, "Game Changer" drew the series' biggest number in that key demo in almost two months—a 3.8 rating (with each point translating into 1.3 million viewers).[2]

In what proved to be merely a temporary setback to the series' reputation, a heated debate ensued in the news media and blogosphere regarding the episode's iPad-centric nature. Two distinct camps emerged: one side considered the iPad integration to be unforgiveable and shameless, a profit-driven partnership of *Modern Family*'s production company, Twentieth Century Fox Television, the ABC network, and Apple. Another faction found it realistic and convincing, a savvy creator-fueled storyline that made sense within the show's fictional world. Characterizing these divergent positions was a widely circulated pair of posts appearing on the "The Live Feed" blog of the *Hollywood Reporter* that involved television editor James Hibberd and *Modern Family* co-creator (with Steve Levitan) Christopher Lloyd. Hibberd suggested that "the iPad scenes felt like an advertisement," the end result being that ABC "water[ed] down a brand with the perception of selling out . . . especially if it didn't sell out."[3] In response, Lloyd claimed, "there was no product placement," though *Modern Family* "ha[d] made those agreements with other companies." In this case, he said, no financial transaction was guiding the iPad's representation, as "it was all story-driven."[4]

The "agreement" that Lloyd refers to here was the season-long product-placement deal for *Modern Family* that ABC had previously struck with Toyota for its Sienna and Prius vehicles. Unlike the iPad, these Toyota product integrations, which had totaled over eight minutes of airtime up to this point, drew virtually no media response.[5] "Game Changer," however, was a different story. Questions arose akin to Hibberd's and Lloyd's contrasting assessments over the motives behind the iPad integration. For instance, had ABC crossed the line in corporate synergy under the influence of Apple CEO Steve Jobs, who, at the time, was the largest shareholder and sat on the board of ABC parent corporation, The Walt Disney Company? Did *Modern Family* violate its trust with the viewing public, as the series had received a Peabody Award for its "distinguished achievement and meritorious public service" on the exact morning that "Game Changer" aired? Did the iPad qualify as product placement, since the device's actual debut was April 3, three days after the episode's airdate?

This brief controversy surrounding the iPad's presence in *Modern Family* highlights the increasingly blurred line between entertainment and marketing that characterizes the contemporary U.S. television landscape. With more viewers making use of ad-skipping digital video recorders, watching TV on DVD, or streaming (or stealing) content off the Internet, marketers have begun to push for more ways to intertwine their products within network programming itself. Product placement, product integration, and branded entertainment—three common terms to describe a form of advertising in which a product, corporate logo, or brand name is positioned as a "prop" in a program or is used as an integral part of the story-line—is one of those strategies. All have become a staple of broadcast and cable television, particularly with the influx of "non-scripted" or reality television since the success of *Survivor* (CBS, 2000–present) in its debut season. FOX's *American Idol* (2002–present), CBS's *The Amazing Race* (2001–present), and Bravo's *Top Chef* (2006–present) all continually weave advertisers' products within their storylines and gameplay. Integration has also found its way into scripted television with such notable examples as NBC's *The Office* (2005–2013) and Staples, *30 Rock* (NBC, 2006–2013) and Snapple, and *Chuck's* (NBC, 2007–2012) season-long Subway integrated sponsorship. *Modern Family's* integration of the iPad, therefore, is more the rule than the exception in today's media landscape.

Timothy Havens and Amanda D. Lotz provide a model that helps to explain how the iPad integration in "Game Changer" underscores the ongoing tensions between art and commerce in the media industries.[6] They propose an "Industrialization of Culture" framework to take into account the wide range of cultural, economic, in-stitutional, professional, and personal forces that lead media practitioners to shape the aesthetic content and ideological meaning of texts on three different levels of in-fluence: mandates, conditions, and practices. A mandate is the primary purpose of an industry organization, its reason for operating, such as profit-seeking or public service. Conditions refer to the broader behavior of the media sectors—the various technologies, regulations, and economics that affect how media industries operate. And practices encompass the myriad of professional roles and activities that make up the day-to-day operations of the media industries. Together with various social trends, tastes, and traditions that media producers might draw on when creating programming, this framework can account for how media industries bring a show into being. Media workers, particularly those in commercial media organizations, have only some degree of individual autonomy, or, as Havens and Lotz call it, "cir-cumscribed agency." Cultures, mandates, conditions, and industry practices invari-ably all work to impinge on the agency of media professionals. Yet, "the drive for popularity," they argue, "and the conflicting and competing interests of a wide range of decision makers involved in creating an individual media text provide opportu-nities for agency and self-expression."[7]

When viewed through this framework of circumscribed agency, the iPad inte-gration and ensuing debate over "Game Changer" exposes the myriad pressures faced by *Modern Family's* creators in constructing an episode of commercial tele-vision. ABC's primary mandate, as one division within a massive publicly traded company, is to make money for its parent company's shareholders. It does this primarily through selling the audiences gathered by its content to advertisers. For instance, the cost of a thirty-second spot for *Modern Family* began at $130,388 in fall 2009 before the show's ratings were proven.[8] However, not all audiences that comprise the value of this spot are created equal. The most coveted demographic for the television industry is 18–49-year-old white, college-educated males with above-average incomes. Advertisers consider such audience members to have more discretionary income and be more susceptible to changing brands than other demographic segments. Networks thus create programs, first and foremost, to serve these specific demographic and advertiser needs.

Since *Modern Family* was designed to attract this demographic, and subsequently has drawn a large portion of it, it is not surprising that ABC would enter into a brand partnership with Apple. While the demographics for a typical Apple user skew differently across product lines, the computer company also pays attention to the psychographic market segment of the "early adopter"—a person who embraces an advantageous new product or technology before others do. A 2007 report conducted by Solutions Research Group on the potential first-generation "early adopters" of the iPhone concluded they were educated men in their thirties, living in New York or California, with household incomes of $75,600 a year.[9] The late thirty-something, affluent, Californian Phil Dunphy—the self-identified "early adopter" himself—makes "Game Changer" a textbook description of this psychographic. A preliminary market research report shortly before the airing of "Game Changer" lends further support to this argument, revealing that 27% in the 18–34 age range (compared to 18% of all consumers) expressed an interest in buying the iPad.[10] Five months after the device's release, iPad users, according to Nielsen, were 65% male and 63% under the age of thirty-five. Additionally, 25% of iPad users had incomes of $100K or more, while 51% had a bachelor's degree or higher.[11] This demographic and psychographic compatibility suggests that integrating the iPad into *Modern Family* was a no-brainer: a high-profile show integrating a highly desired device just days before its launch made perfect sense.

Demographic alliances between brands like ABC and Apple have greatly increased due to profound technological and economic changes in the media industries during the last ten years. These partnerships reflect a volatile historical moment in which networks, advertisers, and viewers are reevaluating the terms of their relationships with one another. Media clutter, audience fragmentation, and digital convergence have increasingly made it more difficult for media companies to reach the younger end of the 18–49 demographic. The increase in the number of media, media outlets, and media technologies has given audiences more choices for consuming entertainment where they want, when they want, and how they want. For instance, almost 36% of TV households (up from 13.5% three years earlier) were equipped with digital video recorders (DVRs) when "Game Changer" aired, while the average American was watching more than ten hours of time-shifted TV per month.[12] Together with viewer erosion, greater competition, and rampant piracy, social and cultural shifts such as these have dramatically reshaped the way the media industries do business with one another.

Increased product placement deals have become one solution to this crisis; integration spending in television, movies, Internet, videogames, and other media totaled $3.61 billion in 2009 and is poised to double by 2014.[13] Certainly, the hostility directed at the iPad integration in "Game Changer" partly had to do with the overwhelming pervasiveness of product placement in contemporary U.S. media. From the standpoint of Apple, the ABC network, and the program's production studio, Twentieth Century Fox Television, *Modern Family* represented a timely marketing opportunity that could attract widespread media publicity for both the iPad and the series while also combating DVR ad-skipping in the home. Many viewers, however, felt that these companies had violated a social contract they had with the series by seemingly joining forces to impose a sales pitch into the narrative fabric of a beloved show purely for profit and marketing purposes. In their mind, the timing of the episode—three days before the release of the iPad—reeked of opportunism at the hands of corporate executives. The iPad integration seemed to be coordinated no differently than the well-timed, multiplatform product placements ever present in reality shows. In cases like *The Amazing Race* or *Survivor*, product integration is to be expected. Not so with scripted comedies and dramas, particularly those series like *Modern Family* that are defined as "quality television" by various interpretive communities.[14] It is assumed that "quality television" series are not inhibited by the same financial constraints, popular trends, and advertising demands that plague most other television productions. *Modern Family* was believed to be above such base commerce for these critics and viewers. Or so they thought.

Even if ABC adhered to its commercial mandate and demanded that Levitan and Lloyd integrate the iPad into *Modern Family* at the behest of Steve Jobs, such an explanation does not fully account for the positive response about the product placement from many fans and critics, for whom Phil Dunphy's excitement over the new device seemed to be a logical extension of his character rather than an advertisement for Apple. Longtime television journalist Josef Adalian of The Wrap personally took Hibberd and CNET's Chris Matyszczyk to task for claiming product integration without proof and for being TV storytelling purists. "If you're trying to tell a story about a character irrationally lusting over a tech product circa spring 2010, spoofing the iPad was the obvious (and reasonable) choice. If it had been spring 2009, Phil would no doubt be praying for a Kindle. And if it were 2011, he'd probably be begging for a 3-D TV set."[15] In fact, Levitan remarked that Phil's frenzy over getting an iPad for his birthday would better tap into the zeitgeist rather than the original choice—a videogame.[16]

The writers of *Modern Family* had made Phil's obsession with technology and gadgets clear earlier that year in "Fifteen Percent" (January 20, 2010). That plotline concerns Claire's inability to work Phil's universal remote for their new theater system. After Claire breaks the remote out of frustration, Phil informs her, "The experts at CNET.com rated it the best remote. They gave it three-and-a-half mice." Following this setup, the iPad in "Game Changer" can appear then to be story-driven and a natural fit for techno-geek Phil. When Phil tells Claire, "Next week! That's like the worst thing you can say to an early adopter," after she fails to get him the iPad on its release day, his words likely rang true for many audience members. Thus, Phil's stroking of his iPad at the end of the episode while whispering "I love you" to it, can easily be perceived as true to character and a satisfying ending to the episode's narrative arc, rather than an awkward product placement.

When viewed as creative synergy between art and commerce rather than corporate synergy among Fox, ABC, and Apple, the general success of the iPad integration can partially be attributed to a certain amount of agency that Levitan, Lloyd, and their writing team had in the decision-making process. Even though the specific nature of their negotiations with executives over the aesthetic and narrative use of the iPad is unknown, the writers' creative agency over the depiction could not have been completely unfettered or unregulated. Thus, when viewed within Havens and Lotz's Industrialization of Culture framework, it becomes apparent that various industrial forces and practices circumscribed their autonomy, shaping how the device would be narrativized in the episode. These concessions—fueled largely by the profit motive of ABC and Apple—may have compromised *Modern Family's* free creative reign and might give validity to viewer claims that the show "sold out." "Organic"—a marketing term that suggests seamless, subtle, or inconspicuous product integration—disguises the notion that the iPad, like any product, must always be presented in a positive, consumer-friendly light. In this vein, one could view Phil's description of the device as "a movie theater, library, and music store all rolled into one awesome pad" as a virtual commercial about the iPad's selling points preapproved by Apple executives.

Or consider the dramatic pause on the exterior of the Apple Store in "Game Changer" as Claire rushes to the back of the line to pick up an iPad from a new shipment. Panning her movement screen right to left in wide shot, the camera momentarily freezes when the Apple logo hits the center of the frame in an aesthetic decision unmotivated by narrative concerns. And one can construe another scene as explicitly promoting Apple, as when Claire presents Phil his virtual birthday cake (after Luke ate the material one) in the form of an iPad app.

As Phil professes his love to his iPad at episode's end, celebratory music kicks in on the soundtrack as family members gather behind him in a picturesque tableau, all equally mesmerized by the iPad. These lines of dialogue and aesthetic choices appear market-driven rather than character-driven, designed to celebrate the device's functionality and splendor. Such a reading is reinforced by the absence

FIGURE 27.1.
Phil blows out the
birthday candles on his
brand new iPad.

of any criticism of the iPad in "Game Changer," though a number of limitations of the device's first version were in fact well known before it became available for purchase. No camera or video recorder, no multitasking capability, no Flash support (the latter a particular complaint since the introduction of the iPhone)—any of these deficiencies could have been addressed in the episode. That they are not suggests the creative limitations placed on the creators of *Modern Family*. Had there been no such limitations surrounding product integration, one might have expected to see an episode in which the Dunphys were terrified of driving their Toyota Sienna after unintended acceleration problems caused the automaker to recall over nine million vehicles in November 2009 and January 2010.

When viewed through this framework of circumscribed agency, it is arguable that whether or not Apple paid for the placement of the iPad in "Game Changer" does not really matter. The episode exposed the internalized logic of American commercial television, one that supports a broader consumerist mindset regardless of actual sponsorship. In fact, "Game Changer" was a textbook example of scripted brand integration of products into a primetime television program, as James Grant Hay, the founder and CEO of Australian brand integration agency InShot, has observed. For Hay, *Modern Family* told the iPad story in a compelling, innovative, and *organic* way: the iPad was strongly integrated into the story narrative, the device was positively mentioned in several different contexts, and the actors emotionally engaged with the product while using it on screen.[17] Apple need not have paid for the iPad placement because the internalized logic of commercial television is to promote consumerism, turn audiences into commodities, and celebrate a product as a vital component of "realism." In the end, a light comedy like *Modern Family* could never critique a real product, questioning the functionality of the iPad or the safety of Toyota cars, as doing so would bristle against the norms of general consumer culture.

Two months after the airing of "Game Changer," Jeff Morton, a producer on *Modern Family*, told attendees at the Produced By Conference that the episode "may have gone a little too far in hindsight." While he confirmed that Apple compensated no one at Twentieth Century Fox Television or ABC for the brand integration, he did acknowledge that "the public thought it was a giant sellout" and that it "sort of backfired on us."[18] Since "Game Changer's" airing, *Modern Family* has not entered into any conspicuously overt product placement like that of the iPad. Or perhaps they have not found any prominent advertiser with whom to strike an iPad-like integration. Then again, there goes Phil, in the season 2 episode, "The Musical Man" (April 13, 2011), hurrying daughter Haley outside the side door of his Toyota van, exclaiming, "The doors slide, the seats slide. What can't the Sienna do?"

NOTES

1. Nellie Andreeva, "Full 2010–2011 TV Series Season Rankings," *Deadline Hollywood*, May 27, 2011, http://www.deadline.com/2011/05/full-2010–11-season-series-rankers/#more-135917.

2. Joe Flint, "'Modern Family' Gives Some Free Love to the iPad," *Los Angeles Times*, Company Town, April 1, 2010, http://latimesblogs.latimes.com/entertainmentnews-buzz/2010/04/modern-family-gives-some-free-love-for-the-ipad.html.

3. James Hibberd, "Release the iPad! Products Disrupt Wednesday Hits," *Hollywood Reporter*'s The Live Feed, April 1, 2010, http://www.hollywoodreporter.com/blogs/live-feed/release-ipad-products-disrupt-wednesday-53365.

4. James Hibberd, "Modern Family Co-Creator Explains iPad Use," *Hollywood Reporter*'s The Live Feed, April 1, 2010, http://www.thrfeed.com/2010/04/modern-family-cocreator-explains-ipad-use.html.

5. Brian Steinberg, "Why Modern Family Still Drives Toyota," *Advertising Age*, March 8, 2010, http://adage.com/article/madisonvine-news/product-placement-modern-family-drives-toyota/142656/.

6. See chapter 1 of Timothy Havens and Amanda D. Lotz, *Understanding Media Industries* (Oxford: Oxford University Press, 2012), 1–26.

7. Ibid., 23.

8. Brian Steinberg, "'Modern Family' Featured an iPad but ABC Didn't Collect," *Advertising Age*, April 1, 2010, http://adage.com/article/mediaworks/modern-family-ipad-abc-collect/143105/.

9. http://www.srgnet.com/pdf/iPhoneBuyersAnalysisJune07.pdf.

10. "Apple Owners Nearly 40 Percent More Interested in the iPad than Non-Apple Owners, According to NPD," NPD Group, March 26, 2010, http://www.npd.com/press/releases/press_100326.html.

11. "State of the Media: The Increasingly Connected Consumer: Connected Devices: A Look Behind the Growing Popularity of iPads, Kindles and Other Devices," Nielsen Media Research, October 2010.

12. Robert Seidman, "DVR Penetration Grows to 39.7% of Households, 42% of Viewers," *TV by the Numbers*, March 23, 2011, http://tvbythenumbers.zap2it.com/2011/03/23/dvr-penetration-grows-to-39-7-of-households-42-2-of-viewers/86819/; "State of the Media: TV Usage Trends: Q3 and Q4 2010," Nielsen Media Research, 2011.

13. Andrew Hampp, "Product Placement Dipped Last Year for the First Time," *Advertising Age*, June 29, 2010, http://adage.com/article/madisonvine-news/product-placement-dipped-year-time/144720/.

14. For the debates about the term "quality" in relation to television, see Jane Feuer, Paul Kerr, and Tise Vahimagi, *MTM: 'Quality Television'* (London: BFI, 1984), Janet McCabe and Kim Akass, eds., *Quality TV: Contemporary American Television and Beyond* (London; I. B. Tauris, 2007); and Mark Jancovich and James Lyons, eds., *Quality Popular Television: Cult TV, the Industry, and Fans* (London: BFI, 2008).

15. Josef Adalian, "The iPad-'Modern Family' Non-troversy: Enough!," *The Wrap*, April 2, 2010, www.thewrap.com/tv/column-post/ipad-modern-family-non-troversy-enough-15905. Adalian was referring to Chris Matyszczyk's online column in which he called the iPad integration on *Modern Family* "less of a product placement and more of product kidnapping a show and holding it by the neck very tightly indeed until it handed over a pile of money." See "30-Minute iPad Ad on 'Modern Family,'" CNET, April 1, 2010, http://news.cnet.com/8301-17852_3-10471959-71.html.

16. Quoted in Sam Schneider and Suzanne Vranica, "iPad Gets Star Turn in Television Comedy," *Wall Street Journal*, April 2, 2010.

17. James Grant Hay, "The Genesis of Apple's 'Modern Family' iPad Story," InShot: Your Brand in Film, Television, and Multimedia, http://inshot.com.au/2010/04/the-genesis-of-apples-modern-family-ipad-story/.

18. Joe Flint, "'Modern Family' Producer Says iPad Episode 'Went Too Far in Hindsight,'" *Los Angeles Times*, Company Town, June 5, 2010, http://latimesblogs.latimes.com/entertainmentnewsbuzz/2010/06/modern-family-producer-says-ipad-episode-went-too-far-in-hindsight.html.

FURTHER READING

Gillan, Jennifer. *Television and New Media: Must-Click TV*. New York: Routledge, 2011.

Gray, Jonathan. *Television Entertainment*. New York: Routledge, 2008.

Havens, Timothy, and Amanda D. Lotz. *Understanding Media Industries*. Oxford: Oxford University Press, 2012.

Mittell, Jason. *Television and American Culture*. Oxford: Oxford University Press, 2010.

28

Monday Night Football
Brand Identity

VICTORIA E. JOHNSON

Abstract: As one of American television's longest-running and most successful primetime programs, *Monday Night Football* demonstrates the central role that sports plays for the medium. Victoria Johnson charts the history of *MNF*, its role in establishing both ABC and the NFL, and its continuing importance on ESPN and in the digital era.

Early in the fall 2011 season of ESPN's *Monday Night Football* (2005–present), a controversy threatened to shift attention from the field of play to a multi-mediated arena where country rock music, politics, and talking-head news programs meet. Hank Williams, Jr., the singer of the *Monday Night Football* opening anthem, "All My Rowdy Friends Are Here on Monday Night," had appeared on *Fox and Friends* (Fox News Channel, 1998–present), where he referred to Adolf Hitler when speaking of President Obama. ESPN immediately removed Williams's song from the *MNF* opening and, within a week, permanently severed ties with him. ESPN's decision to choose this time and venue to distance itself from a performer whose political commitments were neither quiet nor mainstream prior to this event is significant.[1] Williams had challenged the core principles—or principle veneer—of one of the most iconic brands in television history. His statement abruptly threatened to shift *MNF*'s focus as an over forty-year-old U.S. ritual engagement with sport from a shared seasonal cultural forum to a site of segmentation, disjunction and incoherence. The controversy exposed the work that is required to construct *MNF* each week as an unusually *consensual* space characterized by appeals that bridge audience segmentations or divides, whether generational, racial, class-based, gendered, or geographic. This brief rupture encourages us to examine the critical historic and continuing significance of sport TV to networks and media brand identities, and can help explain why such controversies capture wide national attention and concern.

Monday Night Football's (ABC, 1970–2005) popularity through the 1970s and into the 1980s qualified as a genuine cultural phenomenon. While claims that "restaurants closed, theater business fell off, and even doctors refused to deliver babies until the final gun had sounded" are likely exaggerated, its highest-rated games of the three-network era regularly attracted huge audiences with an over 29 rating and over 40 share.[2] Even now, in the multichannel, multiplatform environment, the program's numbers still regularly win its night for all adults aged 18–49, despite the somewhat more limited availability of ESPN compared to broadcast networks. It is no exaggeration to state that *Monday Night Football* resuscitated ABC as a network in the 1970s and ushered in its dominance as the leading broadcaster into the 1980s. Business practices—rights to telecast football and scheduling strategies to counter-program one's rivals—cannot, on their own, create such a huge success, however. *MNF's* status as a cultural phenomenon with unprecedented staying power can be understood only when considering its particularly broad, ritual, and routinized appeal; its aesthetic, aural, narrative, and "casting" conventions and address; and its function as, arguably, one of the lone remaining sites of shared cultural engagement within the U.S. media landscape that is overtly *inclusive*, while remaining adaptive to trends.

In his study *Brands* (2006), Marcel Danesi notes that products, goods, and services with clear brand identities are "imbued with specific kinds of personal and lifestyle meanings" and evoke a constellation of associations "that generate goodwill and care for the product" or corporation whose identity is linked to a set of positive, associated values.[3] Successful branding thus links emotion with a corporate appeal or good, obscuring the market relation between products and brands entirely and subsuming relations of exchange with the resonance of emotional reward.[4] Television networks build powerful brand identities through strong generic cues, casting, visual/sonic codes, scheduling, and commercial unity. Business practices create a symbolic field that signals a coherent destination for a viewer who is addressed and welcomed as belonging to that network's community. Unlike other conventional consumer products and corporations, however, television networks are able to create brand loyalty through the ritual rhythms created by scheduling and the resulting connection to viewers' regular weekly and daily engagements with "must-see" nights of viewing at particular go-to network destinations. Television brands can, in this sense, be sites of community and culture—as something people *do*, engaging a daily or weekly individual ritual, or a shared familial, communal, and even national cultural practice. With its annual, seasonal, and weekly ritual rhythms, yet ever-changing narratives, perhaps no genre serves this role better than sport television.

In the fall of 2011, *NBC's Sunday Night Football* (2006–present) rated higher than any other network reality, drama, or comedy series for the first time in television history.[5] With new rights deals struck by NBC, CBS, FOX, ESPN, and DirecTV through 2022, the National Football League will soon earn almost $6 billion a year in television rights fees alone. Notably, sport TV succeeds according to both the classic logics of broadcast culture—attracting a large, broadly diversified, national audience live, in real-time, defeating DVR technologies or time-shifting—*and* the new profit streams from multiplatform strategies, such as hand-held, online, or digital multiscreening.[6] Indeed, the economic possibility and viability of all such new media endeavors are increasingly dependent upon sports telecast rights. The profitability and fees at stake indicate why networks would be particularly vigilant to protect a successful sport franchise, series, or brand in this climate. But it is important to note that sport TV's relevance to television's institutional profitability and sport's key function in branding network identity have been critical from broadcasting's inception. Through the 1970s, no network was more dependent upon this relationship than ABC, and no series has been more iconic in this regard than *MNF*.

Formed from the sale of RCA's Blue radio network to Edward J. Noble in 1943, ABC was at a competitive disadvantage to distinguish itself upon its entry into television. ABC thus developed a strategy to counter-program its rivals, scheduling genres of musical-variety series and country-and-western programs to attract broad, multigenerational, and predominantly rural family audiences. Through the 1950s, ABC also established partnerships with Warner Bros. and Disney studios to provide original family-friendly and action-oriented programming fare that would have immediate marquee value and advertiser appeal. By the 1960s, these strategies grew ABC's audience numbers but kept the network's profits stagnant, with one exception: sport programming.

In 1960, having proven its ability to schedule for mass audiences and shown profitability with sport programming, ABC took a strategic risk: It signed a five-year, $8.5 million television contract to carry American Football League games.[7] The AFL was perceived as the secondary pro league to the NFL, whose games were, at that time, carried exclusively on top-rated CBS. With the immediate influx of ABC's cash distributed evenly to each of the league's clubs, the AFL was suddenly competitive with the NFL for player contracts and salaries. This sudden viability urged the NFL to consider a league merger, which created a new American Football Conference (AFC) and National Football Conference (NFC) conjoined as a National Football League.[8]

While broadcasters had purchased the rights to air sporting events from early in the network era, a legal change encouraged major professional league television packages for regular season coverage and codified the National Football League as a fundamentally *national* enterprise in ways that have since allowed the league to argue that it has more in common with a public service than with the interests of a private corporation. Specifically, the Sports Broadcasting Act of 1961 made sports leagues exempt from antitrust laws and permitted them to broker broadcasting agreements for all of their teams as a package to networks that successfully bid for telecast rights. As ABC's example in the 1960s proved (and, later, FOX's in the 1990s and NBC's in the 2000s), the viability of both sport leagues *and* television networks has since been staked on winning these rights.[9]

By this exemption, individual NFL teams do not sell and control the television rights within their own local markets. U.S. professional football is, thus, uniquely national in economic organization, institutional identity, and viewer availability. While football fans are well aware that where you live determines what teams you get to see more often than not, even "local" games are negotiated based on League rules and restrictions. Overall, especially for viewers who are out-of-market from a local team, the NFL offers fans of "the League" more national games each week than any other major-league sport, with multiple regular season games airing weekly over seventeen Sundays and Mondays, multiple regular season games airing weekly on eight Thursdays, and all-inclusive playoff coverage following.[10]

Between passage of the Sports Broadcasting Act and the AFL/NFL merger, the NFL's centrality to the profitability of 1960s TV became stunningly apparent when CBS paid $28 million in rights fees for the 1964 and 1965 NFL seasons and was immediately rewarded with sponsorships from Ford and Philip Morris of $14 million each.[11] However, according to the NFL commissioner at the time, Pete Rozelle, such success would be limited if it was confined to Sunday afternoons. Thus, Rozelle sought to expand the audience for football beyond the weekend daytime male viewer to a broad, family viewing audience, and particularly to capture female viewers.[12] This was, of course, the exact audience and genre of programming that ABC knew best.

The network's last-place status led Rozelle to first approach CBS, NBC, and even the new Howard Hughes–owned Sports Network before he would listen to ABC's pitch to be a prime time home for the NFL. But CBS was exceptionally successful on Monday night, with a solid line-up of comedy and variety that already appealed broadly to families and to the female head of household demographic via *Mayberry, RFD, The Doris Day Show,* and *The Carol Burnett Show.* NBC, approached next, had such a vast catalog of films that the network had just added a *Monday Night at the Movies* to its schedule.[13]

Roone Arledge claims that his pitch memo arguing for ABC's acquisition of primetime football was inspired by his wife, Joan, whose people-watching and enjoyment of the ambient activity at a Notre Dame-Army football game made him consider the spectacular and narrative properties of the sport as much as the score or outcome.[14] Arledge argued that—particularly in primetime, with the added drama of nighttime photography, lighting, and effects—*Monday Night*

Football would create a completely "new form of televised sports drama" that would immerse a nation of viewers, together, in the human spectacle of sport.[15] Rather than replicating the view from the stands, Arledge envisioned immersing the viewer in the action itself, as well as offering the best access to all of the ambient sights and sounds of the venue, so that the spectator could "experience the countless things that make up the feeling of the game."[16] While primetime coverage would be visually distinct from daytime games, Arledge also considered *MNF* to be in a separate category from other football coverage in terms of its production value, resource allocation, and attention to narrative depth and detail: these included using three times more cameras to cover the action than during a day game, *MNF*'s innovations in slow-motion and instant-replay photography, and in-depth, behind-the-scenes half-time and sideline reporting featuring players as protagonists to follow during the week's game's story arc. While these techniques are now standard fare in nearly all sport coverage, *MNF* introduced the visual, technical, and narrative grammar for all such production.[17]

MNF's aesthetic and story innovations extended to the aural realm as well. The program experimented with modern sound design and effects, particularly to evoke a sense of consistent movement and to sustain energy throughout each broadcast. By its second season, *MNF*'s distinctive "dun dun dun dun" theme song had established its sonic brand. Titled "Heavy Action," the theme was composed by Johnny Pearson for a British sports competition show, *Superstars,* and was reengineered in 1987 by composer Edd Kalehoff. At various periods in the series' history, other themes have been added to "Heavy Action" in attempts to enhance specific demographic appeals and to promote corporate family members within the program's address. Hank Williams, Jr.'s "All My Rowdy Friends Are Coming Over Tonight" was adapted to commemorate the twentieth anniversary of *Monday Night Football* in 1989, and Williams became a fixture with music video openings adapted for each week's different competitors. In 1993, ABC partnered with rock, rap, and soul artists affiliated with Polygram Records "in favor of a musical approach styled to reach a broader" and ostensibly younger demographic.[18] But Williams soon returned to be featured in subsequent seasons until the 2011 controversy. The value of the ongoing use of the iconic "dun dun dun dun" *MNF* theme and its weekly inclusion from the series' inception to the present were underscored. The classic theme's consistency and familiarity cut through any momentary controversy to call *MNF* viewers back to what "matters," connecting the week's match-up with the seasonal ritual that outlives time-bound incidents, and assuring the continuity of a cultural icon beyond the gridiron.

Monday Night Football's original announcer cast—Howard Cosell, Don Meredith, and Frank Gifford—remained together for only eleven seasons, yet they forged a template for a new mode of sports announcing that has arguably helped usher in sports talk and phenomena such as ESPN itself. As part of a strategy to never allow lapses in interest throughout the broadcast, the booth announcers were "cast" to appeal to the broad, "mass" national viewing audience in a balance of personality types, looks, and expertise that would engage viewers in a volatile mix and encourage living room debates. Howard Cosell was a former lawyer who had risen to fame as a sports announcer particularly due to a close relationship with boxer Muhammad Ali at the height of Ali's career. His persona was unapologetically abrasive and impolitic.[19] Meredith had been the star quarterback for the Dallas Cowboys and was intended to represent a "Middle America" country-boy type, while deflating Cosell as well as providing gentle humor and "straight talk" about the sport itself. Frank Gifford had both a star athlete's background—having been a standout offensive player for the New York Giants—and a celebrity's polish in the broadcast booth. According to Gifford, his role was to be the mediator of the proceedings as "Howard pontificated. Don Meredith was the country guy who kept the big city slicker straight. I kept law and order."[20]

In the multichannel era, ABC's sibling network ESPN has taken up and expanded most of the practices the broadcaster initiated for the digital and multi-platform age. *MNF*'s transition from ABC to ESPN in 2005 was relatively seamless, as, in many ways, it represented a logical transference in an era when broadcasters and cable operators are increasingly siblings with shared interests within the same large conglomerate family wherein cable outlets frequently underwrite the endeavors of their broadcast partners. ESPN was launched independently in 1979 (as the "Entertainment and Sports Programming Network"), but by 1984, Capital Cities/ABC was a majority owner of the channel with the Hearst Corporation. By 2005, *MNF*'s move to cable was supported by ESPN's extensive in-home availability on basic cable packages, as well as its multiple cable outlets, websites, radio networks, mobile apps, magazine, and other extensions of its brand beyond the constraints of ABC's broadcast or affiliate schedules. The transition was further supported by ESPN's comparative content and programming flexibilities, the program's generic fit with ESPN, and the outlet's tremendous profitability. ESPN has since enhanced and capitalized upon cross-platform promotional and coverage possibilities for *Monday Night Football* such as using multiscreen venues for each game (e.g., HD, Spanish language, online, etc.), and beginning *MNF* coverage up to six hours prior to kickoff.

ABC's initial risk in signing the AFL thus paid off in institutional stability, consolidation, and growth for both entities. In the years between its coverage of AFL games and the finalization of the NFL merger and launch of *Monday Night Football*, ABC became the "Worldwide Leader in Sports" as it developed its expertise in Olympics coverage and weekly digest programming with *Wide World of Sports* (1961–1997) and *American Sportsman* (1965–1984), as well as its college

FIGURE 28.1.
The incomparable Howard Cosell jokes with co-host "Dandy Don" Meredith in the first episode of ABC's *Monday Night Football*.

football and college football bowl game coverage. Due largely to *Monday Night Football*, ABC became the top network in the 1970s, adding new affiliates and resurrecting its other program divisions to the extent that it featured fourteen of the top twenty rated programs in primetime. *MNF* is a rare series whose impact on industry history, sport culture, and our ways of visualizing and telling ourselves stories about sport are impossible to overestimate.[21]

Prior to Hank Williams, Jr.'s 2011 firing, it is likely that the most controversial and polarizing merger of music, the NFL, and television occurred with Janet Jackson's "wardrobe malfunction" at Super Bowl XXXVIII in 2004. While shocking to many, the special-event nature of the Super Bowl allowed that controversy to be categorized as exceptional and to be contained. By contrast, until 2011, as a presumptive spokesman for *MNF*, Williams was symbolic of a weekly inclusive and ritually shared broadcast community, *not* of a particularized, segmented, narrowcast-appeal point-of-view. In the fall of 2011, however, his political outspokenness threatened to rupture or expose the constructed nature or vulnerability of television as a site of shared culture. His "rowdiness" risked undermining and altering an engaging weekly ritual, a site of mainstream, "national" inclusiveness. ESPN's swift response to the controversy thus reassured audiences, sponsors, and the NFL that—as the second-longest running series in all of primetime—*MNF* would remain a distinctive cultural focal point that could appeal, live and in real-time, to a multigenerational, multiregional, diversified demographic and market audience.[22] Thus, the *MNF* brand promises the possibility of consensual, broad(cast) culture commitments in an increasingly fragmented media era. This possibility may be a rapidly diminishing and tenuous one, but *MNF*'s continued success points both to its industrial and affective

FIGURE 28.2.
Hank Williams, Jr., along with some of his rowdy friends, record a promo for *MNF* prior to the singer making comments that threatened the program's inclusive brand.

viability with viewers, even in the face of ongoing media transitions and commercial and critical discourses that posit that segmentation and division define the national interest.

NOTES

1. Hank Williams, Jr., began singing "All My Rowdy Friends Are Here on Monday Night" in 1989, during the twentieth anniversary season of *Monday Night Football,* and had participated in every season since, though his song was featured only in the opening game of the 1993 season. Williams is a vocal political conservative who has explored running for office (senator, Tennessee, 2012) and who has written and recorded divisive songs including the 1988 "If the South Woulda Won" (the Civil War).

2. Bert Sugar, *"The Thrill of Victory": The Inside Story of ABC Sports* (New York: Hawthorn Books, Inc., 1978), 278.

3. Marcel Danesi, *Brands* (New York: Routledge, 2006), 1, 7.

4. For a case-study of contemporary branding, see Robert Goldman and Stephen Papson, *Nike Culture: The Sign of the Swoosh* (Thousand Oaks, CA: Sage Publications, 1998).

5. Michael McCarthy, "'Sunday Night Football' Rules Prime Time," *USA Today,* January 5, 2011, 3C.

6. For further discussion of the "new" and "old" value of sport TV, see Victoria E. Johnson, "Everything Old is New Again: Sport Television, Innovation, and Tradition for a Multi-Platform Era," in *Beyond Prime Time: Television Programming in the Post-Network Era,* Amanda D. Lotz, ed. (New York: Routledge, 2009), 114–37.

7. Michael Oriard, *Brand NFL: Making and Selling America's Favorite Sport* (Chapel Hill: University of North Carolina Press, 2007), 19.

8. Sugar, 275. The league's merged schedule began in 1970.

9. John T. Wolohan, "United States," in *TV Rights and Sport: Legal Aspects,* Ian Blackshaw, Steve Cornelius, and Robert Sickmann, eds. (The Hague, The Netherlands: TMC Asser Press, 2009), 569, 575.

10. For a detailed explanation of the NFL's policies regarding local restrictions on coverage and blackout rules for carriage, see Jon Kraszewski, "Pittsburgh in Fort Worth: Football Bars, Sports Television, Sports Fandom, and the Management of Home," *Journal of Sport & Social Issues* 32, 2 (May 2008): 121–38.

11. Erik Barnouw, *Tube of Plenty: The Evolution of American Television*, 2nd rev. ed. (New York: Oxford University Press, 1990), 347.

12. Sugar, 275.

13. Ibid., 276.

14. Marc Gunther and Bill Carter, *Monday Night Mayhem: The Inside Story of ABC's Monday Night Football* (New York: Beech Tree Books, 1988), 18. For more on Arledge, see John Tedesco, "Roone Arledge," in *The Encyclopedia of Television*, Horace Newcomb, ed. (Fitzroy Dearborn, 1997), http://www.museum.tv/eotvsection.php?entrycode=arledgeroon.

15. Benjamin G. Rader, *In Its Own Image: How Television Has Transformed Sports* (New York: The Free Press, 1984), 116.

16. Gunther and Carter, 18.

17. For examples of Arledge's appeal to the "show" of sport, see two ABC-era openings for *Monday Night Football* games available on YouTube as of this writing: from 1973, http://www.youtube.com/watch?v=m8fkMkE2Yjg; and, from 1984, http://www.youtube.com/watch?v=k7LuxcBgSwo&NR=1.

18. J. Max Robins, "MNF Goes from C&W to Rock, Rap," *Daily Variety,* August 6, 1993, 5.

19. Phil Patton, *Razzle-Dazzle: The Curious Marriage of Television and Professional Football* (New York: The Dial Press, 1984), 107.

20. Quoted in Michael McCarthy, "ABC's Monday Night Finale Is a Night of Reckoning," *USA Today,* December 27, 2005, 4C.

21. Christopher Anderson, "American Broadcasting Company," in *Encyclopedia of Television*, 2nd ed., Horace Newcomb, ed. (New York: Fitzroy Dearborn, 2004), 89.

22. The longest-running series in primetime is *60 Minutes* (CBS, 1968–present).

FURTHER READING

Danesi, Marcel. *Brands.* New York: Routledge, 2006.

Johnson, Victoria E. "Everything New Is Old Again: Sport Television, Innovation, and Tradition for a Multi-Platform Era." In *Beyond Prime Time: Television Programming in the Post-Network Era*, Amanda D. Lotz, ed. New York: Routledge, 2009).

Oriard, Michael. *Brand NFL: Making and Selling America's Favorite Sport.* Chapel Hill: University of North Carolina Press, 2007.

29

NYPD Blue
Content Regulation

JENNIFER HOLT

Abstract: Studies of regulation and policy often seem distinct from the analysis of television programming and content. But in this examination of the controversial series *NYPD Blue,* Jennifer Holt traces the show's role in the FCC's history of "policing" controversial content, and thus reveals how the politics of regulation are integral to what we watch on TV.

The critically acclaimed series *NYPD Blue* (ABC, 1993–2005) had a remarkably long run, particularly for a program noted not just for its gritty aesthetic and ensemble of complex characters, but for pushing boundaries in the areas of profane language and nudity on primetime broadcast programming. The show's language and "adult content" inspired protests from religious groups, letter-writing campaigns to the Federal Communications Commission (FCC), citizen boycotts, and blackouts by more than fifty ABC affiliates in its first year. *NYPD Blue* was also embroiled in a long-standing battle with regulators, which heated up at the end of the show's run, as the FCC's philosophy of regulating content turned significantly in 2004. Subsequently, in 2008, the agency fined ABC for nudity in an episode that had aired five years earlier ("Nude Awakening," February 25, 2003). Years of legal arguments ensued, and the ultimate resolution dismissing the fines did little to clear up long-standing confusion about the standards employed to police content on broadcast television.

Indeed, the history of broadcast content regulation is defined more by its struggles than by any coherent set of rules or guidelines. The *NYPD Blue* case marks a critically important moment in this contentious history, challenging the conceptual underpinnings of indecency regulation while the FCC fought vehemently to protect them. Through this protracted battle, industrial, social, and cultural anxieties about nudity and indecent material—and their appropriate televisual manifestations—were also on display. The series and the network's indecency case made cultural politics, and the politicization of the FCC, more public. Exploring the ways in which these aspects of content regulation became embattled during the run of *NYPD Blue*, most notably after the "Nude Awakening" episode, reveals a new layer of drama in ways that policy—and its history—become visible in the television text.

NYPD Blue was co-created by David Milch and Steven Bochco, who had previously collaborated on *Hill St. Blues* (NBC, 1981–1987). The series became most closely associated with Bochco, a writer-producer with a long history of developing successful, stylistic genre programs, such as *Hill St. Blues*, *LA Law* (NBC, 1986–1994), and *Doogie Howser, M.D.* (ABC, 1989–1993). While *Hill St.*'s realist aesthetic and mature content was daring for its time, *NYPD Blue* was clearly Bochco's most controversial effort; he even described it as network television's first R-rated series, and one that would intentionally stretch the boundaries of suitability in broadcasting.[1] Nevertheless, it was a mainstay of commercial broadcast television for twelve years and remains ABC's longest running one-hour drama series.

Set in the fictional 15th precinct, *NYPD Blue* featured an ensemble cast centered on the racist, homophobic—yet somehow redeemable—recovering alcoholic Detective Andy Sipowicz and his succession of police partners. Short, graphic bursts of violence were common, and nudity and foul language were regular components of the program as well. Characters used words like "bitch," "asshole," "bullshit," and "dickhead," along with vivid descriptions of breasts and other body parts never before uttered on primetime network television. The inclusion of these elements was partly a function of the show's commitment to realism—often the justification used by producers. *NYPD Blue*'s substantial critical accolades, including twenty Emmy awards, four Golden Globes, and two Peabody Awards, lauded the show's unflinching look at life on and off the job. As the Peabody announcement in 1996 said, *NYPD Blue* was the police genre at its best, providing "gritty and realistic insight into the dilemmas and tragedies which daily confront those who spend their lives in law enforcement."[2]

The use of "adult content" in *NYPD Blue* was also partly a reaction to the incursion of cable into the media landscape. Between 1981 and 1993, the three major networks saw their average ratings (percentage of TV households tuned in) slide from 50 down to 33.6, in large part due to competition from cable channels with far less strict content standards than broadcast networks. Cable would continue to siphon the broadcast audience throughout the 1990s, and the more graphic depictions of sex and violence allowed on cable were fuel for Bochco's aggressive style. Before the premiere, he told the press, "In 1993, when you're doing a cop show, you're competing with cable. I don't think we can at 10 o'clock with our hour dramas effectively compete any longer unless we can paint with some of the same colors that you can paint with when you make a movie."[3]

Months before *NYPD Blue*'s premiere in September 1993, the *New York Times* called it "simply put, the raciest show ever to appear on the networks' prime-time schedule."[4] Fifty-seven ABC affiliates (roughly 25 percent) declined to show the pilot, citing the show's affection for nudity and foul language.[5] It was criticized (before it ever aired) and boycotted by conservative media watchdog organization American Family Association (AFA), among others. The boycott threats by these conservative lobbyists and protests by a host of special interest groups intimidated major advertisers, and the heavy hitters in primetime drama series (soft drinks, beer, fast food, automobiles) initially stayed away. Eventually, however, as the show received numerous critical accolades and a devoted following, they came around.

Despite the initial boycotts and protests, Bochco and Milch did not shy away from depicting controversial material at any point during the series' run. They had already waited an extra year to get the show on the air because of lengthy disputes with ABC's internal censors, the attorneys in standards and practices.[6] The show's formal qualities and commitment to realism continued to be inflammatory, particularly in the industrial and social climate of the 1990s. The FCC had grown more vulnerable to politicized pressures after the 1980s, when 90 percent of television content regulations were eliminated under the stewardship of Chairman Mark Fowler. Conservative interest groups and lobbyists increasingly called on regulators to censor television content on moral grounds. In response, the "big four" broadcast networks threw their critics a small bone in 1993, when they announced they would display a warning in advance of violent shows.[7] For *NYPD Blue*, ABC settled on "This police drama contains strong language and partial nudity. Viewer discretion advised." There is a long tradition in the media industries of such preemptive strikes against government regulation, and this network strategy worked to calm legislators for a time. However, Bochco's insistence on testing the limits for broadcasting adult content, on top of mounting economic pressures, the escalating culture wars over sex and violence on television, and a slow turn toward stricter regulations at the FCC, would prove to be the perfect storm for an inconsistent, ill-defined indecency policy.

The most graphic departure from customary depictions of the human body on *NYPD Blue* was not the corpses that appeared in various stages of undress, but the naked buttocks of squad members on display in romantic scenes or even less salacious contexts like getting ready for work. All actors had a nudity clause in their contract requiring them to bare their bodies if the script called for their doing so.[8] Even Dennis Franz as Detective Sipowicz, an overweight, middle-aged man who was as far from a conventional sex symbol as one could find on American television, showed the world his bare behind. But it was not Dennis Franz's naked moment that fueled the crisis for ABC, however. Nor was it any of the other

FIGURE 29.1.
Though *NYPD Blue* had repeatedly
incorporated nudity dating back to
its pilot episode in 1993, this potentially "indecent" sequence from the
2003 episode "Nude Awakening"
led to a long-running court battle.

male characters on the show, almost all of whom exposed their bodies in some
fashion. Indeed, while David Caruso's racy love scene in the show's pilot told the
world *NYPD Blue* was not afraid of nudity in primetime, it did not elicit much
of a response from regulators. Instead, it was a woman getting into the shower in
the tenth season that would put ABC, *NYPD Blue,* and the FCC in a heated legal
battle over buttocks and their proper place in American media culture.

The episode in question showed Sipowicz's colleague and future wife, Connie
McDowell, getting into the shower at his house and Sipowicz's young son, Theo,
walking in on her. As Connie prepares to enter the shower and takes off her robe,
there are two shots of her naked bottom that last for a total of four to five seconds. One has a quick tilt up and down her backside; the other includes her full

naked body from the side, cleverly shot so as not to reveal any frontal nudity, though a portion of her breast is visible. Next, there is a cut to Theo waking up, kicking off the covers and walking into the bathroom, and a reverse shot from behind and between Connie's legs (evoking a famous image from *The Graduate*) of Theo in shock when he opens the door and sees her naked. We then see Connie's mortified face (with her breasts obscured by a silhouette of Theo's head and ears), and cut to Theo running out saying "Sorry!" The last shot of the scene is Connie standing in the bathroom fully nude, but covering her breasts and pubic area with her hands calling back weakly, "It's OK. No problem . . . " The entire sequence runs about forty seconds, with roughly seven seconds of partial nudity on screen.

After reviewing what was characterized as "numerous complaints," the Enforcement Bureau of the FCC sent a letter of inquiry to ABC one year after the episode aired.[9] ABC's response, which included a transcript of the show and letters explaining why the episode was not indecent, did not satisfy the FCC. In 2008—five years after the episode was broadcast and three years after the series went off the air—the FCC fined ABC and forty-five of its affiliates $1,237,500 for the scripted nudity. Each affiliate was sued for $27,500, the maximum allowable fine for violating the FCC's indecency policy.

Legislative efforts to censor television content have always been a juggling act, as regulators and lawmakers try to balance the lofty yet elusive construct of the "public interest"; First Amendment values and objectives; the maintenance of diversity over the airwaves and the preservation of a robust marketplace of ideas; and the protection of contemporary community standards. The landmark case of *Miller v. California* established a three-pronged test to determine obscenity, and declared that this form of speech is not protected under the First Amendment:

1. If the work as a whole would appeal to the prurient interests of the average person, applying contemporary community standards;
2. If the work depicts or describes, in a patently offensive way, sexual conduct or excretory functions [as defined by applicable state law];
3. If the work, taken as a whole, lacks serious literary, artistic, political, or scientific value [a national standard].[10]

Material that meets all three criteria is deemed obscene and is never allowed on broadcast television. Indecent speech, on the other hand, is another issue—and the one that has proven to be the most divisive for broadcasters and their regulators. Indecent speech is permitted but restricted to the hours of 10 p.m. and 6 a.m., when it is assumed that children will not be watching or listening. Although the FCC was authorized by Congress to impose fines on those who broadcast obscene, indecent, or profane language in 1960, the agency did not exercise its authority to regulate indecent speech until 1975.[11] This occurred in the famous *Pacifica* case, which concerned the broadcast of George Carlin's "Filthy Words" monologue. Carlin's routine was broadcast on a New York educational, non-profit radio station (owned and licensed to the Pacifica Foundation) in the afternoon hours. In that monologue, Carlin uses a great deal of profane language in a satirical commentary on the absurdity of our culture's obsession with certain words considered to be dirty or taboo, especially for television.

After a complaint from one listener, the FCC sued the broadcaster and the case went all the way to the Supreme Court, which ruled that the FCC could legally fine stations and determine indecency in specific contexts. Still, the Supreme Court found Carlin's routine to be indecent, not obscene, and cautioned that the FCC's power was limited, saying that this ruling did not give the FCC "an unrestricted license to decide what speech, protected in other media, may be banned from the airwaves in order to protect unwilling adults from momentary exposure to it . . . "[12] One of the great and largely unheralded contributions of George Carlin to media culture is that his act of mocking media policy actually helped to legally define it. For many years after the *Pacifica* ruling, the FCC focused its enforcement efforts on the use of Carlin's "seven dirty words."[13]

Throughout the 1990s, shows like *NYPD Blue*, *In Living Color*, and *Married . . . With Children* inserted more "adult content" into primetime television. *NYPD Blue* in particular seemed to directly challenge indecency policy with its language and displays of nudity. In 2001, the FCC issued a set of guidelines to attempt to provide direction for broadcasters regarding indecency.[14] These guidelines, drawing on the *Pacifica* decision, explained that indecent material was that which (1) describes or depicts "sexual or excretory organs or activities"; and (2) is "patently offensive as measured by contemporary community standards for the broadcast medium."[15] Also under the policy, whether a broadcast is patently offensive depends on the following three factors: (1) "the explicitness or graphic nature of the description or depiction"; (2) "whether the material dwells on or repeats at length" the description or depiction; and (3) "whether the material appears to pander or is used to titillate, or whether the materials appears to have been presented for its shock value."[16]

In the span of just a few years, this indecency policy got quite a workout. At the 2002 Billboard Awards, Cher addressed her detractors in a live broadcast audience with the line "so fuck 'em." During the 2003 Golden Globe Awards, Bono said as he picked up his award, "This is really, really, fucking brilliant." That same year at Fox's Billboard Music Awards, Nicole Ritchie used the same word when presenting. One month later, ABC aired the "Nude Awakening" episode of *NYPD*

Blue. In January 2004, Janet Jackson had her infamous "wardrobe malfunction" during the halftime show of Super Bowl XXXVIII, when her breast was exposed during a dance routine.

These incidents helped to fuel the already inflamed culture wars, as broadcasters, producers, interest groups, lawmakers, and consumers clashed over freedom of expression in the arts and the government's authority over this domain. The climate for tolerating indecency had also turned, thanks largely to the organization of conservative lobbyists. In 2000, there were 111 complaints about 111 programs made to the FCC. In 2002, there were almost 14,000 complaints made about 389 programs. The following year there were over 200,000 complaints about 375 programs, and in 2004, there were 1.4 million complaints about 314 programs.[17] This stark increase was mostly thanks to the online efforts of the Parents Television Council, a conservative advocacy organization that created and exploited loopholes in the accounting of indecency complaints in order to drastically distort the percentage of the audience that is actually upset.[18]

In response to these complaints and an increasingly reactionary political climate, the FCC's indecency policy changed. In 2004, the FCC declared "for the first time, that a single, nonliteral use of an expletive (a so-called 'fleeting expletive') could be actionably indecent."[19] Additionally, as part of the fallout from the 2004 Super Bowl halftime show, fines for broadcasters exploded. In 2003, the FCC had imposed $440,000 in fines; in 2004, it imposed $8 million.[20] Two years later, Congress increased the maximum fines for broadcasting indecent material tenfold—from $32,500 to $325,000—as part of the Broadcast Decency Enforcement Act, which passed unanimously in the Senate and had only thirty-five dissenting votes in the House.[21]

ABC's response to *NYPD Blue's* 2008 fine highlights the seemingly absurd and almost comical aspects of defining indecency for regulatory purposes. ABC's original defense was that buttocks are not a sexual or excretory organ because, among other reasons, "they do not have sexual or excretory physiological function." The Commission countered that although buttocks are "not physiologically necessary to procreation or excretion, [they] are widely associated with sexual arousal and closely associated by most people with excretory activities."[22] Many pages, and quite a bit of legal maneuvering, were spent on the appropriate characterization and definition of buttocks for this particular case, and on the part of ABC to present them as part of the body's muscular infrastructure and nothing more.

ABC also contended that the nudity was "not presented in a lewd, prurient, pandering, or titillating way" and that the purpose of the scene was to "illustrate . . . the complexity and awkwardness involved when a single parent brings a new romantic partner into his or her life." Arguing that the nudity was not included to depict an attempted seduction or a sexual response, ABC claimed instead that it contributed to the show's much-heralded aesthetic of realism.[23] The FCC did not accept this argument, and the network and its affiliates wound up in court.

At the same time, ABC was in another lawsuit challenging the FCC's indecency policy, along with Fox, CBS, and various affiliate stations.[24] That case, *Fox Television Stations, Inc. v. FCC*, wound its way up to the Supreme Court and back down, and after four years resulted in the appeals court invalidating the FCC's indecency policy. In 2010, the 2nd Circuit Court ruled that the policy was unconstitutional and produced a "chilling effect" on First Amendment–protected speech.[25] The court's ruling is significant for its statement about the dangers of over-regulating media content:

> If the FCC's policy is allowed to remain in place, there will undoubtedly be countless other situations where broadcasters will exercise their editorial judgment and decline to pursue contentious people or subjects, or will eschew live programming altogether, in order to avoid the FCC's fines . . . This chill reaches speech at the heart of the First Amendment.[26]

Because of the decision in the *Fox* case, ABC asked the court to dismiss the fine for *NYPD Blue*, pointing out that the fine was based on an indecency policy since declared unconstitutional. In January 2011, the fine was thrown out, and the FCC was left with no legal means to regulate indecency.

It is still a bit too early, however, for broadcasters to confidently send naked women back into the shower during primetime. The *Fox* case made its way to the Supreme Court for the second time and the standards and fundamental tenets of regulating broadcast content were on trial once again. In the summer of 2012, the Supreme Court reviewed the *Fox* and *ABC* cases together and unanimously decided that the earlier 2nd Circuit Court was wrong: the FCC can indeed regulate indecency; they just need to work on the way they do so. The ruling essentially said that the FCC did not give the broadcasters "fair notice" before they aired the questionable episodes, and invited the commission to modify their standards into something more clear and specific for broadcasters to use.[27] However, since the Supreme Court's decision notably focused its ruling on process and declined to address the First Amendment issues that have been at the heart of the crisis over indecency regulation, the decision actually offered little clarity for broadcasters and almost guarantees future litigation. Consequently, uncertainty still reigns in the arena of policing content regulation, and in many ways, this continued revaluation of propriety and boundaries on television is *NYPD Blue*'s greatest legacy.

NOTES

1. Edmund Andrews, "Mild Slap at TV Violence," *New York Times*, July 1, 1993, A1.

2. Peabody Awards, *NYPD Blue*, 1996; http://www.peabody.uga.edu/winners/details. php?id=157.

3. Elizabeth Kolbert, "Not Only Bochco's Uniforms are Blue," *New York Times*, July 26, 1993, C11.

4. Ibid.

5. Bryan Curtis, "*NYPD Blue*: The Eroticism of the Cop Show," *Slate*, February 23, 2005, http://www.slate.com/id/2113912/.

6. Elizabeth Kolbert, "What's a Network TV Censor to Do?" *New York Times*, May 23, 1993, http://www.nytimes.com/1993/05/23/arts/television-what-s-a-network-tv-censor-to-do. html?pagewanted=all&src=pm.

7. See Edmund Andrews, "TV Violence Gets a Warning," *New York Times*, July 4, 1993, section 4, p. 2.

8. Greg Kennedy, "Blue, Blue Blue: Sex, Violence will Star in Fall Cop Show," *Ottawa Citizen*, July 28, 1993, B7.

9. *In the Matter of Complaints Against Various Television Licensees Concerning Their February 25, 2003, Broadcast of The Program "NYPD Blue."* Forfeiture Order, FCC 08-55, 23 FCC Rcd 3147 (rel. Feb. 19, 2008).

10. See *Miller v. California*, 413 U.S. 15 (1973).

11. See *Fox Television Stations, Inc. v. FCC*, 613 F.3d 317 (2d Cir. 2010).

12. See *FCC v. Pacifica Found.*, 438 U.S. 726 (1978) at 759–60.

13. The "seven dirty words" are "shit," "piss," "cunt," "fuck," "motherfucker," "cocksucker," and "tits." See *FCC v. Pacifica* for a transcript of Carlin's "Filthy Words." Versions of the monologue can also be heard on Carlin's albums *Class Clown* (1972) and *Occupation: Foole* (1973). Carlin was arrested for performing the monologue live in 1972 but the case was eventually thrown out, as the speech was determined to be indecent, rather than obscene.

14. *Industry Guidance on the Commission's Case Law Interpreting 18 U.S.C. § 1464 and Enforcement Policies Regarding Broadcast Indecency*, 16 FCC Rcd 7999 (2001).

15. Ibid, IA.

16. Ibid, IB.

17. FCC Indecency Complaints and NALs: 1993–2004, March 24, 2005, http://transition.fcc. gov/eb/broadcast/ichart.pdf.

18. See, for example, Adam Thierer, "More Inflated FCC Complaints," *The Technology Liberation Front*, September 9, 2009, http://techliberation.com/2009/09/09/ more-inflated-fcc-indecency-complaints/.

19. *Fox Television Stations, Inc. v. FCC*, 9.

20. Ibid, n. 3

21. Frank Ahrens, "The Price for On-Air Indecency Goes Up," *Washington Post*, June 8, 2006, http://www.washingtonpost.com/wp-dyn/content/article/2006/06/07/AR2006060700287.html.

22. *In the Matter of Complaints Against Various Television Licensees Concerning Their February 25, 2003 Broadcast of The Program "NYPD Blue,"* Forfeiture Order, FCC 08-55, 23 FCC Rcd 3147 (rel. Feb. 19, 2008).

23. Ibid.

24. See *Fox Television Stations, Inc. v. FCC*, 613 F.3d 317 (2d Cir. 2010).

25. Ibid.

26. Ibid, 31.

27. See *Federal Communications Commission et al. v. Fox Television Stations Inc., et al.*, Certiorari to the United States Court of Appeals for the Second Circuit, No. 10–1293, argued January 10, 2012, decided June 21, 2012, http://www.supremecourt.gov/opinions/11pdf/10-1293f3e5.pdf.

FURTHER READING

FCC v. Pacifica Foundation 438 US 726 (1978).

Fairman, Christopher M. *Fuck: Word Taboo and Protecting Our First Amendment Liberties.* Naperville, IL: Sphinx Publishing, 2009.

Freedman, Des. *The Politics of Media Policy.* Malden, MA: Polity, 2008.

Heins, Marjorie. *Not in Front of the Children: "Indecency," Censorship, and the Innocence of Youth.* New Brunswick, NJ: Rutgers University Press, 2007.

Levi, Lilli. "The FCC's Regulation of Indecency," *First Reports* 7, 1 (April, 2008). http://www.firstamendmentcenter.org/madison/wp-content/uploads/2011/03/FirstReport.Indecency.Levi_.final_.pdf.

30

Onion News Network
Flow

ETHAN THOMPSON

Abstract: The "flow" of television segments has long been understood as fundamental to how viewers experience the medium and how programmers direct audience attention from one show to the next. In this look at the *Onion News Network*, Ethan Thompson examines how television's flow has shifted emphasis to brand identity and catering to audience taste, now that convenience technologies such as the DVR have greatly compromised linear models of flow.

On October 4, 2011, a giant asteroid hurtled through space on a path certain to end life as we know it. NASA launched a mission to destroy the asteroid, but the shuttle blew up shortly after takeoff due to the crew's complete lack of aeronautical experience—they were, after all, a single mom, a dancer, an unemployed steel mill worker, and three other "dreamers with heart." Anchor Brooke Alvarez presided over *Onion News Network*'s (IFC, 2011) coverage of "Doomsday 2011" with élan, telling the audience she hoped the segments distracted them from their impending deaths, and imploring them to spend a few of their last minutes alive watching messages from the sponsors. As *ONN*'s thirty-minute block of news programming ended, so did the planet. On-screen graphics reported the asteroid had entered the earth's exosphere, the set shook, and reception grew disrupted before going to static. Then credits rolled and logos for "The Onion Productions" and "IFC Originals" appeared. Maybe it wasn't the end of the world after all.

No public panic followed. Granted, those watching *ONN* were a narrow slice of the TV audience. Narrower still was the slice that watched but didn't already know *ONN* was news parody, or couldn't recognize its parodic cues. In contrast, when CBS broadcast "War of the Worlds" on its coast-to-coast network of radio affiliates seventy-three years earlier, panic ensued. The front page of the *New York Times* reported "a wave of mass hysteria seized thousands of radio listeners throughout the nation" in response to the dramatic performance that included vivid reports of Martians spreading death and destruction across New York and New Jersey.[1] Whether or not genuine hysteria was as widespread as reported is questionable. Even the *Times* noted that in order to mistake the performance for "real news," listeners had to miss Orson Welles's opening introduction and three additional announcements that emphasized the program's fictional nature.

But regardless of whether "War of the Worlds" generated panic of the scale described by the *Times* and ascribed to it in the popular imaginary, the performance undeniably struck a nerve when it was simultaneously broadcast to millions of Americans across the country. The perceived verisimilitude (whether listeners thought it was real or just really entertaining) must in large part be attributed to its structure, which consisted of a variety of programming segments. A weather report and a performance by "Ramon Raquello and His Orchestra" is interrupted by news flashes about strange explosions in New Jersey and an interview with an astronomer played by Welles, followed by more music and additional news reports that became more frequent and increasingly disturbing. While a reporter's description of a "rocket machine" rising from the earth and incinerating a crowd of onlookers might sound utterly unbelievable, the surrounding context of the radio broadcast was perfectly mundane, and thus lent credence to the whole. If listeners tuned in at the beginning or focused on just one segment, they would either know it was a fictional broadcast because they had been told so or they would be skeptical because of the fantastic nature of the individual reports. But by simulating radio's juxtaposition of music, remote interviews, and announcers' interruptions, the notorious broadcast was very much a compellingly "real" radio experience.

In 1974, Raymond Williams described the planned "flow" of broadcast segments, like those constructed by "War of the Worlds," as fundamental to television as a cultural form. Reflecting upon watching a movie cut up and interspersed with commercials, news reports, and network promos, Williams defamiliarized the experience of "watching TV" and posited it was not about experiencing an isolated event, but accessing a multiplicity of events and segments available at the flick of a switch.[2] Historians have blamed prewar tension for the panicked reaction to "War of the Worlds," but have also pointed to flow, speculating that many listeners tuned in during a musical interlude on Edgar Bergen's show on NBC, and thus missed the announcements that what they were hearing wasn't the real news.[3] In today's convergence era, the chances of similarly stumbling upon the *ONN*'s "Asteroids Headed to Earth" seem slim. Today's TV viewers don't switch channels during commercials—they fast-forward through them. And if they do happen to be watching live television while the *ONN* is on, the chances they would flip to it are much, much smaller than in the heydays of network radio or network television. Arguably, the "Asteroids Heading to Earth" episode was never "broadcast" at all. The Independent Film Channel (IFC), which runs *ONN*, doesn't distribute programming over the airwaves owned by the American public, but via satellite, fiber optics, and coaxial cable. Secondly, IFC does not program the *Onion News Network* to target a mass or "broadcast" audience. Instead, it is an example of "narrowcasting," which targets a narrowly defined and from the vantage point of advertisers, "quality" audience. For IFC, that means 18–49-year-old males whom the network's marketing wonks label "authentic influencers" on the young end and "responsible rebels" on the older.[4]

Even though the media landscape has dramatically changed, flow remains a valuable tool for understanding television. Programming executives have long talked about flow, though they tend to focus on the flow of audiences from one program into the next on a given channel. Both scholars and executives alike have spent significant time thinking about how flow changes now that the switch described by Williams accesses a more expansive "multiplicity" that can start and stop at almost any time or place the viewer wants, giving the viewer much more power than simply turning the flow on or off. The viewer can, for example, use the switch to fast-forward through the commercials of a program his or her DVR recorded the day before or months ago, or else stop, search recorded programs, and begin another entirely. As Amanda Lotz points out, control devices such as the DVR have thus disrupted flow as a fundamental characteristic of the medium, at least in terms of the planned sequence being determined by someone other than the viewer.[5]

To what extent, then, does "planned flow" still matter? A close look at "Asteroids Headed to Earth" suggests that in the convergence era, the concept is still important as a structuring mechanism and branding strategy. When IFC announced it was renewing *ONN* for a second season, it also revealed four new original series, including *Whisker Wars,* a reality show about the world of competitive facial hair growing. IFC executive Jennifer Caserta, explained their strategy: "IFC has been laser focused on creating and presenting original series that reflect IFC's brand position, 'Always On, Slightly Off.' The positioning defines our indie perspective on what's worth watching, and doing, in alternative culture. It speaks to people looking for smart, clever and authentic programming."[6] Such PR releases are a boon to the media critic interested in how a channel like IFC frames its audience to prospective advertisers, since they help to explain the decision to program a news parody show (not to mention a reality show about facial hair) on the seemingly misnamed "Independent Film Channel." IFC's programs are "smart"; they are "clever"; they are "authentic." This is the goal of IFC's flow: not just to keep our attention, but to convince us that the content we are seeing, whatever its generic nature or network provenance, is smart, clever, and authentic . . . just like us.

FIGURE 30.1.

Unflappable *Onion News Network* anchor Brooke Alvarez presides over coverage of the eminent destruction of the earth.

The half-hour of *ONN* on my DVR started with the announcement: "You're watching the Onion News Network, presented by Acura" over the last seconds of the previous program's credit roll. Here's what followed:

0:00–10:30. The first "act" of *ONN* is a hefty dose of programming proper, closely mimicking the flow of cable news—this is parody, after all. *ONN* opens with Alvarez's quick note about the upcoming end of the world, followed by a preview of other stories, then the opening credits. This is immediately followed by graphics for "Doomsday 2011" coverage and various exchanges with fake journalists, calls to provide feedback via Twitter, and banter between Alvarez and the *ONN* "First Responders," three pundits who sit behind laptops at a table. The ten minutes ends with a trivia question: What happened to Tucker Hope #8? This is a bid to keep us watching through the commercial as well as a reference to the ongoing joke of Alvarez's interchangeable and disposable line of co-hosts.

10:30–11:00. An integrated promotion follows, as Alvarez announces that *ONN* is presented by Acura and explains that the car company beat out NASA when *ONN* was choosing an integrated sponsor. A clip shows her talking with the First Responders, whose opinions are sponsored by the company. One sits inside an Acura instead of at the desk, and the sequence cuts to a close-up of him saying, "Exactly. . . that is totally Acura-ate," with the words also appearing on screen. This promo cuts to a green screen and the announcement "IFC Onion News Network all new episodes Tuesday 10/9 central, presented by Acura. Acura Advance."

11:00–11:30. Unlike the promo which integrated Acura's brand name and slogan into the *ONN*'s parodic style, the next segment is a straightforward Acura ad devoid of humor. A female athlete transforms into a glamorous model. "It works with people. It works with cars," we are told.

11:30–12:00. A fake promo for the nonexistent show *Onion News Network Declassified* follows. Brooke Alvarez talks about her past and ideas about reporting, and also mentions her new fragrance "Brooke Water . . . available in stores now."

FIGURE 30.2.
As part of a product integration
deal with Acura, one of the *ONN*
"First Responders" comments inside
a car on the set.

This segment does not include any mention of Acura or IFC. It is presented as a "straight" segment like those within the programming of *ONN* proper.

12:00–13:00. Three "normal" ads follow: for Twizzlers candy, for Asics shoes, and for Samuel Adams beer. While there are no direct tie-ins to IFC or *ONN* in the ads, the style and content of each do seem consistent with IFC's "smart, clever, authentic" brand. The first two ads keep the claims and selling points minimal: the Twizzlers ad includes only one line of narration ("The twist you can't resist."), and the Asics ad has no narration at all, just text ("Gravity, meet your archenemy"). The Samuel Adams ad suggests it is no ordinary beer, but a "new seasonal interpretation of the German Märzen style"—that is, a new-yet-authentic beer.

13:00–13:30. In keeping with the "show don't tell" aesthetic of the previous ads, a promo for another IFC original series, *Portlandia,* features music from the indie group Washed Out and minimal text announcing a premiere months away in January, and a quote from MTV that testifies it is "A charming brand of sketch comedy."

13:30–20:15. Doomsday 2011 returns and various *ONN* segments follow, some about the apocalypse (such as "500 sluts and 500 douchebags sequestered in a bunker to repopulate the Earth") and some not (such as one man's struggle to overcome his "goddam stupid looking face"). Alvarez promises that when the show comes back, she'll reveal her one regret, but in the meantime the audience can tweet their guesses about what it might be.

20:15–20:30. An IFC promo for *Malcolm in the Middle* (FOX, 2000–2006) follows, featuring comedian/musician Reggie Watts doing a stream-of-consciousness keyboard and vocal performance about that show. Watts's stylized look and performance, captured via hand-held camera in what appears to be a dimly lit club, rebrands *Malcolm in the Middle* through "hip" connotations. Additionally, IFC has brought the sitcom into the convergence era by ending its promo with the hashtag "#malcolminthemiddle." Watching *Malcolm in the Middle* in 2011 on IFC, in other words, is not like watching *Malcolm in the Middle* on FOX, on your parents' TV, during the first term of George W. Bush.

20:30–21:30. Two thirty-second ads follow. One warns of consequences for "breaking the code" in Las Vegas, which apparently means posting pictures of questionable behavior online. The narrator tells us to "report friends and learn more at visitlasvegas.com" in a way that suggests if not outright parody, then perhaps an ironic "double-address" to both those who have or haven't accepted a culture of perpetual surveillance. Next is an ad for Intuit websites.

21:30–21:45. The last segment before returning to *ONN* is a promo for *The Increasingly Poor Decisions of Todd Margaret*, another IFC original series whose second season is, like *Portlandia*, premiering in January. *Todd Margaret* features David Cross and Will Arnett, two performers currently appearing on IFC in the off-network cult TV show *Arrested Development*.

21:45–25:00. Doomsday 2011 coverage resumes. Alvarez reveals her one regret and reads a couple of guesses from viewers (despite the fact that *ONN* is obviously taped ahead of time). We get an update from Tucker Hope #9 that Republicans are celebrating that the asteroid has fulfilled their goal of making Obama a one-term president, and another segment about a disgraced coupon-counterfeiting mayor. Alvarez checks in with some tweets documenting how viewers are spending their final moments alive, such as "working on the perfect asteroid-destroying-earth joke to post! #asteroid."

25:00–25:15. Next up is a "real" promo for the next episode of *ONN*, and the on-screen graphics announce IFC's slogan/brand positioning for the first time during the thirty-minute block: "IFC. Always on. Slightly off."

25:15–27:15. Five ads follow, and while they advertise a range of goods and services, to different degrees they suggest their products are for the discriminating viewer/consumer. The first features Jimmy Fallon, former *Saturday Night Live* performer and current host of *Late Night* on NBC, pitching the Capital One Cash Rewards card. The next is Hershey's new "Air Delight Kisses"—not your ordinary chocolate candy, just like Samuel Adams is not your ordinary beer. Next is an ad for the online dating site eHarmony, with a guy in a black sweater looking for a "cool great girl" who "lets me be me" while he will "enjoy her being her." He is an IFC guy because he is "authentic"! Next up is McDonald's, which doesn't go to IFC to sell Big Macs or McRibs—at least not directly. Instead, it suggests the IFC viewer "discover 'me time' anytime" and "McCafe your day with McDonalds frappe." You, IFC viewer, are smart enough to know McDonald's is bad for you, but that's what indulgence is about. Why not be true to yourself (authentic!) and go to McDonald's for some "me time"? Next up: the Freecreditscore.com band sings about a girl who goes to college and spends all her parents' money.

27:15–28:15. Another IFC promo brings the channel's different types of programming together. First we see clips from the TV shows, both original and off-network (*Todd Margaret, Portlandia, Malcolm in the Middle, ONN*), then clips from films in rotation (*The Shining, Sin City, Crank, Sweeney Todd, House Party*), then these intermingle with clips featuring characters doing some physical approximation of dancing. As we have been told previously, these IFC characters are "always on" and also "slightly off," but rather than repeat that slogan, the promo ends with a line from Malcolm: "Oh great, so I'm the freak of the freak show?"

28:15–30:00. Doomsday 2011 resumes, and Alvarez tells us that the asteroid is just one mile from earth. The First Responders are in a panic, but Alvarez stands strong as the set shakes and "Asteroid Has Entered Earth's Exosphere" appears on-screen. Static and the credits follow.

Such a segment-by-segment accounting of flow shows that the *ONN* program segments proper are connected via previews of upcoming content, interactive prompts such as trivia questions, and thematic content particular to the episode. But arguably what is most apparent overall is IFC's strategy of hyper-branding, very much designed to combat the decline of flow, whether within the *ONN* proper, its product-integrated segments, IFC promos, or even in relation to the ads. In the convergence era, flow still exists, but is less obviously pointed in any single "linear" direction of audience experience. To use Williams' original phrasing, the flow can still be "switched" on, but for programmers the challenge is no longer to count on a linear experience or sequence of events, but to build the network brand so that each segment of flow is consistent with the brand and connects to another branded segment somewhere at some time—even months away. Thus, in this era where "what's on next" doesn't matter as much as it once did, we are repeatedly reminded IFC is "Always on."

Indeed, there is arguably more flow, not less, across multiple platforms. In the case of *ONN*, there are short podcasts one can view online or subscribe to, *ONN* on the IFC television channel, on the IFC website, on IFC video-on-demand, and even in pirated recordings circulating on peer-to-peer systems. This echoes *The Onion's* own cross-media flow, in that it originated as a print newspaper, then expanded into a website, before beginning the *Onion News Network* video podcasts which are the immediate forerunners to the IFC show. All of those formats continue to exist, and all promise the same smart, satiric take on media and political culture.

In the network, multichannel, and early post-network eras, flow might be likened to a gate being opened on an aqueduct, bringing a steady stream of content down with it. Now it's more like dumping a glass full of content on a table. The programming segments still "flow," but in multiple, sometimes unpredictable, directions. Whatever that flow comes in contact with must stay "wet" with the appropriate brand identity. So when properly integrated into the flow, ads and segments become an organic part of what we have deliberately chosen to spend time with. Thus, when Acura-integrated segments are deleted from fan-curated copies of the program available for download via bit-torrent, or if we fast-forward through them, we feel not only that we may have missed something, but also a kind of betrayal. We should have watched it all, as devoted viewers and fans.[7]

ONN parodies cable news in order to satirize media and political culture, and what ultimately powers a devoted relationship to *ONN* isn't flow, or any content within the flow, but a taste for such satire. Satire has historically been regarded as a sophisticated cultural form, and that cache is now made part of IFC's "smart, clever and authentic" flow. The parodic news genre specifically is hardly a new phenomenon either, though it is arguably more prevalent in media culture than ever before. While some commentators have suggested the popularity of news parody is a sign of cynicism and disengagement, others have suggested fans of shows such as *The Colbert Report* or *The Daily Show with Jon Stewart* experience a sense of community and strengthened political commitment knowing that other "smart people" share the same deep frustrations with the news and what is happening in the world. Viewers may feel that Brooke Alvarez or Stephen Colbert are not only speaking to them and other like-minded fans, but *for* them—fiercely articulating dissatisfaction with the status quo, saying what they don't have the power to say themselves and what no one in the "real" media seems willing to say. Those are powerful feelings, and thus the value of such affirmative satire (it is hoped by the network and advertisers) is that such feelings carry over from the segments parodying the news to the segments selling candy, shoes, beer, and cars.

In assessing the persuasive nature of apocalyptic flow in 1938 or 2011, what matters is not so much whether audiences think that the world is ending at the hands of invading Martians or errant asteroids, but that they *feel* like it might as well be. Audiences in 1938 were subject to "prewar tensions" and rattled by the economic devastation of the Great Depression. In 2011, America was ten years into a "War on Terror" with its state-endorsed anxiety, and also in the midst of the worst economic crisis since the days of the "War of the Worlds" broadcast. News of a quick and fiery death-by-asteroid might seem an ironic end to deep frustration with financial, political, and cultural gridlock. For the responsible rebels if not the authentic influencers, surely there might also be poetic justice in going out like the dinosaurs, currently consumed as fossil fuel in the tanks of Acuras everywhere.

NOTES

1. "Radio Listeners in Panic, Taking War Drama as Fact," *New York Times*, October 31, 1938, 1.

2. Raymond Williams, *Television: Technology and Cultural Form* (London: Routledge, 2003), 87.

3. Michelle Hilmes, *Only Connect: A Cultural History of Broadcasting in the United States* (Belmont, CA: Thomson-Wadsworth, 2007), 100.

4. Dave Itzkoff, "1990s Return on IFC," *New York Times,* December 3, 2010, C2.

5. Amanda Lotz, *The Television Will Be Revolutionized* (New York: New York University Press, 2007), 34.

6. "IFC Renews Onion News Network," *TV by the Numbers,* March 22, 2011, http://tvbythenumbers.zap2it.com/2011/03/22/ifc-renews-onion-news-network-greenlights -four-new-original-series/86693/.

7. Such strategies are known as "affective economics." See Henry Jenkins, *Convergence Culture: Where Old and New Media Collide* (New York: New York University Press, 2006), 61–62.

FURTHER READING

Brooker, Will. "Living on *Dawson's Creek*: Teen Viewers, Cultural Convergence, and Television Overflow." In *The Television Studies Reader,* Robert C. Allen and Annette Hill, eds. New York: Routledge, 2004.

Gray, Jonathan, Jeffrey P. Jones, and Ethan Thompson, eds. *Satire TV: Politics and Comedy in the Post-Network Era.* New York: New York University Press, 2009.

Jaramillo, Deborah L. "The Family Racket: AOL Time Warner, HBO, *The Sopranos,* and the Construction of a Quality Brand." In *Television: The Critical View,* 7th ed., Horace Newcomb, ed. New York: Oxford University Press, 2007.

Lotz, Amanda. *The Television Will Be Revolutionized.* New York: New York University Press, 2007.

McAllister, Matthew P., and J. Matt Giglio. "The Commodity Flow of U.S. Children's Television." In *The Advertising and Consumer Culture Reader,* Joseph Turow and Matthew P. McAllister, eds. New York: Routledge, 2009.

31

The Prisoner
Cult TV Remakes

MATT HILLS

Abstract: Two television trends that have grown more prominent in recent years are American remakes of foreign series and the popularity of cult TV. Matt Hills examines an example of both, the American remake of 1960s British "cult classic" *The Prisoner*, and suggests why such "neocult" programs can fail to capture the appeal of the original and alienate cult fandoms.

How should we analyse TV shows that have taken on cult status? Often science fiction/fantasy, these programs typically have devoted fan followings. Perhaps, then, it is important to consider not only the textual qualities that may have incited a cult following, but also the activities of dedicated fans. However, viewed from a contemporary perspective, cult television is not something created by audience activity alone. It is a label, and a phenomenon, with a televisual history stretching back at least to the 1960s. For example, Sue Short has suggested that British series *The Prisoner* (ITC, 1967–1968) "serves as a . . . precursor to the cult telefantasy shows we see today, by dint of its visual detail and narrative intricacy, [and] its ongoing mysteries," which were "pioneering strategies that would find their way into many subsequent shows."[1]

Over time, "cult" has therefore become an identifiable grouping of TV series with a number of shared textual attributes, meaning that programs can be designed to generate cults. Since the 1980s, cult audiences have become an identifiable group, in turn meaning that generations of fans can now be targeted by TV professionals. Far from being accidental successes triggered by challenging, innovative programming, by the 2000s, cult TV had become one industrial strategy for reaching audiences.

Contemporary cult TV is therefore dialogic: producers can use storytelling techniques and genres to target fans, whilst fans can evaluate shows and share their views via social media, either assenting to their industrial targeting or rejecting it. Appealing to a built-in, loyal audience helps explain why cult shows with established fandoms have frequently been remade, rebooted, or "reimagined." *Star Trek: The Next Generation* (syndicated, 1987–1994) was perhaps the first major example of this phenomenon, thereby indicating that self-conscious cult television was marketable by the late 1980s. But the process of remaking or rebooting has accelerated in recent years, with the likes of *Battlestar Galactica* (ABC, 1978–1979; Sci-Fi, 2003–2009) reborn on the Sci-Fi Channel; *Doctor Who* (BBC, 1963–1989, 2005–present) revitalised by BBC Wales; *The Bionic Woman* (ABC, 1976–1977; NBC, 1977–1978, 2007) and *Wonder Woman* (ABC, 1975–1977; CBS, 1977–1979) short lived or not making it past pilot stage as U.S. network TV shows; as well as relatively unsuccessful *Randall and Hopkirk (Deceased)* (ITV, 1969–1970; BBC, 2000–2001) for the BBC, and *The Prisoner* (2009) remade by U.S. cable channel AMC in partnership with the U.K. commercial producer and broadcaster ITV. What this list demonstrates is that self-conscious cult TV designed to generate passionate audience engagement does not always win the affection of established fan-bases. Remaking cult TV in some ways reduces the program-maker's level of risk by offering an established show that already has some brand recognition, but also introduces a different type of risk wherein fans may judge the new version to be an inauthentic imitation of their beloved series.

Illuminating this process, the 2009 remake of *The Prisoner* can be taken as an example of what might be called "metacult"—that is, a "cult about cult," or "self-conscious cultism."[2] However, what *The Prisoner* remake does is slightly more complicated: like BBC Wales' *Doctor Who*, it uses cult as one of many modes to target audiences, so the term "neocult" would be more accurate. This term suggests that drawing on cult attributes and speaking to cult audiences, for instance, does not rule out "mainstream" audience targeting at the same time. Rather than a focusing on a metacult niche, neocult seeks to combine cult targeting with other, differentiated audience addresses. Shawn Shimpach has recently argued that contemporary TV shows tend to be designed to be highly "translatable" in that they contain composite elements likely to appeal across national borders and across different audience taste cultures. The results are TV dramas that appear on the face of it to have "universal" appeal, whereas in actuality they are carefully crafted to bring together fragmented, differentiated audiences.[3] Considered in this light, neocult combines an appeal to historical, established cult audiences with various "mainstream" audience appeals.

By marked contrast, the original series of seventeen episodes of *The Prisoner* was far less obviously "translatable" or "mainstream" in design. The series starred Patrick McGoohan as "Number Six," an otherwise unnamed character who finds himself a prisoner in a strange, unknown location called "the Village," where everybody is identified only by his or her allocated number. Village society involves

Six being tested by the authorities, with a sequence of different Number Twos (the highest authority besides the mysterious Number One) seeking to discover his secrets, especially why he resigned from his career as a spy. Since McGoohan acted as executive producer and sometime writer-director, as well as playing the titular lead character, he had an exaggerated degree of creative control over the show. As Chris Gregory has pointed out, "The cult of *The Prisoner* is inevitably also a 'cult of McGoohan,' which positions its creator as a transcendent artistic 'genius.'"[4]

McGoohan described "his" show as "an allegorical conundrum," since exactly what it was saying about identity and individuality remained radically unclear.[5] In the final episode, "Fall Out" (February 1, 1968), Number Six discovers that Number One is a version of himself and seems to escape from the Village. Critic Mark Bould has pointed out that strictly speaking, the 1960s series is not an allegory, since this would mean that a clear meaning, or decoding, could be arrived at: "to the extent that it avoids allegory, avoids meaning a particular something, it remains a conundrum." For Bould, it is *The Prisoner*'s persistently enigmatic quality that has been its "source of success and longevity."[6] It also suggests that *The Prisoner* was very much ahead of its time, given that this massively enigmatic quality is one of the key attributes of 2000s TV drama as identified by Shawn Shimpach:

> Programs [in the 2000s] *had to look good in order to attract attention* amid so many alternatives, but increasingly *they also needed to intrigue and sustain interest.* This interest had to be sustained, moreover, not simply long enough to compel a viewer to set his/her remote down, but over an entire afterlife in which the program could be viewed multiple times in multiple contexts for years to come.[7]

McGoohan's *Prisoner* achieved both of these aims—it was "high-end TV" before such a thing became a niche industrial category.[8] It featured extremely distinctive visuals and, by virtue of its puzzling nature, generated intense fan speculation and rewarded fans' close attention when rewatching on video and DVD. With regard to the program's "look[ing] good," Piers Britton and Simon Barker have noted that

> *The Prisoner* represents one of the most striking design packages in the history of screen entertainment . . . [T]he series had a vivid and attractive overall aesthetic. With its primary colors and candy stripes, its architectural potpourri of space-age modernism and picture-postcard prettiness, and even the Albertus graphics used both in the settings and for the title sequences, the crisp character of the aesthetic is in some ways delightful.[9]

FIGURE 31.1.
Star, executive producer, and sometime
writer-director Patrick McGoohan as
the original "Number Six."

Given its impressive televisuality—its designed, aestheticised TV image—and
what might also be called its accompanying teleconceptuality—the use of the TV
image to create conceptual puzzles and conundrums—it is perhaps unsurprising
that *The Prisoner*, being so ahead of its time, achieved a cult status. It was highly
unusual TV drama, challenging norms of genre and representation. Nowadays,
the show is often described as a "cult classic" by academics and critics, as well
as being represented in these same terms in publicity for the AMC remake: the
European DVD, for instance, announces a "reinvention of the 1960s classic cult
thriller." However, *The Prisoner* was not immediately embraced as a TV classic
after its original 1960s broadcast. It would be fairer to say that it has taken on
"classic" status over time and through the championing of its cult devotees and
critics, thereby according with Leon Hunt's observation that in some cases "'classic status' . . . [is] achieved through the currency of cult" and hence via cult audiences' practices of evaluation and valorization.[10] Despite the fact that *The Prisoner*
bewildered much of its 1960s audience, it has thus been recontextualized as a TV
classic, thanks in large part to the long-term aesthetic celebrations and discriminations of its fandom.

The AMC/ITV *Prisoner* is hence not just "cult about cult"; it is also a remake
of a cult TV series now thought of as "classic" television. As such, it self-consciously engages with notions of prestigious as well as cult TV. The AMC press
release repeatedly stresses the "cinematic" and "filmic" nature of the material:

> AMC's reinterpretation of the highly influential 1960s cult classic . . . combines a
> wide range of genres, including espionage, thriller and Sci-Fi, into a unique and
> compelling drama that expands upon the network's distinctive cinematic approach
> to creating high-quality storytelling. . . . Acclaimed film actors Jim Caviezel (*Passion*

of the Christ, The Thin Red Line) and Ian McKellen (*Lord of the Rings, The Da Vinci Code*) will star.[11]

The choice of a six-episode miniseries is significant. This American TV category can be distinguished from "regular" on-going series television, and in recent years it tends to be the culturally highbrow domain of premium cable channels such as HBO. Remaking *The Prisoner* as a "high-quality" miniseries also allows AMC to recruit the likes of Caveziel and McKellen, who would be far less likely to sign on for a twenty-two-episode returning TV series. Furthermore, by opting for a shorter form drama than the original, AMC/ITV can secure a higher per-episode budget, whilst promoting the remake as a "miniseries event" in publicity.[12]

Reinterpreting the show as a miniseries therefore has economic and industrial implications, including allowing this "classic" TV to be positioned as highly cinematic, "event" television in line with AMC's brand identity. Of course, this revision also brings narrative consequences. McGoohan's vision was framed as an episodic series, ending almost every time with the same shot of bars slamming across Number Six's face. It didn't tell a single coherent story across its seventeen episodes, but instead offered a range of takes on its basic premise. Mark Bould observes that despite audience "attempts to impose a story arc, *The Prisoner's* [1960s] episodes generally function . . . with no memory of previous episodes, or consequences in following ones."[13] In fact, McGoohan had originally envisaged the series as being closer to a miniseries, as his "original plan . . . called for just seven episodes; [ITC boss, Lew] Grade . . . ordered nineteen more, to give an American network a half-year series with the potential for renewal. The two settled on a compromise of seventeen episodes, a standard summer run."[14] Although McGoohan had originally planned just seven episodes, the commercial goal of selling the show to America resulted in its being extended into a longer run. In a sense, then, the AMC reinterpretation seemingly moves closer to McGoohan's vision of a coherent, consistent story concept that isn't stretched out into "filler" episodes, as well as moving closer to cult fans' desired, imagined text—again, a coherent, consistent serial.[15]

In reshaping *The Prisoner* as a miniseries, AMC/ITV made a number of key narrative changes. Rather than facing different Number Two opponents, as per the original's episodic format, there is just McKellen as a consistent Number Two, as the miniseries structure (and film star casting) requires just one antagonist for Number Six to struggle against. By introducing different, episodic Twos, the 1960s series created a heightened sense of Village hierarchy existing systematically beyond each specific embodiment, whereas in the AMC rendering the Village is far more conventionally identified with Number Two as a repressive individuated villain. And the remake provides Number Six romantic possibilities in the form of 313 and 4-15. The remake thus introduces a far more culturally "mainstream" and

FIGURE 31.2.
The AMC remake of *The Prisoner* privileged televisual flair and production values over the original's persistently enigmatic quality.

"translatable" emphasis on rival love interests that are very much absent in the original.[16] These narrative choices make sense in terms of strengthening a coherent, single storyline expected of a miniseries, but they work against the distinctiveness of McGoohan's vision. Each narrative shift moves the show away from the out-of-the-ordinary and towards TV drama cliché, turning it into regular rather than "edgy" fare. The remake is also refocused on "universal" meanings of family: Number Two's relationships with his son, 11-12, and his partner, M2, are explored, along with the possibility that Six has a brother, Sixteen. Other "translatable" elements are also highlighted, such as the implication of the existence of a dangerous corporation, Summakor, in the conspiratorial plotlines. Peter Wright has argued that U.S. remakes of British cult TV can manifest, rather than Americanization, a form of cultural imperialism he calls "mainstreaming," or the imposition of conventional, dominant meanings on material that had previously been rather more eccentric, idiosyncratic, or countercultural.[17]

Even more problematically, as a miniseries telling a single overall story, the AMC version moves towards narrative closure, and hence towards a clear explication of its premise. The Village is explained in a way that makes it a well-worn sci-fi trope (a dreamscape created by the character M2) rather than an ongoing mystery. Rover, the Village guardian, is also explained away as one of Six's own projections. And the reason for Six's resignation is likewise explicated. Although Sue Short suggests that the final shots of episode six, "Checkmate" (November 17, 2009), are meant to be "chilling" but are actually "absurd", more significant is the fact that they offer a clear and obvious resolution to the miniseries.[18] An almost catatonic and yet tearful 313 in effect becomes the new M2, responsible for dreaming the Village. And Number Six becomes the new Number Two, in charge of making the Village work. According to episode three, "Anvil" (November 16, 2009), there is no Number One, although the anomalously named M2 is ultimately revealed to have been the first occupant of the Village, whilst Six is revered as "the one" by Villagers prior to taking up the role previously inhabited by

Two. There is precious little to speculate over here, and little for fans to pick over and actively reconstruct. Despite seeming to get closer to the authenticity of McGoohan's original serialized plan and fan readings of the 1960s series, then, the AMC/ITV *Prisoner* replaces enigmatic teleconceptuality with the definite ending and explanatory exposition that are characteristic of a closed miniseries.

Ironically, by distorting McGoohan's vision of a coherent seven-part *Prisoner*, ITC's responses to the commercial forces of 1960s American TV helped create an incoherent, muddled, imperfect show that cult fans could actively reread *as if* it were a miniseries. But by directly crafting the 2000s remake as a miniseries, commercial forces of contemporary U.S. quality TV work *against* the newer show having a cult "afterlife" as an open philosophical conundrum. Viewers are given too much meaning, and are not left to puzzle out events. Although some aspects of the show's paratexts, such as episode titles, also hark back to the original, this act of homage is undercut somewhat by the end credits, which, right from episode one, indicate that Jim Caveziel plays "Michael/Six," thus naming the character and removing a key sense of mystery.

Although failing at the level of teleconceptuality, the AMC *Prisoner* boasts pronounced televisuality, using Namibia as a location, and Swakopmund for the Village, along with Michael Pickwoad's production design. It repeatedly deploys "epic" landscape shots of swirling sands among otherwise untouched dunes, dwarfing Number Six by the immensity of surrounding geography and nature. This visual coding is essential to maintaining AMC's "quality" and "cinematic"-style drama, and hence to the notion of producing prestigious "event" TV which lives up to the standards of a television classic. Appeals to the cult fan audience are also made through production design: a Penny Farthing (an icon of the original Village) is visible in the Go Inside club; Number 93, the old man first encountered by Six, is dressed in a jacket strongly reminiscent of McGoohan's original costume; and the mise-en-scene of the original Six's Village apartment is recreated. The implication is that 93 may have been the McGoohan Number Six, a design strategy which subtly and subtextually repositions the remake as a continuation of the narrative universe beloved by fans. Numerological games are also played with cult fandom intent on reading for clues, with "93" hinting at the number six (9 minus 3), whilst "313" also hints at an unusual status, displaying its number one symmetrically hidden within a six (3 and 3). And this latter clue does, indeed, fit 313's eventual fate, as she becomes the new equivalent of M2 (number one inhabitant of the Village) working alongside Six. Other narrative games are knowingly played with the cult audience, such as the use of almost subliminally edited, fleeting images of Village characters framed in non-Village or "real-world" CCTV footage (e.g., Number Sixteen in "Harmony" and 909 in "Anvil"). These images can be seen if digital freeze-framing or screen-grabbing is used in a manner that suggests that the program-makers expect attentive fans to explore these momentarily flashed-up images and their implications—implications that are solidly confirmed by diegetic explanations given in later episodes. Such investigatory tendencies are frequently a hallmark of cult TV, and their presence strongly suggests that *The Prisoner* was simultaneously targeting *Lost*'s (ABC, 2004–2010) fandom by emulating aspects of that neocult show. For instance, AMC's *The Prisoner* focuses on numerological games and number-spotting; it represents an isolated, mysterious locale; and it features a shadowy, mysterious corporation. There are certainly cult intertextualities on display here, as indeed there were between *Lost* itself and the 1960s *Prisoner*.

Some fans and critics have criticized the AMC *Prisoner* for being an "Americanized" take on a British show.[19] And though it is both Americanized and mainstreamed, seeking to reach a range of different audiences as well as established cult fans, it is the desire to produce "event" TV (i.e. "quality," "cinematic" television) that perhaps most directly counters the effective targeting of cult fans. For it is this drive towards the miniseries centered on (film) star casting and narrative resolution—this attempt to do justice to a "classic" by (mis)understanding its classic status only as a matter of televisual flair and production value—that renders *The Prisoner* an "event" that is ultimately uneventful for established cult fans. It doesn't linger in the mind because it's just so obviously on the money. In neocult TV, cult fandom becomes one audience addressed amongst a multiplicity of others. And whereas the original *Prisoner* was ahead of its time, the 2009 remake is all too strongly of its time. This is true not just in terms of gesturing at post-9/11 meanings (via Summakor's shimmering "twin towers" and references to terrorist attacks), as well as incorporating representations of homosexuality and stronger roles for non-white actors. It is also true in terms of how the remake demonstrates the economic, industrial, and cultural requirements of an "event miniseries" by prioritizing televisuality over and above the original cult's enduring teleconceptuality. In short, AMC's *The Prisoner* highlights one of the dangers of neocult: by targeting established fans of cult TV, along with audiences for contemporary "quality" and "mainstream" television, neocult can end up being dismissed, if not reviled, by the very fans it had hoped to attract.

NOTES

1. Sue Short, *Cult Telefantasy Series* (Jefferson, NC: McFarland, 2011), 196.

2. Umberto Eco, *Faith in Fakes: Travels in Hyperreality* (London: Minerva, 1995), 210; Ernest Mathijs and Jamie Sexton, *Cult Cinema* (Malden and Oxford: Wiley-Blackwell, 2011), 235.

3. Shawn Shimpach, *Television in Transition* (Malden and Oxford: Wiley-Blackwell, 2010), 32.

4. Chris Gregory, *Be Seeing You . . . Decoding The Prisoner* (Luton, UK: University of Luton Press/John Libbey, 1997), 197.

5. Alain Carraze and Helene Oswald, *The Prisoner: A Televisionary Masterpiece* (London: Virgin Books, 1990), 6.

6. Mark Bould, "This is the Modern World: *The Prisoner*, Authorship and Allegory," in *Popular Television Drama*, Jonathan Bignell and Stephen Lacey, eds. (Manchester: Manchester University Press, 2005), 108.

7. Shimpach, 28, my emphasis.

8. Robin Nelson, *State of Play: Contemporary "High-end" TV Drama* (Manchester: Manchester University Press, 2007).

9. Piers D. Britton and Simon J. Barker, *Reading Between Designs: Visual Imagery and the Generation of Meaning in The Avengers, The Prisoner and Doctor Who* (Austin: University of Texas Press, 2003), 130.

10. Leon Hunt, *BFI TV Classics: The League of Gentlemen* (London: BFI, 2008), 17.

11. Available online at http://www.sixofone.org.uk/Prisoner-Remake.htm.

12. Trisha Dunleavy, *Television Drama: Form, Agency, Innovation* (New York and London: Palgrave Macmillan, 2009), 154.

13. Bould, 104.

14. Jeffrey S. Miller, *Something Completely Different: British Television and American Culture* (Minneapolis and London: University of Minnesota Press, 2000), 46.

15. Rupert Booth, *Not a Number: Patrick McGoohan—A Life* (Twickenham, UK: Supernova Books, 2011), 219.

16. Short, 28.

17. Peter Wright, "Expatriate! Expatriate! *Doctor Who: The Movie* and Commercial Negotiation of a Multiple Text," in *British Science Fiction Film and Television,* Tobias Hochscherf and James Leggott, eds. (Jefferson, NC: McFarland, 2011), 142.

18. Short, 29.

19. Russell Lewin, "Spies, Lies and the Lovely Mrs. Peel," in *The Best of British: SFX Collection Special Edition* (Bath, UK: Future Publishing, 2011), 44–51; and see Short, 28.

FURTHER READING

Gregory, Chris. *Be Seeing You . . . Decoding The Prisoner.* Luton, UK: University of Luton Press/John Libbey, 1997.

Johnson, Catherine. *Telefantasy.* London: BFI, 2005.

Short, Sue. *Cult Telefantasy Series.* Jefferson, NC: McFarland, 2011.

Stevens, Alan, and Fiona Moore. *Fall Out: The Unofficial and Unauthorised Guide to The Prisoner.* Tolworth, UK: Telos Publishing, 2007.

32

The Twilight Zone
Landmark Television

DEREK KOMPARE

Abstract: Few programs in television history are as iconic as *The Twilight Zone*, which lingers in cultural memory as one of the medium's most distinctive aesthetic and cultural peaks. Derek Kompare examines the show's signature style and voice of its emblematic creator Rod Serling, exploring how the program's legacy lives on today across genres and eras.

As with any other art form, television history is in large part an assemblage of exemplary works. Industrial practices, cultural influences, and social contexts are certainly primary points of media histories, but these factors are most often recognized and analyzed in the form of individual texts: moments when particular forces temporarily converge in unique combinations, which subsequently function as historical milestones. Regardless of a perceived historical trajectory towards or away from "progress," certain programs have come to represent the confluence of key variables at particular moments: *I Love Lucy* (CBS, 1951–1957) revolutionized sitcom production; *Monday Night Football* (ABC, 1970–2005; ESPN, 2005–present) supercharged the symbiotic relationship of sports and television; *Hill Street Blues* (NBC, 1981–1987) introduced the "quality" serial drama to primetime.

The Twilight Zone (CBS, 1959–1964) is an anomalous case, simultaneously one of the most important and least representative of such milestones. While universally hailed as one of the medium's creative peaks, its actual influence on subsequent programming, unlike that of the examples listed above, has been marginal. Its compact tales of ordinary people encountering extraordinary situations certainly provide some of the most memorable moments in American television history, including episodes like "Time Enough At Last" (November 20, 1959), when fate, and gravity, ruin a bookworm's post-apocalyptic utopia; "The Invaders" (January 27, 1961), a stark lesson in perspective; "The Monsters Are Due on Maple Street" (March 4,

1960) a chillingly plausible vision of social breakdown; and "Walking Distance" (October 30, 1959), a poignant critique of nostalgia. However, its contemporaneous kindred spirit *The Outer Limits* (ABC, 1963–1965) notwithstanding, the series' legacy has not been a line of similarly ambitious, well-executed and well-received anthology dramas, but rather a spotty succession of mostly forgettable "shock" series with plenty of "gotcha" moments, but little of *The Twilight Zone's* signature artistry, candor, or wit. Thus, alongside its celebrated creator and primary writer, Rod Serling, the series has historically suffered the same fate as many of its episodes' protagonists: erudite, witty, passionate, and noble, but ultimately marginalized from a shallow, risk-averse world that can't quite understand it.

Fifty years later, in an era when many television writer-showrunners have become minor celebrities (at least among industry peers, critics, and fans) for creating programs that are said to function "beyond" the normative, "safe" parameters of the medium, it is well worth considering how history has shaped our perceptions of such previous figures and their series. Serling was arguably the first in this incongruous line of the celebrity iconoclast television showrunner. As Jon Kraszewski details in *The New Entrepreneurs*, unlike his fellow "angry young men" of 1950s anthology drama fame, particularly Paddy Chayefsky and Reginald Rose, Serling embraced the commercial and creative demands of the new Hollywood-based production mode of the 1960s.[1] However, in contrast to other celebrity producers of the time, like Desi Arnaz, Lucille Ball, Jack Webb, and even Alfred Hitchcock, and as suggested by his signature series' title, Serling also self-consciously staked out commercial television's creative and ideological frontiers rather than its center. His legacy has thus been not so much the format of *The Twilight Zone*, which followed decades of suspenseful anthology fiction and drama in literature, radio, and television, but rather its combined creative and industrial ethos: ambitious television that simultaneously subverts *and* satisfies the expectations of safe commercial broadcasting—that is, consistently disturbing the boundaries of convention and comfort and raising the medium's aesthetic bar, while still offering a reliable venue for advertisers to hawk cars, cigarettes, and processed food. Accordingly, both Serling and *The Twilight Zone* display many of the contradictions and compromises that have plagued television's most venerated producers and series ever since. Television can be a relatively bold medium, but always within the parameters of its broader commercial and cultural functions.

Rod Serling created *The Twilight Zone* in 1959, during a period when network television was still in the throes of the first of many conceptual shifts, moving from primarily live, New York–based comedy-variety shows and one-off anthology dramas to filmed, Hollywood-produced, and firmly genre-based ongoing series. However, the remaining live anthology series, while clearly on the demise, were still regarded as the standard-bearers of television quality, with critical praise and scrutiny primarily focused on their scripts and writers, in a manner that was in keeping with the format's origins in New York theater. While a burgeoning crop of standardized westerns and private-eye shows dominated the late-1950s schedule, Serling's new filmed anthology series was sold to sponsors largely on his reputation as one of the medium's star writers established in New York anthology dramas like 1957's *Requiem for a Heavyweight*. This wasn't a mere façade, as Serling eventually wrote 92 of the series' 156 episodes. This massive workload, coupled with his other producing tasks and on-screen persona as host, cemented his association with the series; it has since been impossible to separate them.[2] Although many other creative figures were certainly essential factors in the series' success, any historical assessment of *The Twilight Zone* must start with Rod Serling's writing.[3] Indeed, his iconic words and voice open and close every episode, guiding viewers into the Twilight Zone, introducing them to the episode's protagonist and premise, and leaving them with a pithy summation of its theme.

Serling's work on *The Twilight Zone* is "well-crafted." That is, his scripts elegantly and efficiently convey compelling characters and unusual narratives, while also wearing their format-driven labor proudly. Serling's renowned work habits present a classic image of the inspired yet diligent writer: hunched over a typewriter or Dictaphone for hours on end, and fueled with an endless supply of cigarettes and coffee. As Kraszewski argues, this vision of Serling is also emblematic of the mid-century corporate creative: a formidable talent, certainly, but also fully ensconced in the forms of commercial broadcasting and assumed rituals of creative genius.[4] As a career broadcast dramatist, writing dozens of original scripts and adaptations for both radio and television, Serling learned his trade within the frameworks of network and station scheduling, as well as the unavoidable primacy of advertising.

He was not naïve about these limits. Begrudgingly, he regarded them as a necessary price to advance his career. Like many of his colleagues, he became increasingly frustrated by network and advertiser avoidance of discomfort and controversy. Several of his earlier teleplays had been altered to bury any direct reference to ongoing social issues (in particular, race and religion), while others had had dialogue and situations changed to keep sponsors happy, such as avoiding the word "lucky" so as not to suggest the rival Lucky Strike cigarette brand. Indeed, he created *The Twilight Zone* at the peak of his reputation in the industry in large part because he desired greater creative control over his scripts. However, he also realized that he had to keep advertisers satisfied in order for the series to stay on the air. In a filmed pitch to potential advertisers leading in to a screening of the series' pilot, Serling told his audience of ad agents and manufacturers, "We think it's the kind of show that will put people on the edge of their seats, but only for that one half an hour. We fully expect they'll go to the store the following day and buy your products. It's that kind of show."⁵ As the series continued, Serling would similarly slide from incongruous Greek chorus to product pitchman, directly shilling sponsors' products and promoting the CBS schedule. While these sequences were cut from the series' syndication runs, and thus seemingly excised from its history, it is important to remember them in order to better understand Serling's multiple roles in the public eye during its original run.⁶

While Serling's entrepreneurial acumen was significant, he was ultimately selling his writing, and that was what cemented the show's place in television history. The most striking aspect of his scripts (not only his *Twilight Zone* work), especially from the perspective of a half-century later, is the dialogue. Serial dramas today rely on narrative-driven conversation, where every scene advances larger and longer stories that typically transpire across many episodes and seasons. In contrast, and befitting the rapid pace of anthology drama where character arcs play out over minutes rather than hours, *Twilight Zone* scripts center on individual reflection, conveying characters' philosophical speculations on their situations. *Twilight Zone* characters soliloquize rather than converse, and situations aren't resolved as much by characters' narrative actions as by their self-realization. The dialogue is poetic yet direct: rhythmically suited to the modern pace of television at the time (and its aesthetically modern forebears in mid-twentieth-century literature, drama, radio, and film), but also capable of piercing many of the era's normative cultural and social veils.

For instance, in "The Monsters Are Due on Maple Street," suburban neighbors turn on each other in an escalation of suspicion and violence brought on by a power outage. In the final confrontation scene, only Steve, who's been the sole voice of reason throughout the episode, clearly expresses what's happening:

> Let's get it all out. Let's pick out every idiosyncrasy of every single man, woman, and child on the street. And then we might as well set up some kind of citizens' court. How about a firing squad at dawn, Charlie, so we can get rid of all the suspects. Narrow them down. Make it easier for you.

This brash style carried through to Serling's opening and closing comments, which, especially in the case of "Monsters," underlined the episode's argument:

> The tools of conquest do not necessarily come with bombs and explosions and fallout. There are weapons that are simply thoughts, attitudes, prejudices—to be found only in the minds of men. For the record, prejudices can kill and suspicion can destroy, and a thoughtless, frightened search for a scapegoat has a fallout all its own—for the children, and the children yet unborn. And the pity of it is that these things cannot be confined to the Twilight Zone.

Such signature dialogue was in turn enhanced by the expressive resources of the production crew, which combined the sensibilities of both New York drama and Hollywood film. The result was television that regularly departed from the comfort of the normal and focused on existential fears and insecurities, turning those living-room cabinet TV sets into nightmare portals. The series' particular combination of style, efficiency, and narrative impact—entire stories played out in a lean twenty-five minutes—has never been equaled since. Importantly, while both of the series most compared to *The Twilight Zone* tended towards more realist narratives—*The Outer Limits* occupying the generic core of science fiction, and *Alfred Hitchcock Presents* (CBS/NBC, 1955–1965) dealing primarily in mystery and suspense—*The Twilight Zone* took a broader perspective, moving instead into the realm of the vaguely "supernatural."[7] This more diffuse remit granted the series a wider narrative scope, allowing it to focus less on explaining the details of particular fantastic concepts and more on the reactions of its everyday "normal" characters, typically drawn from the era's anthology plays, whose drives, strengths, and insecurities all had to be conveyed within the space of a thirty or sixty-minute teleplay, rather than unfold over the hours and years of typical serial dramas today.

The episode "The Eye of the Beholder" (November 11, 1960), generally considered one of the series' best, exemplifies this efficiency. The main character, Janet Tyler, is in a hospital, late at night, her face swathed in bandages. She yearns not only to be free to see and feel the light and the air on her face again, but also to look "normal." As the episode unfolds, we learn that she is a physical freak, and her society has forced her to undergo treatment to "correct" this deformity. This is her last treatment cycle, and if it fails, she will be forced to live in an internment camp with others "of her kind." At the episode's climax, the bandages are slowly removed, and we realize that the treatment has failed: she is still a horrific freak. However, to our eyes she is beautiful; everyone else in her society is a pig-faced monster (conveyed by William Tuttle's simple yet effective makeup). This reversal is set up not only by Douglas Heyes's exacting direction and George T. Clemens's low-key cinematography (which keep the faces of the entire cast unseen until the climax), but also by Serling's words. Janet's longings move from mundane to existential, as she rails against her looming fate and rebuffs the placating words of her doctor and nurses: "Who makes all these rules and statutes and traditions that the people who are 'different' have to stay away from the people who are 'normal'?" As her bandages are removed, a televised speech from this world's leader (channeling demagogues Hitler, Stalin, and McCarthy) rages against "nonconformity": "We know now that there must be a single purpose, a single norm, a single approach, a single entity of people, a single virtue, a single morality, a single frame of reference, a single philosophy of government. We must cut out all that is different like a cancer itself!" Produced while racial segregation still held sway in much of the United States against an expanding civil rights movement, the episode elegantly makes its allegorical point.

That said, like every landmark series, *The Twilight Zone* is certainly not without its problems. While its standards were generally high, not every concept worked, and a few were complete misfires. Moreover, while its general ethos (and Serling's) was to question conformity, injustice, hypocrisy, and ethical weakness, it did so within the relatively circumscribed parameters of the urbane, Kennedy-era liberalism seen in both "Monster" and "Beholder." The stylistic vehicles of expressive yet efficient anthology writing, directing, and then in-vogue method-acting maximized its impact within this particular range of critique, but no further. Indeed, even its de facto rival *The Outer Limits* was able to experiment a bit more boldly and cryptically at times, as seen, for example, in the bleak time-travel paradox of "The Man Who Was Never Born" (October 28, 1963) and the searing critique of Cold War psychology in "Nightmare" (December 2, 1963). Not surprisingly, the series' most notable blind spot is gender: *The Twilight Zone,* in sync with the dominant representations in U.S. culture in the 1960s, is a thoroughly male-centered universe, with women typically limited to secondary roles. Aside from standout episodes with female protagonists like "Beholder," "The After Hours" (June 10, 1960), and "The Midnight Sun" (November 17, 1961), Serling's scripts generally treat women as either nagging harpies or endless fonts of love and understanding, and only in relation to men.[8]

Still, the series struck a chord in its initial run by appealing to an idealistic but already diminishing expectation that television should fascinate while it entertains. Although when *The Twilight Zone* premiered, *Playhouse 90* (CBS, 1956–1960) and other endangered anthology series still claimed the mantle of "serious" television, by the time of its demise in 1964, Serling's series functioned as the most conspicuous continuation of the style, sensibility, and ethos of the 1950s anthology drama, albeit on film instead of live. The rapid demise of this precise narrative and stylistic balance was evident throughout the remainder of Serling's curtailed life. After *The Twilight Zone* was cancelled, aside from a handful of exceptions like *Star Trek* and *I Spy*, television drama drifted into the mundane waters of bland realism or escapist action-adventure in the late 1960s. Projects that had grander, less formulaic ambitions were either reserved for the new paragon of "quality," the made-for-TV movie, or shunted to the margins of the schedule as "far out" fare. Thus, despite bearing his name and visage as host, *Rod Serling's Night Gallery* (NBC, 1969–72) functioned mostly as a gaudy horror show that, while not without its own particular charms, bore only the most superficial resemblance to *The Twilight Zone*.[9]

In retrospect, *The Twilight Zone's* most distinctive feature, conveyed in the relatively Spartan staging of early 1960s television production design, remains

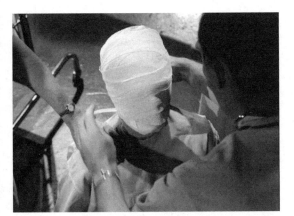

FIGURE 32.1.
Bandages removed from the "freak"
in this episode of the *Twilight Zone*
reveal a beautiful woman, in a typical reversal that echoes Kennedy-era
liberalism in its critique of conformity
and injustice.

its dialogue. Unfortunately, as conventions of film and television dialogue have changed, this style has been hardest to emulate in later incarnations of the series or its ersatz knock-offs.[10] With the anthology format seemingly no longer a viable option, Serling's most recent stylistic heirs would seem to be serial drama writers like David E. Kelley (*Ally McBeal, Boston Legal*), Aaron Sorkin (*The West Wing, The Newsroom*), and Joss Whedon (*Buffy The Vampire Slayer, Firefly*), whose meticulously rhythmic and biting dialogue convey a similar aesthetic function, and whose plots often center on cultural critique. However, their characters also occupy a self-aware space that Serling's did not. Sorkin's dialogue in particular attempts to bring theatrical, Serling-esque speech into the twenty-first century, but ultimately fails to convey the same gravity; his characters sound more like "characters" in our time than Serling's ever did in his. Similarly, writers like Vince Gilligan (*Breaking Bad*), Damon Lindelof (*Lost*), and Ronald D. Moore (*Battlestar Galactica*) have generated deeply relatable characters caught in fantastic situations, but their modus operandi is much more slanted towards conventional realism, favoring showing over telling, putting the weight on performance, composition, mise-en-scene, and editing, with relatively minimalistic dialogue and few of Serling's typical speeches. Moreover, aside from these figures and a handful of others—e.g., David Milch (*Deadwood*), Amy Sherman-Palladino (*Gilmore Girls*), David Simon (*The Wire*)—most television drama today is written collectively. There are certainly showrunners who function as auteurs much as Serling did, but there are almost none with as much direct creative input and public notoriety as he had.[11]

Thus, fifty years later, *The Twilight Zone*'s legacy appears not so much in contemporary programs, but rather in the unabated circulation of the original episodes, and in the even wider spread of its most celebrated moments and of the figure of Serling himself. Still, the spirit of the series can be found in the

FIGURE 32.2.
Twilight Zone creator Rod Serling,
whose iconic voice opens and closes
every episode.

aspirations of would-be television iconoclasts, for whom *The Twilight Zone* and Serling function as key models of attitude if not form. As star writer-producer-director J. J. Abrams gushed in a 2009 interview, "*The Twilight Zone* at its best is better than anything else I've ever seen on television."[12] As a television milestone, *The Twilight Zone* still holds a unique place in the medium's history. While attempts to revive the anthology format are increasingly unlikely in an era reliant on the safety of serial and procedural drama, *The Twilight Zone* will always be there—in reruns, on video, and online—for viewers to visit, representing a particular moment in American cultural history, and reminding us of the range of television's storytelling possibilities.

NOTES

1. Jon Kraszewski, *The New Entrepreneurs* (Middletown, CT: Wesleyan University Press, 2010).

2. In contrast, while Alfred Hitchcock was the executive producer, on-screen host, and occasional director (of 17 out of 268 episodes) of his signature series, *Alfred Hitchcock Presents*, he was still primarily involved in directing feature films, and did not function as the series' showrunner in the same capacity as Serling did on *The Twilight Zone*.

3. Other notable regular contributors included producer Buck Houghton; cinematographer George T. Clemens; director Douglas Heyes; composers Jerry Goldsmith and Bernard Herrmann; writers Charles Beaumont, George Clayton Johnson, and Richard Matheson; and many well-regarded character actors (e.g., John Dehner, Jack Klugman, Lee Marvin, Burgess Meredith, Cliff Robertson).

4. Kraszewski, 139–73.

5. Rod Serling, "Original Network Pitch" (Los Angeles: Cayuga Productions, 1959), available on *The Twilight Zone: Season One,* Blu-Ray (Image Entertainment, 2010).

6. The "Definitive Edition" box set (both on DVD and Blu-Ray) from Image includes examples of Serling seguing from *Twilight Zone* host to sponsor pitchman.

7. That said, there were certainly some *Twilight Zone* stories that fit more comfortably within particular genres, and could easily have aired on either *The Outer Limits* or *Alfred Hitchcock Presents*.

8. See, for example, "The Lonely," "People Are Alike All Over," "Uncle Simon," "A Short Drink from a Certain Fountain," and "Sounds and Silences."

9. The ghosts of *The Twilight Zone* only briefly surfaced in *Night Gallery*, as in Serling's Emmy-nominated script "They're Tearing Down Tim Riley's Bar" (January 20, 1971) in which a world-weary middle-aged man laments the disappearing world of his youth.

10. The production-plagued big-budget anthology film version of the series, with remakes of three original series episodes, though unfortunately known most for a fatal production accident that killed actor Vic Morrow and two child extras, and the subsequent criminal trial of the segment's director, John Landis, was released in 1983 to middling success. An ambitious television revival ran on CBS from 1985 to 1987, and in syndication during 1988–1989, but was unable to garner consistent notice. Similarly, the latest revival, on UPN in 2002–2003, despite solid intentions and high-level talent, made virtually no impact. Copycat series, most produced in the 1980s, concentrated more on outright horror, and have included *Amazing Stories* (NBC, 1985–1987), *Darkroom* (ABC, 1981–1982), and *Tales From the Darkside* (Syndicated, 1983–1988). Of all the attempted latter-day anthology series, the revival of *The Outer Limits* (Showtime/Sci-Fi, 1995–2002) garnered the most consistent commercial and critical success.

11. J. Michael Straczynski, who was involved with the 1980s revival of *The Twilight Zone*, arguably surpassed Serling's control with his space opera *Babylon 5* (Syndicated/TNT, 1993–1998), writing 92 of its 110 episodes (including the entirety of the third and fourth seasons).

12. Quoted in "Top 10 TV Episodes," *Time*, http://www.time.com/time/specials/packages/article/0,28804,1927690_1927684_1927626,00.html.

FURTHER READING

Hill, Rodney. "Mapping *The Twilight Zone*'s Cultural and Mythological Terrain." In *The Essential Science Fiction Television Reader*, J. P. Telotte, ed. Lexington: The University Press of Kentucky, 2008.

Kraszewski, Jon. *The New Entrepreneurs: An Institutional History of Television Anthology Writers*. Middletown, CT: Wesleyan University Press, 2010.

Sander, Gordon F. *Serling: The Rise and Twilight of Television's Last Angry Man*. New York: Plume, 1994.

Worland, Rick. "Sign Posts Up Ahead: *The Twilight Zone, The Outer Limits*, and TV Political Fantasy, 1959–1965." *Science Fiction Studies* 23 (1996): 103–22.

Zicree, Marc Scott. *The Twilight Zone Companion*. New York: Bantam, 1982.

V

TV Practices
Medium, Technology, and Everyday Life

33

Auto-Tune the News
Remix Video

DAVID GURNEY

Abstract: Convergence culture has redefined television in many ways—from what devices we use to watch TV, to who can make TV and how it can be made. In this essay, David Gurney examines how The Gregory Brothers draw upon news coverage and other online videos as raw material for satirically remixed and reconfigured takes on current events and Internet culture.

Amidst the sights and sounds of Katy Perry's "California Gurls," Usher's "OMG," and other bubbly hit songs of summer 2010, one unique single and its accompanying video experienced an unexpected moment in the spotlight with its Auto-Tuned chorus of lines including "Hide yo kids / Hide yo wife" and the repeated "We gon find you / We gon find you" becoming instant catchphrases in the pop lexicon. "Bed Intruder Song" by The Gregory Brothers and Antoine Dodson was not novel in terms of its use of synthesizers, drum machines, or even Auto-Tune pitch-correcting software, but rather because of the original source of its vocal tracks. Lifted from a recording of television news originally broadcast by a local NBC affiliate (WAFF in Huntsville, Alabama), the unintentional catchphrases began as statements from Antoine, whose family's home had been broken into by a perpetrator intent on sexually assaulting one of its female members. Despite sampling's long history in hip-hop, this peculiar source and the extended use of the sample made this a standout track. For The Gregory Brothers, however, re-purposing television news was not so unusual even if it represented a shift from appropriating the words of the powerful to the words of the relatively powerless.

A media phenomenon like "Bed Intruder Song" underscores that when we talk about television in the twenty-first century, we are talking less about a specific media technology and a circumscribed set of behaviors surrounding it, than about an ever-expanding constellation of technologies associated with an increasingly less cohesive set of practices. Really, this has always been the case,

FIGURE 33.1.
Antoine Dodson, auto-tuned
and remixed into "Bed In-
truder" star.

but the continuing proliferation of portable viewing devices (from the Watchman
to smartphones) and platforms for content distribution (from VHS to streamed
FLVs) has made the object described as "television" less stable and well defined.
Alternatingly convergent and divergent digital streams have made television content and conventions increasingly open to audience/user capture and manipulation. While the expanse of online audiovisual media encompasses much more
than just reposted and/or repurposed material that was initially designed for
television, the medium is a defining presence. This essay will examine television's
circulation through networked digital media platforms that have often been described as "viral" by focusing on a particular set of makers, The Gregory Brothers, and their *Auto-Tune the News* series, which serves as both an exemplary and
a unique case of a trend in how television content is drawn in to transmedial
activity and what happens to it in such environs.

While most people use terms like "viral video" or "going viral" to refer to the
user-to-user spread of media content, virality implies at least one other crucial con-
notation—viral recombination.[1] The metaphorical basis of media virality, the biological virus, often becomes most potent when it goes through the process of genetic
recombination. In simplified terms, when two or more viruses enter the same cell,
there is potential for genetic material from each to recombine with the other during
their processes of replication. In some instances, these recombined viruses increase
significantly in potency, as evident in cyclical fears over "swine flu," which are recombinations of influenza viruses separately active in humans and pigs resulting in
a more resistant strain affecting humans. Similarly, cultural code is subject to such
recombinations in many forms even predating digital media. Take, for instance, the
narrative structure of an epic poem like *The Odyssey* being lifted and recontextualized over the course of millennia into works as diverse as James Joyce's modernist
novel *Ulysses* and the Coen brothers' screwball comedy *O Brother, Where Art Thou?*
Comedic practices of satire and parody frequently facilitate such recombinant

work, pulling in cultural codes through techniques such as exaggeration, repetition, and recontextualization to render the source material humorous, often with a critical perspective. It has been through such recombinant practices that The Gregory Brothers have risen to a place of prominence within popular culture.

Starting in 2009, their online series *Auto-Tune the News* almost immediately became widely circulated and recognized. Even though it's not the first case of an online video series finding sizable audiences, the series is distinct in that it so wholeheartedly includes viral recombination, as it is built upon a fairly simple recombinant practice: taking television news coverage as raw material for redaction and reconfiguration. True to its title, *Auto-Tune* finds The Gregory Brothers treating spoken voice samples with Auto-Tune audio processing software and mixing them with contemporary music, typically R&B/hip-hop production elements. Like almost all recombinations, though, this has the effect of casting the source materials into satirical relief, with the Brothers taking the opportunity to critique conventions of reportage—not unlike television news parody of the past, including *That Was The Week That Was* (1964–1965), *Saturday Night Live*'s (NBC, 1975–present) "Weekend Update" segment, and, of course, *The Daily Show with Jon Stewart* (Comedy Central, 1996–present).[2] However, digital media have allowed the Brothers, a group of makers without the initial backing of a major network or production house, to enter this arena on their own terms. Looking at two popular episodes of *Auto-Tune* will illustrate more clearly the style and critical cut of their satire, as well as how the visibility gained through user-generated content can in some cases shift the balance of power between digital media satirists and targets.

To start, a close examination of the second episode of the series, "pirates. drugs. gay marriage" (April 21, 2009), will bring the satirical potentials of viral recombination into focus. The episode opens with a clip from the "Roundtable" segment of the April 12, 2009, episode of ABC's *This Week with George Stephanopoulos* (1981–present) in which *Washington Post* editorialist Ruth Marcus remarks on the significance of the recent Iowa Supreme Court decision that made same-sex marriage legal in the state. Two of the brothers, Michael and Andrew, are composited into the roundtable scene (superimposed over Stephanopoulos and panelist George Will, respectively) from the very opening. Speaking as if interrupting Marcus in the midst of her attempt to underscore the importance of the court's ruling, they begin repeatedly chanting "boring" in her direction, with Michael insisting, "I'm not feeling any love between us right now. You've gotta do it like this . . . Shawty." With the move of addressing Marcus as "Shawty" (a particular inflection on "Shorty," hip-hop lingo for a desirable female), the Auto-Tune effect begins melodizing the spoken dialogue of both the brothers and Marcus. A backing track of tinkling synthesizer accompanies this, effectively rendering the scene with the sonic identity of a contemporary hip-hop track.

FIGURE 33.2.
Andrew, one of The Gregory Brothers behind *Auto-Tune the News,* reacts to news anchor Katie Couric.

With this, "pirates. drugs. gay marriage." enacts the basic *Auto-Tune the News* formula: recombining televised news and political commentary with elements of hip-hop production to create uniquely hybridized content that makes critical statements about television news, political rhetoric, and popular culture in a few notable ways. At a basic level, the interruptions and melodizing serve to deflate the air of authority that the hosts and commentators of Sunday morning television news discussion shows often carry. There is also a clear statement being made regarding an aesthetic and rhetorical gulf between a serious news program like *This Week* and large swaths of the citizenry. The interjections of "boring" are obviously joking, but they point to the reality that a Sunday morning panel program is pitched to a limited demographic or taste culture—one that likely divides along lines of generation, class, and race. In another sense, Michael's use of "shawty" and a subsequent proposal that he and Marcus "get carried away" and "get gay-married today" as a way to steer discussion away from the political stakes of the original clip make a familiar critique of one of popular hip-hop's most prevalent subjects (i.e., attracting women) and its often casual objectification of females. Furthermore, given mainstream hip-hop's record of anti-queer lyrical content, the collapsing of getting "gay-married" into a description of a proposed heterosexual coupling may be highlighting a discomfort with homosexual practice. Of course, the switch from earnest political discussion to more eroticized vocalizing also indicates that the sex lives of the body politic are perhaps better suited to musical expression than legislation. Whatever the particular mix of meanings a viewer takes away from this recombination, at the very least, it has the effect of making one aware of the strange mixing of the sexual and the political that the "real" television news has been carrying on in its coverage of same-sex marriage.

Similar recombinations follow in the episode, including one involving footage of CNN anchor Kiran Chetry describing results of a viewer poll on marijuana legalization, in which a wigged and mustached Michael is inserted in split-screen taking credit for the strong support for legalization found in the poll. In this case, the hip-hop context actually syncs even better with the news content, while putting the topic into a state of refraction similar to the same-sex marriage question. A more elaborate segment has Andrew in gorilla costume doing a split-screen duet with Fox News commentator Sean Hannity. Labeled through on-screen text as "Frank McGee—Angry Gorilla," the character exaggeratedly echoes the already performative anger Hannity is directing toward President Obama for taking "some credit for authorizing the mission" to rescue the captain of the *Maersk Alabama* from his pirate captors. This costume and its associated character subsequently play a recurring role throughout the series, standing in as buffoonish caricature of demagogic pundits attempting to stoke anger and fear in their audiences. With this character, it seems that the series achieves its most transparent critique of television news tropes: a takedown of the blow-hard rhetoric that has come to fill a great deal of the programming hours of cable news networks. While having nowhere near the subtlety of Stephen Colbert, the McGee character does make a shorthand jab at the outrage of pundits overshadowing or, in some cases, supplanting the topics covered by television news.

Including other recombined clips of television news coverage on the *Maersk Alabama* event, climate change, and drug legalization over less than two-and-a-half minutes, the episode operates as a dense interweave of ribald commentary in a tradition consistent with news media parody of the past, yet there are a few key differences. For one, the range of topics covered in this compressed time span means that it moves at a more accelerated pace than much preceding news parody. Furthermore, the hip-hop conceit allows for easy shifting among topics, with clips being treated more as sections of a song (i.e., verse, chorus, bridge) than as rhetorical moments that need logical connections to be made between them. Consequently, the satire is most clearly pitched at television news tropes rather than any specific political issue. Yet what's changed most is that the tools of digital media allowed media outsiders like The Gregory Brothers to more directly take from the media culture that was surrounding them, reconfigure it, and utilize online distribution to reach audiences far beyond what they might have reached only a few years prior. Essentially, their "production" process involves choosing media that strikes them as being (virally) potent and worthy of satirical treatment, recombining it with other cultural codes both original (e.g., Frank McGee—Angry Gorilla) and borrowed (e.g., hip-hop conventions), producing something novel, and using YouTube's distribution power to have their construction with multiple layers of mediation seen widely. As a DIY effort, theirs is clearly a case of the relatively powerless using tools of digital media to take swipes at those with power in television news.

First uploaded only ten days after the first official episode ("march madness. economic woes. pentagon budget cuts."), this second entry in the series built on the popularity of the first and began to find more transmedial mobility. For instance, shortly after this episode began to circulate, three of the four Brothers appeared on *The Rachel Maddow Show* (MSNBC, 2008–present) to discuss the popularity of and logic behind the budding series.[3] This appearance on *Maddow* (as well as coverage in various print publications) stands as a marker of the transmedial nature of viral circulation. While the budding series was being passed around by hyperlink through email, message boards, social networking sites, and political and Internet culture blogs, the interview with Maddow is a clear case of how other media become involved with the spread.[4] This, in turn, raised The Gregory Brothers' profile, making them a somewhat recognizable brand, gaining them YouTube channel subscribers and other social media followers, as well as giving subsequent productions an advantage in terms of their initial visibilities.

While "pirates. drugs. gay marriage." plays out as an exemplary case of the basic template underlying nearly the entire *Auto-Tune the News* series, a later episode, the aforementioned "Bed Intruder Song!" (July 31, 2010) illustrates a shift in the series that sent The Gregory Brothers' work in a slightly different and more questionable direction.[5] The episode fits within the basic form of *Auto-Tune the News*, though in a more streamlined way: rather than featuring various topical television news clips, there is only one clip recombined in this episode. In addition, the clip, though certainly a form of television news, stands apart from the material used for preceding episodes given its regional origins in a broadcast by Huntsville, Alabama, NBC affiliate WAFF. Antoine Dodson, a man who had interrupted and thwarted an attempted assault against his sister, Kelly, dominates the original news report in which he emphatically expresses his mix of anger and resolve towards the unknown intruder whom he forced to leave. Given the rather restricted local audience for the original airing, the clip found a larger audience only because a Huntsville-area viewer was so struck by Antoine's expressiveness that she or he decided to post a link to the video on social news website reddit.[6] As the video began viral circulation on the day following its original airing, The Gregory Brothers quickly joined in the chorus of viral recombinations that were appearing by offering their musical version only a day after the clip's initial posting.

However, as a result of injecting musical comedy into such a situation, the satire becomes more potentially problematic. Certainly, here, as in "pirates. drugs. gay marriage.," television news conventions are a target. The original clip is coverage of a crime, a break-in at the Dodson residence that had the potential to be even worse than it ultimately was. Including eyewitness testimony is a common element of such reporting, and, given that Antoine was the one who stopped the incident from progressing, he is clearly an important witness. Of course, when such events occur, the manner and eloquence of such eyewitness testimony can vary widely. Still, one might want local television news producers to do their part in both preparing their eyewitnesses for the camera and using editing to convey the information as clearly and concisely as possible. In practice, anyone who has seen local television news broadcasts knows that even newsmakers with copious experience in front of cameras have trouble generating flawless, off-the-cuff sound bites. To be sure, the Dodson clip is of the unpracticed ilk; his is an instantaneous response to a violation of his family's safety in its immediate aftermath. His dress, a do-rag and a black tank top, and location, a housing project, belie the Dodson family's limited means. Inasmuch as the reporting of the event is fulfilling the function of notifying the local public of intrusive criminal activity in their community, it can also be seen as exploiting the near tragedy of a poor black family.

What complicates any reading of the original news clip even further is how Antoine's spur-of-the-moment interview actually unfolds. Rather than stumbling over his words or rambling incoherently, he comes across as composed and articulate. He clearly defines the situation in a way that does not cast his family as victims but rather as ever-diligent defenders of their domicile while also urging others to be proactive and issuing an emphatic warning to the perpetrator. His speaking style is charismatically performative, and even rhythmic, with his head swaying back and forth for dramatic emphasis and his pointing at the camera with a rolled tube of paper to underscore his resolve. It is easy to understand why three separate sound bites of his are used in the aired clip: he is a magnetic presence on the camera.

However, while Antoine clearly seized his moment, there is no way to lock down meaning. Especially as the clip began circulating virally online, the initial stakes of the segment (i.e., a report of local crime that a concerned viewer might find alarming) dissipated to the point where Antoine's dress and mannerisms became the main points of focus. The comments resulting from the clip's posting on reddit show that there are significant numbers of viewers who look at Antoine as a cartoonish embodiment of negative stereotypes even as many others see him as an empowered individual asserting defiance. In choosing to recombine such footage, The Gregory Brothers tread a fine line between uplifting their muse and denigrating him. As a self-identified gay African American man living in a housing project, Dodson was a marginalized and underrepresented figure with little control over how he was received by audiences. This led some commentators to question whether the expansive popularity of Dodson and the song were simply because his performative flamboyance played into negative stereotypes, while others worried that the comedy of it obscured or trivialized the terrible event that had spurred the initial report: the attempted rape of a young woman in her family home.[7] Such concerns call attention to a core tension within all viral (and social) media: when audiences have the power to choose what they want to circulate and how they want to see that content recombined, the potential for derogatory or, at the very least, unintended meanings to be made by subsequent audiences only increases.

Furthermore, having already spent over a year as a visible presence in Internet comedy and popular culture, the Brothers had moved from being small operators making catchy musical compositions with television news to being recognized as cunning satirists with an audience large enough to gain them profit-sharing through their YouTube channel and a job creating an "Auto-Tune the Ads" clip to act as a viral component of Sony's 2009 holiday ad campaign. All this is to say that they were no longer so powerless, and in using the footage of Antoine, the power differentials in their work had shifted. In this case, they were established media-makers recombining the words and images of the relatively powerless. In moving from satirical jabs at politically powerful, elite television to engagements with more local news stories and user-generated online content, the dynamics of the Brothers' work shifted, and eventually they created a new series, *Songify This*, to signal the change. As a bridging entry from their initial series, "Bed Intruder Song" became commercially viable as an audio-only digital download through iTunes. With the Brothers sharing revenue with their unintentional singer, they effectively helped Antoine to monetize his fleeting Internet celebrity. This does not control the way in which the song functions for audiences, who might regard it as a celebration of resilience, a jeering takedown of the disenfranchised, or something above or between. The profit-sharing also does not eliminate the power differential (though it did assist in Antione attaining the means to move his family), even if it does position the Brothers more as mindful collaborators than opportunistic vultures.

While such engaged transmedial success is not in any way the dominant experience of viral video-makers or their source materials, *Auto-Tune the News* serves as a clear illustration of just how meaningful transmedial recombinations are within the arena of viral video. As more users are able to gain visibility, and in some cases power, through these practices, the meanings and values of their productions inevitably shift. The popularity of such work is undoubtedly impacting increasing numbers of television viewers (and media audiences in general), causing them to watch for moments of television excellence and excess that might be extracted, posted online, and potentially recombined. This seems like a positive development, attuning, if not awakening, audiences to more active, and potentially critical, viewing practices. The popularity of viral recombinations is in some ways just a modern manifestation of the types of borrowing and circulation that took place within folk cultures of the past, but with the tools of digital media allowing makers like The Gregory Brothers to use these practices to cultivate audiences, it will be important to watch what such empowered makers accomplish with their new pathways to visible commentary.

NOTES

1. An earlier version of this discussion is available in David Gurney, "Recombinant Comedy, Transmedial Mobility, and Viral Video," *Velvet Light Trap* 68 (Fall 2011): 3–13.
2. For more on precedents of parodying of television news, see Jeffrey P. Jones, *Entertaining Politics: Satiric Television and Political Engagement,* 2nd ed. (Lanham, MD: Rowman & Littlefield Publishers, 2010); Jonathan Gray, Jeffrey P. Jones, and Ethan Thompson, eds., *Satire TV: Politics and Comedy in the Post-Network Era* (New York: New York University Press, 2009).
3. "*The Rachel Maddow Show* for Friday, May 1, 2009," MSNBC.com, May 4, 2009, http://www.msnbc.msn.com/id/30561015/#.TlgVOTswnWw.
4. Hey Obama—Get in the Fight!! "Auto-Tune the News #2: pirates. drugs. gay marriage," *Talking Points Memo Reader Blog*, April 24, 2009, http://tpmcafe.talking-pointsmemo.com/talk/blogs/wadeblazingame34/2009/04/auto-tune-the-news-2-pirates-d.php.; Lindsey Weber, "Auto-Tune: Almost Over? Our Favorite Auto-Tune Parodies," *Urlesque*, April 24, 2009, http://www.urlesque.com/2009/04/24/auto-tune-almost-over-our-favorite-auto-tune-parodies/.
5. This is designated as episode 12b of the series and was subsequently retitled "BED INTRUDER SONG!!! (now on iTunes)."
6. panhead. "This actually aired on my local news today." *reddit*, July 28, 2010. http://www.reddit.com/r/funny/comments/cuvn3/this_actually_aired_on_my_local_news_today/.
7. Andy Carvin, "The YouTube 'Bed Intruder' Meme: A Perfect Storm of Race, Music, Comedy And Celebrity," *NPR All Tech Considered*, August 5, 2010, http://www.npr.org/blogs/alltechconsidered/2010/08/05/129005122/youtube-bed-intruder-meme.

FURTHER READING

Burgess, Jean, and Joshua Green. *YouTube: Online Video and Participatory Culture*. Cambridge: Polity Press, 2009.

Gurney, David. "Recombinant Comedy, Transmedial Mobility, and Viral Video." *Velvet Light Trap* 68 (Fall 2011): 3–13.

Jenkins, Henry, Sam Ford, and Joshua Green. *Spreadable Media: Creating Value and Meaning in a Networked Culture*. New York: New York University Press, 2013.

Snickars, Pelle, and Patrick Vonderau, eds. *The YouTube Reader*. Stockholm: National Library of Sweden, 2009.

34

Battlestar Galactica
Fans and Ancillary Content

SUZANNE SCOTT

Abstract: Being a fan of a TV program in the convergence era increasingly means engaging "official" ancillary content such as podcasts and webisodes produced in conjunction with the series itself. Suzanne Scott's examination of such "textual expansions" of *Battlestar Galactica* shows how ancillary content enriches fan experience while also channeling participation in ways that best suit the industry's financial and ideological interests.

Most weeks, the opening credits sequence of the Sci-Fi (now SyFy) Channel's cult hit *Battlestar Galactica* (2003–2009) featured title cards that read: "The Cylons were created by man. They evolved. They rebelled. There are many copies . . . and they have a plan." These lines were designed to summarize the premise of the show for audiences, but they also provide a useful allegory to explore the shifting relationship between the television industry and fans within media convergence. When the first studies of television fans emerged in the early 1990s, scholars focused on the transformative works (fan fiction, fan vids, and fan art) created and circulated within female fan communities.[1] These early studies framed fans as "textual poachers," producing texts that queered, critiqued, or expanded on the source material. Fans weren't passive consumers who were content to follow producers' textual "plan," but rebels waging a tactical resistance on both dominant representations and the intended meanings of the media industry. Alongside the massive growth of online fan culture in the past decade, the television industry's business model evolved to respond to technology's destabilizing effect on the relationships both between producers and consumers and between networks and advertisers. One way the television industry has tried to appeal to fans and acknowledge their growing promotional importance in a post-network business plan has been through ancillary content models.

Located on a television series' official website, ancillary content models consist of webisodes, webcomics, episodic podcasts, blogs/vlogs, alternate reality games (ARGs), and a range of other content aimed at fans. While these textual expansions and supplements are free, ancillary content develops alternate revenue streams for the industry via banner ads and embedded commercials, as well as being designed to reinforce the narrative value of the "primary" television text. It is easy to see how ancillary content enriches fans' experience of consuming a television series, but we must also consider how ancillary content channels fan participation in ways that best suit the industry's financial and ideological interests. Positioning a television series within a web of ancillary content that impacts the unfolding serial narrative offers the audience incentives to watch episodes as they air and eradicate time-shifting (streaming shows online or watching them through a DVR). Ancillary content also uses place-shifting (viewing television on mobile devices such as laptops) to the industry's advantage, encouraging fans to consume online content to achieve a comprehensive understanding of the series' master "plan."[2]

Using *Battlestar Galactica* (*BSG*) as a test case, this essay examines how the television industry's recent attempt to reach out to fans through a continuous flow of ancillary content might have a counterintuitive effect, alienating pre-existing fan communities and negatively impacting fan creativity. Henry Jenkins argues that the transformative works that fans create thrive on textual ambiguities and routinely "work to resolve gaps, to explore excess details and underdeveloped potentials" in the text.[3] As television series begin to strategically fill the narrative and temporal "gaps" between episodes and seasons with ancillary content, certain modes of fan engagement are privileged over others. Through an analysis of the ancillary content surrounding *BSG*'s season 3 premiere episode, "Occupation" (October 6, 2006), we can address broader concerns about the temporal and ideological strictures that ancillary content models place on fans, and consider the affirmational forms of fandom they endorse. Unlike transformative fandom, which values "appropriation over documentation, and multiple interpretations over hierarchical authority," affirmational fandom is characterized by a deep investment in both authorial intent and the "rules" that govern a fictional universe, along with a desire to comprehensively understand that universe.[4] As the television industry begins to reach out to fans, recognizing them as a powerful promotional force, it is important to consider which types of fans, fan practices, and fannish modes of textual engagement the industry is attempting to attract and encourage through ancillary content.

Creator and Executive Producer Ronald D. Moore ("RDM" to fans) launched his re-imagining of ABC's 1978 cult series *Battlestar Galactica* as a three-hour miniseries in 2003, and quickly became a visible and vocal proponent of digital ancillary content.[5] In particular, Moore's weekly podcast commentaries and his avid defense of the narrative value of webisodes during the 2007 Writers Guild of America strike helped to position him not only as *BSG's* primary gatekeeper of information and guardian of narrative continuity, but also as an advocate for integrating ancillary content into viewers' television experience.[6] The webisode series "*Battlestar Galactica*: The Resistance," and Moore's podcast commentary for "Occupation" confirm that the bulk of *BSG's* ancillary content is concerned with executing and justifying Moore's "plan" for the series; at the same time, they also suggest a broader industrial plan to encourage affirmational modes of fan engagement.

Though Moore's *BSG* had always taken its inspiration from post-9/11 culture, the popular press immediately honed in on the season 3 premiere's clear parallels to the U.S. occupation of Iraq, and its sympathetic framing of the show's human characters as insurgents (thereby aligning their once-genocidal Cylon adversaries with American occupying forces). "Occupation" concluded with one of the series' minor human characters, Duck, infiltrating a graduation ceremony for the newly formed "New Caprica Police" (human patrolmen working for the Cylons) as a suicide bomber. Moments before Duck detonates the bomb, he murmurs, "I'll see you soon, Nora." Without further context, fans might have watched the credits roll with questions flooding their brain: What past "mistakes" is Duck referring to as he prays before the bombing? Who is Nora and how did she die? In the past, fans would have immediately begun to pick away at these ambiguities, debating potential answers and scribbling in the textual gaps and margins to create and circulate answers of their own.

Instead, many of these questions were preemptively answered over ten installments of the webisode series "*Battlestar Galactica*: The Resistance," released on Scifi.com in the month prior to "Occupation." Because the webisodes collectively had the same running time as an episode of the television series, were produced by the same creative team, and featured the same cast, many fans viewed them as the first "episode" of season 3. Accordingly, in addition to promoting the season 3 premiere, the webisodes laid the narrative groundwork for the season's first story arc, detailing the early stages of the Cylon resistance movement. Focusing on a pair of minor characters from the *BSG* universe, former Viper pilot Duck and former Galactica deckhand Jammer, each of the two- to four-minute webisodes detailed their motivations to join and betray the resistance movement, respectively.

The content of the webisodes informed the audience's understanding of a number of key narrative developments in season 3. Most prominently, the murder of Duck's wife, Nora, by Cylon Centurians in webisode 4 directly motivated Duck's suicide bombing in "Occupation," as well as dictating the episode's closing line.

FIGURE 34.1. Ancillary content on the official *Battlestar Galactica* website.

Duck's prayers in the temple in "Occupation" resonated more deeply with fans who knew of his conflicted faith from the webisodes. Likewise, Jammer's recruitment to join the New Caprica Police and serve as a Cylon informant in webisodes 7 and 8 enhanced fans' understanding of the death order carried out by Jammer and foreshadowed Jammer's eventual execution later in season 3. Because the webisodes were conceived and shot after filming for season 3 had begun, they ironically replicated fans' own production process, beginning by identifying elusive or ambiguous facets of television episodes and retroactively providing context. Some of these moments of ambiguity in "Occupation" are expressed verbally (e.g., Duck's statement that "Since they killed her, I don't have anything to live for") while others are created aesthetically (e.g., the slow motion shots of Duck during the Pyramid game, signaling his significance, or the pointed close-up of Jammer as Roslin's diary/voiceover notes that those serving the Cylons might be people they "least expect"). Because the webisodes aired prior to "Occupation," they functioned to answer fans' questions before they were given the opportunity to ask, settling debates before they were allowed to grow lively, and exploring the minor character backstories and relationships that were once the domain of fan texts.

If the *BSG* webisodes sought to preemptively resolve narrative ambiguities, Moore's weekly podcast commentaries functioned to retroactively contextualize and justify narrative decisions. Thus, the rise of producer/creator podcasts as a popular component of ancillary content models over the last several years might be viewed as an overt attempt by the industry to maintain interpretive power, while simultaneously providing a space for creators to articulate their "plan" for the series to fans. Jonathan Gray argues that commentaries have always functioned to "add an authorial voice that instructs readers on how to make sense of scenes and themes . . . thus constructing a clear 'proper interpretation'" of the text.[7] Moore's weekly *BSG* podcast commentaries routinely suggest proper interpretations, but they also suggest that the author himself is a key ancillary text for fans to consume.

Recorded in Moore's home, often with his wife Terry Dresbach (or "Mrs. Ron," as she was known on the SciFi.com message boards) present, the podcasts' amateurish aesthetic and their blend of intimacy and authority make them fascinating texts to decode in their own right. For example, the "Occupation" podcast opens with the couple debating whether or not to hold a fan contest to name their newly adopted kittens (a suggestion from Mrs. Ron that Moore quickly rejects). If Moore generally plays the paternalistic role of the all-knowing auteur in the podcasts, laboriously detailing and justifying every editing decision and plot point, Mrs. Ron's role might be seen as lending a "fannish" presence: we hear her complain that she can't hear the episode, gasp at plot twists, and make intertextual references, quipping that Starbuck being held in her domestic prison by Leoben is like "a dark *Groundhog Day*," and humming the theme to *The Patty Duke Show* as Moore discusses the technical logistics of shooting multiple "copies" of Cylon characters. At one point, Mrs. Ron openly privileges her fan identity, noting to her husband, "I'm not listening to you, I'm reading my thread on the SciFi [message] board." Yet, despite these displays of fan participation and Mrs. Ron's complaints that "everyone gets so literal" when interpreting the show, the podcasts work to reinforce the value of Moore's voice and interpretations, and affirmative sites of fan engagement, such as the show's official message board.

Derek Kompare has argued that it is "difficult to conceive of a more direct assertion of authorship" than a commentary, and that weekly creator podcasts make "such authorial exegesis . . . a normal part of the cult television viewing experience."[8] Moore's podcast commentary for "Occupation," which was available for download the day after the episode aired, clearly positions itself both as a central component of fans' viewing experience and a direct assertion of Moore's authorship over the television text as a whole, encompassing both the series and the ancillary content that surrounds it. When Moore presents alternative narratives, in this case reading directly from an early (and ultimately abandoned) draft of "Occupation" that opened with a Cylon propaganda film, he is less concerned with opening up new narrative avenues for fans to explore in their own

FIGURE 34.2.
Fan art of series creator Ron Moore by
Arne Ratermanis.

transformative works than with exhaustively explaining why those roads lead to dead ends. In the case of the propaganda film, Moore simply states that "it just felt like the wrong tone," but there are many other more detailed examples of narrative justification, such as Moore's explanation of the placement of Laura Roslin's "diary" exposition sequence within the episode, or the rationale behind moving Starbuck's captivity plot line from season 2 to season 3.

Even when Moore's exertions of authority are playful (such as when he jokes about killing off a popular character), they ultimately reinforce the power of that authority (the claim is that such a joke would create "300 threads [on fan message boards] in about four minutes."). Moore also uses the "Occupation" podcast to stress the significance of ancillary content, and his role as an authorial overseer of that content. When Moore emphatically states that he's "sure all of you [fans] listening to this have watched [the webisodes] several times," discusses their development and intersection with the series, and emphasizes the need to view them "several times," he accentuates the narrative significance of ancillary content. By framing fans as narrative collectors rather than creators, Moore appears to be equating fan "participation" with consuming ancillary content.

Such ancillary content models could be viewed as a more covert form of cease and desist letters, temporally and ideologically (rather than legally) discouraging fans from certain interpretations of or elaborations on the text. First, there are the intensified consumption patterns that ancillary content models encourage. Because ancillary content is released between seasons or episodes of a show, fans who wish to explore narrative gaps and ambiguities through the creation of their own fan texts increasingly find those gaps either already filled in by the show's creators, or difficult to develop before another piece of ancillary content overwrites or negates it. Thus, while a narrative nugget of information dispatched in ancillary content might inspire fans, the creative window of opportunity for fans to play with it has shrunken considerably. We can read this shrinking window of time for fans to textually engage with an unfolding television series narrative as an exacerbated form of what Matt Hills calls "just-in-time fandom," in which fan productivity "become[s] increasingly enmeshed within the rhythms and temporalities of broadcasting."[9] Ancillary content creates a compounded form of "just-in-time fandom" that encourages an increased rate of consumption and the collection of narrative data, rather than fannish speculation and textual production.

Conversely, being unable to access and consume ancillary content poses a different form of temporal control. Australian media scholar Tama Leaver, writing about his inability to access "The Resistance" webisodes prior to season 3, has expressed concerns about the "tyranny of digital distance" that occurs when the economics that underpin digital distribution are exposed. Leaver argues that because the "expectation of near-synchronous global distribution [was] not fulfilled," fans outside the United States were forced to avoid participating in broader online fan communities for fear of being "spoiled," or to acquire these texts illegally via peer-to-peer file sharing. In deciding to limit the reach of the webisodes, NBC-Universal not only privileged American fans, but also displaced global fans from the intricate rhythms and temporalities their ancillary content created.[10]

Second, ancillary content could be viewed as a mode of ideological control, suggesting "intended" or "preferred" interpretations of the text. Ancillary content not only scribbles in the margins that used to belong to fans; it also encourages them not to color outside of the (often heteronormative) lines. A prime example is *BSG*'s second webisode series, "The Face of the Enemy," released online between December 12, 2008, and January 12, 2009. The first webisode in this series featured a fleeting kiss between Felix Gaeta and Louis Hoshi, alluding to a romantic relationship that Gaeta ultimately breaks off in the final webisode. The lack of prior evidence of Gaeta's bisexuality or his relationship with Hoshi on the television series and (a few knowing glances aside) no subsequent acknowledgement of their relationship for the remainder of the series are telling. Ancillary content models present a less commercially charged space to explore homoerotic storylines and frequently push queer readings or queer characters to the periphery of the narrative. This allows for a concurrent acknowledgment of the latent homoerotic subtext that inspires slash fiction (transformative works that construct a romantic relationship between two characters of the same sex) and a containment of such readings that neatly isolate them from the primary commercial television text.[11] *BSG* writer Jane Espenson claims that Gaeta's sexuality was never mentioned on the television series because sexual orientation was "simply not an issue in their world," but this utopianism doesn't sufficiently explain why some narrative connections between the television show and ancillary content are emphasized, while others remain invisible on the show's margins.[12]

Inevitably, some fans embrace this influx of ancillary content; others argue that interpretive power should belong to the audience for whom exploring ambiguities makes fan participation pleasurable. We shouldn't devalue affirmational forms of participation or presume that this binary between affirmational and transformative modes of fan participation adequately captures the diversity of fan identities or types of engagement. That said, it is worth noting that the affirmational fandom that ancillary content "sanctions" is characterized by more monologic than dialogic relationship with the text and its producers, facilitating the fan's industrial incorporation as a promotional tool. Though ancillary content presents itself as a more participatory model of consumption and appears to be facilitating more points of contact between audiences and creators, it remains firmly rooted in the "old media" broadcast ethos of television. Audiences within the era of ancillary content may have more sanctioned and visible modes of talking back to their television screen online, but these "conversations" are typically one-sided and privilege creators' voices and viewpoints.

The media industry's growing reliance on ancillary content and the corresponding creation of "official" fan sites online privilege affirmational modes of engagement, and reward hegemonic textual interpretations that neatly align with the creator's (or network's or corporation's) preferred understanding of the text. Ultimately, the concern is that ancillary contents' emphasis on affirmational modes of fan engagement may reinforce a hierarchy, legitimating some fan practices and marginalizing others.[13] Because the process of "watching television" now commonly includes consuming ancillary content, fans are presented with the Cylonian options of rebelling (continuing to pry open the text to construct new narratives of their own) or "evolving" (moving along sanctioned narrative paths and accepting the author's "plan"). Whether fans are "affirmational" or "transformative" in their engagement, the industry's "plan" for mobilizing and monetizing fandom and how fans respond to and potentially undermine that plan deserve further study.

NOTES

1. See Camille Bacon-Smith, *Enterprising Women: Television Fandom and the Creation of Popular Myth* (Philadelphia: University of Pennsylvania Press, 1991), and Henry Jenkins, *Textual Poachers: Television Fans and Participatory Culture* (New York: Routledge, 1992).

2. See Cynthia B. Meyers, "From Sponsorship to Spots: Advertising and the Development of Electronic Media," in *Media Industries: History, Theory, and Method*, Jennifer Holt and Alisa Perren, eds. (Oxford: Wiley-Blackwell, 2009), 77.

3. Jenkins, *Textual Poachers*, 278.

4. Julie Levin Russo, "Twansformative? The Future of Fandom on Twitter," paper presented at the Flow Conference, Austin, TX, October 1, 2010, http://j-l-r.org/node/987; "Affirmational fandom vs. Transformational fandom," Obsession_inc, June 1, 2009, http://obsession-inc.dreamwidth.org/82589.html.

5. Created by Glen A. Larson, the original *Battlestar Galactica* ran for only one season on ABC in 1978–1979. It was resurrected as *Galactica 80*, a spin-off that ran for only half a season in 1980.

6. Jenny Hontz, "Webisodes: A Battle Against the Empire," *Newsweek*, October 23, 2006.

7. Jonathan Gray, *Show Sold Separately: Promos, Spoilers, and Other Media Paratexts* (New York: New York University Press, 2010), 89.

8. Derek Kompare, "More 'Moments of Television': Online Cult Television Authorship," in *FlowTV: Television in the Age of Media Convergence*, Michael Kackman, Marnie Binfield, Matthew Thomas Payne, Allison Perlman, and Bryan Sebok, eds. (New York: Routledge, 2011), 107.

9. Matt Hills, *Fan Cultures* (New York: Routledge, 2002), 178–79.

10. Tama Leaver, "Watching *Battlestar Galactica* in Australia and the Tyranny of Digital Distance," http://www.tamaleaver.net/cv/tyranny_postprint.pdf.

11. See Sara Gwenllian Jones, "The Sex Lives of Cult Television Characters," *Screen* 43 (2002): 79–90; and Catherine Tosenberger, "'The Epic Love Story of Sam and Dean': *Supernatural*, Queer Readings, and the Romance of Incestuous Fan Fiction," *Transformative Works and Cultures* 1 (2008), http://journal.transformativeworks.org/index.php/twc/article/view/30/36.

12. Michael Jensen, "Live Chat with Jane Espensen," *AfterElton.com*, March 19, 2009, http://www.afterelton.com/blog/michaeljensen/live-chat-with-jane-espenson. For a discussion of the "persistence of heteronormative containment" on *BSG*, see Julie Levin Russo, "Hera Has Six Mommies (A Transmedia Love Story)," *Flow*, December 19, 2007, http://flowtv.org/2007/12/hera-has-six-mommies-a-transmedia-love-story/.

13. Kristina Busse, "Podcasts and the Fan Experience of Disseminated Media Commentary," paper presented at the Flow Conference, Austin, TX, October 2006, http://www.kristina-busse.com/cv/research/flow06.html.

FURTHER READING

Jenkins, Henry. "*Star Trek* Rerun, Reread, Rewritten: Fan Writing as Textual Poaching." In his *Fans, Bloggers, and Gamers: Exploring Participatory Culture.* New York: New York University Press, 2007.

Kompare, Derek. "More 'Moments of Television': Online Cult Television Authorship." In *Flow TV: Television in the Age of Media Convergence*, Michael Kackman, Marnie Binfield, Matthew Thomas Payne, Allison Perlman, and Bryan Sebok, eds. New York: Routledge, 2011.

Leaver, Tama. "Watching *Battlestar Galactica* in Australia and the Tyranny of Digital Distance," http://www.tamaleaver.net/cv/tyranny_postprint.pdf

Russo, Julie Levin Russo. "User-Penetrated Content: Fan Video in the Age of Convergence." *Cinema Journal* 48, 4 (Summer 2009), 125–30.

Pearson, Roberta. "Fandom in the Digital Era." *Popular Communication* 8, no. 1 (January 2010), 84–95.

35

Everyday Italian
Cultivating Taste

MICHAEL Z. NEWMAN

Abstract: While all commercial television has an investment in promoting consumerism in its audiences, few genres are as focused on the various dimensions of consumption as cooking shows. Michael Z. Newman analyzes Food Network's *Everyday Italian* with Giada De Laurentiis as an instance of lifestyle television, perpetuating cultural norms of gender, class, and taste.

American television is, with rare exceptions, a commercial medium supported by advertising that pays for the programs. A TV show's audience is not only a collection of a large number of persons (a million viewers may not be that many, depending on the network and time of day), but also a commodity whose attention is sold by the TV station or network to the advertisers who want to reach those persons with commercial messages. Making meaningful and entertaining television content may be the agenda of those who create it, but to succeed commercially, TV shows need to attract audiences who are desirable to advertisers in terms of age, gender, and income, among other traits. One central purpose of television in American society is thus to promote consumption of the goods and services advertised during the commercial breaks. Seen this way, television is a consumerist medium, encouraging us to spend our money on burgers and sodas, movie tickets and jeans, smartphones and video games, vacations and cars.

Everyday Italian with Giada De Laurentiis has aired in the United States on the Food Network since 2003 (original episodes were produced through 2008), and has more recently been airing on its spinoff cable outlet, the Cooking Channel. Each episode shows the host in a home kitchen preparing several dishes connected by a theme such as "Italian street food" or "Sicilian summer," as well as brief scenes away from Giada's kitchen discussing the episode's theme, shopping, and dining, often with others. Most of the show is concerned with demonstrating recipes, leading the audience through a series of steps toward serving an impressive and delicious meal. At the same time, cooking shows like *Everyday Italian* epitomize the commercial function of TV, serving as especially sharp examples of television's consumerist mandate.

Everyday Italian explicitly and implicitly promotes consumption in several ways. The thirty-second commercial spots that run in between segments of course do what commercials always do: they address messages to audiences to get them to buy items typically advertised during cooking shows, such as yogurt and paper towels, which often appeal to a household's "grocery decision makers."[1] But the show itself, the content, is also thoroughly commercial and consumerist, exemplifying a growing trend in recent media in which content is itself in some ways like a commercial. For instance, reality shows like *Extreme Makeover: Home Edition* (ABC, 2003–present) promote Sears home improvement products and services, while *American Idol* (Fox, 2002–present) features its contestants in ads for Ford cars. *Everyday Italian* is a food show, so episodes implicitly encourage the audience to shop for groceries to use following Giada's recipes. The setting is a kitchen where the host prepares dishes using a variety of tools, and so the show likewise invites us to acquire similar knives and appliances. Indeed, many cooking show stars, including Giada, endorse lines of kitchenware and prepared food. The Giada De Laurentiis Collection of products for sale at Target department stores includes cookware and bakeware, gadgets and cutlery, and DVDs of her television shows.

We might also think of *Everyday Italian* as an elaborate promotion for Giada herself, a Food TV star whose image and identity sell those cookbooks, knives, casseroles, pans, and jars of pesto that feed her status as a celebrity chef and extend her personal brand beyond TV. This star persona, promoted on her television series as well as in her cookbooks and in magazine interviews, combines a relatable and cheerful guide to cooking Italian food with a young, sexy, even seductive physical presence. For instance, in 2007 Giada appeared in *Esquire* magazine photographed in a skin-tight, low-cut white dress, the top of which resembles a push-up bra, with her hands and lower body drenched in bright red tomatoes, making clear the overlap of food and sex in her public identity. Giada's hyper-feminine and sexualized appearance and performance on *Everyday Italian* makes the show more than mere instruction in culinary technique. By offering up a fantasy of sensuality, *Everyday Italian* promotes not only the consumption of food and other products, but also of Giada herself as an image of sexualized desire and pleasure.[2]

For decades, televised cooking shows have had a strong pedagogical dimension, addressing audiences as students of culinary practice. For instance, Julia Child's *The French Chef* (WGBH, 1963–1973) assured a generation of middle-class American home cooks that they could prepare impressive food themselves with the ingredients and tools available to them, and find satisfaction in the pleasures of cooking and eating.³ Pedagogical food TV since Child has offered instruction to home cooks not only in efficient and practical skills of the kitchen, but also in appreciation of food and its effective preparation as an essential component of the good life. "Dump-and-stir" shows on the Food Network and the Cooking Channel like *Everyday Italian* continue in this tradition, offering lessons in various aspects of cooking as a practice requiring knowledge and skill. Giada De Laurentiis guides us as a peppy teacher instilling good habits and special knowledge about ingredients and techniques. She takes care to describe her ingredients (cinnamon is "warm," parmesan cheese is "nutty," olives are "rich and fruity") and to explain her techniques (shocking vegetables in ice water prevents overcooking, mustard helps bind a vinaigrette). She takes care to introduce unfamiliar viewers to the ingredients and practices of Italian cookery, translating the literal meaning of *biscotti* ("twice cooked" cookies) and explaining the uses of Italian pantry staples like hazelnut chocolate spread and *vin santo,* a dessert wine.

The audience of *Everyday Italian* is addressed in a number of overlapping but distinct ways: as consumers of food and other goods, as subjects submitting to fantasies of sensual experience, and most explicitly as students of kitchen technique. But in addition to the details of this culinary pedagogy, shows like *Everyday Italian* instruct audiences in a more general way of thinking and living. These shows open up viewers to a vision of good taste, presenting a model of how to live that we might attain, but more likely merely aspire to. Cooking shows are one type of "Lifestyle TV," a category of consumerist media including home decorating and personal makeover programs on channels such as HGTV and TLC. These shows are about the consumption of products (like food on cooking shows, furniture on decorating shows, and apparel on makeover shows) that are supposed to realize the viewer's desire for fashioning an identity particularly in terms of social class—or at least to offer an ideal of how this identity might be fashioned. Seen this way, a show like *Everyday Italian* is instructing us not only how to grill shrimp or bake a cake. It is also showing us how to exploit this knowledge as a form of *cultural capital,* a term the French sociologist Pierre Bourdieu coined to describe the way knowledge and skill function as tools for realizing and maintaining distinctions of social power and status. Taste can be very personal, and often seems deceptively simple and natural, as we tend to think of taste as being just good or bad. But it also has a social power to elevate those who assert their good taste and its superiority over those who lack it. Cooking shows cultivate their audience's competence in cooking and eating as part of a wider constellation of consumer choices.

Even as they offer us various kinds of practical knowledge and skill, however, such shows also function as an escape from social realities into a fantasy realm of sensual pleasures. The everyday routines of hurried schedules—of foods chosen more for availability and ease of preparation than nutrition or taste, of banal prepackaged and hastily assembled, good-enough meals—may be cast aside. Turning to a show like *Everyday Italian* at a time of leisure allows for a vicarious indulgence in a seemingly more authentic and dignified, and more satisfying, experience of food preparation and consumption. The fantasy is not merely of having Giada's knowledge and skill, but the time, freedom, counter space, equipment, and grocery budget to indulge in the kind of gustatory pleasures represented in *Everyday Italian*. The idea that the recipes prepared are for "everyday" consumption is evidently more hopeful than practical. While the dishes do not usually involve the elaborate or fancy preparations we might find in another kind of Food Network show hosted by a restaurant chef (e.g., *Emeril Live*, 1997–present), it is also not the "everyday" food typical of American quotidian life.

Giada assures us that her pork chops are "never dry," as she dresses them up in ingredients that are uncommon to American home cooking, such as capers. Her rice (actually *risotto*) is served with porcini mushrooms and Gorgonzola. Rather than pulling the lid off a pint of supermarket ice cream, she churns her own, made from ricotta cheese. This is a marked contrast to the types of food advertised in the show's commercial breaks. During the episodes airing daily in the summer of 2011 on Cooking Channel, for instance, the products advertised repeatedly included DiGiorno frozen pizzas, Hillshire Farms sliced turkey, Honey Nut Cheerios, Hamburger Helper, Keebler cookies, The Laughing Cow cheese, and Hidden Valley ranch dressing. These are convenience or snack foods, often processed and requiring little if any preparation and appealing to a broad mainstream of American consumers. To the extent that any might be considered ethnic, they are among the most commonplace ethnic foods in the American diet. Such items as frozen dinners and bottled dressings are not at all the kinds of ingredients one finds in Giada's dishes, which are presented as authentic, from-scratch preparations, and products of her unique skill and personal touch. This contrast between the food in the episode and the food in the commercials reveals the appeal of shows like *Everyday Italian* as one of escape from the ordinary and into a realm of deeper—if vicarious—pleasure.

Sometimes such vicarious experience of pleasure in cooking shows (as well as in magazines like *Saveur* and *Bon Appetit* and blogs and other websites about cooking and eating) leads to the use of "food porn" as a description of these texts and their appeal.[4] The charged metaphor of porn suggests a number of features of the visual style of food media, and of the reception of shows like *Everyday Italian*. One aspect of food porn is the fetishized emphasis on the desirable object, the food, often depicted in adoring and vivid close-up photography. This is a food equivalent of pornography's graphic depictions of isolated body parts and sexual acts. The *Everyday Italian* episode "Roasting Show" (December 11, 2004) shows us such fetishized views of ingredients in the forms of ripe pears held in the host's bare hands, fresh green stalks of rosemary and grains of salt pinched by her fingers, pale yellow olive oil glistening as it is drizzled over a loin of pork, with Giada's hands working an herb rub into the surface of the meat. The pleasure of this kind of television viewing is highly visual, and it arouses a sensory desire, a wish to feel or taste, which it cannot directly satisfy. Perhaps also like conventional pornography, food porn offers an idealized and unattainable representation, manipulated and stylized by media production techniques in ways that are aimed at maximizing the audience's desire.

But in addition to the appeal of the food, and closely connected to it, the representation of Giada De Laurentiis herself is also in some ways designed to arouse sensual desire and vicarious pleasure. She is obviously represented to have sex appeal, modeling an image of female sexual desirability. We may assume that heterosexual female viewers are expected to idealize this image and that heterosexual male viewers are invited to desire it sexually. This makes shows like *Everyday Italian* appeal to several audience segments, including those straight men who may not be most likely to take her instruction in cooking but still might enjoy the spectacle of her performance in the kitchen. Giada is thin but curvy, in some ways a voluptuous kitchen goddess like Nigella Lawson; though as self-consciously sexualized as Nigella, Giada's Italian ethnic identity conveys sensuality more than Nigella's Englishness could.[5] Rather than wearing chef whites as some Food Network hosts do, Giada dresses in low-cut casual tops in the kitchen, invariably showing her cleavage. In introductory sequences shot away from the kitchen, Giada addresses the camera in more dressy feminine attire like a clingy cocktail dress, with her hair down and more elaborately coiffed, and her face made up glamorously. Her image is one of conventional female attractiveness, the kind on the covers of women's magazines like *Vogue, Redbook*, or *Cosmopolitan* more often than those in the cooking section of the magazine rack. In the kitchen, she often expresses strong feelings about her food, accentuated with bold gestures and bright wide smiles, exuding physical presence. The momentary pleasures she performs when tasting her own cooking at the end of each episode, closing her eyes and enjoying a brief private moment before opening them to describe the flavors and textures while still visibly chewing and swallowing, are voyeuristic offerings to an audience eager for its own desires to be stimulated and satisfied. Giada's image as a fit and sexy woman is also reinforced in her cookbooks. For instance, *Everyday Italian*, a bestselling companion book to the TV series, includes not only the obligatory glossy food shots, but more than fifty images of the chef herself. The pleasures of eating and of sex are of course distinct, but in combining these two forms of sensuality, cooking shows like *Everyday Italian* invite us to consider them together, to see the ways that media forms like the cooking show can create overlapping and intermingling desires and fantasies.

FIGURE 35.1.
Giada in the kitchen on *Everyday Italian*.

In "Roasting Show," we find many of the characteristics of *Everyday Italian* considered so far. Giada prepares roast pork loin with fig sauce, which she introduces by comparison to pork chops and applesauce, a dish more familiar to American viewers. This positions her food as a more Italian, authentic, distinguished version of a familiar combination of pork and fruit and encourages the audience to consume the dish as a means of social distinction. As she pairs the meat with roast fennel and parmesan cheese, the pedagogical dimension of cooking shows is realized in Giada's discussion of possibly unknown ingredients in the savory main and side dishes. The fig sauce contains port wine and rosemary, which she describes as sweet and pine-like, respectively. Giada introduces fennel, "still foreign to a lot people," as her favorite vegetable, and one that is eaten throughout the year in Italy. She excitedly compares its flavor to licorice. The camera closes in for tight shots of the fennel bulbs and fronds, emphasizing its exoticism and enticing green color and soliciting our desire. Giada shows off her ethnic heritage, performing her identity as Italian American, when she articulates terms like *Parmigiano-Reggiano* (Italian parmesan cheese) in a pronounced, affected accent. This is to demonstrate the authenticity of her culinary practice and her authority as a chef. She is also represented visually as a sexually desirable woman, in a scoop-collared top with a plunging neckline and glossy red lips. She often leans forward toward the camera to reach items on the counter or to open the low oven door, revealing more cleavage.

The flow from content to advertising in *Everyday Italian* creates overlapping commercial messages, making repetitive appeals to the audience to consume both food products and the host's star persona. Introductory and interstitial portions (those between the kitchen scenes) show Giada shopping for groceries and chocolate candies, and the commercial spots as recorded during an airing in 2006 feature several advertising foods, including one for "the other white meat." Both content and advertising have redundant consumerist messages, reinforcing one another: eat pork. During the kitchen segments, though, we also find shots of Giada framed by brand-name appliances in the background, and close-ups of her hands chopping fennel give us a nice glimpse of her high-end Global chef's knife. These images also encourage our consumption.

In the episode's concluding segment, Giada sits at an outdoor bistro table covered in a tablecloth sipping from a glass of red wine before tasting the dinner she has prepared. She characteristically pauses to contemplate and savor the first bite of each dish, chewing with eyes closed before proceeding to explain the virtues of the recipes as she has prepared them: "The meat is moist, and the fig sauce is perfectly sweet." Roasting the fennel has mellowed out its licorice flavor, Giada says, and "the cheesy crust from the parmesan cheese, it's salty, buttery, and fantastic!" All of these lines are delivered with accompanying body language, broad hand gestures, and facial expressions to accentuate her satisfaction. Her pleasure in the sensual experience of eating is as important for the show's messages as the more pedagogical moments of explanation and demonstration. A cooking show like *Everyday Italian* is centrally concerned with this representation of distinguished, authentic, gustatory, and even erotic pleasure as an escape from everyday realities. Its ultimate purpose, however, is to return us to the usual experience of familiar supermarket foods that both the content and commercials urge us to consume.

Television can be many things, but our typical experience of TV in the United States is of a medium that encourages us to improve our lives and realize our dreams by exercising our agency as consumers. Such appeals typically involve more than the obvious sales pitches of thirty-second commercials; they can be woven through television's "content" as much as through its ads. Wherever we encounter them, these appeals, explicit or implicit, work by summoning our desires for social status and personal pleasure. Such desires are often aroused through sensual means, such as the audiovisual representations of food and femininity in *Everyday Italian*, in which Giada De Laurentiis's image is offered as a focus for our consumerist fantasies. As in many forms of television—not only lifestyle TV, but programs in many other genres such as game shows, reality series, and dramas—our appetite for consumption is often tempted by combinations of sex, star image, and fantasies of pleasure.

NOTES

1. "Advertise with Us" page of Food Network website, http://www.foodnetwork.com/advertise-with-us-audience-profile/package/index.html.

2. For further considerations of gender politics and representations in recent cooking shows, see Rebecca Swenson, "Domestic Divo? Televised Treatments of Masculinity, Femininity,

and Food," *Critical Studies in Media Communication* 26 (2009): 36–53; and Elizabeth Na-
thanson, "As Easy As Pie: Cooking Shows, Domestic Efficiency, and Postfeminist Temporality," *Television & New Media* 10 (2009): 311–30.

3. Dana Polan, *Julia Child's The French Chef* (Durham, NC: Duke University Press, 2011).

4. For a more elaborate consideration of cooking shows as pornography, see Andrew Chan,
   "*La grande bouffe*: Cooking Shows as Pornography," *Gastronomica: The Journal of Food
   and Culture* 3 (2003): 46–53.

5. Nigella Lawson's shows include *Nigella Bites* (UK Channel 4, 2000–2001; later seen in the
   United States on the Style network) and *Nigella Feasts* (Food Network, 2006–2008).

FURTHER READING

Collins, Kathleen. *Watching What We Eat: The Evolution of Cooking Shows.* New York: Continuum, 2009.

Ketchum, Cheri. "The Essence of Cooking Shows: How the Food Network Constructs Consumer Fantasies." *Journal of Communication Inquiry* 29 (2005): 217–34.

Palmer, Gareth, ed. *Exposing Lifestyle Television: The Big Reveal.* Hampshire, UK: Ashgate,
2008.

Ray, Krishnendu. "Domesticating Cuisine: Food and Aesthetics on American Television."
Gastronomica: The Journal of Food and Culture 7 (2007): 50–64.

36

Gossip Girl
Transmedia Technologies

LOUISA STEIN

Abstract: While television is often thought of as a predigital mass medium distinct from online "new media," contemporary television programs are frequently intertwined with transmedia digital contexts and practices. Louisa Stein examines *Gossip Girl*'s representations of digital technologies, advertising tie-ins, and online extensions to highlight how digital media functions as a central theme, a style of representation, and mode of engagement for this popular teen drama.

According to my Social Climbing agenda, I have a busy few days ahead of me. I'll be attending a charity fundraiser, the Bass Industries Anniversary Party, and the launch of Eleanor Waldorf's fashion line. At these events, I'll be eavesdropping for pieces of scandalous information that I can send to the anonymous blogger, Gossip Girl, to help my pursuit of upward social mobility, and at the same time I'll be hoping to be captured in a cell phone snapshot doing something scandalous, like knocking over a champagne bottle and blaming the mess on someone else. With any luck, I'll earn "spotted points" and "scandal points" and will soon be receiving invites to more intimate events with Upper East Side socialites Blair Waldorf, Chuck Bass, and Serena van der Woodsen. And as I rack up scandal points, I'll be watching the snow fall outside the window of my Vermont home. Because of course I've been describing an online game I was playing in winter 2012—specifically the transmedia game Social Climbing, which extends the storyworld of the television series *Gossip Girl* (CW, 2007–2012) by way of Facebook. From within Facebook, I can consult my Social Climbing agenda and virtually attend fictional gatherings in *Gossip Girl*'s version of New York City. In this way, *Gossip Girl*'s fantasy narrative extends into the everyday digital representations of self and community on Facebook.

The *Gossip Girl* television series revels in the scandals and personal dramas of wealthy teenagers in New York City. The series' characters use digital tools to gain and maintain power and status in an already elite community. With its emphasis on using digital tools to see and be seen, the Social Climbing *Gossip Girl* game, currently still in the initial testing (or "beta") phase, invites me to participate in the TV series' fantasy of digitally infused social power-play from within the frame of my own Facebook account. *Gossip Girl*'s Social Climbing game is the latest in a line of transmedia extensions that have invited viewers to partake in the series' elite social world, a world shaped by consumerist excess and privilege. In all cases, *Gossip Girl*'s online extensions have offered ways for viewers to spend real money to participate in the virtual pleasures connected to *Gossip Girl*. For example, one can purchase additional scandal or spotted points in Social Climbing in order to attain invitations to more intimate gatherings with the key players of the *Gossip Girl* fictional community.

This essay considers *Gossip Girl*'s representation of digital power in its narrative, online extensions, formal elements, and advertising. All four of these dimensions work in unison to depict a digital culture shared by *Gossip Girl* characters and viewers, in which digital tools offer the powers and pleasures of access, networking, and intervention. Transmedia extensions offer an obvious space for film and television to invite viewer participation in a narrative's fantasy world. However, in the case of *Gossip Girl*, the televisual text of the series itself indirectly invites the viewer to intervene in the program's very form, through the integration of do-it-yourself aesthetics into the series' imagery. These indirect invitations to viewer intervention offer an expansive vision of *Gossip Girl* viewers as digital authors, a vision that is also increasingly echoed in its marketing and product advertising. The premise of *Gossip Girl* suggests a double-edged vision of digital culture, where the digital equals both threat and power, but the series' larger transmedia logics mark a turning point in cultural representations of the digital, shedding longstanding fears of the dangers of cyberspace in favor of a more marketable vision of the empowered digital viewer turned cultural author.

Gossip Girl's ambivalent representation of the relationship between young adults and digital technology echoes contradictory public discourses about the new generation of millennial youth growing up in an already digital world. These discourses depict millennials as highly skilled digital "natives" and, at the same time, as potential victims navigating dangerous digital terrain.[1] William Strauss and Neil Howe popularized the vision of "millennials" as a digitally proactive generation who use the tools of the web to enact social change.[2] However, prototypical millennial TV programs like *Buffy the Vampire Slayer* and *Degrassi* tell a different story, featuring storylines about online stalkers (be they supernatural robots or adult men) posing as teen boys to ensnare naïve teen girls.[3] Such episodes and many others like them paint a fearful picture of the dangers facing young people (and especially young women) in the unknown realm of the digital.

Like popular discourse, academic analysis of youth engagement with digital technologies also constructs a contradictory picture. On the one hand, much of academic discourse bolsters perceptions that contemporary youth are digitally savvy, arguing that digital technologies significantly shape the outlook and life experiences of children, teens, and young adults. For example, in *The Young and the Digital,* S. Craig Watkins argues that young people experience their social connections through a mix of in-person and digital interactions.[4] Likewise, the studies represented in Kazys Varnelis's collection *Networked Publics* describe a multifaceted terrain of young people using digital technologies to engage with each other, thus forming and embodying the "networked publics" of the book's title.[5] But academic studies also warn that not all teens have equal access and digital skills, and that intersecting issues of economics, race, and ethnicity shape teens' access to and use of digital networks in significant ways. Watkins has argued that race, ethnicity, geography, and class inform the way young people relate to and deploy technology, and that the resulting differences in technological access and use have in turn created "participation gaps."[6] Other scholars contend that our sense of teens' competency in technology use may be dangerously overstated; for example, all teens do not equally understand the stakes of carefully controlling privacy settings on Facebook, and these differences can have significant ramifications.[7] Thus, both academic and popular discourses acknowledge that many young peoples' lives are infused with and shaped by digital technology, while also calling attention to ways in which the spread of digital technologies have uneven and uncertain outcomes.

The premise of *Gossip Girl* seems likewise ambivalent about the role of digital technologies in millennial lives. On the one hand, it seems to feed off of and fuel anxieties about millennials' overdependence on digital media. *Gossip Girl* features young adults immersed in and dependent on digital technologies. Each episode of the series opens with narration from the pseudonymous blogger, Gossip Girl. Through her blog posts, Gossip Girl sets the social agenda for the teens of New York City's Upper East Side by releasing rumors and scandals, the threat of which cast a pall over the teenagers' lives. The series depicts its teen protagonists trapped by the digital technologies that pervade their lives. Many episodes revolve around the threat that Gossip Girl will reveal personal details that may wreak havoc on the teens' social lives, or even get them kicked out of school. The teens of *Gossip Girl* live in fear that their secrets will be posted on the Gossip Girl blog, and, as the seasons progress, many also live with the ramifications once the private has indeed been made public for the blog-reading masses.

Yet *Gossip Girl* isn't simply a horror show about the terror of digital access. The teens in *Gossip Girl* depend on and revel in their digital networks, and through various digital campaigns, the series hails viewers who are assumed to be equally digitally connected. A late second-season episode entitled "Carnal Knowledge" (February 2, 2009) playfully depicts the teens at a complete loss for how to behave when their teacher demands they hand in their cell phones. The series consistently highlights how its teen characters depend on and utilize the very digital technologies that terrorize them. Indeed, the teens of *Gossip Girl* are their own digital bullies. They gain the upper hand in contested relationships by sending out carefully timed information to Gossip Girl's blog, which she in turn sends out to everyone in "blasts" of digital knowledge-as-power. The season 2 climax ("The Goodbye Gossip Girl," May 18, 2009) hinges on the teens realizing that not only could any one of them be Gossip Girl, but that in a way each one of them is Gossip Girl—that Gossip Girl is a construct of the social and digital network to which they all subscribe and which they together constitute. This ambivalent representation of Gossip Girl (both the blogger and the teens that make up the Gossip Girl network) depicts "her" as simultaneously a source of teen bullying and a source of teen power. And, through the aspirational hailing of *Gossip Girl*'s transmedia extensions, we as viewers are also included in and thus responsible for Gossip Girl's pleasurable network of terror and power.

Gossip Girl thus not only constructs an ambivalent picture of digitally connected millennials, but also goes one step further: it interpellates its viewers into this mixed position by deploying game-like transmedia extensions that allow viewers to play at being part of *Gossip Girl*'s world of digitally networked power and danger. Over its six seasons, *Gossip Girl* offered a range of immersive transmedia experiences that encourage viewers to interact with the storyworld of *Gossip Girl* using digital technologies, and more specifically to participate in the processes of digital gossip and consumerism as featured in the series. The first large-scale transmedia extension took the form of a digital version of the New York City lifestyle featured in the series, represented through the software interface of Second Life. *Gossip Girl*'s Second Life extension allowed viewers to explore a virtual Upper East Side, where they could create an avatar who could shop in digital representations of high-end department stores and attend online parties.[8] In 2008, The CW teamed with fashion retailer Bluefly.com to translate the digital shopping imagined in *Gossip Girl*'s Second Life into actual online shopping. Visitors to Bluefly.com could shop in the *Gossip Girl* "store," where they could purchase not *Gossip Girl* t-shirts and merchandise as one might imagine, but clothing and brands that the characters on the show might wear. The *Gossip Girl* store was divided into sections by character, so viewers-turned-online-consumers could purchase clothes as part of their identification with, or appreciation of, the style of a particular character in the storyworld.

In 2012, both *Gossip Girl*'s Second Life and the *Gossip Girl* Bluefly shop were defunct, but viewers could try out the *Gossip Girl* Social Climbing Facebook

Game. As I described in my opening, *Gossip Girl*'s Social Climbing invites viewers to move directly from their involvement with the "real life" digital social network of Facebook to their engagement with a *Gossip Girl*–based fantasy play-space. As with the Bluefly *Gossip Girl* shop, this digital extension invites players to spend real money in order to purchase enough "scandal" and "spotted" points to have access to the virtual elite of *Gossip Girl*. In Social Climbing, participants fill their appointment books with invitations to activities such as art exhibits and exclusive parties, each of which (if one can afford to enter) becomes the opportunity to be "spotted" by *Gossip Girl* characters or to snap photos of fictional friends as fodder for Gossip Girl's blog. The Facebook Social Climbing game overtly constructs digital ambivalences (of wielding power or being exposed) and offers them as purchasable pleasures that signify inclusion in the *Gossip Girl* fantasy.

But while it's easy to recognize *Gossip Girl*'s more overtly interactive transmedia extensions like the Social Climbing game as key places for immersive viewer participation, what's perhaps more remarkable is how *Gossip Girl* embeds invitations to digital interaction into the television text itself. Indeed, *Gossip Girl*'s transmedia dimensions extend participatory invitations already at work in the televisual text of the series. Sharon Ross describes how TV texts can invite viewer participation through a mix of direct and indirect address to viewer knowledge and viewer interactive practices.[9] For *Gossip Girl*, the series' emphasis on the status of televisual text as representation continually invites viewer participation. At key moments, the series' visual language calls attention to its status as televised fiction and artifice by interrupting or freezing the image, creating an aesthetic of the interrupted process of the celluloid image of film. One of the most iconic—and fan-beloved—of these moments occurs when two fan-favored characters, power-hungry teen Blair Waldorf and power-entrenched teen billionaire Chuck Bass, first become involved with each other. In "Victor/Victrola" (November 7, 2007), Blair and Chuck kiss for the first time in a cab that is racing through a New York City night. As the music crescendos and they lean into a kiss, the image flickers, becomes desaturated, and skips, as if it were simultaneously an old projected silent film with accumulated dust and a skipping TV image. Finally, the image ruptures and burns away, like projected celluloid film on fire. This playful visual imagery layers various indicators of "pastness" in media, collapsing them into a collective aesthetic of nostalgia and emotion conveyed through form. At the same time, the aesthetic play interrupts the series' realism (such as it is) with highly reflexive mediation; that is, the moment calls attention to *Gossip Girl*'s status as television by layering its contemporary televisual brand of melodramatic realism with codes of previous media forms. Thus melodrama overtakes realism and offers a way in for the viewer via the *form* of the series itself, suggesting the possibility of achieving emotionally resonant imagery via invasive editing. This moment invites the viewer to consider all of *Gossip Girl's* status as codified representation. *Gossip Girl's* reflexive framing emerges throughout the series via self-conscious intertextual references: each episode title is modeled after the title of a well-known Hollywood film, and episodes often feature dream-like sequences that cast Blair in the role of a famous figure from classic cinema. For example, the episode "The Blair Bitch Project" (April 21, 2008) opens with a dream sequence in which Blair approximates the role of Holly Golightly in *Breakfast at Tiffany's*, running through the rain in a trench coat to find her cat.

Gossip Girl's consistent play with past media, and more specifically its occasionally aggressive deployment of a nostalgic/analog film aesthetic, is tied to a larger cultural embrace of the digital evocation of celluloid. This trend can be seen recently in mobile apps Hipstamatic and Instagram, both of which simulate analog film aesthetics, approximating through digital means Polaroid and Holga-style imagery to communicate an emotional interpretation of a found moment. This and other instances of formal nostalgic style within *Gossip Girl* draw on current aesthetic vernacular to invite the viewer to enter in and rework the digital text, or at least to imagine doing so. In comparison to the invitations to viewer participation in *Gossip Girl's* transmedia extensions (like Social Climbing and Bluefly), the series' invitation to imagine reworking the televisual text through editing encourages a more open-ended form of viewer engagement, including a marked shift from audience to author. Where the Social Climbing player must navigate the game's restrictions to achieve specifically delineated goals and rewards, *Gossip Girl's* moments of nostalgic, do-it-yourself aesthetics invite viewers to imagine themselves as creators transforming the raw material of the series itself.

And indeed these moments of digital cinematic fissure become favorites in fan re-workings through digital remix. Many fan-made remix videos (known within fan culture as "fanvids") build to the moment described above of Chuck and Blair kissing in the cab, with its skipping image and burning up film strip, using this stylized imagery unaltered at the climax of a song or in its climactic refrain. And many of these and other vids use video-editing filters to create a similar feel of "pastness" throughout their vids, altering more realist *Gossip Girl* footage with sepia filters, or desaturating imagery to black and white, or interrupting footage with white flares that mimic an image burning up.[10] The series aligns emotionally dramatic moments with an emphasis on the TV image's status as representation, thus inviting an aesthetic intervention into televisual language; viewers turned vidders then use digital media tools such as Adobe Premiere and Final Cut Express to explore and expand upon the characters that inspire them to create more storyworld, more narrative, and more analysis.

The series' product advertising in turn builds on this invitation to viewers to intervene with televisual form, for example through the promotional campaign

FIGURE 36.1.

This fan-produced video uses filters to add a layer of nostalgia to footage from *Gossip Girl*.

for the "Nikon Coolpix" digital camera. In spots that ran within commercial breaks, these ads directly reworked *Gossip Girl* scenes. Serving double duty as promotional spots for both the show and the Nikon camera, the advertisements rendered *Gossip Girl* footage in a campy yet nostalgic aesthetic. Like the scene from "Victor/Victrola" analyzed above, these spots refer to a range of past media styles, employing an over-the-top male voiceover, flicker filters for an old home movie feel, a laugh track to add a classic sitcom flavor, and interrupted still images with photo frames. All of these elements reshape carefully selected clips of salacious dialogue between *Gossip Girl*'s romantic pairings, making the series sound like a racy screwball comedy with 1940s pacing and twenty-first-century sexual innuendo. The camera advertised through this playful synthesis features internal editing abilities, with the campaign tagline "create in any light." Its advertising emphasizes the Nikon Coolpix's in-camera special effects tools (including what Nikon terms a "nostalgic sepia" option), framing, and other "creative" filters that could be used for exactly the type of modern/nostalgic remix intervention modeled by the advertisement itself.[11] Thus, both the aesthetics of the advertisement and the digital tool being advertised encourage the viewer to take a position of playful and creative mediation with the televisual text, a position already posited within the program itself. In this way, The CW, *Gossip Girl*, and Nikon together integrate the do-it-yourself practices and aesthetics of remix and fan culture into their joint commercial enterprise.

Gossip Girl mines our culture's deep ambivalence toward and fascination with the spread of the digital. The series' ambitious characters strive for social safety both from and through the tools of digital media. While *Gossip Girl* may depend on our innate sense of ambivalence toward the digital, if there's one takeaway from the show, it's that its millennial characters live in a world inextricably infused with digital media. At least in the upper-class fantasy world of *Gossip Girl*, there's no going back. *Gossip Girl's* transmedia extensions echo this sentiment, especially with the Social Climbing game situated within Facebook users' everyday online experience. But what's most striking perhaps is that both audience-instigated digital productivity and *Gossip Girl's* marketing campaign seem to leave the narrative's ambivalence behind, celebrating the power of transformation through user access to digital tools. On the one hand, it's no surprise that The CW and Nikon would take this opportunity to shed the negative weight of anxieties about the threat of digital culture, capitalizing instead on the market potential for tools of digital authorship like a Nikon camera. But all the same, the result is a celebration of viewer power, a merging of viewer emotional investment in power-hungry characters like Blair Waldorf and Chuck Bass with a sense of assumed viewer right to the power of re-representation and transformation.

From the start, *Gossip Girl* has negotiated between two narratives of the digital—between anxious warnings about the dangers of digital power and visions of digital transformation as power and play. *Gossip Girl* depicts digital technologies as tools of social policing, but also as tools of social mobility through expressive authorship. The series' play with aesthetics of mediation highlights the latter, encouraging the viewer to approach the series as representation—as raw digital material for creative intervention. As the seasons progress, *Gossip Girl's* continued emphasis on playful aesthetic manipulation, echoing and in turn echoed in fan practice, suggests that we are at a watershed for cultural understandings of the digital, in which commercial and vernacular culture both are moving away from a fear of digital dangers and toward an embrace of the powers and pleasures of digital play.

NOTES

1. Marc Prensky, "Digital Natives, Digital Immigrants," *On the Horizon* 9, 5 (2001), http://www.marcprensky.com/writing/prensky%20-%20digital%20natives,%20digital%20immigrants%20-%20part1.pdf

2. Neil Howe and William Strauss, *Millennials Rising* (New York: Vintage, 2000).

3. See *Buffy the Vampire Slayer*, "I Robot, You Jane," April 28, 1997, and *Degrassi: The Next Generation*, "Mother and Child Reunion," July 1, 2002, for examples of millennial televisual narratives representing digital fears.

4. S. Craig Watkins, *The Young and the Digital* (Beacon Press, 2010).

5. Kazys Varnelis, ed. *Networked Publics* (Cambridge: MIT Press, 2008).

6. "The Young and the Digital: Interview with S. Craig Watkins," New Learning Institute (March 2, 2011), http://newlearninginstitute.org/blog/young-and-digital-interview-s-craig-watkins-part-ii.

7. See Chris Jay Hoofnagle, Jennifer King, Su Li, and Joseph Turow, "How Different Are Young Adults from Older Adults When it Comes to Information Privacy Attitudes and Policies?", public comment to Federal Trade Commission roundtable on consumer privacy, April 14, 2010, http://www.ftc.gov/os/comments/privacyroundtable/544506-00125.pdf.

8. Louisa Stein, "Playing Dress-Up: Digital Fashion and Gamic Extensions of Televisual Experience in *Gossip Girl*'s *Second Life*," *Cinema Journal* 48, 3 (2009): 116–22.

9. Sharon Ross, *Beyond the Box: Television and the Internet* (Malden, MA; Blackwell, 2008).

10. For examples of such vids, see the book's website at http://howtowatchtelevision.com/.

11. Coolpix US Sell Sheet, http://cdn.press.nikonusa.com/wp-content/uploads/2011/02/COOL-PIX_P300_US-Sell-Sheet_110202.pdf.

FURTHER READING

Pattee, A. S. "Commodities in Literature, Literature as Commodity: A Close Look at the *Gossip Girl* Series." *Children's Literature Association Quarterly* 31, 2 (2006): 154–75.

Ross, Sharon Marie. *Beyond the Box: Television and the Internet*. Malden, MA: Blackwell Publishers, 2008.

Stein, Louisa. "Playing Dress-Up: Digital Fashion and Gamic Extensions of Televisual Experience in *Gossip Girl*'s *Second Life*." *Cinema Journal* 48, 3 (2009): 116–22.

Watkins, S. Craig. *The Young and the Digital: What the Migration to Social-Network Sites, Games, and Anytime, Anywhere Media Means for Our Future*. Boston: Beacon Press, 2009.

37

It's Fun to Eat
Forgotten Television

DANA POLAN

Abstract: Though select television programs are celebrated in their time and later canonized via reruns on cable channels and in critical anthologies like this one, much television remains ephemeral. In this essay on a forgotten yet unique cooking show, Dana Polan provides a model for researching (and reconstructing) a television program that barely remains accessible—and may never have made much of an impression to begin with.

On the web, there survives a curious bit of early local television programming: a short clip (little more than eleven minutes) showing Latina chef Elena Zelayeta from her 1950s cooking show, *It's Fun to Eat*. Aided by her teenage son Billy, with whom she engages in light comic banter, Elena prepares pickled tuna and cheese biscuits. Billy ends the segment with a plug for the sponsor's product, the Fresherator.[1]

In many ways, *It's Fun to Eat* is typical of the unassuming fare that filled up daytime hours at local stations in the first years of postwar commercial television. This was modest, even minimal, television: modest and minimal in instructional ambition (here just a few simple recipes offered in real time), in visual style (in this case, long shots of the overall action broken up by closer views), and in dramatic quality. Down to the somewhat awkward way in which the transition is made to the plug for the Fresherator, *It's Fun to Eat* looks like what a lot of average daytime television would have looked like at the time. We might think of this as the realm of "forgettable television"—programming designed to be forgotten at virtually the very moment of its original viewing, as most TV was, and thus destined to be forgotten in historical accounts that typically single out canonic and classic shows. That is, this forgettable fare was planned for immediate consumption and assumed to possess no enduring impact. Such evanescent television represents an aspect of television history that we both could stand to learn more about (since it did comprise so much of what was on the daytime airwaves at the time), and yet have a hard time learning about (since its very impermanence means that it generally left few researchable traces behind).

In the case of *It's Fun to Eat*, the desire to know more is amplified no doubt by a striking particularity of the show: Elena did her cooking and instructing as a *blind* person, and this fact can turn the seeming ordinariness of her show into something quite extraordinary. While running a successful San Francisco restaurant in the 1930s, Elena had fully lost vision in both eyes, and retrained herself to cook sightless. Our recognition of the show's unassuming qualities as forgettable daytime programming has to be tempered by a certain admiration for Elena's ability to play to the audience and create an affable persona for cameras she could not see; she evidently was aided in this task a bit by strings attached to her ankles that the crew would tug on so she would know which way to look when there was a cut from one camera to the other. The very premise of this show is pretty amazing. Maybe *It's Fun to Eat* is not so forgettable after all.

The astounding uniqueness of a blind cook working in a medium that is so much about visibility—to the extent that in the clip when Elena plates up a dish, she can ask the viewers without evident irony "Now doesn't that look perfectly beautiful?" as if she and the viewers shared in the vision—in itself makes *It's Fun to Eat* a seductive object for historical analysis. Unfortunately, for the historian, the Internet clip of *It's Fun to Eat* seems to constitute the only surviving footage from the show. There's a lesson here about the vulnerability of so much early television: until 1947, there was no effective mechanism to make recordings of live TV shows, and even after that, generally only night-time programming—for example, successful national network shows, for which copying allowed reruns and syndication and nationwide broadcast across time zones—was deemed to merit preservation. Ephemeral daytime television, such as cooking shows which were often considered lowbrow feminine entertainment, was not so deemed. Thus, it was often only by chance that storage copies of this or that early daytime television were produced, and it is rare that they survive down to the present and sometimes get found by a researcher or archivist.

In the case at hand, the footage from *It's Fun to Eat* was discovered in the underground parking garage of KPIX-TV studios, and here too there's a lesson about early television and its study. As Alex Cherian, archivist at the San Francisco Bay Area Television Archive wryly, albeit sadly, explained to me, "TV stations tend to put equipment and assets in their parking garages when they have no space left. It's usually an unofficial staging ground for stuff which is about to be dumped."[2]

Given that this one clip is all we have of *It's Fun to Eat*, there's a lot about it that remains shrouded in mystery, and there's very little in the historical record

FIGURE 37.1.
Though often appearing
mundane in content and
formal strategies, "forgotten
television" like the obscure
cooking show *It's Fun to Eat*
can produce insights into
media culture.

to help us out.[3] Not only was most daytime programming not felt worthy of preservation, but even at the moment of its initial airing, it was often not given much
more than passing attention. On the production end, channels simply needed
to fill up their airwaves. With their goal being simply to get anything out on
the air, the production staff usually didn't register anything memorable in what
they were doing. Moreover, supporting materials, like studio records, were often thrown out. Likewise, on the reception end, spectators might single out some
particular show as a favorite (and bit by bit, some series started becoming classics
fondly remembered years later) but especially in the early days of television set
acquisition, most viewers were content just to have any images whatsoever, and
could consume hours of quickly forgotten fare. Consequently, when (or if) the researcher finds someone who worked on the show—or watched it—the researcher
may discover that this person may not have accurate memories of it (or even any
memories of it at all), not because it was entirely forgotten but because it never
really made an impression in the first place.

It's not even clear from the website or from the program content when *It's Fun
to Eat* actually aired, and Elena's published autobiography isn't helpful on the
matter either: even to Elena herself, her efforts in television don't seem to have
had much impact on the overall course of an eventful life.[4] Here, too, there's a
lesson for the historian: with some concerted effort, it might be possible to track
down the broadcast dates for *It's Fun to Eat*, but the researcher has to make a serious decision about whether that effort would be worth it. Perhaps, for instance,
some local newspaper might have the information in its TV listings, although
such listings were quite sporadic for newspapers in local TV markets and they
were often inaccurate since shows were moved around or cancelled with little advance notice. Maybe, then, it's enough to know the approximate period of the
show to gesture toward its general fit into its historical moment.[5]

The historian then has to be quite imaginative and creative, within the limits of time, energy, and resources.[6] In this particular case, I followed a number of possible research paths. Predictably perhaps, I started with web searches on "*It's Fun to Eat*" (along with the names of the people associated with its production) and on "Elena Zelayeta" (which led me to six books she authored, including her autobiography), and I even tracked down William Zelayeta (the Billy of the clip), who at age seventy-seven graciously agreed to an interview. But even the best intentions don't matter if the archival material or participant memories aren't there. Thus, there were virtually no hits for the terms online; Elena's books are, as noted, skimpy on details of her television work; and, most important, William Zelayeta had few concrete recollections of the program, in large part because he had been a rambunctious teenager at the time with other things on his mind.

Perhaps with more time and resources, one could follow some other research paths. For instance, in her book *Dreaming of Fred and Ginger: Cinema and Cultural Memory*, British film historian Annette Kuhn explains how she learned a lot about what spectators made of the movies they saw in the 1930s by interviewing people from the era who were now in retirement homes. In similar fashion, perhaps one could interview elderly people in San Francisco or Los Angeles to see if they remember Elena's shows and what their specific recollections are. But, truth be told, that seems to be quite a long shot. Who might remember an ephemeral daytime show from around sixty years ago? In the absence of memories and documentary material, to try to imagine what the television experience of *It's Fun to Eat* might have been like, one needs to move to the context of other comparable programs to reconstruct what television was *generally* like at the time. Once we know some of the general conventions of television style at the time, we can examine how this show worked with them or, perhaps, went off instead in other directions.

Many factors would encourage an overall regularity in the look of 1950s daytime television, especially in the instructional domain. For instance, if the goal is to teach steps in a process such as cooking, it makes sense to proceed chronologically (do this, then do that).[7] And when shooting in real time and transmitting live, as was the case for much of the local daytime programming of the era, chronology seems all the more called for. For example, once a recipe gets going and the food starts to be transformed, it is hard to interrupt the action to go back or forward in time. (But it's not impossible: there are indeed ways of "cheating" chronology, as when Elena explains that her short program doesn't provide time to show the actual, real-time baking of her biscuits so she has made some up in advance.)

For the most part, cooking shows are highly conventionalized in structure (chronological demonstration in real time) and in style (functional alternation of long shots and close-ups to give both the overall picture and the instructive detail). In fact, for all their seeming dynamism (fast, even frenetic cutting), today's cooking shows often are not that far from these conventions set in place early on in instructional television's history. For instance, a randomly chosen episode of Giada De Laurentiis's *Everyday Italian* (Food Network, 2003–2008) about cooking for a beach party ends with a highly edited exterior scene where Giada plays volleyball with her friends. But while she is in the kitchen preparing their picnic, the editing pattern alternating long shots of the whole kitchen and close-ups of her busy hands is the norm just as it was in instructional television's earliest years.[8]

Across its history, instructional television has often been caught in a tension between providing viewers with familiar fare (experiences that were comfortable because they were conventional) *and* with keeping interest going by adding a touch of the different, the daring, the unique, the special. Although it may at first seem paradoxical, I would argue that in fact it's the very uniqueness of *It's Fun to Eat*—the seemingly sole example of a television show built around a blind cook—that contributes to its qualities of average, everyday, ordinary television. Elena's blindness is exceptional for cooking shows, no doubt, but it is often useful for any TV cook to have traits that make their instruction stand out and seem special within the unfolding regularity and ordinariness of so much what's on the air. (In the case of *Everyday Italian*, to return to that more contemporary example for a moment, what's being sold is not just a regularized culinary experience, but the supposed stand-out specialness of a host who, as Michael Newman points out in his essay in this volume, combines cheerfulness with sexiness.)

Certainly, in the case of Elena Zelayeta, it might well be that in concentrating on Mexican and Spanish-inflected dishes, she already stood out from a pedagogy more commonly focused on commonplace American cuisine. Postwar home cooking, and the instructional cooking shows typically devoted to it, had two different responsibilities. On the one hand, with suburbanization, romantic ideologies that were pushing women to marry young (what proto-feminist Betty Friedan would later term "the feminine mystique"), and new modes of mobility (from the new car culture to commercial air travel), more newlywed brides were living away from their mothers and thereby needed instruction in the sorts of domestic activities that in prior times they would likely have learned at home. Thus, it's not surprising that early twentieth-century cookbooks generally included *no* recipes for anodyne staples like bread since it was assumed that these would naturally be part of a housewife's repertoire, whereas mid-twentieth-century cookbooks went to great lengths to spell out every step in making such seemingly basic food items. In such a context, culinary instructors stepped in to offer average citizens lessons in the ordinary practices of everyday life.

On the other hand, there was quite a lot about everyday postwar American middle-class life that had to do with anxieties about one's social standing and with coming off well in the eyes of others. For instance, one narrative motif in the period, common to cooking shows as well as fictional dramas and comedies, had to do with the last-minute guest (often one's boss) who is coming unexpectedly to dinner but who anticipates a great meal, which, if not provided, means the family could be missing out on that raise in salary it has been hoping for.[9] Whether or not real-life social and work-place status was actually decided in this fashion, the pervasiveness of the motif in fiction suggests that even in the seemingly domestic space of the kitchen, concerns about standing and career advancement were being played out.

In such a context, it mattered not only to know how to cook ordinary American fare, but also to create more distinctive, standout dishes. Thus, to take an important example, at the beginning of the 1960s, Julia Child would tap into an American mythology of French culture as a high culture whose practices could grant an average person distinction; both her book *Mastering the Art of French Cooking* and her television show *The French Chef* (WGBII, 1963–1973) served to offer Americans ways to achieve status through haute cuisine. Child functioned as what we might term a "cultural mediator" whose task it was to introduce average citizens to new practices of modernity (in this case, practices of the domestic realm responding to new postwar roles for both men and women at home) and perform a delicate balancing act in which something new was presented, but not something so new as to be frightening—for instance, as late as the 1960s, Julia Child was still persuading average Americans to not be wary of garlic as a taste enhancer.

In these terms, Elena Zelayeta could be said to be a cultural mediator, too. She saw Mexican/Spanish food as offering a celebratory quality that could well contribute to parties and other forms of socializing. Revealingly, her second cookbook is entitled *Elena's Festive Recipes* (1952), while her first, a general introduction entitled *Elena's Famous Mexican and Spanish Recipes* (1944), included special sections on "Company Dinners" and "Fiesta Menus"—with the latter explaining how to make one's table attractive to others by placing green, white, and red carnations on it to emulate the Mexican flag or drawing little pictures of sombreros, cacti, and so on as place settings.[10] Even in the brief *It's Fun to Eat* clip, key moments are dedicated to plating up the food in style. Food here is not only sustenance but also visual seduction. No doubt, Mexican food lacked much of the cultural cachet of haute French cuisine, as Mexican cooking was often imagined to be more boldly spicy than aesthetically subtle, but it was nonetheless an exotic, even exciting, cuisine that could add pizzazz to common American fare.

   Still, Elena insisted on the ways that Mexican food was not so different as to be unachievable by American cooks or unappreciated by American consumers. Just as Julia Child would "translate" French food into an American vernacular—for instance, "boeuf bourguignon," she insisted, was just another name for good old American beef stew—Elena insisted on the translatability of Mexican food. As she put it in the beginning pages of *Elena's Famous Mexican and Spanish Recipes*, "along with giving recipes for traditional Mexican dishes, I have included many American adaptations—easy to prepare, easy to serve."[11] When she explains, for instance, how to make enchiladas, she clarifies that "Typical Mexican enchiladas are not served with a great deal of sauce; however, in my experience of cooking for American people, I have found that they like plenty of sauce and somewhat thicker [preparations]. . . . For them I would suggest that this recipe for sauce be doubled."[12]

   So we can sum up *It's Fun to Eat* as a show that was "in between": in between in its subject matter, which has to do both with satisfying American culinary tastes and yet also with opening them up to new cultural horizons; in between in the mix of its quite ordinary, even quite minimalist style (or rather non-style) and the stand-out appeal of a distinctive host who, although blind, could still play well to the cameras and foster a sense of personality and intimacy; in between in its status as a transitional show between the ephemeral, even forgettable fare of daytime postwar television and later, more celebrated celebrity-driven series, such as Julia Child's *The French Chef* in the 1960s. And as a mysterious, incomplete object for historical research, it also exists somewhere in between all the shows that have been fully forgotten in the ravages of time and those for which we have rich and varied stores of information.[13] In both its typicality and its seeming uniqueness, *It's Fun to Eat* epitomizes so much of what everyday television has been about, and that is what makes it such an enticing object of investigation for the historian.

NOTES

1. The clip can be viewed on the San Francisco Bay Area Television Archive website, where it has been digitized for posterity: https://diva.sfsu.edu/bundles/189406.

2. Personal correspondence with author, September 26, 2011.

3. One researcher, a historian of San Francisco life and lore, Meredith Eliassen, has located in the San Francisco History Center of the San Francisco Public Library a brief clipping about *It's Fun to Eat*, from the February 3, 1953, issue of the *San Francisco Examiner* (no page is indicated). This article (which Eliassen has described to me in an email as a mere "snippet") asserts that *It's Fun to Eat* was filmed in San Francisco, Elena's place of residence, but for distribution to Los Angeles. But even the details of this production history of the show remain unclear (and unconfirmed).

4. Elena Zelayeta, *Elena* (Englewood Cliffs, NJ: Prentice-Hall Inc., 1960), 204–205.

5. From Billy's appearance on camera compared to his birth date (1934), we can guess that the show aired sometime in the early 1950s.

6. I have been much inspired here by British television scholar Jason Jacobs's excellent study *The Intimate Screen: Early British Television Drama* (New York & London: Oxford University Press, 2000). Starting from the fact that almost no British shows survive from before the mid-1950s, Jacobs sets himself the deliberate challenge of trying to figure out what the earliest programming might have looked like, given the absence of the shows themselves. He tries to reconstruct their look and style from production records, autobiographical accounts, journalistic reviews, and other secondary data. It is impressive how much he is able to come up with.

7. At the same time, though, it's often part of an effective instructional strategy to show an example of the finished product at the beginning of the operation to hold out the promise of what the payoff will be if one follows the lesson through to its conclusion. Cooking shows might include a glimpse in the opening moments of a finished dish.

8. For more on *Everyday Italian*, see Michael Newman's essay in this volume.

9. For example, on the TV series *Bewitched*, Darren is constantly bringing his boss, Larry, home for dinner at the last minute, leaving Samantha with the conundrum of deciding whether to use her witch powers or not to get the meal on the table expeditiously.

10. Elena Zelayeta, *Elena's Famous Mexican and Spanish Recipes* (San Francisco: Dettners Printing House, 1944), and *Elena's Fiesta Recipes* (Los Angeles: The Ward Ritchie Press, 1952).

11. *Elena's Famous Mexican and Spanish Recipes*, 6.

12. Ibid., 37.

13. To take just one example, if you want today to study the classic series *The Twilight Zone* (analyzed in this volume by Derek Kompare), you have at your disposal several different DVD box sets (with lots of supplementary material), scholarly books on the show, detailed episode guides, Rod Serling biographies, and on and on.

FURTHER READING

Collins, Kathleen. *Watching What We Eat: The Evolution of Cooking Shows*. New York: Continuum, 2009.

Jacobs, Jason. *The Intimate Screen: Early British Television Drama*. New York & London: Oxford University Press, 2000.

Kuhn, Annette. *Dreaming of Fred and Ginger: Cinema and Cultural Memory*. New York: New York University Press, 2002.

Polan, Dana. "James Beard's Early TV Work: A Report on Research" *Gastronomica*, 10, 3 (Summer 2010): 23–33.

———. *Julia Child's The French Chef*. Durham, NC: Duke University Press, 2011.

38

One Life to Live
Soap Opera Storytelling

ABIGAIL DE KOSNIK

Abstract: Few genres are as associated with the television medium as the soap op-era, which has populated daytime schedules for decades, often with the same shows running for more than the lifetimes of their characters. Abigail De Kosnik provides a long-term view of *One Life to Live* and the lifelong story of one character to high-light the unique narrative possibilities of soap operas and call attention to what might be lost if the genre continues to disappear from television.

In 2012, only four U.S. daytime dramas, or soap operas, remained in produc-tion, while as recently as 1999, twelve soap operas were broadcast daily. The last decade has witnessed a wave of cancellations of soaps, most of which enjoyed tremendous longevity, especially in comparison to primetime TV programs, which rarely reach a tenth season. In recent years, four of the most venerable soaps were terminated: *Guiding Light* (CBS, 1937–2009) ended after seventy-two years of continuous broadcast (fifteen years on the radio and fifty-seven years on television); *As the World Turns* (CBS, 1956–2010) concluded after fifty-four years; *All My Children* (ABC, 1970–2011) ran for forty-one years before its last episode aired; and *One Life to Live* (ABC, 1968–2012) was forty-four years old by its fi-nal broadcast. With four soap operas still airing daily on broadcast television (as of this writing), and soap-like genres growing in popularity outside the United States, the long-running serial television drama is not yet obsolete.

However, the cluster of recent forced finales indicates that U.S. television net-works no longer believe that soaps are worth significant investment. The years 2009–2012 have been a "twilight" period for the American soap opera, with the genre's ranks diminishing swiftly and audiences beginning to accept that soaps, which had always presented themselves as "worlds without end," are headed for extinction. It is possible, even likely, that all U.S. daytime drama production will shut down in the next ten to twenty years.

Therefore, now may be an appropriate time to reflect on what soaps have been uniquely able to present in their extended runs—namely, *lifelong stories*, or stories that span some characters' entire lives. Even though soaps have large ensemble casts, and regular soap viewers follow the plot arcs of dozens of characters, only a handful of characters on each daytime drama have "lived" their entire lives on the show. These characters, in most cases played continuously by one actor, form the core of their respective soap operas, serving as touchstones for all other characters and the fulcrums for many major storylines. On *All My Children*, model-turned-mogul Erica Kane was the most prominent lifelong character; on *One Life to Live*, it was the aristocratic-but-tortured Victoria (Viki) Lord; *Guiding Light*'s most prominent lifelong character was probably attorney Tom Hughes. Erica and Viki were integral to their respective shows from the premieres, and Tom was born five years after the show's debut, but other lifelong characters appeared on their soaps at much later points in the shows' runs, such as *General Hospital*'s (ABC, 1963–present) Robin Scorpio and Lucky Spencer, *Days of Our Lives*' (NBC, 1965–present) Hope Williams Brady, and *Guiding Light*'s Lily Walsh Snyder. What defines lifelong characters is that they are featured on their shows for decades, so that many viewers have a sense of witnessing their entire lifetimes, or a very large portion it. Most of the aforementioned characters started as children or teens on their shows, so viewers feel as if they watched those characters "grow up," or, if they started watching soaps at an early age, that they grew up with the characters. Different generations of soap viewers may attach to different generations of soap characters, and people may miss out on several years of characters' lives if they stop watching soaps for a period of time and then resume regular viewing, but the intergenerational community of soap fans is available to fill in knowledge gaps. Oral histories relayed from fan to fan, as well as elaborate character histories published in book format and online, make it possible for a soap fan to follow, or retrospectively learn about, every major event in a soap character's life.

This essay focuses on the lifelong story of Viki Lord, the central character of *One Life to Live*. Viki's expansive narrative offers clear examples of three key elements of soap opera lifelong storytelling: 1) the *deep seed and long reveal*, 2) *continual reverberation*, and 3) *real-life temporality*. Each storytelling technique, as illustrated with examples from Viki's fictional life, highlights the unique narrative power and possibilities of the soap opera genre. Soap operas are best known for sudden and improbable plot twists, but not all revelations on soaps seemingly come from nowhere. Some "reveals" come after years of story-building and character development. I use the phrase "deep seed and long reveal" to refer to such plot arcs. Soaps have the ability to hint at plot points for decades, heightening tension around certain secrets or hidden aspects of characters' lives that the audience knows about, but that the characters are unaware of until at some point;

often many years after a narrative arc begins, the secret explodes in a ferocious climax with severe narrative ramifications. On *One Life to Live*, the unveiling of the root cause of Viki Lord's psychological illness was the show's most notable deep seed and long reveal.

Viki was shown to suffer from Dissociative Identity Disorder (DID) from *One Life*'s start in 1968. Viki's most dominant "alter," the alternate personality that emerged and overtook Viki's life most often throughout the show's run, was called Niki Smith. Viki's father, millionaire newspaper magnate, Victor Lord, raised Viki strictly, with high expectations, as she was the heir to his fortune and his business empire. As a result, Viki grew up to be elegant, well-spoken, and incredibly responsible in all matters; in contrast, her alternate personality, Niki, was a loud-mouthed, manipulative, promiscuous party girl. Each time Niki surfaced, she wreaked havoc, and each time, Viki successfully suppressed her and repaired the social damage Niki had done. What caused Viki to develop such a destructive alter?

In the late 1960s, Viki uncovered a repressed memory of her mother accidentally falling down a staircase to her death. Viki believed that the trauma of witnessing this horrible event led her psyche to create "Niki." But in the 1990s, Victor Lord's widow and Viki's enemy, Dorian Lord, began to insinuate that the cause of Viki's DID lay in other childhood experiences involving her father, Victor, the memories of which lay buried in Viki's subconscious mind. For almost thirty years, *One Life to Live* viewers had seen Viki refer periodically to her domineering father's rigid expectations and impossibly high standards as sources of psychological pain. During those decades, the audience watched dozens of moments when Viki told stories about, or simply made mention of, Victor Lord, as well as numerous flashback scenes of a young Viki interacting with her father. Over this extended period of time, the viewer gathered many impressions of Viki's relationship with Victor, such as the fact that Victor was obsessed with his daughter, and had an unhealthy need to exercise complete control over every facet of Viki's life. Therefore, when Dorian began to imply that Viki was repressing memories about her father that led to her developing multiple personalities, most viewers heard Dorian's veiled warnings as confirmation of what they already suspected: that Victor had sexually abused Victoria.

In 1995, Dorian finally revealed the truth about Victor's having abused Viki during her childhood, and the knowledge shook Viki to her core. But for the longtime viewer, this reveal was an extraordinary reward for having faithfully followed *One Life to Live* for as many as twenty-seven years. For the possibility that Victor had been an abusive monster to Viki had been planted in the minds of audience members in the 1960s, and that seed of suspicion about Victor grew with every flashback that Viki had about her father, all through the 1970s and 1980s, until in the 1990s, the seed finally reached fruition as spoken dialogue between Dorian and Viki. As Dorian spoke the terrible secret of Viki's early years aloud, the long-time viewer likely thought, "I knew it all along! I always thought that's what must have happened to Viki."

Only long-running soaps can plant such a deep seed of plot, and then have it culminate in a satisfying reveal after such an attenuated length of time. Given the frequent changes in soap staff members, a long-arc plot might be initiated by one head writer or executive producer and then developed by entirely different sets of writers/producers. *One Life*'s decision to "reveal" Viki's childhood sexual abuse in the 1990s may have been motivated by writers of that time picking up on obvious plot threads left behind by earlier writers, or by fans' ongoing speculation about the origins of Viki's DID, or by an increasing awareness in American society of incest and the psychological disorders that often result. Whether or not the deep plot seed of Viki's victimization was intended from the start or not, it struck loyal viewers as faithful to what they knew of Viki's character and her past. A deep seed and long reveal need not have any "authorial" intent behind it, but the reveal must accord with viewers' recollection of characters' histories in order to ring true.

The multiple authoring of soap operas does not always culminate in a powerful plot twist that honors characters' histories while delivering fresh, shockingly dramatic scenes to viewers—some deep seeds and long reveals are better executed than others. But soaps accomplish this combination of history and surprise far more often than comic book reboots or James Bond recastings. Comics, comic-based cartoons and films, and the Bond movies are multiple-authored texts that depict the same moments in key characters' lives over and over (a superhero's origins, his early discovery of his powers, etc.), and *only* depict a limited range of years for characters (typically, the years when they are at their peak physical condition). No matter how long these male-oriented narratives remain a part of the popular cultural landscape, they rarely allow their core characters to substantially age, or to undergo the significant psychological and emotional crises that accompany different stages of life—by their emphasis on repetition rather than character growth, they lack the kind of narrative journey that *One Life to Live* writers were able to give viewers who followed Viki's advancement from youth into middle age.

Of course Viki's struggle with her mental illness did not end when she discovered its traumatic origins. Lifelong stories on soaps never conclude; as soon as a character resolves one long-running plot conflict, other related issues arise. I call this rippling narrative style "continual reverberation." On *One Life to Live*, after having lived for years with DID and repeatedly suffering the dire consequences of the devious actions of her red-headed alter, Niki Smith, Viki made a shocking discovery: her beloved daughter, Jessica, had actually been born a twin, and the twin had been kidnapped from the hospital before Viki even knew of her existence. The secret twin, Natalie, suddenly showed up in Llanview (the fictional Pennsylvania town where *One Life to Live* takes place) in 2001, and was an entirely different creature than the angelic Jessica. Jessica was blonde, and Natalie was a red-head. Jessica was a kind, polite, good-hearted young woman, and Natalie was a brash, self-centered, tough-talking hoyden. Jessica looked and sounded very much like her mother, Viki—but Natalie looked and sounded almost exactly like Viki's alter, Niki. Shortly after Natalie's appearance in Llanview, Natalie's claims to being Viki's biological child led Jessica to doubt that she was even related to Viki (Natalie suggested that perhaps she and Jessica had been switched at birth), and Viki attempted to reassure Jessica (and herself) that Jessica was indeed her child by standing beside Jessica in front of a mirror and forcing Jessica to look at the two of them, side by side. "You are my child!" said Viki. "Do you see how much you look like me?" Just at that moment, Natalie entered the room and paused behind Viki and Jessica, and in the mirror reflection of all three of them, Jessica did look very much like Viki, but Natalie's resemblance to Viki was equally strong.

Although Viki was initially loath to believe that rude, loud Natalie was as much her biological child as sweet, calm Jessica, *One Life*'s viewers recognized Natalie's significance right away. Natalie embodied the side of Viki that Viki could never bring herself to accept: the Niki side. For the progression of Viki's lifelong story, it was important that she be confronted with the physical incarnation, in two distinct bodies that were born of her body, of the "twin" aspects of her psyche. Jessica was a young Viki, but Natalie was a young Niki, and the girls' coexistence in Viki's life forced Viki to acknowledge and appreciate the two very different women as "hers."

The Jessica/Natalie story of the 2000s was not just any "evil twin" plotline, endemic to daytime dramas since the genre's beginnings; it held special resonance for viewers of *One Life to Live* because it provided a physical manifestation of the internal war that had been raging inside of Viki for so long. The Jessica/Natalie plot was a continuation of the Viki/Niki arc that spanned the entire duration of the soap's history. And although Jessica and Natalie became devoted to one another despite their differences, united in a way that Viki could never herself manage to unite the two halves of her personality, the story did not end there. A series of devastating events in 2005 led Jessica to experience a period of blackouts and memory-loss, and Jessica discovered that she, like her mother, suffered from DID. Jessica's wild and conniving alter, Tess, then repeated some of the same clashes that Viki/Niki had enacted years earlier: Tess loved a different man than Jess did; Tess had very different life goals than Jess; Tess's ideas of what constituted

FIGURE 38.1.
Viki's twin daughters, Natalie (left) and Jessica (right), embodied two sides of her personality that she could never reconcile.

happiness and satisfaction were almost totally opposite to Jess's. Moreover, when a pregnant Tess found herself in a crisis, going into labor while totally alone in an abandoned vineyard, it was Niki Smith whom Tess hallucinated to help her through the delivery, as Tess claimed that Niki was the only "mother" that Tess had ever known. In fact, the traumatic event in Jessica's childhood that caused her to develop the Tess personality was an incident of sexual molestation that took place while Niki was running Viki's life (Niki routinely neglected young Jessica whenever she was in charge of Viki's household). The tragedy of Viki/Niki, never fully resolved for Viki, echoed in the tragedies suffered by her children and shaped the trajectories of their lives. For Viki, the knowledge that her beautiful daughter, her greatest accomplishment and joy, suffered from the same horrible illness that had forever plagued Viki was shattering.

Although the emergence of Jessica's alter was one of the more tragic pieces of fallout from Viki's ongoing struggle with DID, other plotlines that flowed from Viki's lifelong story yielded more positive outcomes. Natalie and Jessica's forming a sisterly bond, for instance, was rewarding for viewers who had often longed for Viki to be able to reconcile her dominant self with her Niki personality; the loving relationship that developed between Viki's twins felt like an analog or substitute for the Viki/Niki integration storyline that never played out. Also, the audience's (and Viki's) perception of Dorian shifted dramatically after Dorian informed Viki of her father's abusive behavior. Prior to the revelation about Victor in the 1990s, the audience had known Dorian only as Viki's wicked stepmother and archenemy, who had most likely killed Victor Lord while he was ill; although *One Life to Live* was vague on this plot point, Dorian was always singled out as the most likely murderer. But after Dorian told Viki the truth about Victor, the audience began to see that perhaps Dorian was not entirely a villainess. Perhaps Dorian had facilitated Victor's death, not only in order to inherit his millions, but also from a

desire to enact justice. Perhaps Dorian had long felt animosity towards Viki because Dorian knew that she had avenged Viki's childhood suffering, but Viki did
not know and always treated Dorian with disdain. The reverberations of Viki's
ongoing multiple personality storyline reached far beyond Viki's life and shaped
the stories of a number of other characters on *One Life*'s canvas. Martha Nochimson argues that the forced reconsideration of Dorian's nature and past acts had
the added (potential) effect of raising women viewers' awareness of patriarchal
stereotypes.[1] If viewers re-evaluated Dorian's sometimes ethically questionable decisions as "complex," stemming from deep and various motives, rather than as the
workings of a "simply" cruel woman typical of stereotyped female villains, then it
is possible that the continual reverberations of Viki's long-arc story did more than
entertain; they may have promoted a more feminist mode of interpreting media
texts in fans of *One Life to Live*.

One reason that soaps' long-arc storylines, with their drawn-out plot reveals
and unceasing reverberations, can affect soap viewers deeply is that "soap time" approximates "real time." Unlike the compressed temporalities of a two-hour film or
a one-hour weekly series that runs for only a few years, soap opera events unfold
in a timeline that mirrors viewers' lived time quite closely. A soap opera airs five
days per week for fifty weeks of each year, usually for many decades, and so viewers
have the sense that they live their lives alongside, or in tandem with, soap characters. Even though the events in soap characters' lives are usually far more dramatic
than those taking place in viewers' lives, the parallel between soap time and real
time gives soap operas a certain ongoing realism that other forms of drama rarely
match. Viki uncovered her memories of her father's abuse, not twenty minutes or
two hours after she began to manifest symptoms of DID (as would occur on a primetime television program or in a movie), but twenty-seven years later. The time
that it took Viki to realize what had happened to her in her childhood is, according to Sigmund Freud, a normal amount of time for any adult to "remember, repeat, and work through" early trauma and heal psychologically.[2] Among TV genres,
soaps alone have the ability to show an individual undergoing an intense psychological transformation over decades, which is often the time that people require to
recover from the damage inflicted upon them during their youth. Although soaps
have often been criticized for their outlandish, unbelievable plots, in this respect,
they are highly realistic fictions, resembling many women's actual experiences of
psychological hurt and healing. The open-endedness, persistence, unevenness, and
unpredictability of Viki's struggle against her inner demons, and the fact that it
took her nearly thirty years to realize the most crucial truth of her own childhood,
are what Nochimson values as realistic: a kind of realism that can be achieved in
"soap time" far better than in any other narrative genre's time-frame.

The similitude of "soap time" to real time can lead viewers to feel close, even literally familiar, with soap characters. For example, media theorist Robyn Warhol writes of having moved thirty times in forty-six years and marveled at the fact that "in all those places, only one set of persons has been constantly present, continually and reliably 'there' no matter where: the characters who populate Oakdale, Illinois, the fictive setting of *As the World Turns*."[3] Similarly, Nancy Baym states that soap viewers can feel as if they have formed a strong bond with soap characters—a bond she calls "a parasocial relationship—a kind of family."[4] Neither Baym or Warhol claim that soap viewers are deluded that fictional people are, in fact, members of their family; although some studies of soap opera fans have speculated that fans confuse reality and fantasy, and although this stereotype of regular soap viewers remains popular today, numerous scholars have observed that the reality/fantasy conflation is experienced by only a small percentage of fans, and that the vast majority of viewers clearly understand the boundary between fictional lives and real lives.[5] Rather, Baym and Warhol point to an affective impact that soap operas can have on audiences that no other narrative genre can have by virtue of soaps' duration and the constancy of their casts of characters who come to feel like parts of viewers' families.

The sheer quantity of episodes that soaps produce every year, and the number of years that soaps air, allow soaps to tell "lifelong stories" about "lifelong characters," with deep seeds, long reveals, and continual reverberations of key plot arcs. These soap-specific narrative techniques can generate, in long-term viewers, an intensity of emotional response to plot twists that people usually feel only when they witness family members or close friends experiencing significant or sudden life changes. The unique temporality of soap storytelling, and its impact on audiences, was well understood by one of daytime drama's pioneers, Agnes Nixon, who created *All My Children*, *One Life to Live*, and several other soap operas. Nixon writes:

> The serial form imitates life in that, for its characters, the curtain rises with birth and does not ring down until death. . . . The ingredients are the same [as those] required for any good dramatic fare but with one basic difference: that the continuing form allows a fuller development of characterization while permitting the audience to become more and more involved with the story and its people.[6]

Some soap stories span fictional people's—and real people's—entire lives, and therein lies their effectiveness. If and when soap operas finally disappear from the American television landscape, the force and power of lifelong storytelling will die with them.[7]

NOTES

1. Martha Nochimson, "Amnesia 'R' Us: The Retold Melodrama, Soap Opera, and the Representation of Reality," *Film Quarterly* 50, 3 (Spring 1997), 32.

2. Sigmund Freud, "Remembering, Repeating and Working Through," in *The Standard Edition of the Complete Psychological Works of Sigmund Freud*, vol. 12, James Strachey, trans. and ed. (London: Hogarth Press, 1959), 145–56.

3. Robyn R. Warhol, *Having a Good Cry: Effeminate Feelings and Pop-Culture Forms* (Columbus: Ohio State University Press, 2003), 103.

4. Nancy Baym, "Perspective: Scholar Nancy Baym on Soaps after the O. J. Simpson Trial," in *The Survival of Soap Opera: Transformations for a New Media Era*, Sam Ford, Abigail De Kosnik, and C. Lee Harrington, eds. (Jackson: University Press of Mississippi, 2011), 105.

5. Austin S. Babrow, "An Expectancy-Value Analysis of the Student Soap Opera Audience," *Communication Research* 16, 2 (April 1989): 155–78; Nancy Baym, *Tune In, Log On: Soaps, Fandom, and Online Community* (Thousand Oaks, CA: Sage, 2000), 36–37; Dannielle Blumenthal, *Women and Soap Opera: A Cultural Feminist Perspective* (Westport, CT: Praeger Publishers, 1997), 99–102; C. Lee Harrington and Denise D. Bielby, *Soap Fans: Pursuing Pleasure and Making Meaning in Everyday Life* (Philadelphia: Temple University Press, 1995), 101–108.

6. Agnes Nixon, "Coming of Age in Sudsville," *Television Quarterly* 9 (1970), 63.

7. In 2013, *One Life to Live* and *All My Children* were revived as web series available on Hulu and iTunes via The Online Network. Thus, as this book goes to press, the story of Viki Lord continues.

FURTHER READING

Baym, Nancy K. *Tune In, Log On: Soaps, Fandom, and Online Community.* Thousand Oaks, CA: Sage, 2000.

Ford, Sam, Abigail De Kosnik, and C. Lee Harrington, eds. *The Survival of Soap Opera: Transformations for a New Media Era.* Jackson: University Press of Mississippi, 2011.

Harrington, C. Lee, and Denise D. Bielby. *Soap Fans: Pursuing Pleasure and Making Meaning in Everyday Life.* Philadelphia: Temple University Press, 1995.

Warhol, Robyn R. *Having a Good Cry: Effeminate Feelings and Pop-Culture Forms.* Columbus, Ohio State University Press, 2003.

39

Samurai Champloo
Transnational Viewing

JIWON AHN

Abstract: Television criticism usually addresses "what" TV is watched, and often "who" watches, but "where" TV is watched is less commonly considered vital to understanding it. In this look at the anime program *Samurai Champloo,* Jiwon Ahn argues for the importance of "where" to the meanings and pleasures of texts which—like anime—circulate in television's global flows.

Watching an imported or translated text on television is an increasingly ordinary experience in the current state of globalization. But what unique critical questions should we consider in order to make sense of such viewings? To understand our desire for and pleasure in viewing imported television texts, we need to consider how texts produced for overseas distribution are designed differently for international audiences, and how this design may inflect (or not) our viewing of them. Anime offers a productive example in that the format's long history of international circulation inevitably involved the development of textual strategies suited to transnational consumption, including, notably, an effort to balance exoticism with familiarity in terms of appeal. While the popularity of shows such as *Dragon Ball Z* (Cartoon Network, 1998–2005), *Ranma ½* (Fuji Television, 1989–1992), and *InuYasha* (Cartoon Network, 2000–2004) on U.S. television can be attributed to this mixing of exotic and familiar, this essay focuses on the more recent case of *Samurai Champloo* because of its more self-conscious and playful balancing of these two modes of appeal.

Samurai Champloo is a twenty-six-episode anime series that premiered on Fuji Television in Japan in 2004 and has since been distributed worldwide. In the United States, the show aired on the Cartoon Network as part of Adult Swim until 2006, and was recently redistributed by FUNimation, an anime distribution network that includes a cable TV channel. In order to discuss how to watch *Samurai Champloo* specifically, we need to know what *Samurai Champloo* is, beyond just being a "foreign" text.

We can start by investigating what the curious word "champloo" means. While it's easy to guess that the "samurai" in the title relates to the show's genre affiliation, "champloo" can be understood as signifying the show's eclectic approach to representing time and space in its diegetic world. Coming from the regional language of Okinawa, the tropical southern islands of Japan, *champloo* literally means "something mixed," and is also the name of a popular local dish (*champuru*) created from stir-frying all sorts of different ingredients. Although the show never explains the term's meaning, it would be reasonable to begin our inquiry with an understanding that *Samurai Champloo* is an anime text that uses the genre conventions of samurai, while providing "something mixed" for the viewing pleasure of the contemporary global audience. This essay considers the critical issues involved in viewing *Samurai Champloo* specifically in the transnational context, using the show's first episode, "Tempestuous Temperament" (U.S. airdate May 14, 2005), as its main reference point. By looking at the episode as well as the show more generally, I aim to illustrate how our awareness of the context of viewing informs our reading of the show and intensifies the polysemic pleasures we take from it.

Samurai Champloo follows the genre conventions of *chanbara*—samurai movies—which belong to the larger category of period drama, called *jidai-geki*, in Japanese national cinema. Set in the historical past of the Edo period (1603–1868), the show features three main characters, two of whom are wandering samurai warriors who represent widely different samurai identities. Mugen, the main character, is an unorthodox swordsman whose unlawful past as a pirate keeps haunting him. Jin, on the other hand, is a rogue samurai who is on the run after inadvertently murdering his own teacher. Coming together from two opposite ends of *bushido* (the code of conduct for samurai), the two men set out on a journey toward an unknown destination, aiding Fuu, a tea house waitress, in search of an ever mysterious "samurai who smells of sunflowers."

In "Tempestuous Temperament," the three characters are introduced through a series of brawls in a small town as being, respectively, hopelessly rebellious (Mugen), reclusive yet righteous (Jin), and feisty and determined (Fuu). The show's setting is also established as the Edo period through the costumes characters wear, the architectural style of buildings, and the showcased socio-cultural customs. But while ostensibly a period drama, the program seems less concerned about authentically reproducing historical details than we might expect. The episode begins with a text, written in the format of traditional scroll calligraphy (in English), which reads, "This work of fiction / Is not an accurate / Historical portrayal. / Like we care. / Now shut up and enjoy / the show." Instead of aiming at historical authenticity, *Samurai Champloo* frequently exhibits aspects that do not belong to the period, such as the hip-hop music of the opening credits, the use of scratching as a transitional marker between separate plot points, and the graffiti-style font used in the title sequence. As the episode progresses, it gradually becomes obvious that part of the show's fun is its intentional mixing up of discordant details, as we encounter characters carrying around a boom box and speaking with a contemporary "street" accent on the streets of Edo.

This stylistic mixing is reminiscent of the aesthetic characteristics of director Shinichiro Watanabe's previous work, *Cowboy Bebop*, first aired in the United States on the Cartoon Network from September 2001 until February 2002. *Cowboy Bebop*, which made Watanabe an internationally recognized anime auteur, is considered canonical by many anime fans because of its distinctive form that freely juxtaposes the conventions of different genres including space opera, the western, film noir, and American musical influences of jazz and blues. *Cowboy Bebop* proved especially successful in presenting a chaotically anachronistic atmosphere through its mixing of different historical styles, in spectacular contrast to the blasé attitude of that show's main character, Spike, a bounty hunter who lives in a small, dilapidated spaceship named "Bebop," floating aimlessly in space. It also vividly visualized the sense of alienation in a postindustrial society where the experience of up-rootedness becomes a defining condition of human existence. This anachronistic frenzy of the environment combined with the moody feelings of retreat, embodied by Spike, create a sense of longing, a kind of nostalgia for an unknown time, which can be considered symptomatic of the postmodern experience.

Despite a wide difference in setting (Mars in 2071 versus feudal Japan), *Samurai Champloo* bears a strong resemblance to its predecessor in terms of character development, an episodic narrative design, the use of contemporary music, and most importantly, its bold mixing of existing genres and styles. Unlike the stylized celebration of postmodern nostalgia in *Cowboy Bebop*, however, the mixing of generic and historical iconographies in *Samurai Champloo* contributes to an overall sense of global connectivity by introducing the contemporary international influences of hip hop and graffiti art into feudal Japan. If in *Cowboy Bebop* the temporal mixing of past (cowboy, bebop), present (the current drama), and future (the setting of 2071) holds the key to understanding its theme of existential angst, in *Samurai Champoo* it is the spatial connection, such as the mixing of iconographies of global spaces, that enhances the dramatic quality of the three characters' search for Fuu's absent father, through which process they form a deeper human connection. This connectivity of global spaces is most stunningly exemplified in the show by the graffiti art on the walls of the national monument Osaka Castle in episode 18, "War of the Words" (U.S. airdate, January 5, 2006).

Samurai Champloo is thus a rich text to examine within the analytical frameworks of auteurism and genre theory, inviting us to look comparatively at several works directed by Shinichiro Watanabe and analyze their varying strategies for genre remixing. When we look at *Samurai Champloo* not just as a self-contained

FIGURE 39.1.
Graffiti art adorns the wall of the
famous Osaka Castle, complicating its status as an "authentic"
Japanese monument.

work but as a text received within a specific context of a complex global flow of
ideas and influences, however, critical issues involved in viewing the show inevitably multiply. For example, in order to watch anime on U.S. television, we need
to consider at least four different critical issues: 1) viewing anime outside Japan
as a global media product; 2) viewing anime from a fan's perspective as a source
of global fan culture; 3) watching anime on television, rather than on a computer
screen or on other mobile devices, as a legally distributed televisual text; and 4)
viewing anime on television in the United States. I will focus the current discussion on the question of transnational viewing, which is related to issues 1 and 4
here, and show how our awareness of those issues enables us to understand the
polysemic attractions of the familiar and the exotic that *Samurai Champloo* consciously constructs for the transnational audience.[1]

In the first episode of *Samurai Champloo*, we see a constant negotiation between the familiar and the exotic played out through the show's form and content. What is familiar in this exotic-sounding anime is first its formal style. After
the calligraphic text dismissing concerns about historical authenticity is shown,
the episode opens with a scene of execution in which the two main characters
whom we have already seen in the opening sequence are about to be decapitated.
This scene of high tension is dramatically framed in a mixture of high, low, and
Dutch (canted) angles, and edited at a rapid pace. This is followed by a flashback
showing how the two men got into such a dangerous situation. Yet, instead of
smoothly transitioning to the previous day, the show first displays an intertitle,
"One Day Earlier," and presents a street scene of a contemporary Japanese city
in which cars are busily moving and a boy is dancing in front of the camera to
the beat of hip-hop music. Then the intertitle repeats more insistently, "One Day
Earlier!" with an exclamation point added, and we see what appears to be video
footage rewinding back to the premodern scenery of rural Edo.

These opening scenes are significant for two reasons: first, they reveal the
show's formal sophistication, with its rapid editing, stylized shots, and nonlinear

narrative structure, which more closely align the show with globally influential movies such as *Pulp Fiction* (1994), *Trainspotting* (1996), and *Fight Club* (1999), rather than well-known anime texts such as *Akira* (1988) or *Princess Mononoke* (1997). The reflexivity in the use of subtitles/intertitles also attests to the way that the show positions itself as familiar to global youth audiences who are presumably media-literate enough to handle such a playful and whimsical approach to reality. The episode consistently shows familiar tropes of formal sophistication and reflexivity; for example, the two fights Mugen and Jin get involved in are presented through parallel editing, repeatedly cutting back and forth with scratching sound effects as if the hands of the editor function like those of an invisible DJ.

The show presents a dimension of familiarity through its character development of Mugen and Jin. While ostensibly from seventeenth- or eighteenth-century feudal Japan, the two main characters look perfectly familiar to the contemporary global audience: speaking freely, acting independently, questioning authority, and refusing to compromise their individual freedom, they display an attitude embodied in the existential hero typically found in the genres of the western or the film noir. Throughout the episode and the show more generally, the two male protagonists are presented as the only characters with a sense of humor, and their deadpan jokes guide viewers through alternating moments of tension and danger. The rebellious, anti-authoritarian, and fearless characters of Mugen and Jin, contrasted with greedy, corrupt, and inefficient authority figures, add to the familiarity of the text to the global youth audience.

What is exotic in *Samurai Champloo*, on the other hand, originates unsurprisingly from the show's period setting, which provides abundant opportunities for the show to display the iconography of the exotic for non-Japanese viewers. These include costumes and accessories characters wear (*kimono* dress, *geta* shoes, *kasa* hat), food and drink characters consume (dumplings, skewers, hotpot, *sake*), and buildings characters reside in, as well as music and dance, tea-drinking, sword-fighting, and more. These cultural artifacts, which Susan Hayward argues are part of the process of constructing national identities and myths, are featured casually in *Samurai Champloo* as part of its narrative world, yet function significantly in constructing a unified vision of the Japanese nation, with its own distinctive culture, exotic and mythical to non-Japanese viewers.[2] Even though some of the historical details in question are overtly inauthentic, viewers and fans do not seem to have a problem in accepting them as meaningful markers of characters' national identities, judging from, for example, how readily those characters' outfits are reproduced at "cosplay" ("costume" + "play") events at anime conventions around the globe.[3] This exotic appeal is further accentuated later in the show, when we are introduced to the show's third-person narrator, Manzou the Saw, who functions as a cultural informant and interpreter by explaining the significance of certain cultural practices such as woodblock painting and baseball in Japan to contemporary viewers. Through these efforts to present both familiar and exotic attractions, *Samurai Champloo* positions itself as a singular yet accessible text, offering possibilities for multiple readings and pleasures for diverse transnational audiences.

As mentioned above, viewing anime as a global media product requires us to consider how anime's distribution and consumption contribute to the current formations of geopolitical power relations. Although it may sound odd to suggest that adorable anime characters such as Pikachu and Totoro can be part of a global power struggle, the concerns of cultural imperialism, especially regarding U.S. influence in Latin American countries, have been consistently raised in debates about globalization over the past decades.[4] Sometimes called "Disneyfication" (similar euphemisms include Coca-colonization and McDonaldization), the tendency has prompted concerns that the mass-production and distribution of cultural and media products by multinational corporations (MNC's) will overpower and eradicate more organic developments within local cultures, resulting in the domination of a globally homogeneous monoculture; and that because most MNC's are based in the first world, often in the United States, the resulting global monoculture will impose Western and/or American values and lifestyles on citizens in different parts of the world. When we consider anime as a global media product consumed by viewers outside Japan, the question of cultural imperialism, and the concerns about a global monoculture become complicated because of the unique location of Japan apart from the Western/American paradigm.

The fact that anime texts themselves are produced through a labor-intensive process adds further complexity to considerations of transnational anime texts, since much production of anime has been outsourced to Asian countries since the 1980s, especially in the case of 2D animation, which has been outsourced mainly to South Korea, and to a lesser degree to Taiwan, both of which are former colonies of Japan. Even for cultural products, such as films, television shows, animated series, books, CDs, etc., the practice of outsourcing reproduces asymmetrical relations of production, which Toby Miller and other scholars call the "New International Division of Cultural Labor."[5] Consequently, the implications of consuming cultural texts produced through the problematic process of outsourcing needs to be part of our reception of these texts, as exemplified by Jason Mittell's discussion of *The Simpsons* as paradoxically the most "American" text produced through outsourcing in South Korea.[6] Thus, while non-Japanese involvement in the production of *Samurai Champloo* may be minimal, it is worth considering how the show, set in the often-glorified historical past of the Edo period, embodies the idea of Japan as a nation, promoting values and ways of life as authentically "Japanese."

Additionally, viewing *Samurai Champloo* on television not just outside Japan, but specifically in the United States, needs to be further scrutinized. It is reasonable to assume that the political relations between countries exporting and importing cultural products may affect the reception of texts—and vice versa. For instance, the South Korean government banned Japanese popular cultural imports, including anime, for over forty years from the end of World War II until 1997, due to the history of Japanese colonization. Recent years have seen the emergence of a doctrine of Japanese "soft power," which has led the officials within the Foreign Ministry in Japan to start sending selected teenage girls as "cute ambassadors" to international cultural events, with the hope that such adorable representations of Japan would both promote popular cultural exports and soften its national image.[7]

Certainly the history of past relations between the United States and Japan has impacted the reception of anime in the United States. This may be a factor in the strong subcultural appeal that anime seems to hold for adolescent fans in the United States, arguably more so than other pop culture imports, such as Hong Kong martial art movies, Bollywood musicals, and, more recently, K-pop (South Korean pop music). Japan as a nation has a certain kind of fixed, strong resonance for older generations—whether as a war-crazed totalitarian society or as an economic powerhouse. Viewing anime in the United States and being able to appreciate its seemingly childish yet potentially profound texts distinguish American teenage viewers from preceding generations' presumed lack of openness to cultural otherness. This consideration of the national identity of television shows and their viewers is especially important in the case of *Samurai Champloo*, since the show presents a particularly complicated case of cultural politics in that it both promotes and denies Japanese national culture from the Edo Period as the basis for an authentic national identity. In other words, because *Samurai Champloo* spectacularly showcases a mythical Edo in the text, while at the same time disavowing its authenticity by playfully remixing it with contemporary cultural influences, it is worth considering the show as a Japanese text that presents additional viewing pleasures to American viewers in particular.

These sets of critical issues involved in viewing anime texts on U.S. television respectively correspond to the question of viewing position, or where the viewer is coming from in watching the show, which becomes especially relevant when we consider the meaning of polysemy in transnational television viewing. Described by John Fiske as a site of struggle over the multiple (political) meanings of a text, television's polysemy takes on a new complexity in the process of global exchanges of television shows, formats, and influences, blurring boundaries between dominant and oppositional readings, and producers' and fans' positions.[8]

Samurai Champloo is consciously designed by the show's producers as a combination of exotic Edo period drama, with its traditional Japanese spectacle, and the familiar tale of youthful resistance against authority, represented by the rebellious character of Mugen and the fugitive character Jin. Even though it is obvious

FIGURE 39.2.
Samurai Champloo playfully mixes imagery of Edo period drama and youth rebellion.

that the producers of the show perform a balancing act between the exotic and the familiar, and that the design of the text strategically embeds plenty of details both exotic and familiar, the pleasures we take from viewing *Samurai Champloo* on U.S. television are neither inauthentic nor one-dimensional. In other words, even though anime as global media products are programmed as polysemic in order to address diverse transnational audiences, the polysemic pleasures audiences take differ depending on the situatedness of those audiences. Thus, while transnational viewers find *Samurai Champloo* appealing because of its programmed polysemy of the familiar and the exotic, the polysemy of the text can still function as a site of struggle for political meanings, as is evidenced, for example, in an ongoing debate amongst fans over the possible subplots of romantic relations among the three characters or about the sexual orientation of the protagonists.

Being aware of the show's polysemic design, I would argue, does not limit but rather intensifies the pleasures we take in viewing *Samurai Champloo* on U.S. television. For an awareness of our own position in our involvement with a foreign text only enriches the political meanings we produce from our viewing. Just as *champuru*, the popular Okinawan dish, is savored not because of any particular flavor produced from a known recipe, but because of the flexibility of its form that allows people to experiment with and personalize recipes, *Samurai Champloo* can be fully appreciated only when we understand the specificities of our own local viewing of the transnational text, and participate, knowingly and willingly, in the process of meaning production through polysemic readings.

NOTES

1. For further discussion of the international fan cultures of anime, and more specifically, the debate over the fascination that the "foreign" texts of anime hold over the global youth audiences, see: Annalee Newitz, "Anime Otaku: Japanese Animation Fans Outside Japan," *Bad Subjects,* 13 (April 1994), http://bad.eserver.org/issues/1994/13/newitz.html,

and Henry Jenkins, "Pop Cosmopolitanism: Mapping Cultural Flows in an Age of Media Convergence," in *Globalization: Culture and Education in the New Millennium,* Marcelo M. Suarez-Orozco and Desiree Baolian Qin-Hillard, eds. (Berkeley: University of California Press, 2004), 114–40. While Newitz argues polemically that American "fanboys" enjoy viewing anime because of their nostalgia for the American historical past, when politically incorrect representations could be freely circulated in public media, Jenkins interprets American youth's embrace of foreign cultures such as anime, Bollywood, and Hong Kong action movies more positively, calling it "pop cosmopolitanism" and viewing it as fans' attempts to distinguish themselves from their parents' generation through transcultural consumption.

2. Susan Hayward, *French National Cinema* (London and New York: Routledge, 1993).

3. For just one example, see how the three main characters' outfits are recreated for fans' "cosplay" (character-playing through costuming), http://www.cosplaymagic.com/sachco.html.

4. For an in-depth analysis of cultural imperialism, see John Tomlinson, *Cultural Imperialism: A Critical Introduction* (London and New York: Continuum, 1991).

5. Toby Miller and Geoffrey Lawrence, "Globalization and Culture," in *A Companion to Cultural Studies,* Toby Miller, ed. (Malden, MA: Blackwell Publishing, 2001).

6. Jason Mittell, *Television and American Culture* (New York: Oxford University Press, 2010), 445–48.

7. Isabel Reynolds, "Japan Picks 'Schoolgirl' Among Cute Ambassadors," *Reuters,* March 12, 2009, http://uk.reuters.com/article/2009/03/12/us-japan-ambassadors-cute-idUK-TRE52B4JC20090312. For a discussion of "soft power" in the Japanese context, see Douglas McGray, "Japan's Gross National Cool," *Foreign Policy* (May/June 2002), http://www.foreignpolicy.com/articles/2002/05/01/japans_gross_national_cool.

8. John Fiske, *Television Culture* (London and New York: Routledge, 1987).

FURTHER READING

Desser, David. "Remaking Seven Samurai in World Cinema." In *East Asian Cinemas: Exploring Transnational Connections on Film,* Leon Hunt and Leung Wing-Fai, eds. London: I. B. Tauris, 2008.

Jenkins, Henry. "Pop Cosmopolitanism: Mapping Cultural Flows in an Age of Media Convergence." In *Globalization: Culture and Education in the New Millennium,* Marcelo M. Suarez-Orozco and Desiree Baolian Qin-Hillard, eds. Berkeley: University of California Press, 2004, 114–140.

Miller, Toby, and Geoffrey Lawrence. "Globalization and Culture." In *A Companion to Cultural Studies.* Toby Miller, ed. Malden, MA: Blackwell Publishing, 2001.

Tomlinson, John. *Cultural Imperialism: A Critical Introduction.* London: Continuum, 1991.

40

The Walking Dead
Adapting Comics

HENRY JENKINS

Abstract: One of the key ways that television connects to other media is by adapting pre-existing properties from films, comics, and other formats. Henry Jenkins uses one of the most popular of such recent adaptations, *The Walking Dead*, to highlight the perils and possibilities of adaptations, and how tapping into pre-existing fan bases can pose challenges to television producers.

The comic book industry now functions as Hollywood's research and development department, with a growing number of media properties inspired by graphic novels, including not only superhero films (*Green Lantern, X-Men: First Class, Thor*) and both live-action and animated television series (*Smallville, The Bold and the Brave*), but also films from many other genres (*A History of Violence, American Splendor, 20 Days of Night, Scott Pilgrim vs. the World*). There are many possible explanations for Hollywood's comic book fixation:

1. DC and Marvel are owned by Warner Brothers and Disney, respectively, who cherry pick what they think will satisfy mass audience interests.
2. Comics-based stories are to contemporary cinema what magazine short stories were to classical Hollywood—more or less presold material.
3. Hardcore comics readers fall into a highly desired demographic—teen and twentysomething males—who have abandoned television in recent years for other media.
4. Comic books are a visual medium, offering something like a storyboard establishing basic iconography and visual practices for moving image media.
5. Digital special effects have caught up to comics' most cosmic storytelling, allowing special-effects houses to expand their technical capacities.

6. Contemporary television and comics involve a complex mix of the episodic and the serial, deploying long-form storytelling differently from most films or novels.

7. The streamlined structure of comics offers emotional intensification closely aligned with contemporary screen practices.

Despite such claims, comics adaptations often radically depart from elements popular with their original reading audiences. Mainstream comics readership has been in sharp decline for several decades: today's top-selling title reaches fewer than a hundred thousand readers per month—a drop in the bucket compared with the audiences required for cable success, let alone broadcast networks. Some graphic novels have moved from specialty shops to chain bookstores, attracting a "crossover" readership, including more women and more "casual" fans. Adapting a comic for film or television often involves building on that crossover potential rather than addressing hardcore fans, stripping away encrusted mythology about the nature of comics' popularity.

AMC's *The Walking Dead* (2010–present) is a notable exception, establishing its reputation as "faithful" to the spirit if not the letter of the original, even while introducing its original characters, themes, and storyworld to a new audience. Robert Kirkman's comic series was a key example of the crossover readership that graphic novels can find at mainstream bookstores. Kirkman has freely acknowledged his debts to George Romero's *Living Dead* film series (1968–2010), while others note strong parallels with *28 Days Later* (2002). *The Walking Dead's* success with crossover readers and Kirkman's reliance on formulas from other commercially successful franchises in the genre explain why producers felt they could remain "true" to the comics while reaching a more expansive viewership. Using "Wildfire" (November 28, 2010), the fifth episode from *The Walking Dead's* first season, I will explore what aspects of the comic reached television, what changes occurred, and why hardcore fans accepted some changes and not others. As a longtime *Walking Dead* reader, I am well situated to explore fan response to shifts from the original.

To understand what *The Walking Dead* meant to comics readers, one might well start with its extensive letter column. Here, dedicated fans ask questions and offer opinions about every major plot development. Kirkman established a deeply personal relationship with his fans, sharing behind-the-scenes information about his efforts to get the series optioned and then developed for television, responding to reader controversies, and discussing the comic's core premises and genre conventions ("the rules"). Kirkman summarized his goals in the first *Walking Dead* graphic novel:

With *The Walking Dead*, I want to explore how people deal with extreme situations and how these events CHANGE them. . . . You guys are going to get to see Rick change and mature to the point that when you look back on this book you won't even recognize him. . . . I hope to show you reflections of your friends, your neighbors, your families, and yourselves, and what their reactions are to the extreme situations in this book. . . . This is more about watching Rick survive than it is about watching Zombies pop around the corner and scare you. . . . The idea behind *The Walking Dead* is to stay with the character, in this case, Rick Grimes for as long as is humanly possible. . . . *The Walking Dead* will be the zombie movie that never ends.[1]

If, as Robin Wood formulated, the horror genre examines how normality is threatened by the monstrous, Kirkman's focus is less on the monstrous and more on human costs.[2] The comic's artwork (originally by Tony Moore but mostly by Charlie Adlard) offers gore-hounds detailed renderings of rotting faces (lovingly recreated for the television series by makeup artist Greg Nicotero) and blood splattering as humans and zombies battle, but it is also focused on melodramatic moments, as human characters struggle to maintain normality in the face of the monstrous. This merger of horror and melodrama may explain why, despite its gore, *The Walking Dead* comics appeal almost as much to female readers as they do to the men who constitute the core comics market. Early on, some fans criticized the comic's shambling "pace," going several issues without zombie encounters. However, once they got a taste of Kirkman's storytelling, many realized how these scenes contributed to the reader's deeper investment in the characters' plights.

Given his intimate and ongoing relationship with readers, Kirkman's participation as an executive producer on the television adaptation was key for establishing credibility with his long-term readers. Series publicity tapped Kirkman's street cred alongside AMC's own reputation for groundbreaking, character-focused television dramas (*Mad Men, Breaking Bad*) and the reputations of executive producers Frank Darabont (*The Green Mile, The Shawshank Redemption*) and Gale Anne Hurd (*Aliens, The Abyss, The Terminator* franchise) with filmgoers, establishing an aura of exceptionality.

The Walking Dead was a key discussion topic at the 2010 San Diego Comic-Con, a gathering of more than 200,000 influential fans. Posters, specifically produced for the convention, compared the television characters with their comic-book counterparts. The trade room display reconstructed an iconic comic location, a farmhouse where a family had killed themselves rather than change into zombies. Both tactics reaffirmed that the series was closely based on the comics. And Kirkman was front and center, promising fans that the series would capture the essence of his long-articulated vision. If the producers won the hearts of the hardcore fans, they might count on them to actively rally viewers for the series premiere. Thanks, in part, to the fan support in spreading the word and building enthusiasm, *The Walking Dead* broke all ratings records for basic cable for its debut episode and broke them again with the launch of season 2.

By the time *The Walking Dead* reached the air, Kirkman had produced and published twelve full-length graphic novels, representing more than seventy issues. Yet the first season of the television series covered only the first six issues. On the one hand, this expansive narrative offered a rich roadmap. On the other, it threatened to lock the producers down too much, making it hard for the series to grow on its own terms. Speaking at the Paleyfest in Los Angeles after season 1, Kirkman acknowledged that exploring different paths through the material allowed him to explore roads not taken in his own creative process.

The challenge was to give veteran fans recognizable versions of the established characters and iconic moments. Fans had to be able to follow the story structure in broad outlines, even as the producers were changing major and minor plot points, adding new themes and character moments. The audience anticipated that any changes would be consistent with Kirkman's oft-articulated "ground rules" and yet the producers wanted the freedom to take the story in some new directions. *The Walking Dead* had built its reputation for surprising its readers in every issue—any character could die at any moment, and taboos could be shattered without blinking an eye. How could the television series have that same impact if the most dedicated fans already knew what was going to happen next?

"Wildfire" was perhaps season 1's most emotionally powerful episode, where many core themes came into sharpest focus. It was based upon the final chapter of the first graphic novel, which set the tone for the rest of the comics series. The episode includes several memorable moments from the comics, specifically the death of two major characters (Amy and Jim), yet also several shifts that hint at how dramatically the producers had revised things. Fans embraced some of these changes, while others saw them as violating their collective sense of the franchise.

As "Wildfire" opens, the protagonists are recovering from a traumatic and abrupt zombie attack that killed several recurring characters and forced the survivors to confront the vulnerability of their encampment, thereby preparing them to seek a new "home" elsewhere in what is a recurring quest in the comics. The attack's basic outline remains consistent with the graphic novel. For example, Amy gets caught by surprise when she separates from the others, while Jim gets chomped in the ensuing battle. The brutal attack disrupts a much more peaceful "fish fry" scene, which provides an excuse for characters to reveal bits of their backstory. The ruthless battle shows how each character has begun to acquire self-defense and survival skills.

FIGURE 40.1. This AMC promo suggested that the TV adaptation of *The Walking Dead* would be a mirror image of the comic.

Yet a central emotional incident, Andrea's prolonged watch over her dead sister Amy's body, occupied only two panels of Kirkman's original comic. There, Andrea tells Dale, "I can't let her come back like that," capturing the dread of a loved one transforming into the undead. The television series used this line as a starting point for a much more elaborated character study, built across several episodes as the two sisters, a decade-plus apart in age in this version (though not in the original), offer each other physical and emotional support. The two sisters talk in a boat about the family tradition of fishing and how their father responded to their different needs. Andrea plans to give Amy a birthday present, telling Dale that she was never there for her sister's birthdays growing up. The image of Andrea unwrapping the present and hanging the fishing lure around her dead sister's neck represents the melodramatic payoff fans expect from *The Walking Dead* in whatever medium. The expansion of this incident into a prolonged melodramatic sequence has to do both with issues of modality (the range of subtle facial expressions available to a performer working in live action as opposed to the compression required to convey the same emotional effect through static images) and AMC's branding as a network known for "complex narratives," "mature themes," and "quality acting."

"Wildfire" shows Andrea protecting Amy's body as the others seek to convince her to allow her sister to be buried, We hear the sounds of picks thrashing through the skulls of other zombies in the background and watch bodies being prepared to be burned. And, finally, Amy returns to life for a few seconds. Andrea looks intently into Amy's eyes, seeking any signs of human memory and consciousness, stroking her sister's face as Amy's gasps turn into animalistic grunts. The producers play with these ambiguities through their use of makeup: Amy is more human-looking compared to the other zombies, where the focus is on their bones, teeth, and muscle rather than their eyes, flesh, and hair. In the end, Andrea shoots her sister with the pistol she's been clutching—an act of mercy rather than violence.

FIGURE 40.2.
Andrea watches over Amy's death
in a melodramatic sequence
suited both to live-action TV and
AMC's "quality" branding.

Much of the sequence is shot in tight close-ups, focusing attention all the more directly on the characters' reactions. This is the first time the television series shows humans transition into zombies. Several issues after this point in the story (issue 11), the comic revisits this theme with a troubling story of Hershel, a father who has kept his zombie daughter chained and locked in a barn, unable to accept the irreversibility of her fate (an incident which was enacted on screen near the climax of the series' second season). Here, Andrea's willingness to dispatch Amy is a sign of her determination to live.

By contrast, the comic explores Jim's death in more depth. While Jim's family had been lost in a previous zombie attack, Jim was able to escape because the zombies were so distracted eating his other family members. The book's Jim is a loner who has not forged intimate bonds with the others, but who aggressively defends the camp during the zombie attack. In the comic, Jim is so overwrought with guilt and anger that he smashes one zombie's skull to a pulp. In the television series, this action is shifted onto an abused wife who undergoes a cathartic breakdown while preparing her dead husband for burial. On the one hand, this shift gave a powerful payoff for a new subplot built on the comic's discussion of how the zombie attacks had shifted traditional gender politics, and on the other, it allowed a tighter focus on Jim's slow acceptance of the prospect of becoming a zombie.

In both media, Jim initially hides the reality of being bitten from the other campers. Finally, he breaks down when someone notices his wounds. While the producers used the comic as a visual reference for this iconic moment, there are also substantial differences in the staging, including the shift of the bite from Jim's arm to his stomach and the ways the other campers manhandle him to reveal the bite.

Jim's story conveys the dread with which a bitten human begins preparing for a transformation into a zombie. In both the comic and the television series, Jim asks to be left, propped up against a tree so that he might rejoin his family when the inevitable change comes. Here, again, the television series elaborates on these basic plot details, prolonging his transformation to show the conflicting attitudes of the other campers to his choice. The television series is far more explicit than the comic about parallels with contemporary debates about the right of the terminally ill to control the terms of their own death.

In both sets of changes highlighted here, the television series remains true to the spirit of the original comic if not to the letter—especially in its focus on the processes of mourning and loss and the consequences of violence, both of which are often overlooked in traditional horror narratives. Both represent elaborations and extensions of elements from the original book. And both link these personal narratives with the community's collective experience, as in the scene where many from the camp say goodbye to Jim as he lies against a tree awaiting his fate. Some offer him comfort, others walk past unable to speak.

At the same time, two other "Wildfire" plotlines represent more decisive breaks with the comics: the confrontation between Shane and Rick and the introduction of the Center for Disease Control. Rick had been cut off from his wife and son when Shane, his best friend, helped them escape, while Rick was lying comatose in the hospital. Believing Rick to be dead, Laurie and Shane couple until Rick finds his way back to his family. In Kirkman's original, Dale warns Rick that Shane made advances on Laurie. In the television series, Rick has no idea of the potential infidelity, but the audience knows that Shane and Laurie have made love. In the graphic novel, the two men go out to the woods to have it out. In the final panels of the first graphic novel, Shane attempts to kill Rick and is shot in the head by Rick's eight-year-old son, Carl. The boy collapses in his father's arms and says, "It's not the same as killing the dead ones, Daddy." Rick responds, "It never should be, Son. It never should be."

In "Wildfire," tension mounts throughout the episode as the two men clash over what the group should do next. Both turn to Laurie for moral support, which she is unable to offer, saying instead that "Neither one of you were entirely wrong." In the television version, Shane initially mistakes Rick for a deer in the woods until he has his friend in his gun sights and then finds himself unable to draw down. Dale, rather than Carl, comes upon the two men, ending Shane's moral dilemma. When he returns from the woods, Shane seems ready to accept Rick's leadership. Shane's survival represents a decisive shift from the original, though by the season's end, its ramifications were not clear. Perhaps this is a case where Kirkman saw unrealized potentials that, given a chance, he wanted to mine more deeply.

But, in removing Carl from the scene, the television producers could be accused of pulling punches, given how central the sequence of the young boy shooting the adult male had been in the comic's original version (and its refusal to engage in sentimental constructions of childhood innocence). Carl's repeated brushes with violence, and his willingness to take action when adults hesitate, are recurring motifs throughout the books. If the comics often shocked readers by abruptly killing off long- established characters, here the producers surprised some viewers by refusing to kill a character whose death represented an early turning point in the comics.

The visit to the Center for Disease Control, which is introduced in the closing scenes of "Wildfire" and becomes the focus for the season's final episode, "TS-19," has no direct counterpart in the comic book series. One of the hard and fast rules Kirkman established in the comics was that he was never going to provide a rational explanation for how the zombie outbreak occurred. As Kirkman argues in an early letter column:

> As far as the explanation for the zombies go, I think that aside from the zombies being in the book, this is a fairly realistic story, and that's what makes it work. The people do real things, and it's all very down to Earth . . . almost normal. ANY explanation would be borderline science fiction . . . and it would disrupt the normalness. In my mind, the story has moved on. I'm more interested in what happens next then what happened before that caused it all.[3]

One reason Kirkman has Rick in a coma at the start of the comic series is so that the audience is not exposed to the inevitable theorizing which would surround a society coping with such a catastrophe. (A web series, produced for the launch of the second season, further explored what had happened when Rick was in his coma, offering a range of contradictory possible explanations for the zombie epidemic.)

Many fans were anxious about the introduction of the CDC subplot, which implied a medical explanation. At the same time, the closing scenes at the CDC also represent the first time we've cut away from Rick or the other members of his party to see another perspective on the unfolding events (in this case, that of an exhausted and suicidal scientist). For both reasons, many fans saw this subplot as another dramatic break with the spirit of the comic.

And it came at an unfortunate moment—at the end of the abbreviated first season, as the last taste before an almost year-long hiatus. If the series' publicity and presentation had largely reassured long time readers that the series would follow the established "rules," these final developments cost the producers some hard-won credibility, especially when coupled with news that the production company had fired most of the staff writers who worked on the first season, that AMC was reducing the budget per episode for the series, and that producer Frank Darabont was also leaving under duress.

By this point, *The Walking Dead* was the biggest ratings success in AMC's history, leaving many comics fans to worry whether their support was still necessary for the series' success. It would not be the first time that a series acknowledged a cult audience's support only long enough to expand its following, and then pivoted to focus on the new viewers who constituted the bulk of its rating points.

As this *Walking Dead* example suggests, there is no easy path for adapting comics for the small screen. There are strong connections between the ways seriality works in comics and television, but also significant differences that make a one-to-one mapping less desirable than it might seem. Television producers want to leave their own marks on the material by exploring new paths and occasionally surprising their loyal fans. The challenge is how to make these adjustments consistent not with the details of the original stories, but with their "ground rules," their underlying logic, and one good place to watch this informal "contract" between reader and creators take shape is through the letter columns published in the back of the comics. It is through this process that the producers can help figure out what they owe to the comics and to their readers.

NOTES

1. Robert Kirkman, *The Walking Dead Vol. 1: Days Gone By* (New York: Image, 2006).
2. Robin Wood, "An Introduction to the American Horror Film," in *Movies and Methods*, vol. 2, Bill Nichols, ed. (Berkeley: University of California Press, 1985).
3. Robert Kirkman, "Letter Hacks," *The Walking Dead* 8 (July 2004).

FURTHER READING

Gardner, Jared. *Projections: Comics and the History of Twenty-First-Century Storytelling*. Palo Alto, CA: Stanford University Press, 2012.

Gordon, Ian, Mark Jancovich, and Matthew P. McAllister, eds. *Film and Comic Books*. Jackson: University Press of Mississippi, 2007.

McRobbie, Angela. *The Horror Sensorium: Media and the Senses*. Jefferson, NC: McFarland, 2013.

Pustz, Matthew. *Comic Book Culture: Fan Boys and True Believers*. Jackson, MI: University Press of Mississippi, 2000.

Smith, Matthew J., and Randy Duncan, eds. *Critical Approaches to Comics: Theories and Methods*. New York: Routledge, 2011.

Contributors

Christine Acham is Associate Professor in the Program for African American and African Studies at the University of California, Davis. She is the author of *Revolution Televised: Prime Time and the Struggle for Black Power* and numerous articles. She is also the co-director of the documentary film *Infiltrating Hollywood: The Rise and Fall of The Spook Who Sat by the Door.*

Jiwon Ahn is Associate Professor in Film Studies at Keene State College, New Hampshire. Her research interests lie in global media fan cultures, transnational film genres, and lifestyle television.

Evelyn Alsultany is Associate Professor in the Department of American Culture at the University of Michigan. She is the author of *Arabs and Muslims in the Media: Race and Representation after 9/11* (New York University Press, 2012). She is co-editor of *Arab and Arab American Feminisms: Gender, Violence, and Belonging* and *Between the Middle East and the Americas: The Cultural Politics of Diaspora.* She is also guest curator of the Arab American National Museum's online exhibit, *Reclaiming Identity: Dismantling Arab Stereotypes* (www.arabstereotypes.org).

Hector Amaya (University of Virginia) is the author of *Screening Cuba: Film Criticism as Political Performance During the Cold War* and *Citizenship Excess: Latinas/os, Media, and the Ethics of Nation* (New York University Press, 2013). His articles on globalization, the cultural production of political identities, Latin American film/media, and Latino/a media studies have appeared in numerous journals.

Ben Aslinger is Assistant Professor in the Department of English and Media Studies at Bentley University. His work has appeared in numerous collections, and he is co-editor of the anthologies *Gaming Globally: Production, Play, and Place* and *Locating Emerging Media* (forthcoming).

Miranda J. Banks is Assistant Professor of Visual and Media Arts at Emerson College. She is a co-editor of *Production Studies: Cultural Studies of Media*

Industries. Her work has appeared in *Television & New Media*, *Popular Communication*, *Cinema Journal* and *Flow*, and a number of anthologies. Her book, *Scripted Labor: A History of American Screen Writing and the Writers Guild* is forthcoming.

Geoffrey Baym is Associate Professor of Media Studies at the University of North Carolina, Greensboro. He is the author of the award-winning *From Cronkite to Colbert: The Evolution of Broadcast News*, and co-editor of *News Parody and Political Satire Across the Globe*. His research on the changing nature of news and public affairs media has also appeared in numerous anthologies and scholarly journals.

Christine Becker is Associate Professor in the Department of Film, Television, and Theatre at the University of Notre Dame, specializing in film and television history and critical analysis. She is the author of *It's the Pictures That Got Small: Hollywood Film Stars on 1950s Television*. She is currently working on a research project comparing contemporary American and British television production and programming.

Ron Becker is Associate Professor of Media Communication at Miami University of Ohio and the author of *Gay TV and Straight America*. His work has also appeared in numerous anthologies and journals.

Jeremy G. Butler has taught television, film, and new media courses since 1977, at Northwestern University, the University of Alabama, and the University of Arizona. To support his television courses, he wrote the textbook *Television: Critical Methods and Applications,* and he is the author of *Television Style*. He has edited one anthology, *Star Texts: Image and Performance in Film and Television*, and published articles on *Mad Men, ER, Roseanne, Miami Vice, Imitation of Life*, soap opera, the sitcom, and other topics in a range of journals.

Abigail De Kosnik is Assistant Professor at the University of California, Berkeley, in the Berkeley Center for New Media and the Department of Theater, Dance & Performance Studies. She is the co-editor, with Sam Ford and C. Lee Harrington, of *The Survival of Soap Opera: Transformations for a New Media Era*. She has published articles on popular digital culture in several peer-reviewed journals.

Susan J. Douglas is the Catherine Neafie Kellogg Professor of Communication Studies at The University of Michigan and Chair of the Department. She is author of *Enlightened Sexism: How Pop Culture Took Us From Girl Power to Girls Gone Wild*; *The Mommy Myth: The Idealization of Motherhood and How it Undermines Women* (with Meredith Michaels); *Listening In: Radio and the American Imagination*, which won the Hacker Prize in 2000 for the best popular book about technology and culture; *Where The Girls Are: Growing Up Female with the Mass Media* and *Inventing American Broadcasting, 1899–1922*.

Colby Gottert is a documentary filmmaker. The founder of the multimedia production company Digital Development Communications, he has traveled extensively across Africa, Asia, and Latin America to document the work of public health, environmental conservation, and social development organizations. His films have screened at several international film festivals and on PBS.

Jonathan Gray is Professor of Media and Cultural Studies at University of Wisconsin, Madison. He is the author of *Television Entertainment*; *Show Sold Separately: Promos, Spoilers, and Other Media Paratexts* (New York University Press, 2010); and *Watching with The Simpsons: Television, Parody, and Intertextuality*; as well as co-author, with Amanda D. Lotz, of *Television Studies*. He is co-editor of *A Companion to Media Authorship*; *Satire TV: Politics and Comedy in the Post-Network Era* (New York University Press, 2009); *Battleground: The Media*; and *Fandom: Identities and Communities in a Mediated World* (New York University Press, 2007).

David Gurney is Assistant Professor in the Department of Communication and Media at Texas A&M University, Corpus Christi. His work has appeared in *Velvet Light Trap*, *Flow TV*, and in several anthologies. He is currently working on a manuscript dealing with viral video form and aesthetics.

Bambi L. Haggins is Associate Professor in Film and Media Studies at Arizona State University. Her research explores issues of representation in American media, comedy, and media literacy. Her book, *Laughing Mad: The Black Comic Persona in Post Soul America*, received the Katherine Singer Kovacs Award from the Society for Cinema and Media Studies. Her current project deals with the history of women in contemporary American comedy.

Heather Hendershot is professor of film and media at MIT. Her two most recent books are *Shaking the World for Jesus: Media and Conservative Evangelical Culture*, and *What's Fair on the Air? Cold War Right-Wing Broadcasting and the Public Interest*. For five years she was the editor of *Cinema Journal*, the official publication of the Society for Cinema and Media Studies.

Matt Hills is Professor in Film and TV Studies at Aberystwyth University in Wales. He is the author of five books including *Fan Cultures, The Pleasures of Horror*, and *Triumph of a Time Lord*. He has published widely on cult TV and fandom, and is currently editing a collection on *Doctor Who* and completing a book on *Torchwood*.

Jennifer Holt is Associate Professor of Film and Media Studies at the University of California, Santa Barbara. She is the author of *Empires of Entertainment* and co-editor of *Media Industries: History, Theory, Method*. Her work has also appeared in numerous journals and anthologies.

Henry Jenkins is Provost's Professor of Communication, Journalism, and Cinematic Arts at the University of Southern California. He is the author and/or editor of fifteen books on various aspects of media and popular culture, including *Textual Poachers: Television Fans and Participatory Culture; Convergence Culture: Where Old and New Media Collide* (New York University Press, 2006); and *Fans, Bloggers and Gamers: Exploring Participatory Culture* (New York University Press, 2006). His newest books include *Spreadable Media: Creating Meaning and Value in a Networked Culture* (New York University Press, 2013) and *Reading in a Participatory Culture*.

Victoria E. Johnson is Associate Professor of Film and Media Studies at the University of California, Irvine. She has published articles and chapters in numerous journals and collections. Her *Heartland TV: Prime Time Television and the Struggle for U.S. Identity* (New York University Press, 2008) received the Society for Cinema and Media Studies' Katherine Singer Kovacs Book Award.

Jeffrey P. Jones is the Lambdin Kay Chair for the Peabodys and Director of the George Foster Peabody Awards at the University of Georgia. He is the author and editor of five books, including *Entertaining Politics: Satiric Television and Political Engagement*, and most recently (with Geoffrey Baym), *News Parody and Political Satire Across the Globe*.

Derek Kompare is Associate Professor of Film and Media Arts at Southern Methodist University. He is the author of *CSI* and *Rerun Nation: How Repeats Invented American Television*, and has published work on television history and form in several journals and anthologies, on issues ranging from genre hybridity in reality television to the construction of authorship in transmedia cultural production.

Elana Levine is Associate Professor in the Department of Journalism, Advertising, and Media Studies at the University of Wisconsin-Milwaukee. She is the author of *Wallowing in Sex: The New Sexual Culture of 1970s American Television*; co-editor of *Undead TV: Essays on Buffy the Vampire Slayer*; and co-author, with Michael Z. Newman, of *Legitimating Television: Media Convergence and Cultural Status*.

Amanda D. Lotz is Associate Professor of Communication Studies at the University of Michigan. She is the author of *Cable Guys: Television and Masculinities in the Twenty-First Century* (New York University Press, forthcoming 2014), *The Television Will Be Revolutionized* (New York University Press, 2007), and *Redesigning Women: Television After the Network Era*, as well as editor of *Beyond Prime Time: Television Programming in the Post-Network Era*. She is co-author, with Timothy Havens, of *Understanding Media Industries* and, with Jonathan Gray, of *Television Studies*.

Daniel Marcus is Associate Professor of Communication and Media Studies at Goucher College in Baltimore. He is the author of *Happy Days and Wonder Years: The Fifties and the Sixties in Contemporary Cultural Politics*, and writes on documentary, alternative media projects, and notions of history and economic issues in media and popular culture.

Nick Marx is Assistant Professor in the Department of Communication Studies at Colorado State University. He is co-editor of *Saturday Night Live and American TV*, and his work has appeared in *The Velvet Light Trap* and *The Journal of Film and Video*.

Quinn Miller is an Assistant Professor of Film and Media Studies at the University of Oregon. His work has appeared in numerous collections, and he is currently working on a book entitled *Camp TV: Trans Gender Queer Television History*.

Jason Mittell is Professor of American Studies and Film and Media Culture at Middlebury College. He is the author of *Genre and Television: From Cop Shows to Cartoons in American Culture*; *Television and American Culture*; *Complex TV: The Poetics of Contemporary Television Storytelling* (New York University Press, forthcoming), and the blog *Just TV*.

Noel Murray is a critic and pop culture journalist whose work has appeared in *The A.V. Club*, *The Los Angeles Times*, *The Hollywood Reporter*, *Nashville Scene*, and *Performing Songwriter*. He lives in Conway, Arkansas, where he's written frequently about episodic television, including examining the cultural and aesthetic history of the medium in his *A.V. Club* column "A Very Special Episode." He's currently a staff writer for the website *The Dissolve*.

Michael Z. Newman is Associate Professor in the Department of Journalism, Advertising, and Media Studies at the University of Wisconsin–Milwaukee. He is the author of *Indie: An American Film Culture* and co-author, with Elana Levine, of *Legitimating Television: Media Convergence and Cultural Status*.

Sean O'Sullivan is Associate Professor of English at The Ohio State University. He is the author of *Mike Leigh* and has written numerous articles on serial narrative, including such topics as poetry and television; *Deadwood* and Charles Dickens; the structure of *Mad Men*; and third seasons.

Laurie Ouellette is Associate Professor in the Department of Communication Studies at the University of Minnesota. She is co-author with James Hay of *Better Living through Reality TV: Television and Post-Welfare Citizenship*, co-editor with Susan Murray of *Reality TV: Remaking Television Culture* (New York University Press, 2008), author of *Viewers Like You? How Public TV Failed the People*, and editor of *The Media Studies Reader*.

Roberta Pearson is Professor of Film and Television Studies and Head of the Department of Culture, Film and Media at the University of Nottingham. She has written and edited numerous books on topics including cult television, early cinema, and *Lost*, and written several essays on *Star Trek*.

Anne Helen Petersen is Visiting Assistant Professor of Film and Media Studies at Whitman College. Her work has been published in numerous journals and edited collections. She writes the blog *Celebrity Gossip, Academic Style*.

Dana Polan is Professor of Cinema Studies at New York University. He is author of numerous books, including most recently, *Julia Child's The French Chef*.

Kevin Sandler is Associate Professor of Film and Media Studies in the Department of English at Arizona State University. He is the author of *The Naked Truth: Why Hollywood Doesn't Make X-Rated Movies*, the editor of *Reading the Rabbit: Explorations in Warner Bros. Animation*, the co-editor of *Titanic: Anatomy of a Blockbuster*, and co-author with Daniel Bernardi of an upcoming book on *The Shield*.

Jeffrey Sconce is Associate Professor in the Screen Cultures Program at Northwestern University. He is the author of *Haunted Media: Electronic Presence from*

Telegraphy to Television and the editor of *Sleaze Artists: Cinema at the Margins of Taste, Style, and Financing.*

Suzanne Scott is an Assistant Professor of Film and Media Studies at Arizona State University. Her work on fandom within convergence culture, transmedia storytelling, and ancillary content has appeared in numerous journals and anthologies. She also contributed to the twentieth anniversary edition of Henry Jenkins's *Textual Poachers: Television Fans and Participatory Culture.*

Louisa Stein is Assistant Professor of Film & Media Culture at Middlebury College. Her work on gender and generation in media culture and transmedia authorship has appeared in numerous journals and anthologies. She is co-editor of the collections *Teen Television* and *Sherlock and Transmedia Fandom.* Her current book project is entitled *Millennial Media: Fandom and the Transmedia Generation.*

Ethan Thompson is Associate Professor of Communication at Texas A&M University, Corpus Christi, where he teaches courses in media and cultural studies. He is the author of *Parody and Taste in Postwar American Television Culture* and the co-editor of *Satire TV: Politics and Comedy in the Post-Network Era* (New York University Press, 2009).

Index